WORLD POLITICS IN THE GENERAL ASSEMBLY

YALE STUDIES IN POLITICAL SCIENCE, 15

PUBLISHED UNDER THE DIRECTION OF THE

DEPARTMENT OF POLITICAL SCIENCE

HAYWARD R. ALKER, JR., AND BRUCE M. RUSSETT

# WORLD POLITICS
## IN THE
# GENERAL ASSEMBLY

NEW HAVEN AND LONDON, YALE UNIVERSITY PRESS

Copyright © 1965 by Yale University.
Second printing, April 1967.
Designed by Arthur G. Beckenstein,
set in Baskerville type,
and printed in the United States of America by
The Murray Printing Company,
Forge Village, Massachusetts.
Distributed in Canada by McGill University Press.
Library of Congress catalog card number: 65-22313
Published with assistance from the foundation
established in memory of Calvin Chapin
of the Class of 1788, Yale College

# Preface

The coauthors of this book each bring prior substantive and methodological interests to the empirical study of the United Nations. As a graduate student at Yale, Alker felt that both one-dimensional views of policy differences and Charter-based interpretations were inadequate descriptions of the political process in the General Assembly. He decided that studies of the American political process by Robert Dahl, Duncan MacRae, and David Truman were theoretically and methodologically suggestive of ways in which roll-call data could be used to test for the existence of a pluralistic political process in a quasi-legislative international organization. At Robert Abelson's suggestion, factor analysis, a technique invented by psychologists interested in determining the dimensions of human intelligence, was chosen as an appropriate statistical technique for identifying the dimensions of conflict underlying the political process in the General Assembly.

Russett, then teaching at the Massachusetts Institute of Technology, became interested in analyzing the UN as a political system in some ways analogous to national systems. His reading of the theoretical and empirical literature on voting behavior, both about the electorate in general and about legislators, convinced him that despite the obvious differences between national and international systems there might be enough similarities to make exploration of them worthwhile. Accordingly he began to develop a theory about the implications of various distributions of preferences, intensities of attitude, and cross-pressures. He also started work, with James Eagle, on a computational method for analyzing roll-call votes to provide some of the data necessary to test his hypotheses.

At that point we became aware of each other's interests, and Alker accepted Russett's invitation to collaborate on a limited basis. Russett was willing to use the results of Alker's factor analyses as relevant for testing some of his theoretical propositions, while Alker agreed with Russett's commitment to test hypotheses derived from national political systems against politics in the United Nations.

This book, the result of our labor, points up rather clearly what we have done and what we have left undone. The analysis of conflict dimensions in Part I represents, we believe, an important substantive and methodological advance over earlier work. In Part II we make some further methodological innovations and explore some of the implications of a new theoretical approach. That section brings forward at least as many new questions as it answers—perhaps that is the way it should be at this stage of theory building. As to further avenues of exploration, Russett is interested in the use of UN data as one index of regional integration, while Alker would like to apply content analysis to speeches in the General Assembly in order better to understand nationally perceived benefits and disadvantages of decision-making in the context of supranational institutions.

Though each of us must take full responsibility for the final product, and all sections of this book have benefited from the ideas or criticisms of both authors, it is important to make clear the principal contributions of each author. Chapter 1 and Part I, the analysis of issues and alignments, are essentially Alker's work, from the first half of his Yale Ph.D. dissertation. Part II draws on Part I, and starting with Russett's analytic construct in Chapter 8 contains contributions from both authors. Chapters 10 and 12 are primarily Russett's work, as Chapters 9 and 11 represent a rewriting by Alker of parts of his dissertation. The discussion of the relevance and interpretation of the environmental correlations is a joint product. Chapter 13 was mostly drafted by Alker in an attempt to summarize the main points of the book in an historical perspective, and to clarify differences in emphasis and interpretation that can be found in the ideas of both authors in the earlier chapters of the book.

As to the division of labor in collecting the data used in our analyses, Russett is responsible for the final form of the data on national characteristics used in Part II, except for the regional groupings, several changes in which he suggested. Alker, on the other hand, is responsible for the interview material introduced at various points in the text, and for the roll-call votes collected in conjunction with his wife. The speech frequencies for the Second Assembly were originally collected by Alker for the purpose of measuring the opportunity costs of national participation in the Assembly. He prepared a detailed set of coding instructions for counting speeches relevant to particular factors in Assembly voting which Russett found relevant to his concern with the distribution of intensities and attitudes. These were used by Mrs. Dorothy Reynolds, with the assistance of Alker, and under the supervision of Russett, in collecting the remaining speech frequencies used in Part II of this book.

We are indebted to many individuals and institutions for intellectual and financial assistance. The contributions of several diplomats should be personally acknowledged, but the dictates of diplomacy require that their names not be mentioned. Helpful comments and criticisms on all or part of the book have come from Robert P. Abelson, James D. Barber, Daniel Cheever, Karl W. Deutsch, Ernst B. Haas, Thomas Hovet, Jr., Harold D. Lasswell, Myres McDougal, Talcott Parsons, and Walter Sharp. Painstaking editorial assistance from Ruth Davis and Marian Ash of the Yale University Press also helped save us from many obscurities. Robert Bunselmeyer, Douglas Condie, Lois Frampton, Robert Grey, Joel Jutkowitz, Dorothy Reynolds, and Seth Singleton have given various kinds of research assistance. Joan Amore, Iris David, Kay Latona, and Ruth Yaffee have helped type the manuscript for publication. Ann Alker has contributed editorial advice, typing assistance, and chart drawing skills. Norman Hix is responsible for the final versions of the many charts and figures. All who have come in contact with the various stages of the manuscript have contributed ideas and time above and beyond their strict role requirements as critics, research assistants, typists, and draftsmen. None of them, however, shares with us the responsibility for the deficiencies of the final product.

Financially, each of us has several obligations. The contribution of Yale's International Relations Concilium to the costs of Alker's thesis research was stretched by the Yale Computer Center's bargain basement rates for student research and the availability of experienced programming consultants. When programs got too large to handle at Yale, the Computation Center at M.I.T. provided free computer time on its IBM 7090. Russett's earlier work and some of Alker's later computer expenses were paid for out of Russett's grant from the Social Science Research Council. Both authors have been materially and financially assisted by the resources of the Yale Political Data Program (supported by a grant from the National Science

Foundation). Portions of this study have appeared elsewhere. Alker's Ph.D. dissertation, "Dimensions of Voting in the General Assembly," formed the basis of his contribution to this book and to his article, "Dimensions of Conflict in the General Assembly," which appeared in the September 1964 issue of the *American Political Science Review*. Russett's paper, "Toward a Model of Competitive International Politics," appeared in the May 1963 issue of the *Journal of Politics*. Parts of Chapters 8, 10, and 12 appeared in his *Trends in World Politics*, published by The Macmillan Company in 1965.

# CONTENTS

PART II   THE CONTEXT OF UN POLITICS

# LIST OF TABLES

LIST OF FIGURES

xvii

This book draws on two special vocabularies and creates one of its own. United Nations abbreviations are often bewildering, even to the professional student of international politics; the statistically specialized language of factor analysis is equally inaccessible. From these two languages, this book has created a third one, describing particular dimensions of United Nations voting using factor analytic techniques.

A list of explanations for frequently used terms from all three of these vocabularies is appended below. (Since factor labels are defined and summarized in Chapter 7, they will not be repeated here.) The abbreviations and short descriptions are in no way intended as exhaustive or definitive. Nonetheless they may serve as a ready reference for the reader, who, if dissatisfied, should refer to the relevant chapters and references for greater detail.

| TERM | EXPLANATION |
|---|---|
| ADDITIVE RELATIONSHIP | Some fathers would like to think that their *family* income could be computed by multiplying together incomes for *individual* family members; in fact, these terms obey an additive relationship. In this book voting positions on particular roll calls are assumed additively to result from positions on several underlying voting components (factors) rather than from some more exotic formula of combination. |
| AFRICANS | Normally, those states belonging to the African caucusing group. In Part II, the term "Africans" has usually been restricted to mean only those Africans that are not also members of the Arab caucusing group. |

AHC

Ad Hoc Committee (on Palestine). See **SPC**

ARABS

National member of the Arab caucusing group in the General Assembly: these states also belong to the Arab League.

ASIANS

In Part I this term has either a geographic reference or it refers to Asian members of the Afro–Asian caucusing group. In Part II, for analytical purposes, "Asians" refers to non-Arab and non-African members of the Afro–Asian caucus.

BIMODAL

Cold War attitudes are bimodally distributed if large numbers of nations are on both sides of the issue, and few others can be found anywhere in between. The frequency distribution of such attitudes has two noticeable peaks rather than one. Speechmaking patterns or national characteristics like average per capita income might also appear bimodally distributed.

BRAZZAVILLE GROUP

A caucusing group at the 16th General Assembly consisting entirely of African ex-colonies of France.

CASABLANCA GROUP

A caucusing group at the 16th Assembly resulting from the Casablanca Conference. Prominent members include the UAR, Mali, Guinea, and Ghana.

C1, C2, etc,

UN abbreviations for the First Committee, the Second Committee, etc., of the General Assembly. Each nation in the Assembly is represented on C1 through C6 and on the Special Political Committee.

CINSGT

The authors' abbreviation for the Committee on Information from Non-Self-Governing Territories.

COMMUNALITY

That fraction of a roll call's total "variance" that is accounted for by a factor analysis.

CORRELATION

A measure of association between two variables, e.g. two roll calls. It is defined as the average product of standard scores, and ranges from $-1.0$ (perfect negative association) to $0$ (no association) to $+1.0$ (perfect positive association).

COMMON VARIANCE

The amount of total roll-call variance accounted for by interpretable factors common to more than one roll call.

DPI

Department of Public Information.

ECOSOC

Economic and Social Council.

EEC

European Economic Community (the Common Market).

ECAFE

Economic Commission for Asia and the Far East.

EIGEN VALUE

Represented by the Greek letter $\lambda$ (lambda), the eigen value of a particular factor indicates the amount of roll-call variance the factor contains. Each roll call is assumed to have a variance of one.

FACTOR

A "factor" is a hypothetical construct; roll calls are assumed to be combinations of voting factors. Factors are inferred from a matrix of roll-call correlations by assuming the validity of the "factor model" (see below). The term "factor" is used interchangeably with voting "component," "dimension," or "super-issue."

FACTOR ANALYSIS

A mathematical technique for reducing a large number of intercorrelated variables to a small number of distinct underlying variables. In the past factor analysis has been used to uncover the dimensions (verbal, numerical, etc.) of human ability.

FACTOR LOADINGS

The weighting coefficients in the factor model. They are mathematically derived from the matrix of correlations among roll calls.

FACTOR MODEL

The factor model is an equation stating that votes on each roll call can at least partly be explained by a weighted sum of factor scores on several different factors.

FACTOR PATTERN

The array (matrix) of factor loadings.

FACTOR MATRIX

When factors are uncorrelated (as in the original factor analyses in this book), the factor pattern and the factor structure are identical. Either or both may be referred to as the factor matrix.

FACTOR SCORES

An index of national positions on a factor computed from factor loadings as a weighted sum of voting ranks on roll calls known to be related to a particular factor.

FACTOR STRUCTURE

The array (matrix) of correlations between roll calls and factor scores.

FREQUENCY DISTRIBUTION

The frequency (number) of different scores on any variable can be summarized in tabular or graphic form. Graphically, different ranges of the variable are marked off on the horizontal axis; frequencies are usually plotted against a vertical axis.

GA

General Assembly.

GC

General Committee (also known as "le Bureau," from which comes its official abbreviation, BUR).

INSGT

"Information from non-self-governing territories," an abbreviation.

ICAO

International Civil Aviation Organization.

ILC

International Law Commission.

INTENSITY SCORE

An attempt to measure the overall intensity of national or group policy positions on a particular super-issue in the General Assembly. Constructed by dividing the average number of speeches on the super-issue by the percentage of common voting variance accounted for by that voting dimension.

LAMBDA ($\lambda$)

See "Eigen Value."

LOAD

See "factor loading." For the factor analyses in Part I, when an issue "loads" on a factor to a certain extent, one could equivalently say that voting scores on the issue *correlate* with factor scores to that extent.

MEAN

Average, in the sense that the "mean of X" ($\overline{X}$) is the average value of X:

$$\overline{X} = \frac{1}{N} \sum_{i=1}^{N} X_i$$

MEDIAN

Given a set of nations with different voting scores on a particular issue or factor, the median voting score has the same number of national scores above it as there are national scores below it.

MODE

A mode is a high point (very frequent position) on a frequency distribution.

NSGT

Non-self-governing territory.

NORMAL DISTRIBUTION

A bell-shaped frequency distribution, with several attractive statistical properties. One of them is that its mean, median, and mode all coincide.

OBLIQUE

In a word, correlated. Oblique factor analysis does not require factors to be uncorrelated with each other.

OLD COMMONWEALTH        Commonwealth members that have been independent since before World War II. An informal caucusing group.

OLD EUROPEANS          A group of states frequently voting together, comprised of several caucusing groups as well as several non-caucusing group members: West Europeans, Scandinavians, the United States, and the Old Commonwealth.

ONUC                   Acronym for the United Nations forces in the Congo. ONU is the French abbreviation equivalent to UN.

ORTHOGONAL             A fancy way of saying "uncorrelated" or, geometrically, "perpendicular." Unrotated factors are all orthogonal to each other. So are rotated ones.

PROMINENCE             A word for referring to the eigen value of a particular factor.

ROTATED FACTORS        It is easy to visualize the meaning of rotated factors by thinking of a 3-dimensional space in which all roll calls have particular locations and coordinates (loadings) on three perpendicular axes in the space. Holding the configuration of roll calls fixed, imagine the first three fingers on your right hand to be the perpendicular axes. *Identify factors* with the *axes* of the roll-call space. Twist your hand keeping the three fingers perpendicular to each other. Roll-call coordinates (factor loadings) will change—you are rotating factors!

SC                     Security Council.

SG                     Secretary-General.

SIMPLE STRUCTURE       When do you want to stop rotating your three fingers? Several sensible answers exist (see also the discussion of "unrotated factors" below). A perfect, simply structured factor matrix will be one where the coordinates of each roll call are 0.0 on two factor axes, and 1.0 on a third axis. Rotating factors to the best possible approximation of such a factor matrix maximizes the substantive interpretability of factor axes (columns in the factor matrix).

SKEWED DISTRIBUTION

A frequency distribution in which more items are to one side of the mean than the other. As a result the mean and the median do not coincide.

SPC

Special Political Committee. All UN members are represented on this committee which used to be the Ad Hoc Committee on Palestine. Now it hears "overflow" items from the First (Political) Committee.

STANDARD DEVIATION

If variable $X_i$ takes on N values ($i = 1, 2, \ldots, N$), its standard deviation ($S_x$) is

$$S_x = \sqrt{\sum_{i=1}^{N} \frac{(X_i - \overline{X})^2}{N}}$$

The standard deviation of X is often referred to as a "root mean square" (of X), by which is meant "the square root of the average squared deviation of X." It is not wholly misleading to think of the standard deviation of X as a more complicated version of an average (absolute) deviation from the mean of X.

STANDARD SCORE

For any variable $X_i$ ($i = 1, \ldots, N$) with mean $\overline{X}$ and standard deviation $S_x$, the standardized score of any individual i on X ($Z_x(i)$) is merely

$$Z_x(i) = \frac{X_i - \overline{X}}{S_x}$$

Voting scores used in this book are standardized voting ranks; they have the

|  | typical properties of standard scores: means of zero, standard deviations of unity. |
| TC | Trusteeship Council. |
| UNCURK | United Nations Commission for the Unification and Reconstruction of Korea. |
| UNIMODAL | A frequency distribution is unimodal if it has only one high point (the mode). Strictly speaking, unimodal means that a frequency distribution always slopes downward and away from the mode. |
| UNEF | United Nations Emergency Force (formed during the Suez Crisis in 1956). |
| UNRWAPRNE | United Nations Relief and Works Agency For Palestine Refugees in the Near East. |
| UNSCOP | United Nations Special Committee on Palestine. A select committee that in 1947 recommended the partition of Palestine. |
| UNSCEAR | United Nations Special Committee on the Effects of Atomic Radiation. |
| UNROTATED FACTOR MATRIX | In this book, the factor matrix derived by the principal component method of factor analysis. Although each column of factor loadings is uncorrelated with any other column in the factor matrix, the first explains as much roll-call variance as any one factor can, the second column gets as much remaining variance as a single factor can, etc. |
| VARIANCE | The variance $(S_x^2)$ of variable (or roll call) X is the average squared deviation of scores on X. As its symbol $(S_x^2)$ implies, a variance is just a squared standard deviation. Because roll-call ranks are standardized scores, total roll-call variance of a single roll call is one. |
| Z-SCORE | A short way of referring to $Z_x(i)$, which is a standard score for individual (nation) i on variable (roll call) X. |

# CHAPTER 1

# A United Nations Perspective

Predispositions shape and twist perspectives. Each of us, faced with the same body of information, may organize it differently and draw somewhat different conclusions. If we start with strongly held and distinctive ideological presuppositions, we are likely to disagree even about the significance of major political events. How, for instance, should we compare or contrast current international politics with the world of twenty years ago? Have the Sino–Soviet split, fissions within NATO, and the emergence of the new nations drastically altered the conflicts preoccupying national foreign policies, or are these controversies essentially unchanged? Many interpretations exist.

Some Western leaders, even if not subscribers to the "protracted conflict" school, nevertheless see the cold war as the overriding and continuing fact of international life. Similarly, the 1961 Program of the Communist Party of the Soviet Union states that "the basic contradiction of the contemporary world [is] the contradiction between socialism and imperialism." [1] Military power and total ideological commitment provide the foci for this kind of interpretation. Other Western analysts, stressing changes in the international situation, in the means of warfare, or in the nature and leadership of Soviet society, regard the "protracted conflict" view as increasingly unrealistic. Similarly, in at least part of the communist world the possibility of "peaceful coexistence" is a tenet of the reigning ideology.

Neutralist statesmen often express similar views. U Thant, for example, thinks that the West's emphasis on military alliances became outdated in the post-Stalin era, and in fact has been "perhaps

---

1. Quoted by Alexander Dallin, "The Soviet View of the United Nations," *International Organization, 16* (1962), 20.

partly responsible for many independent countries pursuing a policy of non-alignment." In this perspective, early bipolar East–West confrontations were gradually replaced by an East–Neutral–West political configuration. Recently, the Secretary-General further suggested that this tripolar situation has "been superseded by *a complex and fluid pattern of international relations.*" In the light of these developments he urged the United States and the Soviet Union to make more use of the General Assembly of the United Nations as a *realistic representation of the present day world* in settling, by give and take, the issues between them.[2]

But even the Secretary-General's remarks are subject to diverse interpretations. At one point he argued that the primary problems in world politics are those of the developing countries.[3] In another context he predicted that the main political configuration of the 1970s, "if there are any '70s," will contain four centers of power— the United States, Europe, Russia and China.[4] This projection, although suggesting more dimensions of conflict than just a simple East–West one, appears to be oversimplified; the place of the developing countries of Latin America, Africa, and Southern Asia is unspecified and seemingly unimportant.

These conflicting interpretations focus on several related questions. First of all, has there been an evolving complexity and fluidity in international relations since the Second World War? Within the pattern that has evolved, has the cold war increased or decreased in intensity? What are the resulting prospects for the stability or even the survival of international society and politics as we know them?

One way to answer these questions is from a United Nations perspective. Broadening, for analytical purposes, U Thant's claim that the General Assembly is a "realistic representation of the present day world," the approach of this book will be to study these developments as reflected in its debates and decisions. The choice of such an arena for primary analysis may, of course, be disputed or defended by those whose interests have been offended or gratified by these decisions. It is our hope that the objectivity

2. This summary of the Secretary-General's views, as well as the direct quotations (with our emphasis) are from a news item, "Thant Asks Give and Take to Settle East–West Issues," *New York Times* (December 3, 1962).
3. Ibid.
4. "Thant Envisions 4 Power Groups," *New York Times* (June 29, 1963).

and reproducibility of modern social science techniques will help to control for such predispositions affecting our own viewpoints. We shall return to the valid questions of how "realistic" are the politics of the General Assembly in the following chapters.

Our central concern will be, then, to assess the pattern of international relations as it has developed and been reflected in the United Nations. Certainly this problem has at least five major aspects. (1) What are the main, distinctive *issues* that appear in the decisions of the General Assembly? (2) What are the *alignments* of states on these issues? How strongly, with what intensity, are these positions held? A satisfactory understanding and assessment of these issues, alignments, and intensities involves at least three more questions: (3) *What influences the states* within the United Nations to vote the way they do on the different issues before them? To urge a change in national foreign policies, as Thant has done, one must first understand the conditions for them. (4) Which states have been most successful in getting their way on the different issues? In other words, one must examine the *structure of power* within the General Assembly. (5) Finally, also implied in the Secretary-General's remarks is the crucial assumption that using General Assembly procedures will improve East–West relations, as well as give more satisfaction to the less developed nations represented there. We shall consider what have been and what could be the post-decisional *consequences* of political practices within the General Assembly. How do decisions in the United Nations affect the stability, development, and responsiveness of international politics?

Implicit in the rephrasing of our central concern is a *time* dimension. Change is inherent in the claim that the East–West confrontation is no longer the primary one within the United Nations, or, perhaps, even in international relations outside the General Assembly. For each of our questions we should have asked: What have been the main political developments within the United Nations General Assembly at different times, and what might they be in the future? After a discussion of data and methods of analysis in Chapter 2, the next four chapters will discuss the issues and alignments that have appeared in four different sessions of the General Assembly, and Chapter 7 will attempt to assess trends and future projections of their common elements.

Part Two of this book seeks to answer questions about the deter-minants of national voting behavior and the resulting power structure in the General Assembly. Trends and prospects regarding the consequences of these votes will also be assessed. We shall compare the pattern of politics that has developed in the Assembly with a model of one kind of relatively stable international system. With such a model, specific changing conditions and patterns can be assessed in terms of their impact on the stability and responsiveness of the world political system.

The remainder of this chapter outlines prospective answers to the questions noted above, laying a basis for the more detailed year-by-year discussions to follow.

### ISSUES AND ALIGNMENTS IN THE GENERAL ASSEMBLY

Substantive classifications of issues before the United Nations have usually been similar to those used by Thomas Hovet in his *Bloc Politics in the United Nations,* and those in *International Concilation's* annual review of issues before the next General Assembly. Both approaches represent a refinement of the subject categories formally assigned to the Main Committees of the Assembly; these categories, in turn, are spelled out in varying degrees by the Charter of the organization. In summary, Hovet distinguishes:

  a.  Collective measures, including such issues as regulation of armaments
  b.  Peaceful settlement
  c.  Self-determination
  d.  Economic cooperation
  e.  Social and cultural matters
  f.  Humanitarian cooperation (i.e. relief and short-term social cooperation)
  g.  Human rights
  h.  Development of international law
  i.  Administrative, procedural, and structural matters [5]

The obvious advantage of such a classification is that an issue like the

5. Thomas Hovet, Jr., *Bloc Politics in the United Nations* (Cambridge, Harvard University Press, 1960), pp. 24 ff. The issue categories used by Robert E. Riggs in his *Politics in the United Nations* (Urbana, University of Illinois Press, 1958) correspond more closely to Committee distinctions than to Hovet's less arbitrary classification.

future of West Irian, which was discussed in the First Committee (formally concerned with Political and Security Affairs), can be listed both as a question of peaceful settlement and also as involving, in some views, self-determination. Clearly colonialism's many aspects are by no means confined to the Fourth Committee (entrusted with trusteeship questions, including non-self-governing territories). Despite their superiority over committee-based distinctions, such single or multiple assignments must still be based on scholarly judgments, which, it appears, are not easy to replicate.

Hovet's major concern is with bloc (or more accurately, caucusing or interest group) politics in the Assembly. Methodologically his approach reduces to an interesting discussion of the degree of cohesion of different groups over time on votes classified according to his issue categories listed above. Although it provides an important focus for the study of regional cooperation or integration, this approach does not help significantly to elucidate his principal concern, the political process of the General Assembly, *considering*  *simultaneously the interaction of different groups with each other.*

Other studies have used the "bloc voting" framework of analysis. Although limited to the study of several votes from each of the first four sessions of the Assembly, M. Margaret Ball's early paper [6] has the advantage of analyzing specific issues, such as Spanish membership, the partition of Palestine, South West Africa, and the admission of China, in concrete detail. Her substantive conclusions are similar to Hovet's for the same period; she too does not generalize about when, how, and why groups differ from each other.

Geoffrey Goodwin has also assessed the voting behavior of the different caucusing groups on specific issues, including Hungary, Chinese membership, West Irian, and the future of the Cameroons. He concluded that voting figures do not reflect all of the deliberations' consequences nor the intensities of national involvements. In response to charges that bloc voting by the anticolonial countries is "irresponsible," Goodwin demonstrated that the voting patterns are not always simple ones and argued that organized groups within the United Nations add much needed coherence to its political process and do, by and large, reflect the state of world politics as

6. M. Margaret Ball, "Bloc Voting in the General Assembly," *International Organization,* 5 (1951), 3–31.

it is today.[7] The implicit assumption of the critics of bloc voting is that the colonial powers more and more frequently find themselves in an isolated minority. This claim and Goodwin's defense we shall investigate more thoroughly.

Sydney Bailey's perceptive description of the political process within the General Assembly gives an overview missing in most previous roll-call analyses:

> The outstanding fact about the way States associate in the General Assembly is the tendency of Member States to affiliate differently for different purposes. Liberia and the Philippines, for example, usually associate with the heterogeneous group of States which vote with the United States on Cold War issues, but on colonial questions they associate with the even more heterogeneous anti-colonial group. The Western States, to take another example, present a united front on most cold war questions, but split on certain issues involving human rights, colonial matters, the question of domestic jurisdiction, and Chinese representation.[8]

Among the bloc voting studies, Hovet's has the advantage of issue classifications that are generalized sufficiently to allow for summary statements and trend analyses. However, because the particular items within his issue categories are not identified, his descriptions lack the graphic nature of the more selective discussions by Ball, Goodwin, and Bailey.

Serious misperceptions may result from too great a preoccupation with the bloc phenomenon. A relevant example of bloc preoccupation in American policy making is a State Department summary form for describing votes in the United Nations.[9] Roll calls are described briefly down the left side of the page in chronological

7. Geoffrey Goodwin, "The Expanding UN: I. Voting Patterns," *International Affairs* (London), *36* (1960) , 174–87.

8. Sydney D. Bailey, "Coalitions, Groups and Blocs in the Assembly," Chap. 2 of his *The General Assembly of the United Nations: A Study of Procedure and Practice* (New York, Praeger, 1961). In the chapters of *Politics in the United States* not containing roll-call analyses, Riggs descriptions of the Assembly's political process are also quite revealing.

9. H. G. Nicholas believes that "much of the exaggerated concern over bloc voting proceeds from an exaggerated respect for voting as such." See his *The United Nations as a Political Institution* (New York, Oxford University Press, 1959), pp. 120 ff. The sheet to be described was shown to one of the authors by an acquaintance in the State Department.

order. Across the top countries are listed by region, with their votes on the various roll calls given underneath. The results are summarized by giving four figures: the number of votes with the United States, the number with the Soviet Union, the number with both, and the number with neither. Neutral positions of sorts are included, but no attention is given in the summary to the substance or nuance of an issue. On whose initiative or with what consequences were these votes cast? It may just as well be that Russia is voting with the neutrals as that they are voting with the Russians. And of course from the standpoint of American policy considerations some votes are much more important than others, besides representing very different issues.

The absence of these distinctions may also be noted in some diplomats' statements that the Latin Americans never voted against the United States before the Castro regime came to power in Cuba, or that all the neutrals or all the Western powers vote the same way. As all careful voting analyses have shown, only the Soviet bloc, with a few exceptions, mostly in 1946 and 1947, has been consistently united.[10]

A final important contribution to the literature on decision making in the UN is a theoretical interpretation offered by Ernst Haas.[11] Writing in 1956, when the membership of nonaligned states in the United Nations had recently increased, Haas suggested that collective security efforts for the different regional groupings in the UN were translated into two operational maxims: permissive enforcement, and balancing. In line with the first maxim, different groupings of states have tried to obtain United Nations legitimization of their policies. After a related countermove, balancing attempts based on compromises within and between regional groupings have tried to avert a clear-cut victory by either side. Thus, in Korea, first the West and then the Communists sought UN endorsement of their plans for POW exchange. The final decision was largely based

10. Hovet, p. 128. While not at all preoccupied with cold war issues, it is disappointing that the main methodological improvement of Hovets recent *Africa in the United Nations* (Evanston, Northwestern University Press, 1963) is to give percentage agreement scores for various groups with both the United States and the Soviet Union. No other polarizing pairs of nations, such as Israel and the Arabs or South Africa and "Black Africa," are similarly treated.

11. Ernst Haas, "Regionalism, Functionalism and Universal International Organization," *World Politics, 8* (1956), 238–63. Haas cites earlier works by George Liska and Cora Bell.

on Indian proposals which fitted somewhere between the positions held by the two camps.

Haas concentrates more on the different functional concerns of international decision making than on the "who's with us and who's not" tendencies of bloc analysis. As the primary functional concerns constituting the balancing process within and between the Western countries, the nonaligned countries, and to some extent even the Soviet bloc, he sees "security issues, colonial aspirations, and economic demands."

We may detail two additional examples of the balancing process in operation. Because of their desire to enlist the majority of the nonaligned states in the cause of their security concerns, both the United States and the Soviet Union had to give considerable ground in their original opposition to a Special United Nations Fund. Similarly, America was eager to have the United Nations approve the self-governing status of Puerto Rico. The Russians desired to compound the problems of the colonial powers by means of a resolution on the specifics of decisions regarding the self-governing nature of certain territories. The result was a compromise package containing both measures. Neither great power felt it could protest. The most important assumption of Haas' analysis is that permissive enforcement efforts by any major regional grouping will be resisted by a balancing bloc *and* by dissent within the contending regional systems, leading to the presentation of attractive compromise solutions.[12] In this regard, bloc analysis in terms of general issue categories such as "peaceful settlement" or even "colonialism" is not sufficiently precise to say when and on what issues there is dissent within groups along dimensions where potential balancing states exist.

Building from both the contributions and the gaps in earlier work

---

12. Haas, p. 260. Without stressing the importance of internal regional dissent, Kock and Triska make a similar point: "In terms of the Cold War . . . the primary function of the Asian–African coalition has been prophylactic: by withholding support from the West on certain issues, it has indicated areas of Western vulnerability; and when aligning itself with the West it has drawn attention to communist excesses." Jan Triska and Howard Kock, "Asian–African Coalition and International Organization: Third Force or Collective Impotence?" *The Review of Politics,* 21 (1959), 417–55. For a careful and illuminating published account of the Assembly's decision process on the Special United Nations Fund, see J. G. Hadwen and J. Kaufman, *How United Nations Decisions Are Made* (New York, Oceana, 1961).

we may suggest the following questions about issues and alignments in Assembly voting:

1. Numerous uncertainties and misperceptions continue regarding the nature of the distinct issues before the United Nations. Can we find a way of naturally and objectively summarizing the issues before the General Assembly without losing their specific content?

2. Could such an analysis be relatively comprehensive, rather than merely illustrative?

3. Could it also allow us to study the cohesion of the different groupings within the United Nations and the meaning and direction of dissent within them?

4. Could it describe simultaneously and precisely the policy positions of all the states involved in bloc, caucusing, or regional group disagreements? The relations between issues and groups should be clearly drawn.

5. Could we also describe all the main, perhaps functionally specific, issues before the Assembly in summary terms whose interrelations and trends would be meaningful?

6. Finally, could we discover something about the significance or prominence of different questions that UN members discuss? As Haas notes,[13] consequential balancing or compromising of interests, with a possibly related reduction in international tensions, cannot occur over issues of little interest to the nations involved.

### THE DISTRIBUTION OF POWER IN THE GENERAL ASSEMBLY

As mentioned previously, U Thant has urged the great powers to make more use of the General Assembly as a realistic representation of the present-day world, a world containing many other issues distinct from the cold war. Crucial to his analysis is the assumption of a growing diffusion of power in international relations. Compared with the Security Council's veto privilege for great powers, the General Assembly's political formula of one nation—one vote is, at least potentially, radically decentralized. As issues and alignments distinct from the cold war arise, the power of cold war bloc leaders is also likely to decline. To urge greater use of the General Assembly is therefore to favor the continuation of this diffusion of power.

13. Ibid., p. 250.

Other observers have noted the decentralization of power within the United Nations.[14] From one such view the reinstatement of a decentralized international balance of power system, supported by a nuclear stalemate, may be the key to world stability in the future.[15] The Secretary-General's view may be a similar one, although it certainly involves enhanced peacekeeping and policymaking activities in the United Nations context as well.

There also exist diametrically opposed views about the reality and/or the desirability of such developments. Morton Kaplan views world politics as bipolarity structured, based on highly centralized nuclear resources. He believes that there will be no unbearable proliferation of nuclear powers; instead, within a generation one side of the East–West struggle will prevail.[16] And of course the orthodox communist sees the world headed toward the inevitable triumph of socialism over capitalism, rather than perpetual peaceful co-existence.

Yet another possibility is that of a stabilized bipolar world order. While agreeing that "the polarization of the world community between the so-called free world and the Communist bloc is clearly the most immediate source of the danger of general war," Talcott Parsons has suggested that this very aspect of the international situation presents an attractive opportunity. The development of communications and other aspects of interdependence have compelled all nations to be aware of important events everywhere. And the common recognition of an ideological "battle" between

14. For instance, Lincoln Bloomfield believes "power has become diffused and is likely to become more so." Cf. his "The New Diplomacy in the United Nations," in Francis O. Wilcox and H. Field Haviland, eds., *The United States and the United Nations* (Baltimore, Johns Hopkins University Press, 1961), p. 72.

15. In the summary of his "A Multi-Bloc Model of the International System," Roger Masters sees "five or more integrated regional blocs [participating] in a 'balance of power' system not unlike the traditional historical system of European nation-states. This implies a considerable flexibility in alignments, a willingness to limit all warfare (especially in order not to destroy a major bloc) and a tendency to absorb all uncommitted states into one or another bloc. . . . The introduction of an invulnerable nuclear capability considerably alters the influence of numbers by reducing the desirability of alliance as a means of achieving objectives." *American Political Science Review, 55* (1961), 780–98.

16. Morton Kaplan, "Bipolarity in A Revolutionary Age," in Kaplan, ed., *Revolution in World Politics* (New York, Wiley, 1962), p. 266. Personal communications have brought out this view.

East and West presumes "a common frame of reference in terms of which ideological differences make sense. . . . In so far as [such] a conflict of orientations can be defined as 'political' and in so far as it occurs within a pattern of order rather than a Hobbesian state of nature," Parsons suggests that we can refer to the existence of a stabilizing "two party system" in international relations.[17]

Perhaps some additional insights into the distribution of power within the Assembly can be derived from the literature on American community power structures. The recent writing contains an important distinction that has cropped up implicitly in each of the summary questions we have so far discussed. In the terms of an early article, what is the "dimensionality of influence?"[18] For instance, Robert Dahl has taken three "issue-areas"—political nominations, urban redevelopment, and public education—as representative of key decisions made in New Haven.[19] The distribution of power in one substantive area may not correspond to that in another. One must look at a fair number of actual decisions in carefully defined issue-areas over a period of years in order accurately to describe changes in the distribution of power and of other rewards. Such evidence is necessary for any comprehension of the likely stabilizing or destabilizing consequences of a bipolar or multipolar international system. The appropriateness of such models for the international system will be discussed at length in Part Two.

DETERMINANTS OF VOTING BEHAVIOR IN THE UNITED NATIONS

We may paraphrase an often heard point of view about the events and forces that influence the Assembly: "The United Nations is a mirror of the world around it; if the reflection is ugly, the organization should not be blamed."[20] More technically, Ernst Haas has made a similar point in describing the United Nations as a multi-

17. Talcott Parsons, "Polarization and the Problem of International Order," in Morton Deutsch, ed., *Preventing World War Three* (New York, Simon & Schuster, 1963).

18. James March, "An Introduction to the Theory and Measurement of Influence," *American Political Science Review*, 49 (1955), 431–51.

19. Robert A. Dahl, *Who Governs?* (New Haven, Yale University Press, 1961).

20. See Bloomfield, "The New Diplomacy," p. 51. Sir Gladwyn Jebb is credited with the original language of this remark.

phase system "whose characteristics and evolutionary potential must be specified in terms of the changing environment in which it operates." [21]

Of course what happens in the immediate context of UN activities, be it in New York, Palestine, or the Congo, also shapes to some extent the policies enunciated by nations in the General Assembly. The empirical justification of those who emphasize the phenomenon of bloc voting must be that groupings which exist *there* are the most significant or accurate predictors of foreign policies expressed in the Assembly. The counterargument is that particular or common *national* concerns are in the long run more determinative of voting behavior. Such concerns may or may not be shared through caucusing group activities. In brief, the world environment, not the UN process as such, shapes more of the decisions. From this view the phenomenon of bloc voting might be explained by geopolitically similar interests rather than by caucusing bloc pressures.[22]

Personal predispositions help to determine the level of analysis from which one approaches voting behavior in the UN.[23] The optimistic observer will claim as the best predictors or explanations of such behavior those instruments of influence over which he believes he has the greatest control; the pessimist, on the other hand, would probably stress influences he appeared to control least. For instance, some diplomats in the UN verbally single out the eccentricities of particular ambassadors or the behind-the-scenes negotiating process between caucusing groups. Others recall positions determined by foreign ministers. Some military or economic aid administrators, as well as some Congressmen voting for such programs, would see foreign aid and trade as the main sources of pro-Western voting.

21. Ernst Haas, "Dynamic Environment and Static System: Revolutionary Regimes in the United Nations," in Kaplan, p. 278. Italics omitted.

22. Whether the votes of the newer and smaller nations in the UN are commensurate with their role in international relations is another question. Some observers, such as Senator Henry Jackson, have demanded a deemphasis of the United Nations in American foreign policy. They claim that the one nation–one vote system is far from a realistic representation of the present day world, and that to overemphasize strategies designed to succeed within the organization is to invite disaster in the real world arena.

23. James Rosenau, "Pre-Theories and Theories of Foreign Policy" (mimeo., 1964), has suggested that such predispositions might be called pre-theories about what kinds of variables will be most determinative of national policies in an international arena. In his view the *validity* of a particular pre-theory depends, among other things, on the size, development, and competitiveness of the state being considered.

Ideologists on both sides of the Iron Curtain stress competing economic and political systems as the essential characteristic of conflicts in the world today. Cynics have offered the related hypothesis that "the more Communists you have, the more aid you are likely to receive." Two mythmakers, Lenin and Rostow, have plausibly asserted that the stage of a nation's economic development might be a more important influence on voting behavior.

J. David Singer has summarized current literature on international relations theory in terms of the link between the internal and external forces at work upon the nation and its general foreign policy behavior. For him the question is which level of analysis— a systemic analysis of world politics or the level of subsystem components, nation states—is the most profitable. He concludes:

> In terms of description, we find that the systemic level produces a more comprehensive and total picture of international relations than does the national or sub-systemic level. On the other hand, the atomized and less coherent image produced by the lower level of analysis is somewhat balanced by its richer detail, greater depth, and more intensive portrayal.[24]

In Part Two we shall study both systemwide and subsystem influences on voting in the General Assembly. It will thus be possible to use both environmental variables, such as national economic and political development, and regional or caucusing group variables in explaining behavior on the different dimensions of voting in the General Assembly.

### STABILITY AND CHANGE IN THE INTERNATIONAL SYSTEM

The responsiveness of the international system to a multiplicity of changing demands is often thought to be related to its stability. Functionalist theory, for example, asserts that economic and social cooperation in specific and primarily nonpolitical tasks provides a way to mitigate conflicts both within and between states. The pragmatic development of special-purpose organizations will bring about procedural systems and areas of cooperation with "the various strata

---

24. J. David Singer, "The Level-of-Analysis Problem in International Relations," *World Politics*, 14 (1961), 89. Rosenau, "Toward A Pre-Theory," sees five possible levels of analysis: personal idiosyncracies, roles, intragovernmental variables, societal factors, and systemic effects.

of social need which cut across national dividing lines." [25] This is a widely held view. The balancing process suggested by Haas, Chadwick Alger's hypotheses regarding "overlapping conflict systems," [26] Parsons' analysis of crosscutting interests or solidarities in world politics,[27] and the moderating effects of "multiple memberships" suggested by students of American politics [28] all imply distinctive, perhaps functional, dimensions of conflict as part of the international political process.

The functionalist school looks for the mitigation of conflict in the development of nonpolitical ties. Other theorists, such as Haas, Alger, and Parsons, hope for cross-national allegiances to develop *through* the political process. Taking a term from the political theory of national systems, we may label these writers "political pluralists," to distinguish them from apolitical functionalists. These two groups share a common concern with restructuring allegiances and interests in a way conducive to peaceful international development.

Both voluntaristic and deterministic interpretations of the consequences of changing issues, alignments, and power structures are possible. An increase of crosscutting and negotiable "political" or "nonpolitical" interests, without sharply increasing or decreasing power for some of the major states involved, may deterministically imply more flexible and pragmatic, less dogmatic and less unstabilizing policies. The converse of this hypothesis, which may be argued from either a functionalist or a pluralist point of view, suggests that changing voting positions that vastly increase the voting power of some nations at the expense of others will decrease the possibilities of a mutually profitable balancing process in the United Nations.

25. See Inis L. Claude, Jr., *Swords into Plowshares* (2d ed. New York, Random House, 1961), Chap. 16, for an elaboration and criticism of the functionalist literature.

26. Chadwick Alger, "Non-Resolution Consequences of the United Nations and Their Effect on International Conflict," *Journal of Conflict Resolution*, 5 (1961), 128–47.

27. Parsons, "Polarization and the Problem of International Order."

28. For instance we might cite the works of de Tocqueville, the voting literature, and David Truman's *The Governmental Process* (New York, Albert A. Knopf, 1951). Since most of our own ideas about possible influences on international conflict are drawn from domestic political examples, it may not be inappropriate at this point to note that the functionalist approach to world peace also owes much to ideas about various national forms of political pluralism, such as guild socialism. See Harold E. Engle, "A Critical Study of the Functionalist Approach to International Organization" (unpublished Ph.D. dissertation, Columbia University, 1957).

And such a decline will negatively influence the authority or effectiveness of UN conflict resolution procedures.

On the other hand, even when structural or environmental bases
for conflict appear to be multiplying, statesmanlike political leadership (or bargaining) may be increasingly effective in averting strife.
Such actions might cause systemic or environmental predictors of
policy positions to break down. A careful look at the issues and
years when voting does not appear so closely linked to caucusing
group memberships, foreign aid, military or colonial ties, or immediate economic or security needs might be worthwhile in studying freedom of action in Assembly voting and its consequences.

In some manageable fashion, then, one would want to know about
developments in the General Assembly on policy agreements and
disagreements, successes and failures. When, for whom, on what
issues, and, if possible, why, have they occurred? With some tentative
answers to these questions we will be in a position to assess the
consequences—be they stable or unstable, favorable or unfavorable
—of the changing patterns of power and policy in the General Assembly.

PART I

# Issues and Alignments

# CHAPTER 2

# The Analysis of Assembly Roll Calls

To be feasible, a balanced appraisal of voting dimensions must be selective; for such an analysis to be objective, its methods should be appropriate and its results reproducible. Any examination of politics in the United Nations requires selection among the various organs, activities, and decisions. We shall concentrate on the General Assembly and its main committees in assessing developing issues and alignments. All member states are represented in the Assembly, and these states are repeatedly required to take formal positions on almost every issue of importance before the United Nations. The Assembly has several advantages as the subject of study: its comprehensive membership, agenda, records, and frequent roll-call votes. These votes may occur any time at the request of any member, and record the different national foreign policy positions with unparalleled completeness. No publicly available information about any other UN body is nearly as adequate for our purposes.[1]

Other methodological decisions remain to be made. Which debates, votes, and supplementary materials should be used, and what techniques of analysis are best, or most feasible, for the subject of this inquiry?

1. A limitation in restricting the detailed analysis to issues on which roll-call votes appear is that step by step consensus-building achievements of the United Nations often do not appear in these votes. Among others, Nicholas, *The UN as a Political Institution*, p. 120, has criticized Western and neutral nations for "maximizing votes rather than maximizing agreement." But just because roll calls more often express disagreements than agreements, they are useful summaries of voting alignments.

Diplomats interviewed in New York stress the elaborate behind-the-scenes negotiations that take place about the kinds of resolutions to be introduced, by whom, in return for what services, etc. Yet even if some diplomats believe that "half the Assembly's decisions are made in the Delegates' Lounge" (what about the capitals of the world?), the most controversial and important ones will probably be *reflected* in roll-call voting.

## THE GROWTH OF THE GENERAL ASSEMBLY

Certain sessions of the General Assembly must be singled out for special attention. The problem of selecting years for the description of United Nations voting behavior has been approached in various ways by different scholars. Some have studied specific time periods, such as several consecutive sessions, or the years before or after Stalin's death. Thomas Hovet, in the most exhaustive study yet published, included all the roll-call votes from each of the first thirteen regular Assembly sessions.[2] Our resources demanded that only a few years be chosen, but the need for comprehensiveness and an interest in trends required that they be taken from various periods in UN history.

There is fair agreement among scholars as to what these periods in the growth of the General Assembly have been. Elmore Jackson has characterized the beginning of the United Nations as the period of the Security Council, marked by an effort to make the United Nations work as it was originally conceived.[3] Similarly, Ernst Haas has described an early "honeymoon period" of attempted unity among the great powers.[4] With the intensification of the cold war, this period came to its end. Bloomfield felt the disillusionment of "morning after" by the middle of 1947.[5] While Jackson gives no specific terminal date before 1950, Haas mentions 1947 as the last year of this first period.

In Bloomfield's view, the year 1950 "began with the Communist countries progressively boycotting the United Nations, and it culminated in a war. There followed a period in which, among other things, the Soviet Union did its best to make an 'unperson,' in the Orwellian sense, of the Secretary General." Jackson considers the years 1950 to 1955 the period of the General Assembly, symbolized by the Uniting for Peace Resolution adopted to deal with Soviet vetoes in the Security Council over Korea. For Haas the UN's second

2. Hovet, *Bloc Politics in the UN.*

3. This description and those attributed to Jackson that follow are taken from Elmore Jackson, "The Future Development of the United Nations: Some Suggestions for Research," *Journal of Conflict Resolution,* 5 (1961), 119–28.

4. Ernst Haas, "Dynamic Environment and Static System," pp. 279 ff., is the source for all of Haas' remarks cited in this section.

5. Bloomfield, "The New Diplomacy in the United Nations," pp. 49–50. Other references to Bloomfield's views in this section are from the same source.

phase was one of American dominance and successful enlistment of Assembly majorities. The emphasis of all three of these views is essentially the same.

The admission of sixteen new states in December 1955 symbolized a new period in the United Nations' history. Haas sees this enlargement and the decline of American dominance as a culmination of changes taking place in the world environment in 1953 and 1954.[6] As mentioned in the previous chapter, he views the third phase of the United Nations as characterized by bargaining between regions and bargaining between countries primarily concerned with different issues. The setting is one in which the colonial and human rights issues have furnished the dominant motif, with the practice of collective security increasingly subordinated to it in terms of the kind of support forthcoming for Western bloc demands.

Again in terms of structural modifications of the United Nations, Elmore Jackson considers this third stage in the UN's life the period of the Secretary-General. Operating against the background of a veto-inhibited Security Council and a large and unwieldy Assembly unable to issue precise instructions, "Mr. Hammarskjold developed the executive arm of the United Nations into a formidable tool of international diplomacy." His handling of the Suez Crisis was the most outstanding instance of this development.

The Congo crisis, East–West competition over the role of the United Nations there, Russian rejection of Hammarskjold, his death, and the appointment of an Asian Acting Secretary-General, symbolized a new stage in United Nations concerns and capacities. While the majority of the new states admitted in 1955 had been European, *all* of the 23 new members admitted between 1956 and 1960 were African or Asian, bringing the United Nations' total membership close to 100. Jackson describes the present period as "a basic struggle for control of the organization" in the presence of Afro–Asian majorities. With the end of the colonial issue as a dominant theme Professor Haas believes the Assembly's fourth phase will involve increased economic demands on East and West

6. In addition to McCarthyism we would mention the inconclusive end to the Korean War, improved East–West relations in part due to Stalin's death, and the Colombo Conference of 1954, setting the stage for the Bandung Conference in the spring of 1955. Riggs, p. 174, and Hovet, p. 104, also note a decline in American influence in 1953 and 1954.

and, perhaps, the funneling by the Soviet bloc and certain under-developed allies of their "collective security" needs into the General Assembly.

It seemed reasonable, then, to choose four years, each from a different period of the United Nations, to test these views of UN developments.[7] Each period contains special crises which, if they continued to be of concern, would be found in the voting in subsequent years. Rather than risk having almost all the votes in 1950 or 1956 or 1960 reveal only a cold war, Suez, or Congo align-ment, and to catch the cumulative effects of these crises, years follow-ing them have been chosen. The somewhat atypical nature of the first session suggested that it also be excluded. Taking evenly spaced years from those remaining under consideration, and including the Sixteenth Session—the latest one for which records were available at the beginning of this research—the Second, Seventh, Twelfth, and Sixteenth Sessions were chosen for intensive study. These are the regular sessions commencing in 1947, 1952, 1957, and 1961.[8]

### SELECTING "IMPORTANT" ROLL CALLS

Within the four sessions chosen for intensive analysis, the decision was made to collect all roll calls and then decide which were the most important in terms of explicit criteria. For the principal analyses, the final result was the selection of 48 important roll calls for the Second Assembly, 63 for the Seventh, 50 for the Twelfth, and

7. Certainly other historical interpretations exist, as a reading of the Carnegie Endowment's National Studies on International Organization would show. We have already discussed U Thant's interpretation of UN developments. Soviet views and those of other non-Western states will be reviewed in the appropriate chapters below.

8. The detailed analysis of all sixteen regular sessions and of the several special and emergency sessions of the Assembly would of course be preferable if the resources were available. The time and the effort necessary to do an intensive and comprehensive analysis required the sampling of developments in the United Nations, rather than the careful analysis of all of them. The validity of the characteristics and of the trends thus established will be subject to the peculiarities of the sessions we have chosen; their atypicality will be assessed in the summary chapters. But as the reader will see, in the four sessions chosen there are a number of regularities that do allow for some confidence in generalizing these findings to the years in between as well. A further test of some of these interpretations, using the records of several emergency sessions, may be found in H. R. Alker, Jr., "The Politics of Supranationalism in the United Nations," *Proceedings of the Second Peace Research Conference*, Chicago, 1964 (forthcoming).

70 for the Sixteenth. For each year they represent about one third of all the roll calls recorded.[9]

It would of course be valuable to have some other source of information on attitudes. Nevertheless, and despite its limitations, the study of roll calls is now a generally accepted procedure in research on representative bodies. As David Truman has pointed out in another context, "The public character of the choices recorded in . . . roll calls . . . considerably enhances their value as data. In particular it narrows somewhat the problem of attaching meaning or intent to the vote. The registered choice is one [the state] . . . is willing to have . . . available for whatever use both opponents and supporters may wish to make of it."[10] To supplement this information on the *direction* of attitudes, data on *intensity* i.e. how strongly a delegation feels about a particular viewpoint, were also collected; the particular measures of intensity are described in Part II.

### An Earlier Approach

Which roll calls should be selected? The extent of procedural voting and the amount of duplication on resolutions voted on both in committee and plenary caused Thomas Hovet to "adjust" the number of roll calls in his study to a size more accurately representing the degree of bloc voting involved. His "adjusted gross" set includes:

> 1. All substantive roll-call votes in the plenary except issues which were overwhelmingly defeated in the main committee paragraph-by-paragraph, in which case only one plenary roll call will be included—the key paragraph vote which set the voting trend.

9. Hovet, p. 14, records that of 8,917 votes in the plenary or main committees of the General Assembly in its first thirteen regular sessions, only 1,908, or about 22% of them, were roll-call votes. The others were "show-of-hands" votes or motions "adopted-without-objection." While votes of this last sort are not very interesting, it is clear that many of the "show-of-hands" votes would be worth considering for analysis—if one knew how each nation had voted on them. Professor Hovet does have this information, but only in strict confidence from several different delegations.

10. David Truman, *The Congressional Party* (New York, Wiley, 1959), p. 13. As noted from time to time in the text, interviews with UN diplomats as well as their published writings have also been very helpful in interpreting our findings.

2. Substantive roll-call votes of the main committees which were overruled by the plenary.

3. Only the most important procedural roll calls in the main committees and plenary.[11]

Procedural questions aside, all plenary votes except "spite votes" are included. All but exceptional committee votes, i.e. those reversed by a switch of a few votes in the plenary or by the stiffer two-thirds majority required there, are excluded.

## The Approach of This Study

In terms of our own special concerns, several problems arose in attempting to select important roll calls by these criteria. Generally they involved trying not to omit the most interesting committee votes. Hovet's first criterion legitimately emphasizes the importance of omitting spite votes. In some cases, however, it seems too strict, in others, too unfair a criterion. A study of voting alignments might well omit all but one vote on a resolution on which some sponsor received identical rebuffs, paragraph by paragraph, for propaganda purposes. It often happens, however, that spite resolutions reveal quite different responses. Many Afro–Asians and some Latin Americans will abstain on or vote for the more innocuous paragraphs of a Russian resolution, but vote against harsh or condemnatory wording and the resolution as a whole. For example, on the ten separate votes asked by the Russians on their resolution in the First Committee in 1947 on the Balkan situation, 36 states did not oppose a recommendation that conventions for the regulation of frontier incidents be established, while only 17 states did not oppose the whole resolution holding Greece responsible. One might legitimately want to analyze more than the one plenary agenda vote on the subject. On the other hand, when six identically worded resolutions asking the Security Council to reconsider membership applications vetoed by Russia were overwhelmingly passed in plenary session by virtually the same margin, one might equally suspect the West of propaganda efforts in requiring roll calls on all these votes.

Hovet's second criterion is rather arbitrary. Of course, subjects important enough to be voted upon by roll call in committee and plenary, with substantial realignments in between, are especially

11. Hovet, pp. 20–22.

interesting and worthy of attention. While most important resolutions do appear in plenary roll calls, it may happen that no one will request a roll call for a contest already over. Retaining only committee votes overruled by the plenary seems a poor way of keeping the most important earlier votes. Some of these issues may appear in plenary only as show-of-hand votes; some may not appear at all; and some of them may be virtually the same roll call passed by a 50 per cent majority in committee, but failing of two-thirds support in the plenary. In the latter case there is some not very interesting duplication.

For example, let us consider the votes discussed above. The varying positions taken in committee on the controversial issue of the Balkan conflict never appeared as roll calls in plenary voting. Issues and alignments that are heatedly debated and repeatedly voted on by roll call in committee, but not in plenary, belong in a consideration of important alignments. As we have noted, such votes from the Second, Third, Fifth, and Sixth Committees would be interesting, especially if they were considered important enough by some members to be decided by roll calls. The tendency of plenary voting to be preoccupied with urgent political or colonial issues should not exclude at least some representation of other issues.

Hovet's third criterion seems unexceptionable: the exclusion of unimportant procedural roll calls in committee and plenary. They usually, but not always, duplicate other votes of clearer substantive import. As Hovet notes, *important* procedural votes are best determined contextually. Clearest among them are controversies over whether an item (such as Chinese membership) should be put on the agenda and votes deciding whether a simple or a two-thirds majority will be required to pass a resolution. Heated procedural debates with substantive overtones producing alignments not found in other roll calls were also included.

Working with simplified categories of group cohesion (unanimous, unanimous except for abstentions, or divided) Hovet could ignore with relative ease a problem that must be faced in a study of voting alignments: what should one do about absentee states? When evidence from other votes suggests an absent state would have voted differently from other group members, omitting that state from consideration may be misleading about the exact degree of group solidarity; it certainly will distort our empirical assessment of the policy position of that particular state. *When a state is absent in protest, its position is usually quite clear on the issues being discussed and can be reliably estimated.* To leave out such an estimate of this position would be not to take full advantage of fairly reliable information. Even on issues which appear peripheral to a state's concerns, to treat its absence as an abstention might misrepresent that state's relation to either extreme. (As explained below, we need not invariably assign a middle position to abstentions.) *If a state is absent because it is apathetic, a better estimate would be to assign the state a middle position between both extremes.* On the other hand, diplomats report that sometimes an absence really does mean an abstention—a state is too torn to be listed with either side, but does not want the embarrassment of public indecision. *For states that are clearly cross-pressured an abstention would be the appropriate estimate.* In the original tabulation of the roll calls, the decision was made to estimate the voting positions of absent states by the criteria of this paragraph.[12] Even assuming only 50 per cent reliability in these estimates, resulting inaccuracies would rarely change the relation between a roll call and a voting dimension by as much as two per cent.

Unanimous or nearly unanimous roll calls were also excluded. Statistically, such votes inform us of few or no policy differences, and they tend to have few high intercorrelations with other roll calls evidencing greater divisions. Substantively, virtually unanimous agreements may represent a considerable achievement in the building of consensus, but they are not useful in describing voting dimensions. One deficiency of this approach should also be mentioned. The main information loss resulting from eliminating really unanimous roll calls has to do not so much with changes in the *ranking* of states along a particular dimension—South Africa will always appear very procolonial even if the 100–1 votes against her are excluded—but with how accurately we have assessed the *distance* between the most extreme and the less extreme exponents of a particular view.[13]

12. A further insight into the specifics of such estimates may be gleaned from the discussion of voting scores in the following section. The one or two states each with more than 30% absenteeism were eliminated from the factor analysis in order to keep down the number of estimates required.

13. One solution of the distance problem, which in statistical terminology is the problem of establishing an interval scale of measurement, is somehow to include the

We may summarize and make more precise the above discussion by stating the four criteria used in this study for selecting important roll calls:

1. *Include all substantive votes in plenary; only "key votes," however, will be taken from resolutions voted upon paragraph-by paragraph and overwhelmingly passed or defeated in committee or plenary.* "Key votes" are those giving the clearest indication of the issue at hand, as well as the clearest example (s) within a resolution of significantly different viewpoints, if any are found. An "overwhelming majority" may arbitrarily be taken to be greater than three out of four voters.

2. *Include "key" substantive committee votes when such votes, or their rough equivalents, do not appear in plenary roll calls; in particular, be sure to keep committee roll calls on which there is a sizable shift in alignments between committee and plenary hearings.* "Key" votes are as defined under rule 1 above. A fairly reasonable criterion for "rough equivalence" between two votes on the same subject matter is that fewer than ten states shift their votes by one position. (From "Yes" to "No" consists of *two* such shifts: "Yes" to "Abstain" to "No.") When "Abstain" is the most negative vote, a weaker version of this "shifts" criterion may be applied. This revision of Hovet's second criterion enables the inclusion of quite a few more committee votes in our analysis.

3. *Include procedural roll-call votes in plenary or committee (a) placing a controversial item on the agenda; (b) deciding if a two-thirds majority is required; or (c) having clear substantive implications not duplicated in other roll calls included.*

4. *No virtually unanimous roll calls will be included.* Roll calls will be considered virtually unanimous if they are within five single shifts of complete agreement.[14]

effects of almost unanimous votes. A modest beginning along these lines is indicated in H. R. Alker, Jr., "Dimensions of Conflict in the General Assembly," *American Political Science Review, 56* (1964), 642–57. Another possibility would be to estimate distances from interviews or the content of related debates.

14. The 104 states participating in the Sixteenth Session of the General Assembly were so many that the shifts criteria of the second and fourth rules were revised upward by 50%. The large number of plenary and committee roll calls on different subjects in the Seventh and, particularly, the Sixteenth Sessions led to a slightly more stringent application of the key vote references mentioned above. Details will be given in the appropriate chapters.

### FACTOR ANALYZING ROLL-CALL VOTES

As we have seen, a careful delineation of issues and alignments in United Nations voting is necessary for the detailed study of its political process. As reviewed in Chapter 1, "bloc analysis" techniques are clearly not adequate for our purposes. The six methodological questions asked there bear repeating in summary form. We would like a technique or techniques for meaningfully and objectively (1) summarizing the main distinctive issues before the UN, (2) in a comprehensive way, (3) allowing us to study group cohesion and the direction of dissent, (4) while at the same time allowing us to consider the positions on these issues of all the states involved, (5) in a manner facilitating comparisons, (6) and suggesting some idea of the importance of the different issues and alignments involved. Answering these questions takes us into an area of statistics unfamiliar to the ordinary reader. The exposition below is designed, wherever possible, to discuss in a nonmathematical fashion the decisions to be made.

### Guttman Scaling or Factor Analysis?

Leroy Rieselbach has suggested that a Guttman scale, unlike bloc analysis techniques, "provides a single continuum for rating the performance of individual countries," as well as blocs, and that the unidimensionality of a Guttman scale "ensures that we are dealing with a single or related groups of attitudes." [15]

The essential principle of Guttman scaling is this:

> The items can be arranged in an order so that an individual who agrees with or responds to any particular item also responds positively to all items of lower rank order. The rank order of items is the scale of items; the scale of persons is very similar, people being arranged in order according to the highest rank order of items (agreed to), which is equivalent to the number of positive responses in a perfect scale. [16]

Rieselbach, for example, presents a group of eight colonial ques-

15. Leroy Rieselbach, "Quantitative Techniques for Studying Voting Behavior in the UN General Assembly," *International Organization,* 14 (1960), 291–306.

16. Bert F. Green, "Attitude Measurement," in Gardner Lindzey, ed., *Handbook of Social Psychology* (2 vols. Cambridge, Addison-Wesley, 1954), 2, 353.

tions that form a Guttman scale. They range from voting against discussing the treatment of people of Indian origin in South Africa (which only Italy and South Africa opposed) to French accomplishments in Togoland, which all but the Soviet bloc and some Arab states approved. On intermediate issues, like a resolution calling for time estimates regarding eventual colonial self-government, states at either extreme voted as might be expected—the more anticolonial Latin Americans agreed and their more procolonial neighbors abstained.

As described, this colonial scale is an oversimplification. Hardly ever is unidimensionality so perfect that there are no variations within a scale, no "errors" where a nation is, say, more procolonial than its other votes would lead one to expect. But by convention, if no more than one nation in ten "errs" on any single issue and the total number of errors does not exceed 10 per cent, a scale is considered sufficiently reproducible from the nations' most extreme positions to be acceptable for analysis. When a collection of important votes has been divided into subsets of roll calls that "scale" with each other to this extent, one can then study group cohesion by seeing how close members of a caucus are to each other (in scale ranks) on "super-issues" that we know are perceived (voted upon) by nearly all members in a similar way.

Factor analysis may loosely be considered a multidimensional generalization of Guttman scale analysis.[17] It was chosen for the present study because of advantages over Guttman scaling as a technique of roll-call analysis. First, it takes explicitly into consideration the meaningful roll calls or individual votes that do not scale and therefore are left out of any Guttman analysis. Secondly, it infers *all* the distinct (uncorrelated) factors or super-issues that can be said to underlie a given set of data. Scales that are highly intercorrelated or roll calls that could fit in several different scales are not satisfactorily interpreted by Guttman scaling. Thus, for example, Rieselbach had to assign roll calls with several European

17. The methodologically inclined reader may be interested, however, in Guttman's demonstration of the differences between scales and factors. Louis Guttman, Chap. 4, in Samuel A. Stouffer et al., *Measurement and Prediction* (Princeton, Princeton University Press, 1950). Multidimensional scaling techniques, such as those described by Warren Torgerson in Chap. 11 of his *Theory and Methods of Scaling* (New York, Wiley, 1958) might be considered more natural generalizations of Guttman scaling than multidimensional factor analysis.

abstentions to a rather procolonial position because that position least affected the reproducibility of a Guttman scale. Factor analysis automatically checks individual hesitations to see if another consistent dimension of opinion is involved. From looking at the particular votes that Rieselbach puts all into one scale, one also wonders if some of them, for instance those on West Irian, reflect super-issues different in substance from the South African situation or France's termination of her Togoland trusteeship under UN guidance. Factor analysis allows for a more satisfactory identification of the principal components of these roll calls and a more accurate location of states on these voting components.

## Assigning Vote Scores

The first necessity in a factor analysis is to arrive at a method of assigning a number to each nation's vote on a roll call so that its positions on the implicit factors or super-issues might be determined. No sacrosanct technique exists for transforming "Yes," "Abstain," or "No" into ranks (*ordinal* measurement) or regular numbers with meaningful distances between them (an interval level of measurement). Several possibilities were considered.[18]

It was finally decided to use the ranks held by each state on a roll call. Thus "No" got the lowest rank, "Abstain" a higher rank, and "Yes" the highest rank. For example, on a roll call with ten "No" votes, 30 "Abstain" votes, and 60 "Yes" votes, the rank assigned to the ten countries in the negative would be their *average* rank, 5.5. Similarly, abstentions would merit 25.5; and affirmative votes would receive a rank of 70.5. Subtracting these ranks from the average

18. Robert Abelson suggested a number of transformations of the standardized ranks that were finally used. All would spread out voting positions to give more nearly normal frequency distributions. One such technique would be to find the percentile of a particular vote and find the corresponding z-score for a normal distribution, which might be a more plausible approximation to the underlying position of the state. Cf. Robert Abelson and John Tukey, "Efficient Conversion of Non-Metric Information into Metric Information," *Proceedings of the Social Statistics Section, 1959* (Washington, American Statistical Association, 1960), pp. 226–30.

An alternative technique would be to use the sum of rank reversals, as in Kendall's measures of ordinal correlation. This procedure, however, does not lend itself to as nice an operational interpretation as does the standardized rank for our data. On this and other methods, cf. John B. Carroll, "The Nature of the Data, or How to Choose a Correlation Coefficient," *Psychometrika, 26* (1961), 347–72. Cf. also L. Guttman, "Metricizing Rank-ordered or Unordered Data for a Linear Factor Analysis," *Sankhya, 2* (1959), 257–68.

rank of all nations that are voting (50.5), and standardizing the results so that the new voting scores have a mean of zero and an average squared value of one, the "standardized ranks" that result (indicated by Z's) would be Z(Yes) = 0.80, Z(Abstain) = −1.00, and Z(No) = −1.80. We see that voting affirmatively when 59 other nations do also gives a nation a positive score that is much smaller in magnitude (0.80) than the −1.80 given to the "extremists" in the negative. By these assignments, there are no completely neutral countries. Those abstaining against the pressure of a sizable majority come out closer to the scores of those who said No than they do to those in the affirmative.

Certainly many diplomats explain abstentions on such votes in a similar way. We believe that standardized ranks calculated in this manner contain more useful information than the usual bloc voting method of assigning a +1 score for any Yes and a zero or −1 score for any No, no matter how extreme or moderate the vote is in its context. This approach also allows more flexibility in estimating the voting position of absent nations: when available information did not suggest that either a Yes, No, or Abstain was an appropriate voting estimate, the state was given a truly middle position, the average standardized rank, namely zero.[19]

## Correlating Roll Calls

The correlation coefficient is a statistician's way of precisely measuring the *extent* to which two variables (e.g. roll calls) are associated with each other. Weighing each nation's vote equally, it allows him to answer the diplomat's question: *Do two roll calls reflect the same alignment and, if so, to what extent?* An understanding of this coefficient is worth the effort required: many of the results of Part I and Part II will be stated in such terms.

19. If $X_i$ is country $i$'s voting rank, $\overline{X}$ is the average voting rank, and $S_x$ is the standard deviation of the $X_i$'s $(S_x^2 = \frac{1}{N} \sum_{i=1}^{N} (X_i - \overline{X})^2)$, then a standardized voting rank $(Z_x(i))$ is given by the formula $Z_x(i) = \dfrac{X_i - \overline{X}}{S_x}$ (1)

For UN roll calls the range of the standardized rank (called a "Z-score") is from about 2.5 to −2.5. These ranks are almost the same as the figures used in Spearman's ordinal correlation coefficient, *rho*. Slight differences exist because the number of absentees given 0.0 Z-scores (after initial ranks were assigned) necessitates slight adjustments in Z-scores for other countries in order to keep the resulting ranks standardized.

The meaning of the correlation coefficient can most easily be explained in terms of standardized scores (Z-scores) for any two variables. Reverting to the specific example of two roll calls (call them X and Y respectively) from an Assembly with N members, it is convenient to represent the standardized voting ranks of any country i (where i is an index number ranging from 1 to N) by the expressions $Z_x(i)$ and $Z_y(i)$. It should be clear to the reader that when both $Z_x(i)$ and $Z_y(i)$ are above zero, roll calls X and Y are evoking similar positive or negative responses from country i. If for most other countries the same coincidence of high or low $Z_x$ and $Z_y$ occurs, we would wish to say that roll calls X and Y are positively correlated. The alignments they induce are positively associated with each other.

Statistically, it is possible to define a correlation coefficient that reflects the arguments suggested above. The necessary mathematical insight for designing such a coefficient is the realization that when $Z_x(i)$ and $Z_y(i)$ are *both* either positive *or* negative, the *product* of the two Z-scores is *always* positive. Because of the ways they are defined, adding and averaging Z-score products gives a measure of association that ranges from r = +1.0 (the case of perfect association, i.e. exactly corresponding alignments) to r = −1.0 (the case of perfect negative association, where all the Yesses on one roll call correspond to Noes on another, and vice versa).[20]

Besides saying that *the correlation between two roll calls X and Y is just the average product of their standard scores,* another simple and useful interpretation is possible. In calculating standard voting scores, it is desirable that their average squared value be one. This useful number, the average squared deviation of a variable about its mean, is called a variance.[21] A relatively easy mathematical derivation, which will not be reproduced here, allows us to conclude that

---

20. Such a definition is formalized in Equation (2) where the summation sign (called a sigma) means add the numbers after the sigma for all N values of i:

$$r_{xy} = \frac{1}{N} \sum_{i=1}^{N} Z_x(i) Z_y(i) \tag{2}$$

21. Symbolically, the variance of voting ranks on roll call Y, $S^2_y$, is defined by Equation (3):

$$S^2_y = \frac{1}{N} \sum_{i=1}^{N} (Y_i - Y)^2 \tag{3}$$

the *squared correlation coefficient* $r^2_{xy}$ *gives the fraction of total variance in Y that can be explained by X;* the same coefficient is also equal to the fraction of total variance in X that can be explained by Y. (In both instances a linear [straight line] relationship between X and Y is being assumed.)

### The Factor Model

In our context, *the goal of factor analysis is to get at the basic issues and alignments underlying a wide variety of roll-call votes.* The problem is not unlike the task of the diplomat who, from a wide range of contradictory experience, must decide who is against whom, and on what kind of issues. His need for useful and simple ways of organizing his everyday experience parallels the scientist's concern with objectively describing empirical reality. The scientific approach, however, uses as descriptive criteria such principles as theoretical elegance, parsimony, and intersubjective verifiability. Considerations of national expediency should play a minimal role.

The basic assumption of factor analysis is that if two roll calls involve a common element, there will be a correlation between them. The inductive problem is to go back from the correlations among roll calls to parsimonious and comprehensive descriptions of these common elements, which will be interchangeably described as underlying voting "factors," "components," "dimensions" or "super-issues." In the language of the philosophy of science, this is the task of reducing a large number of operational indicators (e.g. roll calls) to a small number of basic conceptual variables.

Factor analysis is a partly mathematical and partly subjective technique for making these inferences. The particular mathematical model assumed by the "principal component method of factor analysis" [22] states that a nation's vote on a roll call may be thought of as the sum of its positions on the underlying factors involved, each position weighted by a measure of the "loading" or relevance of the underlying factor to the vote at hand. Given the correlation matrix among roll calls, this method finds a matrix $A$ (with entries $a_{jk}$) of these weights. The weights (loadings) measure how substantially each underlying factor score should be used in obtaining a best

22. For a more detailed explanation see Harry H. Harman, *Modern Factor Analysis* (Chicago, University of Chicago Press, 1960), Chaps. 1, 2, and 9. A more readable text is R. B. Cattell, *Factor Analysis* (New York, Harper, 1952).

linear estimate of a nation's Z-score on a particular roll call. If, for example, three distinct factors are found sufficient for a satisfactory interpretation of a set of issues (roll calls) ,[23] then we can mathematically state the implied relationship between each roll call $j$ and factor $k$ ($k$ will equal 1, 2, or 3) . *The factor model relating standardized ranks ($Z_{ji}$'s) on any one issue to national factor scores ($F_{ki}$) in terms of the factor loadings ($a_{jk}$'s) is as follows:*

$$Z_{ji} = a_{j1}F_{1i} + a_{j2}F_{2i} + a_{j3}F_{3i} + U_{ji} \qquad (4)$$

As before, the $i$ subscript indicates any one of N participating nations. An additional $j$ subscript, however, is used to refer to any one of $n$ different rolls calls; the $k$ subscript (actually 1, 2, or 3) on the factor scores ($F_{ki}$) and the factor loadings ($a_{jk}$) labels the particular factor being discussed. $U_{ji}$ represents the "uniqueness" of variable $j$ for nation $i$, the part of its vote that cannot be explained in terms of the inferred common underlying factors.

An additional interpretation of factor loadings should also be mentioned: whenever factors are uncorrelated, the $a_{jk}$'s can be thought of as *correlations* between roll calls and factor scores. Considered as factor loadings, the matrix $A$ is called a factor *pattern*. For correlations, it is called a factor *structure*. We shall use the term factor matrix to refer either to the factor pattern or the factor structure. These two interpretations suggest that a *factor may be thought of either behaviorally, as a major voting alignment* (given by factor scores) *or, substantively, as a component of several concrete issues* (a column of factor loadings).

### The Unrotated and the Rotated Factor Patterns

There are two ways in which the matrix $A$ of factor loadings is usually arrived at, each resulting from a different mix of theoretical elegance and scientific parsimony. Each unrotated factor derived by the principal component method parsimoniously explains as much roll-call variance as possible. "Eigen values" (referred to by

23. The criterion used here in determining "the number of common factors that are necessary, reliable, and meaningful for the explanation of the correlations among the variables" is that "the number of common factors should be equal to the number of eigen values greater than one in the correlation matrix (with unities in the diagonal) ." See Henry Kaiser's paper, "Applications of Computers to Psychological Problems," cited in Harmon, p. 363 n., and published in *Educational and Psychological Measurement, 20* (1960) , 141–51.

the Greek letter lambda: $\lambda$) tell how much roll-call variance each factor accounts for.[24] A lambda of 2.5, for example, indicates that a factor contains roll-call variance equivalent to the entire variability of two-and-one-half roll calls.

Another useful number, the communality (symbolized $h^2$), can be calculated from a factor pattern (See Table 2.1). While the eigen values distinguish among factors, communalities distinguish among roll calls. Each number serves a useful purpose: eigen values give us a way of measuring the prominence or quantitative significance of a particular underlying voting component; while communalities indicate the extent to which the variance of voting ranks on any roll call can be accounted for by common underlying factors.

The hypothetical unrotated factor pattern in Table 2.1A will help us summarize the properties of such a matrix. First of all, note how the eigen values descend rapidly from the first unrotated factor to the second, etc. In fact, each column of factor loadings is chosen to get as much voting variance as possible after previous factors, if any, have been a matrix of roll-call intercorrelations. Secondly, notice how the set of numbers in one column seems unrelated to the set of numbers in any other. As is only approximately true in the hypothetical example, columns of unrotated factor loadings, like unrotated factor scores, are uncorrelated with each other. (The same results hold true for orthogonally or perpendicularly rotated factors, but not for obliquely rotated factors as discussed in note 25 below). Finally, the communalities ($h^2$'s) in Table 2.1A tell how much of each roll call's unit variance is interpretable in a three-factor fashion. Notice these range from about one third to nearly two thirds for the various roll calls.

Just looking at Table 2.1B suggests a satisfying way of interpreting a rotated factor pattern. Most of the high entries are no longer in the first column; each column has several distinctive high factor loadings. If we consider any three-factor analysis of six roll calls as parsimonious as another, and no longer worry about explaining

---

24. In a somewhat simplified form, the basic matrix equation from which $\lambda$k's and $a_{jk}$'s are solved for is

$$a_k \cdot R = \lambda_k a_k$$

The matrix of roll-call correlations is denoted by $R$, while the vector $a_k$ includes one factor loading for each roll call.

as much voting variance as possible by the first one or two factors, Table 2.1B suggests that we can recalculate an equivalent set of rotated factor loadings with clearer theoretical significance.[25] Along these lines Thurstone has proposed the concept of "simple structure" to refer to a factor matrix in which there are as many entries approximating zero or unity as possible. A widely accepted means of operationalizing this concept is Kaiser's "normal" varimax technique for simplifying the columns of the factor matrix.[26] Table 2.1B indicates how an unrotated factor matrix might be restructured by such a technique.

Finally, we are ready to discuss the most important subjective element in the interpretation of unrotated and rotated factor patterns: factors are not born with names, but must be christened by their parents, who may not be able to agree on what they should be called. From Table 2.1A it is not immediately clear how the first unrotated factor should be labeled. Both "cold war" issues like Chinese representation and Hungary and "anticolonial" topics like South Africa and Algerian independence are involved; the dominating presence of the first factor also makes the others harder to name. In the rotated factor pattern, however, all three factors

25. The geometric term "rotating" refers to an "issue space" in which each roll call is located by its factor loadings on different (perpendicular) factor axes. In the hypothetical diagram below, four roll calls are plotted as X's in a two dimensional issue space. Axis I indicated the direction in the issue space along which the greatest possible amount of roll-call variance is explained. It might be hard to label axes I and II, however, because each of the roll calls has sizable non-zero coordinates on both axes. The primed axes indicate how, after rotation, a simpler matrix of factor loadings could have been obtained. Note how only two roll calls have two large non-zero coordinates. As a consequence, axis I′ should be substantively easier to identify than either I or II.

Tilting axis II′ even a little farther to the right while keeping I′ fixed would give an even simpler set of entries in the factor matrix. Nonperpendicular axes are referred to as "oblique rotations."

26. For details see Harman, pp. 301–08.

have two rather distinct loadings which suggest, at least to the authors, the labels "self-determination" (anticolonialism), "cold war," and "UN supranationalism"—more about these choices will be discussed in subsequent chapters. Others may disagree, but their

### Table 2.1. Unrotated and Rotated Factor Patterns

**A.** A Hypothetical Unrotated Factor Pattern
(emphasis on parsimony and frequency of voting behavior)

LOADINGS ON

| ROLL CALL | Factor 1 (East–West) | Factor 2 (North–South) | Factor 3 (China) | h2 |
|---|---|---|---|---|
| 1. UNEF | .45 | .55 | .05 | .51 |
| 2. Chinese representation | .50 | .10 | .45 | .46 |
| 3. Algerian independence | .75 | .10 | .15 | .60 |
| 4. Indians in S. Africa | .70 | .25 | .10 | .56 |
| 5. Hungary on agenda | .50 | .10 | .35 | .38 |
| 6. Increase UN economic aid | .40 | .40 | .05 | .32 |
| Eigen values | $\lambda = 1.92$ | $\lambda = .86$ | $\lambda = .36$ | |

**B.** A Hypothetical Rotated Factor Pattern
(emphasis on theoretical elegance, i.e. easier conceptualization and a simple factor structure)

LOADINGS ON

| ROLL CALL | Factor 1 (self-determination) | Factor 2 (cold war) | Factor 3 (UN supranationalism) | h2 |
|---|---|---|---|---|
| 1. UNEF | .15 | .00 | .70 | .51 |
| 2. Chinese representation | .05 | .60 | .10 | .37 |
| 3. Algerian independence | .85 | .05 | .00 | .73 |
| 4. Indians in S. Africa | .75 | .00 | .05 | .57 |
| 5. Hungary on agenda | .20 | .70 | .05 | .53 |
| 6. Increase UN economic aid | .25 | .05 | .60 | .43 |
| Eigen values | $\lambda = 1.41$ | $\lambda = .86$ | $\lambda = .87$ | |

*Note:* Eigen values ($\lambda$) for any factor can be calculated by summing squared *column* entries; communalities (h2) for any roll call equal the sum of squared *row* entries. If Table 2.1B had resulted from Table 2.1A, communalities, but not eigen values, would correspond. Factor loadings above 0.50 in magnitude have been italicized for convenience. Negative factor loadings mean that high voting ranks (Yesses) correspond to negative factor scores.

interpretations must also be argued and tested, and must predict similar properties of the conflicts they have named.

### Factor Scores

Factor scores may be thought of as national positions on factors underlying roll-call votes. Philosophers might call them "intervening variables." Although not directly observable (they are assumed to intervene between reality and observed events), they may be estimated by linear combinations of voting positions on roll calls related to the factor being described.[27] Calculating and examining national factor scores is one helpful way of getting further insights into the nature of conflicts underlying General Assembly voting patterns. Such an approach, for example, has been especially useful in choosing labels for the first and second unrotated factors in the analysis below. The factor *pattern* should help cognitively to identify the super-issues involved; factor *scores,* which may be correlated with environmental variables, serve to summarize voting behavior.

We can summarize our brief review of factor analysis in terms of the six questions asked at the beginning of this section.

1. Interpretable either in rotated or unrotated form, the uncorrelated, unidimensional factors inferred in terms of a linear factor model can provide a clear and objective way of summarizing the main components of voting in the United Nations.

2. All important roll calls can be included in such an analysis. Entries in the factor pattern tell how much of the voting on any roll call loads on the distinct factors that are inferred to exist. A distinctive roll call will produce a distinctive factor, and a roll call with several different aspects will load proportionately on the relevant factors.

3. Listing factor scores or plotting them graphically for the different voting factors will allow us to see how cohesive members

27. Rotated and unrotated factor scores (component scores) were calculated from a matrix equation derived from Equation (4):
$$F = (A'A)^{-1} A'Z$$
For more details see Henry Kaiser, "Formulas for Component Scores," *Psychometrika,* 27 (1962), 83–88. Revised rotated factor scores were calculated from this equation ignoring the contributions of roll calls with very low factor loadings. Details are given below; the revised rotated factor scores in general show small or moderate intercorrelations.

of the different groups are, as well as the direction of dissent of deviant members.

4. Either a list or a graph will allow easy simultaneous consideration of the locations of *all* the participating states.

5. Because the roll calls in a factor pattern may be identified as to substantive content, and because we have explicit measures of the positions of different states on the separate factors, it will be relatively easy to compare factors from year to year to see how many substantive and alignment changes have occurred in them, and what the trends have been regarding particular issues or general factors.

6. The amount of variance explained by rotated or unrotated factors gives a precise measure of the frequency or relative prominence of the main super-issues before the General Assembly. With such information, for example, we can see whether or not the cold war or colonialism has increasingly preoccupied the United Nations. Measures of the importance of these and other issues for individual states will require additional information.[28]

28. It should be reemphasized at this point that each nation's vote (standardized rank) and each roll call are given equal weight in determining the factors underlying UN voting and their relative prominence. Weighing standardized ranks equally in calculating the correlation matrix from which factors are derived corresponds to the one nation–one vote rule used in the General Assembly. Although frequently done, considering roll calls to be of equal importance (quantitatively) has no similar justification. Our criteria for selecting "important" votes do suggest, however, that these issues have crossed a certain threshold of intensive debate for at least some member states. In later chapters we shall introduce a measure of the intensity behind each nation's attitude on a particular issue.

# CHAPTER 3

# Issues and Alignments
# at the Second General Assembly

### IN THE AFTERMATH OF WAR

The outstanding political achievement of the first part of the first session of the General Assembly was the resolution on atomic energy; the comparable achievement of the second part of the session was the resolution on the general regulation and reduction of armaments. The Atomic Energy Commission has worked hard . . . but the . . . problem still presents many points of disagreement and delay. The Commission on Conventional Armaments has made little progress beyond the adoption of a general plan of work. Thus the two most significant resolutions of the General Assembly still require positive implementation.[1]

While much of the world was slow in giving up its cherished hopes for great power cooperation after the war, tactics in the United Nations very quickly adjusted themselves to emerging conflicts. West, neutrals, and Russians alike felt the growing inadequacy of the Security Council for positive action. For example, during the first session of the Assembly, members of the Security Council took the Spanish situation off its agenda so that the Assembly might discuss it and make recommendations. India brought her disputes with the Union of South Africa directly to the Assembly, and Russia initiated discussion there of the reduction of national arms and armed forces.[2]

In another major dispute, the British government requested that

1. Trygve Lie, "Introduction to the Annual Report of the Secretary-General on the Work of the Organization, 1947," reprinted in *International Conciliation*, No. 433 (September 1947), pp. 510–14.

2. This review draws heavily upon "The United Nations General Assembly: Its Expanding Role and the Issues before the Second Session," *International Conciliation*, No. 433 (September 1947), pp. 479–509.

the question of Palestine be put on the agenda of the second regular session of the Assembly after prior discussion by a special Assembly committee. In August 1947, the United Nations Special Committee on Palestine (UNSCOP) submitted its report containing a majority proposal for a Plan of Partition with Economic Union and a minority proposal for a Palestinian Federal State.[3]

In the same month the United States requested that "threats to the political independence and territorial integrity of Greece" be discussed at the forthcoming General Assembly. After an American resolution in the Security Council asking for Assembly recommendations was vetoed by the Soviets, the United States was successful on September 15 in passing a procedural resolution stating that the Council was no longer "seized" by the Greek question. This question was therefore potentially another important issue which might come up in Assembly debates. A final example of American initiative in enhancing the Assembly's role in matters with which the Security Council would continue to concern itself, but not in a wholly satisfactory way, was a September proposal for the "Establishment of an Interim Committee of the General Assembly on Peace and Security." When it finally met in the months after the second Assembly session, it was called the "Interim Committee of the General Assembly." In the Russian view at least, it had been designed by the United States as a substitute for the Security Council.

## IMPORTANT ISSUES AT THE SECOND SESSION

Before performing a factor analysis of important roll calls at the Second Assembly, some notion of their substance and context is desirable. It will be convenient to group and discuss these issues by their committee of origin, both because verbal descriptions of Assembly activities are usually given in this manner, and because particular voting factors may appear with unusual frequency in certain functional committees.[4]

3. Department of Public Information, *Yearbook of the United Nations, 1947–48* (Lake Success, N.Y., 1949), pp. 228–29. This volume and others in the same series will hereafter be cited as *U.N. Yearbook, 1947–48,* with the correct years inserted. Riggs, *Politics in the U.N.,* is also of special value on the Palestine problem.

4. If an important issue was originally referred to the Assembly by the General Committee (e.g. the inclusion of a controversial item on the agenda) or was debated directly in plenary without being first discussed in a main committee, it is grouped with votes from the main committee where the issue usually appeared.

## The Question of Palestine

Because both the United States and the Soviet Union were reluctant to endorse UNSCOP's majority proposal, neither came out definitely in favor of the partition plan until after more than two weeks of debate in the Ad Hoc Committee on the Question of Palestine. The Arab strategy was to present attractive alternatives to the Assembly, delaying the final decision. If these failed, an all-out attempt was to be made to prevent partition forces from achieving the two-thirds majority required for plenary passage.

A roll call (vote 0002) [5] referring to the International Court of Justice the question of the UN's competence to recommend or enforce any proposal regarding the future of Palestine that was contrary to the wishes of her inhabitants was narrowly defeated by a vote of 20-21-13 (20 for, 21 against, and 13 abstentions). The first operative paragraph of a resolution on Jewish refugees and displaced persons asking their countries of origin to take back and resettle them (vote 0003) actually received support from a majority of those taking sides. The vote was 17 for, 14 against, with 23 abstentions. The whole resolution on repatriation or proportional resettlement of refugees in terms of quotas assigned by a UN committee (vote 0007) failed by only one vote to achieve a majority sufficient to include it in the Ad Hoc Committee's report to the General Assembly (16 for, 16 against, 23 abstentions). On all three of these votes regional groups were united except for the Arab states. West Europeans (but not France) were generally opposed; Latin Americans were sharply divided; most Eastern European nations sided with Western Europe and the United States; nearly all Afro–Asians, except Ethiopia and Turkey, supported the Arabs.

The partition resolution (which passed the Ad Hoc Committee by less than a two-thirds majority, 25-13-17) was finally passed in plenary by a 33-13-10 vote, after much last minute lobbying (roll call 8033). At that time, except for the Latin Americans of whom a slim majority favored partition, voting had solidified along regional

5. The vote numbers correspond to those used in the factor pattern presented below. The first digit represents the Committee where the vote occurred (0 stands for the Ad Hoc Committee, later the Special Political Committee; 8 for plenary roll calls; other first digits correspond to their respective committee numbers); the next three digits give the temporal order in which the vote occurred in the particular committee.

lines: East and West Europeans, except for Greece and the United Kingdom, voted in favor of partition; Arabs and other Afro–Asians (except for the Philippines and Liberia) voted against it. This last vote was the only plenary roll call on Palestine at the Second Assembly.

## Political and Security Affairs

Despite the considerable activity in the Assembly during its first session on the control of atomic energy and the general reduction of armaments, these matters were not discussed in the First Committee during the Assembly's second regular session. This striking omission was compensated for by the detailed consideration these questions were given by their respective commissions, in addition to the limited debate on them by the Security Council during and after the fall of 1947.

Of the agenda items discussed in the First Committee, almost all were decided or deferred in some way by roll-call votes.[6] These included fourteen committee and three plenary roll calls on the Greek border question; two committee and six plenary requests for the Security Council to reconsider some of its membership rejections; seven roll calls on relations with Spain; eight votes on Indians in South Africa; scattered votes on emergency assistance for Trieste, the independence of Korea, or the removal of foreign troops there; and Soviet suggestions that the United Nations take measures against bellicose propaganda and inciters of a new war.

## Economic and Financial Questions

The two issues to reach roll-call votes in the Second Committee, which spent almost all its time discussing parts of the report of the Economic and Social Council, were both in response to Soviet bloc initiatives. Vote 2001 was an American amendment revising a Polish recommendation that all fundamental international

6. See the discussion and roll calls in the *Official Records of the General Assembly;* the wording of resolutions may be found in the *Annexes* to the Official Records, all published each session for each committee by the United Nations. Although it does not contain all the details or innuendoes, the *U.N. Yearbook, 1947–1948,* is an extremely useful and fairly comprehensive summary of the major arguments. Its most serious omissions, especially for the earlier years of the Assembly, are the roll-call votes and debates which form the basic research material for this study.

economic problems should be dealt with through the United Nations. Much of the debate was in criticism and defense of the Marshall Plan. While Arab nations abstained, East European countries resisted the American change.[7]

Similarly, Russia sponsored resolutions in committee (vote 2002) and in plenary (vote 8006) giving to the Economic Commission for Asia and the Far East (ECAFE) the final decision whether non-self-governing territories could participate directly in its work. The plenary vote involved eleven vote shifts by Arab and Latin countries, mostly away from the Soviet position. By the criteria given in Chapter 2, such a change was significant enough to suggest keeping both roll calls in our important set.

### Social, Humanitarian, and Cultural Issues

Of the issues reaching roll-call votes in the Third Committee only one (after eleven vote shifts) had plenary roll-call status. In Committee, Russia requested the deletion of the colonial exemption clause from earlier League of Nations Conventions on traffic in women, children, and obscene publications. The unusual Soviet committee victory was reversed by a plenary roll call requested by the United Kingdom (votes 3001 and 8002). Although still rather split in their voting, Scandinavian, Latin American, and Arab shifts took away the Soviet majority.

Two other issues in the Third Committee that never reached the plenary session are worth noting. Vote 3002 deleted an enumeration of trade union rights, including full employment, a just share of wages, social security, and the right to collective bargaining. Despite its attractiveness, the list was successfully opposed by both the United States and the Soviet Union. A week later, Western and Eastern Europeans were joined by some Latin Americans in rejecting an Indian proposal that "in view of the difficulty of consulting the free will of the peoples of non-self-governing territories" immigration to these territories should not at present take place (vote 3003).

H. G. Nicholas has optimistically suggested "welfare internationalism" to be one of the philosophical foundations of the United Nations:

7. Because vote 2001 was within eight shifts of the cold war alignment on the Greek question (vote 8003) and because it was also within ten shifts of vote 8006, it was not included in the factor analysis.

Just as the nation-state has carried its provision of domestic services far beyond such bare essentials as roads and post offices and now provides for health, employment and higher productivity to such an extent that we speak of "the welfare state," so at the international level by 1945 expectations of what world organization could and should do had passed far beyond the limited, though solid, achievements of the "World Services" side of the League.[8]

Our evidence, the sharp disagreement between the developed and underdeveloped countries on votes 3002 and 3003, suggests skepticism about the degree to which consensus on social welfare questions exists in the United Nations. In explaining its vote, the United States objected to an enumeration of all the trade union rights suggested by a report of the International Labor Organization as "unnecessary," while the Soviet Union rejected the ILO list by claiming that workers in the Soviet Union were "more equal" than managers, a principle not recognized by the ILO. In addition to the expectable reaction of most North Atlantic countries to the immigration resolution, the Soviets, for reasons of their own, insisted that the consent of the country of origin is necessary to prevent immigration that might disturb friendly relations among states. In each of the subsequent Assembly sessions that we shall consider, major differences on basic humanitarian and economic rights such as these continually reappear.

### Trusteeship and Non-Self-Governing Territories

In 1947 it certainly was not unusual for questions regarding non-self-governing territories to arise in more than one committee. Besides several votes on a request for a UN trusteeship over South West Africa (in which India, the United States, and Denmark played important roles), two other important issues in the Fourth Committee were the establishment of a Committee on Information from Non-Self-Governing Territories (vote 8014) and a resolution (originally introduced by India and China) stating that the international trusteeship system was the "surest and quickest" way to self-government (vote 8011).

The Fourth Committee also accepted a proposed trusteeship

8. Nicholas, *The U. N. as a Political Institution*, p. 21.

agreement for Nauru (to be held jointly by the United Kingdom, New Zealand, and Australia). While Latin Americans and Asians frequently differed among themselves on other Fourth Committee questions, the Nauru vote (4004) found the Soviet countries alone on the losing side of a 41–6 majority.

One more issue needs to be mentioned. Vote 8012 saw five Latin Americans, six East European countries, and seven Afro–Asian countries (including Haiti, Cuba, Mexico, China, Ethiopia, and Liberia) protesting the deletion of a specific reference to relations between non-self-governing territories and their metropolitan countries as a subject for statistical analyses in the Secretary-General's summaries of information from these territories.

### Administrative and Budgetary Issues

All the items before the Fourth Committee reached roll-call votes; the Fifth and Sixth Committees were also fairly well represented in roll-call voting at the second session. First, several votes (including votes 5001 and 5012) attempted to cut the budget of the Department of Public Information. The great powers and the Arab–Asians were not able to rally sufficient strength to overcome solid Latin American support for these programs. Secondly, most other West Europeans and the United States joined in opposing a Belgian proposal that additional budget contributions be demanded of countries still requiring their nationals in the Secretariat to pay domestic income taxes (vote 5004). Additional opposition to the Belgian proposal was almost entirely confined to a group of states frequently referred to as the Old Commonwealth—the United Kingdom, Canada, New Zealand, Australia, and South Africa. On another issue, Arab abstentions and almost solid Soviet and Latin American opposition were enough to block a move increasing the number of official records reproduced only in the working languages of the UN, English and French (vote 5008). Also with Arab abstentions, North Atlantic and East European countries were barely able to defeat a Colombian request for Secretariat quotas of at least three persons per country (vote 5010). Finally, votes 8016 and 8017 represent a successful attempt to have the third session of the General Assembly held in Europe with its extra expenses coming out of regular budgetary sources.

## Legal Questions

Soviet resolutions regarding the prosecution of war criminals (votes 6002 and 6009), and small power attemps to speed the work of the Economic and Social Council (ECOSOC) in drawing up a Convention on Genocide in cooperation with the International Law Commission (votes 6010, 8030, 8031, 8032) complete our set of important roll calls.

### VOTING DIMENSIONS IN 1947

The unrotated factor pattern (matrix) is displayed in Table 3.1. As an aid in summarizing the results there, factor loadings between 0.50 and 0.60 in magnitude have been set in italic type; those above 0.60 have been printed in boldface type. (Recall that for uncorrelated factors, like those in Tables 3.1 and 3.2, factor loadings can also be interpreted as correlations between roll calls and factors.) Immediately below each column in the factor matrix an eigen value ($\lambda$) tells how much roll-call variance the factor explains. As previously mentioned, each roll call has a variance of unity, so a lambda of 2.5, for example, indicates that the factor has as much variance as there is in two-and-one half roll calls.

Squaring the correlations in the factor pattern tells how much of the voting variance in each roll call can be explained by each factor. Summing squared pattern entries across a row (producing "communalities") gives the total fraction of voting on a particular issue that can be interpreted in the general terms of the underlying factors.

One preliminary result of the factor analysis should immediately be noticed: it turns out that every important Second Assembly vote but one (8015, on extra Assembly expenses in Europe) had a communality ($h^2$) greater than 0.66. In fact, about 81 per cent of all important voting in 1947 can parsimoniously be explained in terms of eight uncorrelated factors with $\lambda$'s greater than unity: this large portion of the voting that can be interpreted in such general terms we have called the "general" or "common" voting variance. Putting this result another way, actual voting positions on 48 important roll calls could have been predicted (with a correlation

# Table 3.1. Dimensions of Voting in 1947: Unrotated Factor Matrix

FACTORS

| ROLL CALLS | 1 | 2 | 3 | 4 | 5 | 6 | 7 | 8 |
|---|---|---|---|---|---|---|---|---|
| 0002. Palestine; ask ICJ | .24 | .63 | —.26 | .40 | —.06 | .22 | .14 | —.30 |
| 0003. Repatriate Jewish refugees | .35 | .60 | —.38 | .12 | .16 | .22 | —.17 | —.16 |
| 0007. Palestine: Arab resolution | .33 | .69 | —.20 | .29 | .05 | —.00 | —.04 | —.24 |
| 8033. Partition Palestine | —.33 | —.58 | .34 | —.33 | .04 | —.06 | —.04 | .11 |
| 8003. Threats to Greece | —.71 | .35 | .23 | .13 | —.24 | —.07 | .29 | .04 |
| 8004. Greece; Polish resolution | .81 | —.18 | —.21 | .03 | .25 | —.04 | —.27 | .02 |
| 1007. Greece; restore diplomatic ties | .77 | —.11 | .14 | .05 | —.08 | —.04 | —.03 | —.32 |
| 8005. Greece; USSR resolution | .83 | —.16 | —.33 | —.08 | .06 | .02 | —.10 | .03 |
| 8019. SC reconsider Portugal's membership | —.68 | .47 | .20 | .11 | .18 | —.15 | .02 | —.06 |
| 1018. Spain; unqualified for membership | .10 | —.58 | .64 | .31 | —.15 | .10 | .04 | —.04 |
| 8024. SG report on steps taken (Spain) | .12 | —.60 | .63 | .34 | —.18 | .05 | .04 | —.04 |
| 8025. Spain; unqualified for membership | .44 | —.39 | .43 | .24 | .06 | .07 | .22 | —.16 |
| 8026. Confidence in SC re Spain | .15 | —.58 | .61 | .35 | —.21 | .05 | —.02 | .03 |
| 1021. Earlier S. Africa resolution noted | .75 | .14 | .28 | .13 | .06 | —.08 | .04 | —.09 |
| 8027. Indian S. Africa round table request | .81 | .23 | .23 | .03 | —.09 | —.06 | .23 | —.04 |
| 8028. India; S. Africa to ICJ | —.83 | —.18 | —.14 | —.13 | .08 | .12 | —.17 | .13 |
| 1027. Measures vs. new war propaganda | .82 | —.04 | —.01 | —.17 | .03 | .04 | .14 | .17 |
| 8001. Korea on agenda | —.79 | .21 | .40 | .13 | —.14 | .12 | .02 | —.02 |
| 8015. USSR: withdraw troops in Korea | .81 | —.22 | —.12 | —.05 | .17 | —.13 | —.24 | —.12 |
| 8029. Assist Trieste | —.17 | —.57 | .27 | —.30 | —.38 | —.14 | —.07 | —.13 |
| 2002. Allow NSGTs in ECAFE | .82 | .22 | —.12 | —.14 | —.10 | .05 | .03 | —.03 |
| 8006. Participation of NSGTs in ECAFE | .87 | .20 | —.05 | —.15 | —.21 | .02 | —.03 | .09 |
| 3001. Delete colonial exemption clause | .71 | .10 | .17 | —.26 | .09 | .28 | —.22 | —.08 |
| 8002. Delete colonial exemption clause | —.72 | —.02 | —.31 | .06 | .02 | —.28 | .20 | —.07 |
| 3002. Employment a fundamental right | .15 | .72 | .04 | .10 | —.22 | .13 | .18 | .32 |
| 3003. Immigration to NSGTs | .19 | .68 | —.22 | .34 | —.04 | .00 | .04 | .02 |
| 8007. S.W. Africa important? | —.87 | —.11 | —.03 | —.13 | .23 | .17 | .03 | —.04 |
| 8008. No S.W. Africa deadline | .45 | .24 | .50 | .14 | .41 | .04 | —.14 | .30 |
| 8009. S.W. Africa trusteeship request | .65 | .06 | .52 | .11 | .37 | .16 | .04 | .12 |
| 8010. S.W. Africa trusteeship request | .65 | .06 | .52 | .11 | .37 | .16 | .04 | .12 |

# Table 3.1. Dimensions of Voting in 1947: Unrotated Factor Matrix

| ROLL CALLS | FACTORS 1 | 2 | 3 | 4 | 5 | 6 | 7 | 8 |
|---|---|---|---|---|---|---|---|---|
| 8011. Trusteeship "sure and quick" | .85 | .30 | .04 | .01 | —.18 | —.05 | —.03 | .07 |
| 8012. Statistics on NSGTs | —.85 | —.07 | —.12 | —.09 | .34 | —.00 | .01 | .07 |
| 8013. Is CINSGT important? | —.82 | —.10 | —.10 | —.13 | .34 | .12 | .02 | .03 |
| 8014. Establish CINSGT | .80 | .03 | .02 | .10 | —.42 | —.14 | —.06 | .11 |
| 4004. Accept Nauru trusteeship | —.60 | .61 | .20 | .30 | .15 | —.10 | .01 | .04 |
| 5001. Cut public information allotment | .39 | —.35 | —.50 | .28 | .28 | —.22 | .32 | .07 |
| 5012. Smaller DPI cut | .42 | —.28 | —.50 | .46 | .04 | —.16 | .21 | .23 |
| 5004. Reimburse Secretariat local taxes | .43 | .33 | —.16 | —.51 | —.05 | .28 | .31 | .28 |
| 5008. Fewer languages for UN records | —.17 | —.10 | —.11 | .79 | .27 | —.16 | —.25 | .20 |
| 5010. Secretariat quotas: 3/country | .11 | .77 | .18 | —.21 | —.15 | —.02 | .25 | .01 |
| 8016. GA host pays extra expenses | —.13 | .61 | —.04 | —.04 | —.28 | .04 | —.34 | .05 |
| 8017. European site for third GA | .33 | —.21 | .15 | —.24 | .57 | —.03 | .36 | —.25 |
| 6002. Extradite war criminals | .56 | —.36 | .03 | —.35 | .09 | —.31 | .03 | .13 |
| 6009. USSR resolution on war criminals | .81 | —.19 | —.23 | —.13 | .19 | —.26 | —.01 | —.00 |
| 6010. Consider genocide convention later | .05 | —.52 | —.41 | .26 | —.27 | .30 | .00 | .21 |
| 8030. Consult ILC on genocide | —.12 | .57 | .32 | —.12 | —.16 | —.61 | —.07 | .07 |
| 8031. Don't await comments on genocide | .02 | .81 | .43 | —.18 | .19 | —.03 | —.02 | —.02 |
| 8032. ECOSOC proceed on Genocide Convention | —.09 | .67 | .49 | —.09 | .21 | —.14 | —.16 | .08 |
| Roll-call variance accounted for by factor (eigen values) | λ=16.5 | λ=8.5 | λ=4.8 | λ=2.9 | λ=2.4 | λ=1.4 | λ=1.2 | λ=1.0 |

of about 0.90) from national scores on only eight super-issues *if* the appropriate loadings were also known.

To help interpret the two most pervasive unrotated factors in Table 3.1, let us first look at the corresponding factor scores as plotted in Figure 3.1. From the figure, and the caucusing groups circled there, a geopolitical East–West versus North–South interpretation of the two most prominent voting alignments is compelling. Note how West Europeans, the Soviet bloc, most Latin Americans, and all Arabs are in the appropriate quadrants. Even though no formal Afro–Asian caucusing group existed at the Second Assembly, only Algeria (and Turkey) did not take a South–Eastern position on these two conflicts.

Figure 3.1. Unrotated Factor Scores on the East–West and North–South Issues at the 2nd General Assembly

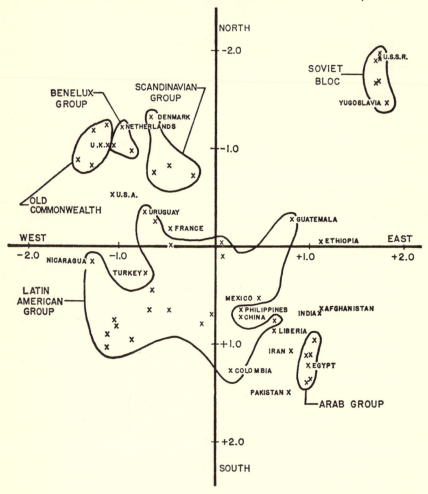

Table 3.1 suggests that "East–West" voting (the first factor) occurred on a variety of cold war and colonial issues, including Greece, Korea, South Africa, and non-self-governing territories. In a corresponding geographic fashion, North–South voting (the second factor) appeared in a multitude of issues: Palestine, relations

with Spain, Secretariat quotas, and the Genocide Convention. Generally, East and West Europeans and Old Commonwealth members took the same positions on these issues; they backed partition in Palestine, supported Security Council competence regarding the Spanish issue, opposed Secretariat quotas, and wanted to proceed more cautiously on a Genocide Convention.

Dividing the first lambda by the sum of all the lambda's tells us that East–West voting underlies about 40 per cent of the common variation in 1947's important roll calls. The second $\lambda$ tells us that a little less than 20 per cent of important voting differences in 1947 were along North–South lines.

### The Rotated Factor Pattern

The rotated factor pattern (see Table 3.2) is supposed to provide simpler substantive factor interpretations: these may be seen from an issue oriented point of view that *complements but does not contradict* the emphasis on frequent or pervasive voting alignments suggested by the unrotated factor pattern. The less frequent general voting components usually take on new and clearer meaning in the rotated matrix.

After rotation of the factor pattern to its most simple structure, factor interpretations become remarkably clear. Rotation does not seem markedly to have affected the unrotated East–West super-issue. The highest loadings on the "rotated East–West" factor again appear on cold war and colonial questions; except for a vote or two on South West Africa, similar boxed entries show its substance to be almost the same as the first unrotated factor. The first rotated factor $\lambda$ of 14.9 closely approximates the unrotated one of 16.5. This equivalence is also clear from a comparison of the rotated and unrotated East–West factor scores in Figures 3.2 and 3.1 (which are actually correlated around 0.95!).

The only issues loading heavily on the second rotated voting component have to do with "relations of UN members with Spain." Many Latin states, most Arabs, and some Europeans would not reaffirm the suspension of diplomatic ties suggested by an earlier resolution. A considerable majority supported the great powers (by a vote of 36-4-12) regarding the Security Council's competence in the matter.

The third principal component of Assembly voting may be

# Table 3.2. Dimensions of Voting in 1947: Rotated Factor Matrix

| ROLL CALLS | 1 | 2 | 3 | 4 | 5 | 6 | 7 | 8 |
|---|---|---|---|---|---|---|---|---|
| 0002. Palestine; ask ICJ | .13 | .04 | .04 | **.90** | —.07 | —.03 | .08 | —.01 |
| 0003. Repatriate Jewish refugees | .27 | .40 | .14 | **.70** | .16 | .01 | —.07 | .01 |
| 0007. Palestine: Arab resolution | .26 | .17 | .00 | **.78** | .03 | —.24 | —.07 | .01 |
| 8033. Partition Palestine | —.26 | —.18 | .10 | **—.76** | .01 | .05 | —.04 | —.09 |
| 8003. Threats to Greece | **—.69** | —.16 | —.04 | .13 | —.23 | —.39 | .28 | .20 |
| 8004. Greece; Polish resolution | .77 | .13 | —.11 | .03 | .29 | .25 | —.29 | —.14 |
| 1007. Greece; restore diplomatic ties | .75 | —.29 | .13 | .12 | —.01 | .02 | —.11 | —.21 |
| 8005. Greece; USSR resolution | .81 | .18 | —.09 | .05 | .12 | .34 | —.05 | —.12 |
| 8019. SC reconsider Portugal's membership | —.69 | .08 | .00 | .20 | .01 | —.51 | —.07 | .03 |
| 1018. Spain; unqualified for membership | .05 | —.86 | .04 | —.32 | .13 | .13 | —.09 | —.02 |
| 8024. SG report on steps taken (Spain) | .08 | —.88 | —.00 | —.32 | .10 | .12 | —.11 | —.01 |
| 8025. Spain; unqualified for membership | .33 | —.64 | —.03 | —.07 | .16 | .11 | —.01 | —.32 |
| 8026. Confidence in SG re Spain | .11 | —.85 | —.02 | —.33 | .13 | .13 | —.12 | .09 |
| 1021. Earlier S. Africa resolution noted | .67 | —.26 | —.02 | .22 | .25 | —.20 | .02 | —.16 |
| 8027. Indian S. Africa round table request | .74 | —.23 | —.04 | .26 | .14 | —.21 | .27 | —.15 |
| 8028. India; S. Africa to ICJ | —.77 | .23 | .09 | —.31 | —.07 | .16 | —.12 | .17 |
| 1027. Measures vs. new war propaganda | .77 | .02 | —.08 | —.02 | .24 | .11 | .27 | —.15 |
| 8001. Korea on agenda | —.79 | —.25 | .21 | .02 | —.05 | —.30 | .08 | .24 |
| 8015. USSR: withdraw troops in Korea | .81 | .05 | —.03 | —.04 | .16 | .16 | —.29 | —.20 |
| 8029. Assist Trieste | —.00 | —.30 | .22 | —.65 | —.38 | .05 | —.05 | .05 |
| 2002. Allow NSGTs in ECAFE | .80 | .12 | .06 | .25 | .08 | .01 | .19 | —.06 |
| 8006. Participation of NSGTs in ECAFE | .87 | .07 | .05 | .17 | .11 | —.02 | .24 | .08 |
| 3001. Delete colonial exemption clause | .66 | .03 | .41 | .05 | .37 | .02 | .05 | —.10 |
| 8002. Delete colonial exemption clause | —.65 | .21 | —.28 | —.04 | —.43 | —.04 | —.08 | —.06 |
| 3002. Employment a fundamental right | .09 | .10 | —.06 | .48 | .17 | —.31 | .50 | .34 |
| 3003. Immigration to NSGTs | .12 | .17 | —.15 | **.72** | .05 | —.20 | .09 | .19 |
| 8007. S.W. Africa important? | —.87 | .16 | .15 | —.21 | —.05 | .07 | —.06 | —.10 |
| 8008. No S.W. Africa deadline | .29 | —.17 | —.06 | .09 | **.76** | —.32 | —.02 | —.04 |
| 8009. S.W. Africa trusteeship request | .46 | —.33 | .03 | .08 | **.68** | —.15 | .08 | —.26 |
| 8010. S.W. Africa trusteeship request | .46 | —.33 | .03 | .08 | **.68** | —.15 | .08 | —.26 |

# Table 3.2. Dimensions of Voting in 1947: Rotated Factor Matrix

| ROLL CALLS | FACTORS | | | | | | | |
|---|---|---|---|---|---|---|---|---|
| | 1 | 2 | 3 | 4 | 5 | 6 | 7 | 8 |
| 8011. Trusteeship "sure and quick" | .83 | —.03 | —.02 | .28 | .14 | —.15 | .17 | .10 |
| 8012. Statistics on NSGTs | —.85 | .28 | —.05 | —.20 | —.00 | .01 | —.13 | —.10 |
| 8013. Is CINSGT important | —.84 | .26 | .05 | —.21 | .03 | .08 | —.09 | —.13 |
| 8014. Establish CINSGT | .85 | —.20 | —.12 | .11 | —.05 | —.01 | .12 | .26 |
| 4004. Accept Nauru trusteeship | —.66 | .02 | —.08 | .38 | .11 | —.53 | —.04 | .17 |
| 5001. Cut public information allotment | .31 | .08 | —.64 | .09 | —.04 | .42 | —.09 | —.36 |
| 5012. Smaller DPI cut | .35 | —.02 | —.69 | .18 | —.04 | .46 | —.07 | —.03 |
| 5004. Reimburse Secretariat local taxes | .39 | .39 | .13 | .06 | .17 | .03 | .69 | —.07 |
| 5008. Fewer languages for UN records | —.27 | —.19 | —.53 | .25 | .26 | .15 | —.54 | .22 |
| 5010. Secretariat quotas: 3/country | .10 | .16 | .16 | .37 | .00 | —.57 | .49 | .05 |
| 8016. GA host pays extra expenses | —.04 | .26 | .25 | .31 | —.03 | —.32 | .03 | .50 |
| 8017. European site for third GA | .21 | —.03 | —.01 | —.13 | .21 | —.02 | .04 | —.80 |
| 6002. Extradite war criminals | .62 | .07 | —.16 | —.46 | .05 | .00 | .02 | —.23 |
| 6009. USSR resolution on war criminals | .82 | .16 | —.24 | —.07 | .08 | .12 | —.12 | —.29 |
| 6010. Consider genocide convention later | .04 | —.11 | —.19 | —.07 | —.12 | .76 | .02 | .25 |
| 8030. Consult ILC on genocide | .03 | .09 | —.10 | .01 | —.13 | —.87 | .02 | .23 |
| 8031. Don't await comments on genocide | —.03 | .14 | .27 | .32 | .33 | —.75 | .19 | —.02 |
| 8032. ECOSOC proceed on Genocide Convention | —.12 | .07 | .17 | .17 | .37 | —.77 | .03 | .08 |

Roll-call variance accounted for by factor (eigen values)    $\lambda=14.9$   $\lambda=4.3$   $\lambda=2.0$   $\lambda=5.4$   $\lambda=2.9$   $\lambda=4.9$   $\lambda=2.2$   $\lambda=2.2$

labeled "support for UN information programs." With a rotated lambda of only 2.0, this general issue was certainly not extremely prominent, but the collaboration of some colonial Europeans, most Soviet allies, and most Arabs does suggest a set of financial interests cutting across both the East–West and Spanish components of voting in the UN that we have just discussed. After the attempted budgetary reductions of votes 5001 and 5012, the third highest loader on the third rotated factor is vote 5008, on which Latin America (except for Portuguese-speaking Brazil) was again solidly opposed to informational restrictions in printing UN records.

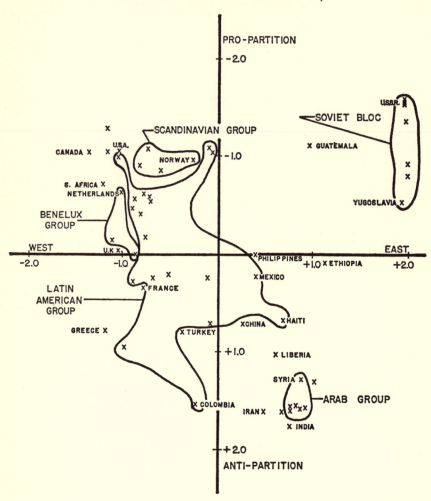

Figure 3.2. Rotated Factor Scores on the East–West and Palestine Issues at the 2nd General Assembly

The rotated fourth factor has the next-to-highest lambda after rotation: $\lambda = 5.4$. Except possibly for the Trieste vote, this fourth distinct component of important voting consists of opposition to UN-sponsored Palestine partition. The interpretation is again straightforward. Solid Arab opposition to partition, to immigration (a key issue in the Palestine controversy), and to extraordinary budgetary expenditures for precedent setting peacekeeping activities in Trieste (vote 8028) explains the common element of all the votes loading heavily on the fourth factor. Split Latin American support and relatively solid Soviet, North Atlantic, and Old Commonwealth approval of partition complete the major aspects of this alignment, the factor scores for which are plotted in Figure 3.2.[9]

The fifth factor, with a lambda of 2.9, appeared strongly in three votes on a proposed "trusteeship for South West Africa." Unlike an almost solid East–West alignment on the importance of a trustee-ship for South West Africa (vote 8008), votes 8009 and 8010 reflect the reluctance of Belgium, the Old Commonwealth, and several "conservative" Latin Americans (e.g. Argentina, Bolivia, Cuba, and Nicaragua) to approve UN interference. Considerable European and Latin support for the trusteeship proposal makes the voting on this issue unlike the typical cold war or colonial issues loading heavily on Factor 1.

With a λ of 4.9, important roll calls in 1947 on a "Genocide Convention" constituted the third most frequent voting issue. Latin Americans, Scandinavians, and Afro–Asians were virtually unani-mous in protesting stalling efforts by Benelux, Old Commonwealth, and Soviet bloc countries (vote 8031 was passed 38-0-14). Unlike its European allies, the United States was consistently on the side of the smaller states, which skeptics accused of trying to legislate inter-national morality. The fairly substantial loading of membership votes like 8018 (discussed in Chapter 2) on factor 6 also reflect a quasi-legislative universalism to which most colonial and Soviet countries objected, at least in 1947. "Small power supranationalism" of this sort also is evidenced by the relatively high loading of vote 5010 (Secretariat quotas for the small powers) on this factor.

The seventh and eighth rotated factors suggest two more distinctive budgetary issues in the Fifth Committee. We have already reviewed

9. The factor scores actually plotted are slightly correlated (r = 0.16). This result occurred because the contributions of roll calls with factor loadings in the rotated factor pattern less than 0.25 in size were eliminated in the calculation of revised rotated factor scores. The same minimal level of significant relationship to the sub-stance of the rotated factor is generally used in other *rotated* factor scores presented in this book. The final (slightly) correlated factor scores might be considered the result of a slight further oblique rotation of the columns of the rotated factor matrix in the interests of increased substantive interpretability. The resulting factor patterns (with more zero entries) would look much the same; the corresponding factor scores correspond much more closely to the alignments of the highest loading roll calls.

the Scandinavian, American, and Old Commonwealth protests to additional budget items for "Secretariat taxes" that were still imposed (vote 5004, the essence of factor 7). Only scattered voices supported Soviet and West European arguments for a "Third General Assembly in Europe," the substance of factor 8.

As was noted in Chapter 2, great power initiative and dominance characterized early voting on the main issues before the United Nations.[10] Although American majorities and Soviet vetoes were frequent, Russian and American agreement on partition of Palestine (for whatever reasons) [11] represented the most important great power cooperation of the honeymoon period.

Structurally speaking, the period of the Security Council is perhaps misnamed. During these years great powers repeatedly brought such issues as atomic energy, Korea, the Balkan crisis, Palestine, and relations with Spain before the Assembly, or possibly, the "Little Assembly," the Interim Committee. The "Uniting for Peace Resolution" in 1950 only formalized a frequent practice of earlier years.[12]

In 1947 East–West conflict was already the most frequent voting alignment in the General Assembly. It consisted of such specific cold war issues as UN membership and the Balkan crisis, as well as policy toward non-self-governing territories. North–South issues, on which most North Atlantic powers and the Eastern European countries agreed, for various reasons, were the second most prevalent voting pattern. (The alignments on the unrotated first two

10. Riggs, pp. 2–3, quoted Leland Goodrich's view (in early 1952) that "No important action can be undertaken by the United Nations with any reasonable prospect of success in the face of United States opposition. Conversely, if the United States gives full support to a proposal, its chances of being adopted must be considered very good, unless of course the veto operates." "American National Interests and the Responsibilities of United Nations Membership," *International Organization, 6* (1952), 376.

11. Dallin suggests a certain lack of definition and inconsistency in early Soviet policies toward non-Western countries. The rejection of "bourgeois nationalism" in Indonesia and India was shortsighted in terms of later policy shifts. "In the Palestine crisis, the Soviet Union was consistent only so far as its anti-British objectives were concerned." Arab states were later to become some of Russia's closest allies in the United Nations (but not domestically). Cf. Alexander Dallin, *The Soviet Union at the United Nations* (New York, Praeger, 1962), p. 30.

12. Similarly, Leland Goodrich, *The United Nations* (New York, Thomas Crowell, 1959), p. 122, shows that in 1948–49 there was a shift away from the Security Council toward the General Assembly in the number of "substantive political issues" discussed.

factors were given in Figure 3.1; they will be discussed and interpreted in more detail in Chapter 7.)

After rotation, issues loading moderately on the North–South factor were distinguished into three sets: votes on Palestine partition, its alternatives and consequences; votes on past and future relations with Spain; and roll calls about the Genocide Convention. Latin Americans were extremely split (but not in the same way) on these two major aspects of North–South voting. Arab–Asians were united on Palestine, but split on the question of relations with Spain. Europeans were also divided on the best Spanish policy. Attempts by the United States and most of the small powers to speed the Genocide Convention were in general not supported by the other great powers. Such efforts might appropriately be described as legislative supranationalism by those on either side of the issue. Finally, different elements of the North and South were aligned against each other on questions about South West African Trusteeship, Secretariat tax exemptions, a European Assembly, and UN informational programs.

All these issues were clearly distinguishable in terms of both their substantive content and state alignments on them. Their classification by functional committee has proved to be analytically convenient, but not substantively important. Granting the important conclusion that there are several main distinct substantive issues in the Assembly, it must also be stressed that early in the Assembly's history East–West and North–South politics frequently underlay these voting patterns.

# CHAPTER 4

# Issues and Alignments
# at the Seventh General Assembly

### ACCOMMODATION AFTER KOREA

If there is any difference between the atmosphere of this Assembly and of previous sessions, it is a subtle one. The expectation of imminent world war has lessened; in its place are signs of a growing awareness that continuing tension may be in store. In 1952 the relevant question about many problems, and not only about those involving the Soviet bloc and the rest of the world, seems to be not "how can it be solved?" but "can an accommodation be reached?" [1]

In this chapter we shall test and enlarge upon suggested features of a second phase in the history of the United Nations, the "period of the General Assembly." If the lesson of the preceding chapter is correct, we should doubt that all years between the Uniting for Peace Resolution and the admission of 16 new members in 1955 can adequately be characterized by the United States' "successful enlistment of Assembly majorities." Soon after the Uniting for Peace resolution increased the powers of the Assembly to deal with the Korean War, stalemate and accommodation were as frequent as victories for the American point of view.

When the General Assembly convened in the fall of 1952, all but one of the important provisions of the Korean armistice had been agreed upon. That one was the issue of voluntary repatriation of prisoners, a problem of secondary importance in fighting the war, which was nearly over.

---

1. "Issues before the Seventh General Assembly," *International Conciliation*, No. 484 (October 1952), p. 363.

Along with the end of the Korean War, prospects included new Soviet leadership and an American Administration committed to "bring the boys home from Korea." With the change in administration would come new Congressional investigations. Already in 1952 a Senate Subcommittee on Internal Security became concerned about the question of American Communists within the United Nations staff and began a series of hearings, as an indirect result of which about forty staff members were dismissed by the Secretary-General." During the Seventh Assembly these events aroused considerable foreign criticism of American actions affecting the United Nations.[2]

Western control over the organs of the UN was further weakened by Soviet success in protesting Trygve Lie's cold war policies; he offered his resignation in November 1952, before it was due.

A development of greater long-range significance, however, was the emergence into self-conscious independence of the Arab–Asian states, with greater potentialities for compromising conflicts between East and West as well as achieving desired policies of their own.

> When the shooting war broke out in Asia itself, on the Korean peninsula, the Asian states were galvanized into efforts to achieve a Korean solution . . . [in] the General Assembly. Last year again [1951] the Asian–Arab states played a significant role in the discussions on dependent peoples in the Fourth Committee. They also had a large share of responsibility in the Covenant on Human Rights, [including] a provision . . . on international respect for the self-determination of peoples. This problem will no doubt be one of the most pervasive and controversial subjects under debate this year [1952].[3]

In the Seventh Assembly, India sponsored resolutions on P.O.W. repatriation reflecting a conscious mediating role. And the great

2. Clyde Eagleton, "Current Problems of the United Nations," in Clyde Eagleton and Richard Swift, eds., *Annual Review of United Nations Affairs, 1953* (New York, New York University Press, 1954), p. 4.

3. "Issues before the Seventh General Assembly," p. 364. Kock and Triska, "Asian–African Coalition," sketch the extremely interesting history of African and Asian associations. Not until 1950 did "occasional association begin to assume the characteristic of a formal alignment. . . . Late in 1951, this *ad hoc* consultative arrangement was transformed into what was often known as the Arab–Asian group, upon the initiatives of . . . Indonesia, Pakistan, Syria, Egypt and India" (pp. 422 ff.). Hovet, *Bloc Politics*, gives exact group memberships since the First General Assembly.

number of issues discussed and voted upon in the Second, Third, and Fourth Committees strikingly emphasized increased concern with self-determination in the General Assembly, as we shall see.

## IMPORTANT ISSUES AT THE SEVENTH SESSION

### Political and Security Affairs

The first plenary roll call (vote 8001) [4] defeated (25-27-8) a Polish proposal to the effect that the Chairman of the Ad Hoc Political Committee be given membership and the right to vote on the General Committee, the steering committee of the General Assembly. Although in many ways a procedural question, its structural implications, including one more non-great power on the General Committee, reflect a continuing and important conflict in the Assembly. All geopolitical groupings were not in perfect agreement among themselves, but French abstention and American, British, and Chinese negatives suggest that the vote contained a threat to the Western great powers. West European and Old Commonwealth states were generally opposed; Latins were very split; a majority of Arab–Asians agreed with the Soviets, somewhat along cold war lines.

As in 1947, the treatment of people of Indian origin in South Africa was discussed as a political issue. The Benelux countries, France, the Old Commonwealth, Turkey, and scattered Latin American nations were the only states to oppose the inclusion of the item on the agenda (vote 8003). The crucial committee vote (0001) on a resolution calling for the suspension of the Group Areas Act pending negotiations under the auspices of a Good Offices Commission passed by a 30-16-12 margin. Bolivia, Chile, Guatemala, Haiti, and Mexico were the principal Latin nations opposed. The plenary vote on the whole resolution (8015) had a more lopsided majority (41-1-15), similar to that on vote 8003.

Overruling South African protests that the matter was one of "domestic jurisdiction" (vote 8016), the Assembly also discussed "the question of race conflict in South Africa." As they had on the question of Indians in South Africa, thirteen Arab–Asians jointly sponsored this item. By a narrow (35-17-7) two-thirds majority, they

4. We are again briefly discussing important roll-call votes. They are numbered as they appear in the unrotated and rotated factor patterns presented below.

were successful on a key paragraph vote (8017) establishing a commission to study and report on the South African racial situation. The whole resolution (vote 8018) then passed by a 35-1-23 majority. Solid European opposition (excluding the Soviet bloc, of course), American and Chinese abstentions, and negatives from the Dominican Republic, Nicaragua, and Peru were not sufficient to produce the one-third necessary to stop a newly self-conscious Afro–Asian unanimity.

Scandinavian attempts at a mild and conciliatory resolution (no mention of South Africa) affirming policies directed toward "racial harmony" produced an unusual coalition. In committee, South Africa and the Soviet bloc were opposed to this resolution (vote 0006). In plenary, only South Africa voiced opposition to the Scandinavian resolution (vote 8019). But the abstentions by most Benelux and Old Commonwealth states, both "left" and "right" Latin Americans (e.g. Haiti and the Dominican Republic) and all Soviet and Arab–Asian states (except Pakistan and China) produced a total of 34 abstentions, ten more than the number of states (including the United States) that supported the resolution.[5]

Despite American backing, resolutions reaffirming the goals and continuing the work of the Conciliation Commission on Palestine did not do as well at the Seventh Assembly as they had in previous years. The Soviet bloc abstained in committee (vote 0009), but fairly strong Latin American support reaffirmed the Commission's work in the Committee vote by a 32-13-13 majority. Philippine efforts to direct the Commission's work "on the basis of" rather than "bearing in mind" earlier UN resolutions did not receive the required two-thirds majority (vote 8026, 26-24-10). And a Philippine amendment emphasizing in particular "the principle of internationalization of Jerusalem" (vote 8027) failed similarly by a 28-20-12 margin. (The pro-Arab position since Israeli expansion after the 1947 partition has been to cite earlier Assembly resolutions on refugee resettlement, territorial boundaries, and respect for the Holy Places.)

In plenary only eight Latins concurred in an appreciation of the Conciliation Commission (vote 8028); the Soviets voted against it

5. The sources for the brief summaries of the important issues before the Assembly are the *Annexes* and *Official Records of the General Assembly* for the Seventh regular session, the *U.N. Yearbook, 1952*, and the two issues of *International Conciliation* cited in notes 1 and 2 above.

(opposing the existence of a Conciliation Commission and American domination of it), while Yugoslavia and Burma were alone among nonaligned states in supporting the resolution. As a result, the American position failed by a vote of 24-15-21 to receive the required two-thirds majority. No further resolutions on Palestine were adopted at the Seventh Assembly, as Arab-sponsored efforts failed by much wider margins.

Although descriptions of the Seventh General Assembly's accomplishments with regard to the Korean War loom large in the summary descriptions of its activities,[6] less than ten per cent of the Assembly's 180 odd roll calls dealt with this subject. Bacteriological warfare charges and prisoner repatriation were the main concerns. Only scattered Arab and Asian abstentions mitigated Soviet isolation on its charges of "brutalities" against prisoners of war (vote 8048) and its opposition to an impartial investigation of charges of bacteriological warfare (vote 8049). A Russian proposal for an immediate cease-fire and complete repatriation (vote 8010) was opposed even by Yugoslavia; it received abstentions only from Afghanistan, India, Indonesia, Iran, Saudi Arabia, Yemen, Egypt, and Syria. On the final Indian repatriation compromise (vote 8013) only China abstained, with all other UN members except the Soviet bloc voting affirmatively.[7]

As Korean questions were not a new subject in 1952, so membership recommendations tied to cold war concerns continued to appear in important roll calls. Regarding Japanese membership in the International Civil Aviation Organization, Assembly unanimity on an American, Canadian, Peruvian, and Venezuelan resolution was marred only by Philippine and Soviet bloc abstentions (vote 8009). On a recommendation to the Security Council regarding Japanese fitness for UN membership, only the Philippines, Israel, Sweden, and Guatemala failed to protest the negative position of the Soviet bloc. No Indian reservations were in evidence as they had been

6. For instance, the *U.N. Yearbook, 1952,* spends almost half of its discussion of political and security questions on topics related to Korea.

7. There were only three *committee* roll calls on Korea, which, because duplicated by votes 8010 and 8013, were excluded from the factor analysis. Five plenary roll calls virtually identical (with less than four switches) to 8010 or 8013 were also excluded as spite votes or procedural (agenda) matters appearing elsewhere. Several of them referred to including Communist Chinese and North Korean delegates in UN discussions or activities.

regarding similar questions at the Second General Assembly. Four Committee votes recommended memberships for Japan, Vietnam, and Libya; they were not included in the factor analysis because they were duplicated by plenary voting on similar issues, except for a few more Latin and Asian abstentions. Vote 8042, a Latin and Scandinavian proposal for a membership study, produced six Asian abstentions and Soviet bloc protests (the vote was 48–6–5). More important, of the two direct (plus several indirect) procedural votes on Chinese representation, only one (vote 8008) was included in the factor analysis. Several Arab, Asian, and Latin states abstained. Only Sweden and Burma sided with the Soviet minority.

Two plenary votes and ten First Committee votes dealt with French relations with Tunisia and Morocco. In committee, mixed Latin support for UN assistance in independence negotiations supplemented generally favorable Arab–Asian votes. Western (including American) opposition was successful in defeating the more extreme suggestions (1011 and 1013). Worried about enhancing the UN on self-determination questions, the Soviets abstained on votes 1006 and 1013. In plenary, eleven Latin states were successful (by a 29-8-22 vote) in adding "due regard to the legitimate rights and interests under the established norms and practices of the law of nations" to an urgent appeal for the development of free political institutions for Morocco (vote 8029). Again on the final resolution (8030, approved 45–3–11) we find Soviet, Benelux, and Old Commonwealth countries virtually alone in abstention or opposition. The United States supported this statement of confidence in France, the hope for negotiations to develop Moroccan political institutions, and appeals for restraint on both sides.

## Economic and Financial Questions

In contrast to the three "economic" roll calls in the Second Assembly, all on Russian initiatives, seventeen committee and four plenary roll calls at the Seventh Session dealt with Second Committee concerns.

After several amendments, a Uruguayan resolution (8045) recommending agreements between states on emigrant resettlements that would help economic development was supported by all but Soviet, Arab, and southern Old Commonwealth members.

None of the remaining Second Committee issues were sponsored or significantly amended by either the United States or the Soviet Union. Eleven of the Western European powers were unable (19-22-13) to define the establishment of "just . . . wage levels" as an objective and a responsibility of the underdeveloped countries themselves (vote 2004). On a successful Brazilian amendment recommending bilateral as well as multilateral agreements for stabilizing international primary commodity prices (vote 2008, 27-15-13), only Pakistan joined the United States, West Europeans, and the Old Commonwealth (frequent voting allies whom we may collectively identify as "Old Europeans") in protest. On votes 2004 and 2008 the Soviet bloc stood between the positions of Old Europeans and the rest of the United Nations. Responding to another European-sponsored amendment the Soviets voted with the underdeveloped countries to defeat (16-32-7) a mildly worded suggestion on commodity trade problems that noted adverse effects on "the ability of [the underdeveloped] countries to finance the purchase of capital goods" (vote 2005). The final plenary vote (8044) on stabilizing primary commodity trade (35-15-9) shows virtually all Latin, African, and Asian states in the affirmative, the Soviets sitting on the fence, and the older Western countries, including the United States, in a negative minority.

Votes 8046 and 8047 were initiatives by Uruguay, Bolivia, and India regarding "the right to exploit freely natural wealth and resources." The Soviets objected to an Indian proposal in favor of "maintaining the flow of capital in conditions of security" (vote 8046; the "bad" word is "capital"), while most Western developed countries abstained. On the final resolution (8047) the Soviets supported (against isolated American and British opposition) a 36-4-20 endorsement of the sovereign right "of any state over its natural resources." [8]

8. A Latin American diplomat interviewed ten years later recalled this triumph with pride. Lincoln Bloomfield has summarized some of the relevant implications: "On certain issues the trend is indeed away from a majority position for the United States. This has in fact already happened on a number of issues in the field of economic planning, such as the proposals for U.N. financing of *economic development*, and in discussions of international pricing of *primary commodities*, as well as in the tendency to define *self-determination* in terms of the right to nationalize foreign-owned property with or without fair compensation." Lincoln Bloomfield, *The United Nations and U.S. Foreign Policy* (Boston, Little, Brown, 1960), p. 11 (emphasis added).

### Social, Humanitarian, and Cultural Issues

As the scope and frequency of roll calls in the Second Committee increased from 1947 to 1952, human rights questions in the Third Committee underwent a similarly remarkable expansion. Neither Soviets nor most Old Europeans were happy with resolutions sponsored by a variety of states (including France, Egypt, and Yugoslavia) urging ratification of an irrevocable convention on the freedom of correcting false information (vote 3003). A somewhat crude attempt by Afghanistan (at Soviet behest?) to sanction the right to nationalize foreign information enterprises (vote 3008) received support only from Bolivia, Indonesia, Iran, Iraq, Yemen, and Liberia outside of the Soviet bloc. On an additional information question, only four Arab–Asian countries supported a Soviet attempt to reaffirm and promote "measures against war propaganda" suggested in 1947. However, fourteen Arab–Asians and Latins abstained (vote 8022).

Among the human rights issues voted on in both committee and plenary, the rights of women and of self-determination were most discussed. In committee, Soviet abstentions and Benelux, French, and Old Commonwealth objections did not deter a 38-7-8 majority (vote 3018) favoring continued study by the Commission on Human Rights of measures to develop international respect for the "rights of people to self-determination." All Old Europeans (including Scandinavians, other West Europeans, the Old Commonwealth, and the United States) objected to resolutions favoring the realization of self-determination through the use of plebiscites and direct participation of indigenous populations in government organs, particularly in non-self-governing territories (votes 8024 and 8025). Soviet reservations in committee on the use of plebiscites disappeared when the resolutions' anticolonial nature became clear.

On the final resolution opening for signature a convention on equal political rights for women (8034), only Soviet and several Moslem states abstained. Regarding the deletion of a possibly superfluous reference to "discrimination," all Old European states and about half of Latin America were willing to go along (8031). An Indonesian addition of the same word (8032) in another paragraph evoked only partial European opposition as well as certain

Latin and pro-West Asian reservations. A badly divided Latin American group made it impossible for other Western states to get two-thirds support for a proposal (vote 8033) that all territories under a state's care, except those stipulated at ratification time, should come under the conditions of the convention. The colonial powers' argument was that some such territories *are* self-governing in social matters and should be given the choice of ratification themselves. Soviet and Arab–Asian reservations about this interpretation need not be elaborated upon.

## Trusteeship and Non-Self-Governing Territories

Despite some nations' continued preoccupation with Korea in the fall of 1952, trusteeship questions and self-determination issues of various sorts almost monopolized the "nonpolitical" committees of the Seventh General Assembly. Besides the discussions in the Second and Third Committees reviewed above, 50 roll calls occurred in the Fourth Committee, one more than the *total* number of plenary roll calls.

The main issues in the Fourth Committee were British treatment of the Wa-Merus in East Africa, the possible unification of Ewe and Togoland, a list of factors for judging whether or not a territory was "self-governing," and the renewal of the Committee on Information from Non-Self-Governing Territories. Split Latin voting, Soviet abstentions and Arab protests assured a 21-21-16 defeat for a final watered-down resolution (8040) on British expulsion of the Wa-Merus from their homelands in Tanganyika. Split Latin voting also accounted for the failure of the Soviet bloc and almost all Afro–Asians to achieve a two-thirds majority inviting Wa-Meru return and agricultural retraining (vote 8038, 28-20-10). Except for Soviet abstentions, a somewhat similar alignment occurred on vote 8039 asking the Administrative Authority to relieve the hardships of the Meru people. In committee, relatively mild amendments by Brazil, Ecuador, and Peru disapproving British actions (vote 4032) had received a 27-17-8 majority (Soviets, Arabs, and several Latins thought they were too mild), while a request for compensation to the expelled natives (vote 4035) had only nine (Benelux and Old Commonwealth) dissents.

American and Venezuelan sponsorship barely succeeded (22-20-12, vote 4009) in including the phrase "unless otherwise decided by the

General Assembly" in a resolution renewing the Committee on Information from Non-Self-Governing Territories. Almost all of the 40-12-2 opposition to vote 4013 renewing the Information Committee came from Old Europeans. Related votes approved a much debated list of factors to aid in the determination by the Information Committee of which countries were in fact "self-governing" (vote 8021, 36-15-7); Latins and some Asians succeeded in calling this decision a "provisional" approval (vote 4021, 23-4-28). An American amendment (vote 4016) deleting the suggestion that the Committee on Information directly associate inhabitants from the non-self-governing territories in its discussion of educational, economic, and social questions was unsuccessful (17-22-15); Latins usually abstained, Old Europeans favored the amendment; most remaining UN members opposed it.

Power struggles between the conservative membership of the Trusteeship Council and the more radical views of the Fourth Committee colored a good many of the votes on Ewe and Togoland and administrative unions. The United Kingdom was unsuccessful (vote 4005; 15-30-8, along familiar lines) in a key procedural vote to have the Chairman of the Togoland Congress address himself first to the Trusteeship Council and *then* to the Fourth Committee if unsatisfied. The United States and Brazil were successful (with only Soviet and a few colonial objections) in expressing the wish that administrative authorities consult the Trusteeship Council about possible administrative unions. The committee resolution (4046) urging British and French reestablishment of a Joint Council for Togoland Affairs (with membership drawn from the two adjoining Trust Territories) received a 30-11-9 majority, despite Old European reservations (except for Greece) and several Latin abstentions. In plenary a paragraph requesting revised trusteeship agreements in conformity with the desires of the inhabitants was not supported by most Western hemisphere states and pro-Western Asians; the Soviet bloc abstained (vote 8036, 18-22-18).

Finally, the Fourth Committee produced scattered Latin, Soviet, and Afro–Asian opposition to an American request for delayed committee action pending the results of Trusteeship resolutions on the participation of indigenous inhabitants in the government of Trusteeship Territories and the work of the Trusteeshop Council (vote 4041). Only the Soviets and a few colonial countries objected to another Fourth Committee request (vote 8041) that the Trustee-ship Council consider a questionnaire and a separate visiting mission to Italian Somaliland, in view of its "independence within the next eight years." Soviet votes appeared to be against even that long a delay in both these cases.

### Administrative and Budgetary Issues

With such heated discussions going on elsewhere, budgetary questions were very much underrepresented in roll-call voting at the Seventh Assembly. The single Fifth Committee roll call (5001) recommended Spanish as a working language of the Economic and Social Council. Only the Soviets and Scandinavians showed any determined resistance (the vote was 43-1-11). Indian and Indonesian absences perhaps indicated an incomplete willingness to support the Latin request.

### Legal Questions

Neither did any legal questions achieve plenary roll call status. Three of the fourteen Sixth Committee roll calls were included in the factor analysis. Almost all Western nations objected to a Czech amendment that Assembly Committees "may consult" (rather than "should consult") the Legal Committee on important legal aspects of a particular question (vote 6005). On the subject of defining aggression, the Soviet Union and the United States were defeated (26-6-22, vote 6011) in objecting to the study of all related problems on the "assumption of a definition being adopted by the General Assembly." The Soviets then joined the Assembly majority on the whole resolution (vote 6012, 36-9-9) sponsored by Afghanistan, Yugoslavia, Iran, the Netherlands, and six Latin American states.

### VOTING DIMENSIONS IN 1952

How many voting dimensions underlay these important Assembly roll calls? Looking at the unrotated factor matrix in Table 4.1, we see that by 1952 the complexity of voting patterns had increased to encompass ten general independent voting components.[9] With 63

9. In Tables 4.1 and 4.2 the tenth factor has been omitted. Its unrotated eigen value was 1.1 (after rotation 1.3). In both cases its highest loadings (0.48 and 0.59, respectively) come from vote 6005 on *"legal consultation"* with the Sixth Committee.

important roll calls (15 more than in 1947), some increase in factors with λ's greater than 1.0 is, however, to be expected.

Adding these lambdas and dividing by 63, the total roll-call variance indicates that ten distinct factors account for 82.3 per cent of all important voting variance in 1952. The pervasiveness of these ten underlying voting components is also evidenced by the fact that only votes on General Committee membership, refugee re-settlement, and Wa-Meru compensation (8001, 8045, 4035) were less than 70 per cent interpretable in terms of these general voting components. (Their respective communalities were 0.65, 0.66, and 0.62.)

Before turning to a more detailed examination of the rotated factor pattern (matrix), a look at the alignments of states on the first and second unrotated factors (Figure 4.1) and at Table 4.1 suggests that East–West and North–South are again appropriate labels for the Assembly's two most frequent voting components. The U.S., Old Commonwealth, West Europeans, and Scandinavians can be nicely grouped in the Northwest quadrant; other regional caucusing groups are quite cohesive and in their appropriate corners. Only Latin Americans reveal a sizable "Eastern" inclination.

East–West voting of the sort summarized along the horizontal axis of Figure 4.1 dominated a wide range of conflict situations, including Palestine and South Africa, as well as key votes on economic development, commodity trade, natural resources, Tunisian self-determination, and a list of factors for deciding if a territory is "self-governing." Only on issues with fairly high North–South loadings (UN membership, prisoner repatriation, scattered colonial and rights questions, the secure flow of aid capital, and Spanish as a working language of ECOSOC) was the United States able to command a large anti-Soviet majority. Occasionally the Soviets and certain colonial powers shared a negative interest in some such moderate anticolonial measures; occasionally too (e.g. vote 6011) the United States and the Soviets shared a Northern minority position. Often these resolutions, like that on repatriation, were *not* American or even Western initiatives.

---

Danish and Norwegian approval of optional consultation, Burmese, Indian, Turkish, and Liberian objections to this provision are the most pronounced departures from an East versus West overall alignment.

Figure 4.1. Unrotated Factor Scores on the East–West and
North–South Issues at the 7th General Assembly

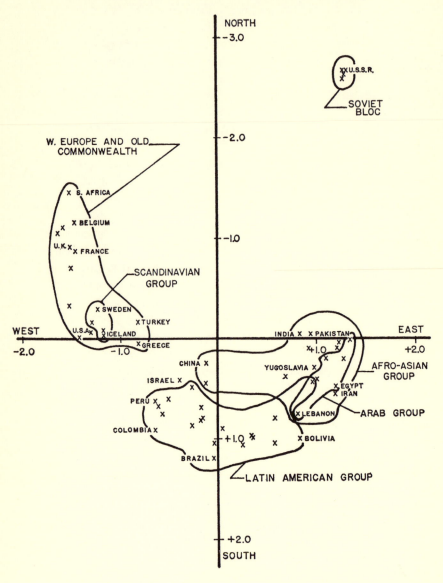

# Table 4.1. Dimensions of Voting in 1952: Unrotated Factor Matrix

### FACTORS

| ROLL CALLS | 1 | 2 | 3 | 4 | 5 | 6 | 7 | 8 | 9 |
|---|---|---|---|---|---|---|---|---|---|
| 8001. Put chairman of AHC on G.C. | .69 | —.06 | —.06 | —.14 | —.01 | .02 | .13 | —.24 | .05 |
| 8003. Indians in S. Africa on agenda | .65 | .19 | —.46 | .35 | —.17 | .02 | .16 | —.14 | —.05 |
| 0001. S. Africa: suspend group area act | .87 | .07 | —.15 | .14 | —.10 | .08 | —.05 | .07 | —.20 |
| 8015. Help Indians—S. Africa discussions | .66 | .17 | —.50 | .31 | —.14 | .15 | .07 | —.04 | —.17 |
| 8016. Race conflict a domestic issue? | —.66 | —.24 | .52 | —.27 | .02 | —.11 | —.05 | .04 | .09 |
| 8017. Commission on race conflict | .86 | .17 | —.20 | —.06 | —.06 | .03 | .06 | .09 | —.17 |
| 8018. Commission to study and report | .85 | .13 | —.19 | —.04 | —.10 | .09 | .07 | .07 | —.19 |
| 0006. Charter asks for race harmony | —.45 | .56 | —.35 | .17 | .22 | —.13 | .03 | —.28 | —.05 |
| 8019. Approve of multiracial harmony | —.24 | .41 | —.53 | .11 | .10 | —.19 | —.02 | —.41 | —.22 |
| 0009. Asks negotiations on Palestine: | —.63 | .10 | —.45 | —.35 | —.04 | .19 | —.24 | .15 | —.10 |
| 8026. on the basis of prior resolutions | .43 | .44 | .57 | .11 | .03 | —.30 | .17 | —.02 | .02 |
| 8027. Internationalize Jerusalem | .34 | .53 | .47 | —.04 | .19 | —.24 | .19 | —.17 | —.01 |
| 8028. Appreciate Pal. Council. Comm. | —.75 | .14 | —.34 | —.14 | —.06 | .29 | —.13 | .09 | —.03 |
| 8048. Brutal murder of Communist POWs | .67 | —.53 | .03 | .11 | .29 | .17 | .20 | —.03 | .08 |
| 8049. Study bacteriological warfare | —.50 | .65 | .19 | .06 | —.25 | —.01 | —.25 | —.07 | —.04 |
| 8010. Immediate cease-fire | .65 | —.53 | .01 | .05 | .28 | .20 | .22 | —.00 | .17 |
| 8013. Korean repatriation | —.35 | .73 | .32 | .08 | .00 | .31 | —.01 | .05 | —.12 |
| 8008. Seating of China | —.58 | .48 | .18 | —.11 | —.17 | —.11 | —.03 | —.00 | .12 |
| 8009. Japan in ICAO | —.39 | .71 | .28 | .13 | .14 | .21 | —.02 | .05 | —.13 |
| 8043. Japan in UN | —.32 | .61 | .43 | .08 | .17 | .18 | .05 | .03 | —.01 |
| 8042. Est. Committee on New States | —.53 | .60 | .13 | .00 | —.25 | —.01 | —.17 | —.09 | .16 |
| 1006. Regrets French absence (Tunisia) | .63 | .13 | .17 | .55 | .11 | —.10 | —.09 | .05 | .10 |
| 1011. Tunisian self-determination | .86 | —.15 | .18 | .27 | —.01 | —.15 | —.05 | .00 | —.01 |
| 1013. GA President and Tunisia | .80 | —.00 | .28 | .34 | .06 | —.09 | —.10 | —.01 | —.05 |
| 8029. Morocco's political development | —.54 | .56 | —.35 | —.11 | .11 | .05 | .00 | .04 | .16 |

# Table 4.1. Dimensions of Voting in 1952: Unrotated Factor Matrix

| ROLL CALLS | 1 | 2 | 3 | 4 | 5 | 6 | 7 | 8 | 9 |
|---|---|---|---|---|---|---|---|---|---|
| 8030. Confidence in France on Morocco | .12 | .71 | —.19 | .26 | .18 | .05 | .02 | .23 | .31 |
| 8045. Ask immigration for development | .39 | .39 | —.25 | —.16 | .16 | —.21 | .23 | —.23 | —.23 |
| 8046. Protect flow of capital | .18 | .72 | .19 | —.05 | .16 | .28 | .04 | .10 | —.19 |
| 8047. Sovereignty over natural resources | .79 | .15 | .00 | —.16 | .21 | .11 | .04 | —.13 | —.15 |
| 2004. Wages are natural responsibility | .61 | —.44 | —.03 | .34 | —.15 | —.15 | —.22 | .19 | —.10 |
| 2005. Help primary producers | —.75 | —.22 | .12 | .45 | —.17 | —.08 | —.01 | .06 | —.10 |
| 2008. Agreements on commodities | .51 | .60 | —.18 | —.34 | —.02 | —.11 | —.04 | .00 | .25 |
| 8022. Measures vs. war propaganda | .81 | —.33 | .12 | .08 | .19 | .13 | —.13 | —.08 | —.06 |
| 8024. Participation in NGSTs | .83 | .22 | —.16 | —.17 | .17 | —.20 | —.15 | .10 | —.05 |
| 8025. Right of self-determination | .83 | .25 | —.02 | —.23 | .09 | —.25 | —.01 | —.01 | .09 |
| 3018. Human rights and self-determination | .44 | .68 | —.23 | .27 | .11 | —.05 | —.05 | .11 | .01 |
| 8031. Remove word "discrimination" | .76 | .02 | —.04 | .23 | —.27 | —.07 | .24 | —.11 | .01 |
| 8032. Add "no discrimination" | .46 | —.02 | —.14 | —.04 | .49 | —.15 | —.44 | .23 | —.09 |
| 8033. No exclusions re rights of women | —.79 | .18 | —.18 | —.02 | .03 | .01 | .32 | .22 | .05 |
| 8034. Convention on women's rights | .45 | .52 | —.00 | .08 | —.02 | —.31 | —.07 | .11 | —.40 |
| 3003. Always correct false information | .27 | .68 | —.02 | —.29 | —.08 | .19 | —.11 | —.16 | .02 |
| 3008. Sovereignty over one's resources | .76 | —.16 | .03 | —.10 | .14 | .15 | —.27 | —.10 | .03 |
| 8041. Discuss Italian Somaliland? | —.04 | .66 | —.13 | .27 | .13 | .17 | .00 | .19 | .09 |
| 4021. "Provisional" SGT factors | .30 | .56 | —.16 | —.16 | —.28 | —.25 | —.02 | .16 | .31 |
| 4009. Renewable CINSGT | .75 | .11 | —.11 | .12 | .00 | —.02 | .14 | .11 | .27 |
| 4013. Continue CINSGT | .81 | .28 | —.12 | —.18 | .04 | —.19 | .08 | .04 | .02 |
| 8020. Automatic CINSGT | .81 | —.04 | —.20 | —.21 | —.12 | —.15 | .04 | .08 | —.09 |
| 8021. List of NSGT factors | .87 | .17 | —.00 | —.08 | —.15 | —.10 | .08 | .18 | .07 |
| 4032. Delete "disapproval" (Wa-Meru) | .79 | .16 | —.11 | .00 | .30 | —.06 | .22 | .08 | .02 |
| 4035. Compensate Wa-Merus | .56 | .16 | —.29 | .26 | —.26 | .01 | .11 | .06 | .08 |
| 8038. Wa-Meru expulsion | .90 | .01 | .13 | .03 | —.20 | —.01 | .06 | .05 | —.04 |
| 8039. Relieve hardship of Wa-Meru | —.79 | —.11 | —.34 | —.04 | .21 | —.02 | .14 | —.02 | .11 |

## Table 4.1. Dimensions of Voting in 1952: Unrotated Factor Matrix

| ROLL CALLS | FACTORS | | | | | | | | |
|---|---|---|---|---|---|---|---|---|---|
| | 1 | 2 | 3 | 4 | 5 | 6 | 7 | 8 | 9 |
| 8040. Regrets Wa-Meru expulsion | —.76 | —.22 | —.34 | .05 | .21 | —.16 | .03 | —.05 | .03 |
| 4005. Address TC first (re Togo) | —.84 | —.10 | .06 | .08 | .05 | .12 | .04 | —.21 | .05 |
| 4046. Resolve Ewe and Togo split | .84 | .14 | —.02 | —.02 | —.08 | —.10 | .05 | .11 | —.01 |
| 8036. Allow their unification | .69 | .20 | .16 | .01 | —.21 | .23 | .25 | —.01 | —.09 |
| 4016. NSGTs in CINSGT | —.79 | .06 | .07 | .03 | —.14 | .00 | —.09 | —.18 | —.12 |
| 4039. Consult TC on unions | .07 | .87 | —.08 | .33 | .07 | .06 | —.03 | .07 | .10 |
| 4041. Note TC consideration | —.78 | .00 | .09 | .21 | .15 | —.19 | —.13 | —.04 | —.05 |
| 5001. Spanish a working language | .11 | .67 | .36 | —.26 | —.02 | .01 | .12 | .07 | —.19 |
| 6005. Others may consult C6 | .50 | —.26 | —.04 | .43 | .00 | .05 | —.16 | —.15 | .19 |
| 6011. Assume aggression defined | .30 | .61 | .18 | .03 | .02 | .08 | —.14 | —.40 | .20 |
| 6012. Draft defs. of aggression | .62 | .07 | —.15 | —.07 | —.13 | .09 | —.25 | —.32 | .23 |

Roll-call variance accounted
for by factor (eigen values)λ=26.0 λ=10.6 λ=3.9 λ=2.8 λ=1.8 λ=1.6 λ=1.4 λ=1.4 λ=1.3

Even after eliminating several cold war "spite" procedural roll calls from plenary voting, East–West voting appears more frequently in 1952 than it did in 1947. Of the common variance, just over half (50.1 per cent) is interpretable as East–West voting. Despite the ten per cent increase in East–West concern since 1947, North–South voting again explains one fifth (20.5 per cent) of the common voting variation. Other factors, however, are not as easy to conceptualize from the unrotated factor matrix.

### The Rotated Factor Pattern

As defined by the criterion of simple structure, the first six rotated factors are all fairly prominent and easy to identify (see Table 4.2). All with small eigen values, the seventh through tenth factors may be more briefly described as scattered opposition to an additional discrimination reference, support for "defining aggression," for "colonial moderation" (especially vote 8030), and for legal consultation.[10] Each of the other six rotated factors (all with rotated λ's greater than 4.0) will be discussed in more detail.

10. See note 9 above, regarding the tenth factor.

# Table 4.2. Dimensions of Voting in 1952: Rotated Factor Matrix

| ROLL CALLS | FACTORS | | | | | | | | |
|---|---|---|---|---|---|---|---|---|---|
| | 1 | 2 | 3 | 4 | 5 | 6 | 7 | 8 | 9 |
| 8001. Put chairman of AHC on G.C. | .54 | —.14 | .22 | .17 | .34 | .01 | .09 | —.33 | —.08 |
| 8003. Indians in S. Africa on agenda | .35 | —.06 | .18 | .81 | .10 | —.12 | .07 | —.10 | .05 |
| 0001. S. Africa: suspend group area act | .54 | —.01 | .24 | .60 | .17 | .20 | —.18 | —.06 | —.17 |
| 8015. Help Indians; S. Africa discussions | .37 | —.01 | .04 | .86 | .13 | —.04 | —.03 | —.03 | —.05 |
| 8016. Race conflict a domestic issue? | —.42 | —.02 | —.04 | —.80 | —.14 | .11 | .10 | .04 | —.04 |
| 8017. Commission on race conflict | .72 | —.00 | .16 | .50 | .16 | .11 | —.10 | .01 | —.10 |
| 8018. Commission to study and report | .68 | —.01 | .15 | .52 | .17 | .14 | —.05 | —.00 | —.15 |
| 0006. Charter asks for race harmony | —.20 | .34 | —.17 | .10 | —.26 | —.71 | —.01 | —.01 | .18 |
| 8019. Approve of multi-racial harmony | —.06 | .10 | —.17 | .26 | —.21 | —.78 | —.05 | —.16 | —.01 |
| 0009. Asks negotiations on Palestine: | —.17 | .03 | —.84 | —.13 | —.28 | —.17 | —.09 | .06 | —.00 |
| 8026. On the basis of prior resolutions | .35 | .36 | .75 | —.06 | —.14 | .04 | .06 | .08 | .05 |
| 8027. Internationalize Jerusalem | .41 | .43 | .60 | —.15 | —.10 | —.17 | .08 | .08 | .00 |
| 8028. Appreciate Pal. Council. Comm. | —.38 | .16 | —.75 | —.10 | —.25 | —.15 | .05 | .03 | .04 |
| 8048. Brutal murder of Communist POWs | .22 | —.28 | .29 | .15 | .77 | .23 | —.06 | —.05 | —.06 |
| 8049. Study bacteriological warfare | —.22 | .51 | —.07 | —.07 | —.71 | —.11 | .07 | —.06 | —.00 |
| 8010. Immediate cease-fire | .25 | —.30 | .23 | .12 | .77 | .27 | —.03 | —.04 | .01 |
| 8013. Korean repatriation | —.14 | .86 | —.07 | —.07 | —.31 | —.03 | .11 | .02 | —.04 |
| 8008. Seating of China | —.18 | .33 | —.11 | —.29 | —.60 | —.13 | .21 | .10 | .17 |
| 8009. Japan in ICAO | —.20 | .84 | —.04 | —.11 | —.23 | —.15 | —.00 | .01 | .00 |
| 8043. Japan in UN | —.14 | .77 | .09 | —.22 | —.18 | —.05 | .08 | .08 | .05 |
| 8042. Est. Committee on New States | —.19 | .43 | —.12 | —.14 | —.67 | —.10 | .17 | —.09 | .16 |
| 1006. Regrets French absence (Tunisia) | .11 | .15 | .63 | .41 | .17 | .17 | —.28 | —.16 | .15 |
| 1011. Tunisian self-determination | .36 | —.16 | .62 | .34 | .26 | .28 | —.21 | —.16 | —.06 |
| 1013. GA President & Tunisia | .30 | .04 | .67 | .32 | .22 | .24 | —.26 | —.17 | —.10 |
| 8029. Morocco's political development | —.09 | .38 | —.49 | —.06 | —.29 | —.40 | .04 | .04 | .36 |

## Table 4.2. Dimensions of Voting in 1952: Rotated Factor Matrix

| ROLL CALLS | FACTORS | | | | | | | | |
|---|---|---|---|---|---|---|---|---|---|
| | 1 | 2 | 3 | 4 | 5 | 6 | 7 | 8 | 9 |
| 8030. Confidence in France on Morocco | .18 | .55 | .01 | .33 | −.11 | −.10 | −.13 | .05 | .56 |
| 8045. Ask immigration for development | −.01 | .19 | −.17 | −.11 | −.15 | −.70 | .12 | .08 | −.01 |
| 8046. Protect flow of capital | .33 | .79 | .02 | .06 | −.02 | −.04 | −.03 | .01 | −.07 |
| 8047. Sovereignty over natural resources | .70 | .11 | .23 | .22 | .30 | .00 | −.11 | −.03 | −.22 |
| 2004. Wages are natural responsibility | −.76 | −.32 | −.12 | −.03 | −.21 | .09 | −.17 | .16 | −.01 |
| 2005. Help primary producers | −.88 | −.05 | −.01 | −.06 | −.22 | −.01 | .07 | .12 | −.01 |
| 2008. Agreements on commodities | .79 | .21 | .01 | .11 | −.18 | −.10 | −.03 | −.20 | .31 |
| 8022. Measures vs. war propaganda | .36 | −.16 | .35 | .20 | .51 | .29 | −.27 | −.22 | −.24 |
| 8024. Participation in NSGTs | .78 | −.02 | .23 | .25 | .09 | −.01 | −.39 | −.06 | .03 |
| 8025. Right of self-determination | .82 | −.02 | .35 | .13 | .07 | −.01 | −.18 | −.12 | .10 |
| 3018. Human rights and self-determination | .38 | .44 | .17 | .52 | −.12 | −.16 | −.24 | −.01 | .27 |
| 8031. Remove word "discrimination" | −.64 | .01 | −.14 | −.05 | −.28 | −.24 | .41 | .05 | .10 |
| 8032. Add "no discrimination" | .34 | −.04 | .06 | .04 | .20 | .00 | −.77 | −.00 | .02 |
| 8033. No exclusions re rights of women | −.42 | .20 | −.42 | −.19 | −.13 | −.28 | .26 | .32 | .30 |
| 8034. Convention of women's rights | −.18 | .36 | −.01 | −.01 | −.52 | −.40 | −.14 | .23 | −.07 |
| 3003. Always correct false information | .57 | .45 | −.10 | .10 | −.31 | −.06 | .08 | −.13 | −.04 |
| 3008. Sovereignty over one's resources | .50 | −.12 | .18 | .15 | .32 | .27 | −.29 | −.27 | −.18 |
| 8041. Discuss Italian Somaliland? | −.01 | .66 | −.08 | .26 | −.03 | −.14 | −.11 | −.13 | .35 |
| 4021. "Provisional" SGT factors | .53 | .13 | .04 | .16 | −.38 | −.01 | .03 | −.17 | .44 |
| 4009. Renewable CINSGT | −.53 | .11 | −.29 | −.18 | −.19 | −.17 | .19 | .15 | .41 |
| 4013. Continue CINSGT | .81 | .00 | .27 | .26 | .09 | −.02 | −.11 | −.04 | .10 |
| 8020. Automatic CINSGT | .72 | −.28 | .17 | .32 | .13 | .10 | −.10 | −.02 | −.07 |
| 8021. List of NSGT factors | .74 | −.02 | .33 | .33 | .09 | .25 | −.03 | −.05 | .10 |
| 4032. Delete "disapproval" (Wa-Meru) | −.46 | .22 | −.31 | −.30 | −.06 | −.42 | .08 | .32 | .25 |
| 4035. Compensate Wa-Merus | .31 | −.02 | .15 | .61 | .06 | .09 | .06 | −.18 | .18 |
| 8038. Wa-Meru expulsion | .59 | −.06 | .45 | .36 | .17 | .33 | −.00 | −.14 | −.11 |
| 8039. Relieve hardship of Wa-Meru | −.50 | −.10 | −.49 | −.24 | −.01 | −.41 | .09 | .20 | .24 |

## Table 4.2. Dimensions of Voting in 1952: Rotated Factor Matrix

### FACTORS

| ROLL CALLS | 1 | 2 | 3 | 4 | 5 | 6 | 7 | 8 | 9 |
|---|---|---|---|---|---|---|---|---|---|
| 8070. Regrets Wa-Meru expulsion | —.57 | —.23 | —.37 | —.20 | —.05 | —.43 | —.03 | .21 | .17 |
| 4005. Address TC first (re Togo) | —.70 | .07 | —.28 | —.34 | —.08 | —.22 | .22 | —.02 | —.01 |
| 4046. Resolve Ewe and Togo split | .67 | —.03 | .35 | .36 | .11 | .18 | —.09 | —.03 | .02 |
| 8036. Allow their unification | .51 | .21 | .29 | .35 | .17 | .26 | .25 | —.05 | —.16 |
| 4016. NSGTs in CINSGT | —.58 | .11 | —.25 | —.26 | —.37 | —.21 | .16 | —.03 | —.13 |
| 4039. Consult TC on unions | .11 | .72 | .09 | .35 | —.22 | —.20 | —.09 | —.14 | .34 |
| 4041. Note TC consideration | —.69 | .08 | —.07 | —.30 | —.25 | —.29 | —.11 | .10 | .06 |
| 5001. Spanish a working language | .42 | .60 | .15 | —.14 | —.28 | —.03 | .14 | .15 | —.12 |
| 6005. Others may consult C6 | .02 | —.27 | .34 | .44 | .15 | .24 | —.14 | —.06 | .02 |
| 6011. Assume aggression defined | .30 | .50 | .26 | .04 | —.11 | —.14 | .04 | —.58 | .06 |
| 6012. Draft defs. of aggression | .46 | —.08 | .09 | .23 | .10 | .06 | —.07 | —.68 | .01 |

Roll-call variance accounted
for by factor (eigen values) λ=14.8 λ=7.3 λ=6.5 λ=6.5  λ=5.4 λ=4.1 λ=2.1 λ=1.9 λ=2.0

The three heaviest loadings on the first rotated factor are: (1) the defeat of an Old Commonwealth, Scandinavian, and Benelux initiated amendment (vote 2005) that governments try to minimize the adverse effects of primary commodity price changes, in particular "the ability of these countries to finance the purchase of capital goods"; (2) vote 8025 upholding the principle of self-determination (with opposition from Old Europeans); and (3) a Fourth Committee vote (4013) renewing the Committee on Information from Non-Self-Governing Territories (again over American and other Old European opposition). As a review of the other votes loading highly on the first rotated factor suggests, the issue of "economic and anti-colonial self-determination" was the most frequent substantively interpretable voting alignment in 1952. This voting dimension accounted for about three tenths (29 per cent) of the common variance after rotation. It is rather remarkable that anti-Old European voting (we include the United States among Old Europeans) was at least twice as frequent as any other substantively interpretable

76

voting alignment *during* the Korean War.[11] In effect, both pro-Western Asians and most Latin Americans voted against their Old European allies on self-determination questions.

What happened to the cold war? Related issues appear mostly in factor five and, possibly, in factor two. The fifth factor, with $\lambda =$ 5.4, is very clearly "the cold war" as it is usually perceived: membership questions and controversies over the Korean conflict are the only loadings on it above 0.60. In terms of the alignments involved, the East, the neutrals (between four and eleven of them), and the West are clearly distinguishable from the individual votes or the factor scores.

Factor two appears to contain a good deal of anti-Soviet and some anticolonial voting. Substantively, Korean repatriation, Japanese membership, guaranteeing the secure flow of capital, Somalian independence, and Trusteeship Council consultation on administrative unions all involve some aspect of UN supranationalism, different both from the cold war and anticolonial self-determination super-issues. In UN terms, the Soviets and the more extreme colonial powers have been the states most consistently trying to thwart supranational efforts of Assembly majorities. Such supranational efforts ranged from peaceful settlement issues (the Korean armistice) to constructive efforts toward decolonization. As one might expect, the highest contributor (vote 8030) to colonial moderation (factor nine) is also strongly related to UN supranationalism.[12] For fuller corroboration, of course, this factor label needs to be checked against

11. While it should be noted that five plenary roll calls relating to the cold war were excluded from the important set of votes that were factor analyzed, about 40 Fourth Committee votes were also excluded (see note 8). If by 1952 diplomats were succeeding in keeping muted an obvious conflict, their degree of success was impressive.

12. The next highest loadings on factor nine (votes 4021 and 4009 "provisionalizing" factors for defining Self-Governing Territories and supporting a renewable Information Committee from Non-Self-Governing Territories) load slightly higher on the anti-colonial first rotated factor than they do on the ninth rotated factor (colonial moderation), but do not contribute to UN supranationalism as we have tentatively defined it. Vote 8030 (favoring Moroccan independence while also expressing confidence in France) has equal supranationalism and colonial moderation aspects, with little anticolonialism of the first factor. Of course the uncorrelated nature of the first, second, and ninth factors does not allow one roll call to load very highly on several of them at once. If one agrees with these (to some extent subjective) factor labels, which survive nicely the more detailed analysis of this note, they help identify substantive implications of certain conflicts with remarkable clarity.

additional data on national attitudes and behavior regarding the United Nations.

Looking at Table 4.2 (the rotated factor matrix) suggests that in 1952 UN supranationalism was more a North–South than an East–West issue: the high loadings on the rotated second factor are similar to those on the unrotated North–South factor. The correlation between North–South factor scores and revised supranationalism scores is a high 0.88. At least in its economic and social aspects, UN supranationalism may be one of the alternatives to the East–West controversy and the cold war that U Thant has called to our attention.[13]

The third factor contains issues that correlated most heavily with the unrotated East–West voting alignment. Substantively it is limited to Arab questions, "Palestine and Tunisia." While the Latin American states had sided with the Afro–Asians and the Soviets against Old Europeans on the self-determination issues of factor 1, three quarters of them supported the efforts of the Conciliation Commission for Palestine along with the Old Europeans (vote 0009). Though this support for the American and Old European position dwindled on vote 8026 to something like the extreme splits of Latin voting on Palestine in 1947, a similar high degree of Latin unity with Old Europeans is found on vote 1013, the highest Tunisian vote loading on the third factor.

Both of these issues contributed heavily to the unrotated East–West voting component in the geographical sense that Old Europeans and Latin Americans—the West—opposed the East, a majority of the Afro–Asian states. They would have contributed even more were it not also the case that on all three of these votes (and others loading on the third rotated factor) the Soviet bloc abstained. As we have seen, eventual Soviet opposition to the Conciliation Commission (vote 8028) killed a further resolution on this subject. Since all of these votes (except for 0009) failed of adoption, inconclusive East–West voting on Palestine and Tunisia in 1952 (with the Soviets somewhat undecided where they belonged) also did not produce constructive decisions at that time.

Votes on Indians and race conflict in South Africa also loaded

13. After describing the evolution of an East–Neutral–West situation (see Chap. 1), U Thant emphasized issues that seem more of a North–South or supranational sort. "The time has come for us to direct our attention more to the economic and social structure of society and particularly to the disparity in the wealth of nations which is one of the root causes of political tension." *New York Times* (December 3, 1962), p. 9.

heavily on the unrotated East–West factor; after rotation, they reflect the similar views of Western anti-interventionists (factor 4).[14] South Africa pleaded domestic jurisdiction against Afro–Asian inquiries. The Soviets backed the Afro–Asians; and so did the states usually thought of as pro-Western Asians. Among Westerners, Scandinavians, the United States, Israel, and sometimes Greece supported the majority. Benelux, the Old Commonwealth, and certain Latins (Argentina, Colombia, Dominican Republic, Nicaragua, and Venezuela) usually opposed the interventionist majority. In terms of their political structure and ideology the Latin members of the defensive coalition were certainly among the more rightist or conservative Latin states.[15] The main coalition members were the most committed colonial powers among the Old Europeans.

The ideals of "liberal interventionists" stand out in the racial harmony and migration-for-development issues composing the sixth unrotated factor. These votes show Western anti-interventionists sharing the skepticism of almost all the Eastern states toward the humanitarian suggestions of the more liberal Westerners. As noted before, in the discussion of humanitarian questions before the Third Committee in 1947, consensus on "welfare internationalism" among United Nations members is extremely hard to find in roll-call voting. (The three or four virtually unanimous roll calls that did occur were usually on first paragraphs of colonial questions—e.g Charter citations. In the First Committee an "earnest appeal for agreement on an Austrian peace treaty" received only two abstentions, but probably because the Soviet bloc was "not participating" in the vote.) As it turned out, neither of these East–West voting subcomponents had much effect on South African policies.

The Uniting for Peace resolution in 1950 appears to have been the high point of the period of Western success in the enlistment of anti-Soviet Assembly majorities. By 1952, Western initiatives obtained large majorities only against extremely implausible Soviet propaganda charges and some membership questions. Afro–Asian (Indian) initiatives (or balancing) characterized the final prisoner

14. Correlations with revised rotated factor scores confirm the above interpretation. Both the Palestine and anti-interventionist alignments correlate .81 with East–West positions. After revision, these two rotated factors are quite highly correlated ($r = 0.60$).

15. They also were among the firmer adherents to the principle of nonintervention (by the United States) in the Western hemisphere.

## Figure 4.2. Rotated Factor Scores on Cold War and Self-Determination Issues at the 7th General Assembly

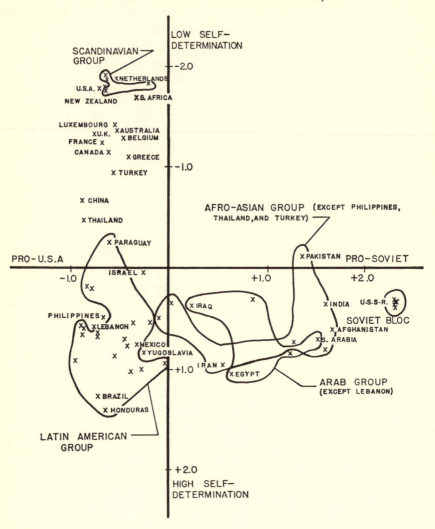

repatriation solution, which with Western support was the only Korean question on which all neutral nations voted with the United States. Southern states also initiated successful moderate resolutions on Morocco, economic development, the right of self-determination and Italian Somaliland. In fact, however, these North–South votes were the only important exceptions to the much more prevalent East–West alignment that appeared on a variety of topics.

In terms of substantively identifiable issues, anti-European majorities on self-determination concerns of the Soviets, Afro–Asians, and most Latins occurred much more frequently than the voting alignments specific to cold war issues. Such issues included information from non-self-governing territories, sovereignty over natural resources, British treatment of Wa-Merus, commodity price stabilization, and Ewe–Togoland unification. Neither liberal nor conservative Westerners were able to achieve the results they desired on South Africa or the Palestine question, which were becoming increasingly East–West concerns.

On closer analysis, then, six prominent and four less frequent distinct aspects of UN voting were found. Related to overall East–West voting were self-determination, the cold war, Palestine anti-interventionism, and liberal interventionism. Among these factors, however, both self-determination and the cold war had a considerable North–South flavor. Closer to the unrotated North–South voting component was the important factor of UN supranationalism. The four less frequent voting components might be labeled "discrimination rewording," "defining aggression," "colonial moderation," and "legal consultation." Only on some aspects of defining aggression and legal consultation did affirmative Soviet and American agreement appear.

We have noted that moderate anticolonial efforts and a successful Korean prisoner repatriation decision loaded heavily on the unrotated North–South and also the related rotated supranationalism factors. An important implication is that UN supranationalism efforts that tend to be most often successful in and outside of the UN are those issues appearing to most members as more North vs. South than East vs. West. A plainer way of restating this hypothesis is to say that, in UN terms, the Soviets and the more extreme colonial powers (often together) have been the states most consistently trying to thwart supranational efforts of Assembly majorities. When they did not succeed, important increments to UN authority occurred.

At this point it also seems appropriate to note that characteristic voting behavior and substantive interpretations of the major factors in Assembly voting appear to have been successfully identified. Considerable continuity on major issues and alignments occurred from 1947 through 1952. The factor labels we have offered even allow cautious interpretation of issues loading significantly on several factors simultaneously.

# CHAPTER 5

# Issues and Alignments
# at the Twelfth General Assembly

## AFTER SUEZ AND HUNGARY

The ineffectiveness of UN efforts in Hungary contrasted sharply with Secretary-General Hammarskjold's successful handling of the Suez affair. The second half of the 1950s was indeed a period of eminence for the Secretary-General. Hammarskjold's astute "quiet diplomacy" and his "diplomacy of reconciliation" have merited considerable attention among scholars and diplomats. Naming this period after the Secretary-General does in some sense reflect his position as the locus of hopes for UN development (the role previously held by the Security Council and then by the Assembly). In the light of more recent developments, however, this interpretation needs to be reassessed.

Russian attitudes toward the United Nations in particular, as well as the whole tenor of international affairs after Suez, are especially worth noting. Alexander Dallin has suggested that within a year after the Western division over Suez the Soviet mood was one of "exuberant optimism." The West had split badly in 1956. An apparent shift in the world power balance had occurred, symbolized by the first Sputnik launched on October 4, 1957. These events evoked jubilance on the part of the Soviets—the West was having difficulty in controlling a majority of UN votes.

Moscow saw defeat for the "imperialists" in the inclusion on the Assembly's agenda of such questions as West Irian, Algeria, racial discrimination in South Africa, and the definition of aggression. Soviet officials, in 1957–58, rather openly talked of a future situation in which the Soviet Union and Communist

> China—once it was seated—would be joined by another perma-
> nent member and perhaps a majority of nonpermanent mem-
> bers on the Security Council.[1]

Dallin suggests very clearly the mechanism of Soviet involvement.
Rooted in their perception of the world political arena is

> a dilemma the Kremlin may scarcely be aware of: the tension
> between the impulses toward universality and exclusiveness.
> From its beginnings, Bolshevism has been impelled, on the one
> hand, to "go it alone," to limit the movement to an elite of
> devoted, professional revolutionaries, and, on the other hand,
> to seek a mass following, a broad base of support, and "allies"
> well beyond its own ranks. . . . The result is a split in atti-
> tudes, encompassing elements of both inferiority and superior-
> ity, and a conflict between the search for worldwide acceptance
> and legitimacy and a sense of proud self-sufficiency.[2]

A vision of a future in which the Soviets might command frequent
majorities in the United Nations would certainly increase the likelihood of their continued participation in a balancing process within
a UN framework (assuming continued Western participation).

Soviet walkouts and withdrawal threats had been frequent during
the first years of the Korean War. In 1953, however, they and the
Chinese Communists accepted or tolerated a face-saving, UN-
sponsored repatriation compromise in a war they no longer wanted
to pursue vigorously. Certainly by 1957 Soviet appraisals of the UN
as a useful political arena had changed, and their alignment with the
unaligned countries had increased. Hammarskjold was useful to them
in the sense that he had effectively supported neutralist sentiments
and actions in the Suez crisis. Concomitantly, however, the Western
nations must have been reevaluating the usefulness of the United
Nations in their diplomacy.[3] Anti-Soviet majorities were certainly

1. Dallin, *The Soviet Union*, pp. 122–23.
2. Ibid., pp. 5–6.
3. For instance, Stanley Hoffman, "The Role of International Organization,"
*International Organization 10* (1956), 357–72, and Vernon Aspaturian, "The Meta-
morphosis of the United Nations," *Yale Review, 46* (1957), 551–65, reflected the critical
attitudes of many Western scholars and statesmen. Although somewhat more favorable
in their evaluations, Kock and Triska addressed themselves to a similar problem
in their article entitled "Asian–African Coalition and International Organization: Third
Force or Collective Impotence?"

harder to achieve. We shall now review the important votes at the Twelfth Assembly to see how far in fact the UN had been transformed from its earlier appearance.

## IMPORTANT ISSUES AT THE TWELFTH SESSION

### Special Political Questions

Included among roll-call votes in the Special Political Committee (which in 1952 had been called the Ad Hoc Committee) were such recurring items as the question of new members, including the Republics of Korea and Vietnam, the issue of race conflict in South Africa, and the treatment of peoples of Indian and Pakistani origin in South Africa. The novelty of "imperialist" defeat regarding the United Nations' concern with South Africa was a Soviet invention (see Dallin's summary above) because the agenda votes in 1957 (8002 and 8003) were much the same as the 1952 agenda vote of 45-6-8 on the question of Indians in South Africa. Final votes (8022, 8023) "deploring" and "regretting" South African failures in these problem areas were harsher than the inquiry efforts of the Seventh Session; and the majorities were bigger (59-6-14 and 64-0-15). But, as we have already seen, conservative European minorities on these questions were not new.

On the 4th of October 1957, the day the Space Age began, Czechoslovakia asked that the question of the composition of the General Committee be placed on the agenda of the Twelfth Session as a matter of urgency, in the interests of equitable geographical distribution.[4] One of the opposing Western arguments was that since the Special Political Committee had recently decided to postpone considering the enlargement of the membership of the Security Council, ECOSOC, and the International Court of Justice, similar action would be warranted in this case. The Russian position on such enlargements has been, since 1957, that they would be acceptable to the Soviet Union only after Communist China was seated on the Security Council.[5]

4. The issue summaries are drawn from the *Official Reports of the General Assembly* for the Twelfth Session, their *Annexes*, "Issues before the Twelfth General Assembly," "Issues before the Thirteenth General Assembly," *International Conciliation*, No. 519 (September 1958), and *The U.N. Yearbook, 1957.* Sydney Bailey, *The General Assembly*, Chap. 5, gives an interesting summary of the work of the General Committee and debates about its composition.

5. Dallin, p. 57.

In the interests of appearing as the champion of the newer members of the United Nations, while sacrificing at least the rigor of her logic concerning Chinese membership in the Security Council, the Soviet Union joined other states in creating three additional African and Asian vice-presidencies of the General Assembly. A last-minute concession that one of the vice-presidents of the General Assembly be a non-great power member of the Commonwealth (vote 8029) paved the way for a nearly unanimous acceptance of change (vote 8030, 49-1-27). With both East and West trying to please or at least not displease the newer nations, we have a good example of bargaining or balancing of the interests of the major UN groupings into a solution not totally unacceptable to any one of them.

A resolution in the Special Political Committee (vote 0001) requesting further examination of questions regarding new members failed by a 33-37-10 vote despite Asian and Soviet support. Over Soviet objections, the Committee reaffirmed its belief that Vietnam should be admitted to the UN (vote 0003, 49-9-22).

Four important procedural votes on Chinese representation occurred in plenary session. Increased Afro–Asian and Scandinavian support brought about a closer division than had previously occurred in 1952: 46 states opposed discussing Chinese representation, 27 wanted to do so, and 10 abstained. The United States and her allies therefore again succeeded in keeping Communist China out of the United Nations (votes 8005 to 8008).

## Political and Security Affairs

As the Special Political Committee was considering the above issues, the First Committee concerned itself with other, but related, problems. Korea, Algeria, Cyprus, West Irian, the suspension of nuclear tests, and disarmament were of sufficient importance to produce roll-call votes. Unlike the relatively happy compromise with respect to increasing the membership of the General Committee, Japanese and Indian efforts to achieve a middle ground between Western insistence on controlled tests suspension and the Russian proposal of a five-year uninspected moratorium did not succeed. A Western resolution, urging states to agree on the suspension of nuclear tests and production of fissionable materials under open inspection, passed the General Assembly by a vote of 56-9-15 (vote 8012 on Table 5.1 and 5.2 below). Similarly, an Indian attempt in committtee and plenary failed to receive support for the nomination of a tripartite scientific commission to recommend adequate inspection systems to the Disarmament Commission (vote 8014). The Assembly, over protests of inadequate representation of the Soviet viewpoint, enlarged the existing Disarmament Commission by adding fourteen new members (vote 8015 below); the Soviets then refused to take part in the Commission. The Japanese attempted to compromise the two opposing viewpoints: they requested that the Disarmament Commission's subcommittee be reconvened to discuss unsettled points between the two sides—including inspection—and called for the suspension of tests *before* agreement was reached. This proposal evoked the disapproval of both superpowers (vote 1004 below). Discussions in the First Committee also produced the usual cold war alignments on Korea (1008 and 8024).

The Soviet-supported discussion of West Irian (actually an Arab–Asian initiative) did isolate the Old European states (vote 8004, 49-21-11). A final resolution (vote 8025) calling for negotiations between the Dutch and Indonesians failed to receive a two-thirds majority because of fairly substantial Old European and Latin American objections (41-29-11). The United States, several Latin Americans, Turkey, and Finland abstained. Finally, the First Committee rejected (vote 1012, 37-37-6) a compromise resolution calling for a "democratic future" for Algeria and produced a small majority asking discussions on Cyprus that would include the prospect of self-determination (vote 8034).

### Economic and Financial Questions

The most significant vote in the Second Committee was probably the unanimous one (72-0-0) establishing the Special Fund for Economic Development, whose history and balancing aspects have been described elsewhere.[6] After relatively little discussion in plenary and

6. Hadwen and Kaufman, *How UN Decisions Are Made.* Their description of Soviet and American maneuvering conforms closely to the main factors in UN voting that we have previously noted. The United States (along cold war lines) wanted to make disarmament a precondition for increased economic aid through the United Nations. The Russians tried to develop the anticolonial theme that Western aid programs would be a form of capitalist exploitation. Afro–Asians, many pro-Western Latin Americans, and increasing numbers of smaller European states merged along supranationalist lines in favor of increased multilateral aid largely financed by the great powers.

committee, a resolution entitled "The Expansion of International Trade," urging approval by member states of the Agreement on the Organization for Trade Cooperation (vote 8021), was approved over Soviet bloc objection and Arab abstentions.

### Humanitarian and Social Concerns

The Third Committee was prolific both in its roll-call votes and in the generality of its resolutions: they concerned the rights of women, self-determination, the Draft Convention of Economic, Social, and Cultural Rights, and a Convention on Civil and Political Rights. More will be said below about the latter.

### Trusteeship and Non-Self-Governing Territories

After considering the question of South West Africa, and recommending (with Soviet opposition and scattered abstentions from Asian and African countries) the establishment of a three-member Good Offices Commission (vote 8011 in plenary), the Fourth Committee became preoccupied with French Togoland (five roll calls) and the Cameroons (eight roll calls). After lengthy deliberations a unanimous committee vote (50-0-26) was reached appreciating the previous Commission's report on Togoland and electing a Commissioner to supervise coming elections. In plenary (vote 8028) only Ghana [7] objected to this result, while the Soviet bloc and most Asians and Arabs (but not Tunisia, Lebanon, Ceylon, Malaya, Laos and a few others) abstained.

The final result of the debates on the Cameroons was a plenary resolution (vote 8031), again with the Soviets and some Arabs abstaining, "noting disturbances" in the area of the Cameroons under French administration and hoping for the promulgation of an amnesty law and appropriate steps by both administering powers toward achievement of the final objective of the trusteeship system. From reviewing the much stiffer wordings that failed to pass the Fourth Committee (4014, 4015) and vote 4020, an unacceptable watered-down resolution, one can infer that the Afro-Asians and perhaps the Soviets were cross-pressured by desires to be as strongly anticolonial as possible, while not appearing to the majority as

7. Ghana's special interests in neighboring Togoland as well as the background of the issues there are well described in James S. Coleman's "Togoland," *International Conciliation*, No. 509 (September 1956).

obstructing the eventual independence of Togoland. As on earlier resolutions, involving free elections in colonial questions (see Chapter 3), we might expect some care on the Russian side not to endorse this principle too completely.

### Administrative and Budgetary Concerns

Only two roll calls occurred in the Fifth Committee. One (5001) limited the maximum contribution of any one member state to ordinary UN expenses to 30 per cent. The Soviet Union abstained,[8] while Australia and New Zealand, most Arabs, and some Latin Americans and Asians opposed the United States. The other vote (5002) set up a committee to review the work of the Department of Public Information.

### Legal Questions

Although the Sixth Committee also considered actions by the International Law Commission and the International Court of Justice, a familiar subject, defining aggression, alone produced roll-call votes. The United Kingdom failed to delete an expression of gratitude for the previous work of the Special Committee on Defining Aggression; nor did a similar attempt (vote 6003) prevent the reestablishment of an expanded Special Committee. In plenary, a resolution taking note of the earlier Special Committee's report (vote 8026) asked for new members' opinions on defining aggression and left to the Special Committee the decision whether the matter should be discussed at the next General Assembly. The majority of Arab states, as well as the Soviet bloc, were against establishing the Special Committee at all.

### VOTING DIMENSIONS IN 1957

How many distinctive super-issues were there in important United Nations roll calls at the Twelfth Session? Looking at the unrotated factor pattern (Table 5.1) of 50 important roll calls, we find that seven uncorrelated factors are needed to explain the matrix of correlations between the 50 roll calls. Together they account for about 80 percent of all votes cast. Looking at the communality problem in a slightly different way, the smallest communalities are

8. Six out of nine members of the Soviet bloc actually voted for this resolution.

likely to result from roll calls with no especially high factor loadings. Using a rather strong cutoff point, it turns out that only three votes —Commonwealth representation on the General Committee, enlarging the Disarmament Commission, and the rejection of the death penalty—had no loadings above 0.55, while the last two both had two loadings at least in the 0.40s.

The first factor in Table 5.1 accounts for roughly 50 per cent of all important votes in 1957. In fact, over 62 per cent of the common variance is explained by factor 1 alone. Looking at those items that correlate especially highly with it—membership questions, two Disarmament Commission votes, both Korean votes, both defining aggression votes, and about two thirds of the colonial issues—we can again justify an East–West label for this factor. Looking again at these original roll-call votes corroborates this impression of a common voting alignment.

The second unrotated factor accounts for only about 11 per cent of all voting (about 15 per cent of the common voting variance). Its highest correlate, vote 4020, was an unsuccessful attempt to compromise competing interests on the Cameroons issue. Most of the NATO powers (except Greece) voted against this resolution because of its specific reference to nonpromulgation of the amnesty law and the "debate" on the Cameroons in the Fourth Committee. The Arabs and Soviets abstained because an attempt (4015) to place the blame for violence on the administering powers had failed.

The second highest correlation with the unrotated second factor is vote 4005. On it Latin Americans and the Soviet bloc joined Africans and Asians in asking the administering authorities of non-self-governing territories to transmit information on the association of these territories with the European Economic Community. Votes 4020 and 4005, when reanalyzed, suggest we again identify unrotated factor 2 as a mixed anticolonial or North–South alignment, with the Soviets and some Arabs voting against Assembly majorities sometimes in a manner similar to the most conservative colonial powers.

Turning to Figure 5.1, we see that our geopolitical expectations about the alignments on the two most prominent super-issues before the General Assembly are again justified. The North–South alignment has the Russians voting with the South, including most Latin Americans, or sometimes standing between the South and the colonial powers. Scandinavians were strongly Northern on colonial

# Table 5.1. Dimensions of Voting in 1957: Unrotated Factor Matrix

| ROLL CALLS | FACTORS | | | | | | |
|---|---|---|---|---|---|---|---|
| | 1 | 2 | 3 | 4 | 5 | 6 | 7 |
| 8002. Race conflict on agenda | .60 | —.52 | .32 | —.35 | —.21 | —.07 | .08 |
| 8003. Indians in S. Africa on agenda | .62 | —.51 | .33 | —.31 | —.18 | —.07 | .04 |
| 8022. Deplores S. African actions | .66 | —.46 | .32 | —.25 | —.16 | —.08 | .06 |
| 8023. Regrets S. Af. failure to negotiate | .59 | —.51 | .30 | —.32 | —.18 | —.16 | .06 |
| 8017. Appreciates UNEF contributions | —.64 | —.04 | .35 | .23 | .20 | —.04 | .06 |
| 8029. Commonwealth on General Comm. | .54 | —.27 | —.12 | .11 | .01 | .01 | —.27 |
| 8030. Constitute General Comm. | .76 | —.45 | —.10 | .10 | .13 | .01 | —.20 |
| 0006. Constitute General Comm. | .74 | —.52 | —.12 | .04 | .17 | —.08 | —.17 |
| 0001. SC to review membership criteria | .84 | .17 | .19 | .12 | .09 | .10 | —.01 |
| 0003. Admit Vietnam | —.81 | —.36 | .05 | .04 | —.18 | .06 | .08 |
| 8004. West Irian on agenda | .76 | —.45 | —.04 | —.02 | —.04 | .11 | .07 |
| 8025. Resolution on West Irian | .84 | —.27 | —.03 | .16 | .07 | —.11 | .15 |
| 8005. Chinese representation | .73 | .43 | .40 | —.11 | .09 | .11 | —.04 |
| 8006. Chinese representation | —.70 | —.47 | —.41 | .15 | —.12 | —.11 | .04 |
| 8007. Chinese rep. off agenda | —.70 | —.49 | —.41 | .13 | —.09 | —.12 | .05 |
| 8008. Chinese representation | —.69 | —.50 | —.44 | .17 | —.13 | —.09 | .03 |
| 8010. Adjourn debate on Syria | .66 | —.09 | —.10 | .05 | —.24 | .34 | .37 |
| 8012. Suspend nuclear tests | —.77 | —.40 | .02 | .15 | —.19 | —.09 | .00 |
| 8013. Asks disarmament publicity | —.58 | —.39 | .41 | .45 | .04 | —.02 | —.05 |
| 8014. Scientific study of disarm. | .85 | .15 | .10 | .07 | 13 | .03 | —.05 |
| 8015. Permanent Disarm. Commission | .84 | .27 | —.11 | —.03 | .06 | .04 | —.07 |
| 8016. Enlarge Disarm. Commission | —.50 | —.35 | .15 | .52 | —.12 | .22 | —.01 |
| 1004. Suspend tests, then inspect | .31 | —.39 | .58 | .34 | .06 | —.06 | .04 |
| 8024. Support unified Korea | —.82 | —.43 | .00 | .14 | —.18 | —.11 | .08 |
| 1008. N. Korean report to UNCURK | .85 | .31 | .25 | .02 | .01 | —.00 | .07 |
| 1012. Democratic Algerian future | —.83 | .01 | .09 | —.26 | —.03 | .25 | —.19 |
| 8034. Cyprus self-determination | .73 | —.27 | —.07 | —.11 | —.20 | .26 | .16 |
| 8021. Organization for trade cooperation | —.66 | —.17 | .20 | .21 | .33 | —.07 | .06 |
| 3005. Cultural rights include schools | —.59 | —.46 | .05 | —.18 | .26 | .20 | —.21 |
| 3007. Protect scientists' interests | —.78 | —.13 | .24 | —.01 | .11 | .33 | .07 |
| 3008. Science for "peace and cooperation" | .78 | .28 | — .04 | .00 | .16 | —.11 | —.21 |
| 3009. No death penalty | —.41 | —.39 | —.12 | —.29 | .18 | .45 | —.26 |
| 3011. Only for serious crimes | .07 | —.12 | —.33 | —.19 | .69 | —.01 | .48 |

Table 5.1. Dimensions of Voting in 1957: Unrotated Factor Matrix

| ROLL CALLS | 1 | 2 | 3 | 4 | 5 | 6 | 7 |
|---|---|---|---|---|---|---|---|
| | | | **FACTORS** | | | | |
| 3012. Death penalty limitations | .57 | —.31 | —.02 | —.06 | .34 | —.10 | .24 |
| 3013. Right of self-determination | .62 | —.57 | .02 | —.20 | .02 | —.08 | —.06 |
| 4015. Renounce violence: Cameroons | .88 | .01 | —.02 | .27 | —.04 | —.07 | .07 |
| 4018. Asks expression re future status | .83 | —.21 | —.09 | .21 | .03 | —.06 | —.10 |
| 4020. Resolution on Cameroons | .51 | —.62 | —.04 | .04 | .28 | .13 | —.05 |
| 8031. Cameroons' trusteeship | —.71 | —.24 | .32 | .06 | .28 | —.03 | —.03 |
| 8011. Asks good offices for S.W. Africa | —.83 | —.16 | .19 | .01 | .08 | —.25 | .05 |
| 4001. Charter and S.W. Africa | .73 | —.21 | —.13 | .13 | —.06 | .22 | —.22 |
| 8018. INSGT important? | —.89 | .10 | .03 | —.23 | .05 | —.02 | —.12 |
| 8019. SG summarizes for CINSGT | .85 | —.26 | —.02 | .16 | —.03 | .07 | —.03 |
| 8028. UN supervises Togo elections | —.80 | —.12 | .03 | —.12 | .00 | —.06 | —.06 |
| 4005. NSGTs and EEC | .67 | —.59 | —.15 | —.06 | .21 | —.08 | —.12 |
| 5001. 30% maximum contributions | —.22 | —.21 | —.08 | —.66 | —.07 | —.23 | —.01 |
| 5002. Review DPI effectiveness | —.62 | —.16 | .05 | —.17 | .02 | .50 | .24 |
| 8032. 3 Secretariat members per country | .83 | .16 | —.13 | .07 | .01 | —.16 | .02 |
| 8026. Defining aggression | —.86 | —.05 | .09 | —.16 | .17 | —.14 | —.09 |
| 6003. Defining aggression | .83 | —.12 | —.14 | .19 | —.07 | .18 | .01 |
| Roll-call variance accounted for by factor (eigen values) | λ=25.2 | λ=6.0 | λ=2.4 | λ=2.3 | λ=1.6 | λ=1.4 | λ=1.6 |

issues (a fact not often recognized) and also Eastern regarding Chinese representation questions. In 1947 the Russians generally voted for Palestinian partition, the biggest single component in North–South voting in that year; in 1952 Korean repatriation and partial rejection of bourgeois anticolonialism pushed them North. Now their more Southern position seems tactically more expedient.

*The rotated factor pattern* is presented in Table 5.2. It will be recalled that varimax rotation approximates, as well as possible, achieving a structure of zeros and ones allowing us to interpret each factor substantively as consisting of only those items with which it is highly correlated. After this operation the transformed factors become remarkably clear in content. The first factor appears quite specific, and is confined only to the most obvious cold war issues (membership, nuclear testing, disarmament, and Korea). This state-

# Table 5.2. Dimensions of Voting in 1957: Rotated Factor Matrix

FACTORS

| ROLL CALLS | 1 | 2 | 3 | 4 | 5 | 6 | 7 |
|---|---|---|---|---|---|---|---|
| 8002. Race conflict on agenda | .15 | —.35 | —.03 | —.86 | —.02 | —.03 | .13 |
| 8003. Indians in S. Africa on agenda | .18 | —.39 | —.01 | —.83 | —.03 | —.03 | .12 |
| 8022. Deplores S. African actions | .22 | —.41 | .01 | —.78 | —.01 | —.09 | .13 |
| 8023. Regrets S. Af. failure to negotiate | .13 | —.37 | —.03 | —.84 | —.01 | —.09 | .06 |
| 8017. Appreciates UNEF contributions | —.25 | .38 | .56 | .16 | .04 | .15 | —.24 |
| 8029. Commonwealth on General Comm. | .13 | —.63 | —.09 | —.12 | —.11 | —.07 | .04 |
| 8030. Constitute General Comm. | .18 | —.85 | —.04 | —.27 | .05 | —.09 | .08 |
| 0006. Constitute General Comm. | .12 | —.86 | —.06 | —.34 | .13 | —.11 | .02 |
| 0001. SC to review membership criteria | .70 | —.42 | .02 | —.13 | .00 | —.24 | .23 |
| 0003. Admit Vietnam | —.72 | .37 | .28 | —.00 | —.10 | .30 | —.05 |
| 8004. West Irian on agenda | .17 | —.66 | —.07 | —.44 | .10 | —.08 | .34 |
| 8025. Resolution on West Irian | .28 | —.65 | —.01 | —.31 | .19 | —.38 | .25 |
| 8005. Chinese representation | .91 | —.11 | —.03 | —.18 | —.05 | —.14 | .12 |
| 8006. Chinese representation | —.94 | .05 | .04 | .17 | .03 | .12 | —.08 |
| 8007. Chinese rep. off agenda | —.94 | .05 | .04 | .15 | .06 | .13 | —.10 |
| 8008. Chinese representation | —.96 | .02 | .04 | .17 | .02 | .12 | —.06 |
| 8010. Adjourn debate on Syria | .25 | —.31 | —.14 | —.23 | .08 | —.13 | .72 |
| 8012. Suspend nuclear tests | —.77 | .27 | .31 | .01 | —.15 | .16 | —.14 |
| 8013. Asks disarmament publicity | —.45 | .11 | .77 | .03 | —.15 | .13 | —.16 |
| 8014. Scientific study of disarm. | .66 | —.48 | —.07 | —.12 | .04 | —.26 | .16 |
| 8015. Permanent Disarm. Commission | .64 | —.43 | —.32 | —.03 | .04 | —.25 | .18 |
| 8016. Enlarge Disarm. Commission | —.49 | .02 | .58 | .19 | —.23 | .17 | .15 |
| 1004. Suspend tests, then inspect | .15 | —.31 | .65 | —.38 | —.06 | —.14 | .05 |
| 8024. Support unified Korea | —.83 | .31 | .31 | —.00 | —.09 | .14 | —.13 |
| 1008. N. Korean report to UNCURK | .78 | —.26 | —.05 | —.20 | —.00 | —.35 | .22 |
| 1012. Democratic Algerian future | —.34 | .52 | .04 | .15 | —.18 | .60 | —.22 |
| 8034. Cyprus self-determination | .23 | —.47 | —.20 | —.41 | .03 | —.04 | .52 |
| 8021. Organization for trade cooperation | —.37 | .25 | .52 | .19 | .20 | .19 | —.30 |
| 3005. Cultural rights include schools | —.44 | .02 | .20 | —.03 | .08 | .64 | —.29 |
| 3007. Protect scientists' interests | —.35 | .45 | .40 | .13 | .02 | .54 | —.04 |
| 3008. Science for "peace and cooperation" | .65 | —.44 | —.24 | .00 | .01 | —.29 | —.05 |
| 3009. No death penalty | —.32 | —.07 | —.02 | .01 | .03 | .78 | —.06 |

## Table 5.2. Dimensions of Voting in 1957: Rotated Factor Matrix

| ROLL CALLS | FACTORS | | | | | | |
| --- | --- | --- | --- | --- | --- | --- | --- |
| | 1 | 2 | 3 | 4 | 5 | 6 | 7 |
| 3011. Only for serious crimes | —.02 | —.11 | —.10 | .07 | **.91** | .09 | .00 |
| 3012. Death penalty limitations | .20 | —.46 | .01 | —.31 | .48 | —.14 | .08 |
| 3013. Right of self-determination | .07 | —.63 | —.09 | —.59 | .10 | —.01 | .04 |
| 4015. Renounce violence: Cameroons | .44 | —.56 | —.04 | —.14 | .02 | —.48 | .31 |
| 4018. Asks expression re future status | .31 | —.73 | —.05 | —.18 | .01 | —.30 | .17 |
| 4020. Resolution on Cameroons | .02 | —.74 | .11 | —.31 | .25 | .15 | .09 |
| 8031. Cameroons' trusteeship | —.36 | .30 | .51 | .05 | .10 | .33 | —.36 |
| 8011. Asks good offices for S.W. Africa | —.54 | .48 | .35 | .04 | .05 | .12 | —.40 |
| 4001. Charter and S.W. Africa | .28 | —.71 | —.12 | —.11 | —.14 | —.04 | .28 |
| 8018. INSGT important? | —.40 | **.60** | .03 | .20 | —.05 | .38 | —.39 |
| 8019. SG summarizes for CINSGT | .32 | —.70 | —.03 | —.27 | —.00 | —.22 | .30 |
| 8028. UN supervise Togo elections | —.52 | .43 | .13 | .09 | —.04 | .31 | —.31 |
| 4005. NSGTs and EEC | .05 | —.81 | —.09 | —.40 | .22 | —.03 | —.01 |
| 5001. 30% maximum contributions | —.26 | .21 | —.39 | —.42 | .12 | .21 | —.31 |
| 5002. Review DPI effectiveness | —.34 | .40 | .16 | .05 | .13 | **.60** | .23 |
| 8032. 3 Secretariat members per country | .49 | —.46 | —.26 | —.09 | .08 | —.46 | .16 |
| 8026. Defining aggression | —.45 | .50 | .17 | .12 | .05 | .32 | —.48 |
| 6003. Defining aggression | .35 | —.64 | —.12 | —.13 | —.02 | —.21 | .43 |
| Roll-call variance accounted for by factor (eigen values) | λ=11.4 | λ=11.3 | λ=3.5 | λ=5.0 | λ=1.6 | λ=4.2 | λ=3.0 |

ment applies to correlations in the factor matrix equal to or greater than 0.60, which imply that about one half of the common variation in a roll call is explainable in cold war terms. Vote 3008, a Czech initiative that states have the right to limit freedom of speech in the interests of "international peace and security," had the only "high" correlation with cold war voting outside of the two political committees.[9]

After rotation, thirteen different votes have loadings above 0.60 on the rotated second factor. Included were all votes on the composition of the General Committee, both votes on West Irian, a vote on

9. The revised rotated scores on this factor, including contributions from all roll calls loading more highly than 0.35 on it, are pictured in Figure 5.2.

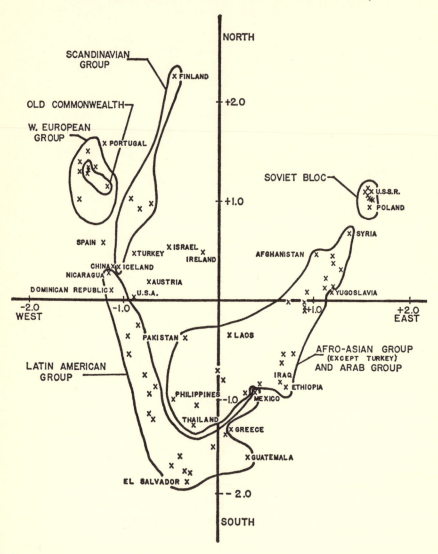

Figure 5.1. Unrotated Factor Scores on the East–West and North–South Issues at the 12th General Assembly

including the right of self-determination in the Convention on Civil and Political Rights (3013), two votes on the French Cameroons, votes continuing the Committee on Information from Non-Self-Governing Territories, vote 4005 on the economic relations of these territories with the European Economic Community, and vote 6003 on defining aggression.

Substantively, the rotated second factor consists almost entirely of certain "self-determination" issues, perceived by UN members to be quite distinct from the cold war. In terms of political alignments, the votes loading heavily on this self-determination factor are anti-European votes on which most Latin Americans and many pro-Western Asians vote against the North Atlantic Community and Old Commonwealth. Vote 0006 on the composition of the General Committee reveals most clearly the power aspirations of Afro–Asians and Latin Americans for a greater say in UN affairs. Soviet and Arab and scattered Asian objections to defining aggression reveal either its low priority in their concerns, or a fear that the definition may be used against them.

The third general factor in General Assembly voting may be called "small power supranationalism." In 1957 it was substantively linked to a fear of destruction. Its highest correlate, vote 3012, was on Article 6 of the Draft Convention on Civil and Political Rights limiting the use of the death penalty to justly tried crimes of the most serious nature. Vote 1004, it will be recalled, was the Japanese plea for the suspension of tests and for inspection negotiations that both the United States and the Soviet Union voted against. Whereas vote 3012 on the death penalty saw the United States in a very isolated minority abstention, the request (vote 8013) that the Disarmament Commission make recommendations on how to conduct a publicity campaign on disarmament found the Soviet bloc on the losing side by 71-9-1.

The United Nations Emergency Force (UNEF) vote (8017) [10] takes on a new aspect in this light. Both the Soviet bloc and most European powers were skeptical about continuing the Force because of its costs, its implications for future actions, and perhaps because it limited their and Arab freedom of action in the area. Other nations supporting UNEF generally have done so out of a fear of far greater destruction if the great powers were unleashed. This interpretation suggests that these hopes and fears were a more im-

10. UNEF was first discussed at the Twelfth Session in plenary meetings. The Fifth Committee then considered its budgetary implications in more detail. It was decided to discuss the single roll-call vote on UNEF at the Twelfth Session *after* the rotated factor pattern was presented, making clearer some of its implications.

portant determinant of alignments on the issue than either feelings
about self-determination or one's favorite in the cold war within the
UN.

In terms of the larger groupings of states by which we have usually
characterized political alignments, the votes that make up our fourth
rotated factor are the most free of common group positions. The
Soviet bloc was so unclear in its signals or intentions that a majority
of its members voted with the United States, but against Belgium,
South Africa, the United Kingdom, and most Arabs on a maximum
contribution figure for ordinary United Nations expenses (vote
5001). A similar North Atlantic cleavage between the United States
and Scandinavians on one side and colonial Westerners on the other
is expressed in the votes on South African racial policy.

Substantively, all these votes reflect some of the Northern powers'
moral or financial commitment to the ordinary work of the United
Nations, in particular regarding South African problems. For
Southern nations, their votes on 5001 suggest their degree of sym-
pathy with Northern reservations. In terms of alignments, we see by
referring to the unrotated factor pattern that both votes 8022 and
8023 on South Africa have heavy East–West and North–South
political aspects. Vote 5001 loads heavily on unrotated factor 3,
where American and Soviet views coincided regarding disarmament
questions. By searching for substantive content in rotated factor 4
issues, we have tentatively distinguished differing perceptions and
alignments that would be nearly submerged in terms of a geopolitical
analysis. Such an analysis suggests more sophisticated international
behavior than East–West or North–South terms will allow.

The capital punishment compromise vote (3011) of which factor
5 almost entirely consists, is an attempt to reconcile the various
amendments to Article 6 of the Draft Convention of Civil and
Political Rights. The changes left most Arabs and some Westerners
unsatisfied by allowing the death penalty to be carried out on the
final judgment of a competent court if a country has not abolished
the penalty altogether.

With a λ of 4.2, the sixth factor is the fourth most frequent issue
in the rotated factor pattern. It can perhaps be interpreted as
"Western humanitarianism." Loading most highly on it is a Colombian and Uruguayan amendment (3009) that the "death penalty shall
not be imposed on any person." Vote 1012 represents an Afro–Asian

resolution recognizing the right of the Algerian people to self-determination, successfully amended by Canada, Ireland, and Norway to a recognition that "the people of Algeria are entitled to work out their own future in a democratic way." Humanitarian revulsion at the violence and torture in Algeria coupled with due respect for the *colon* minorities in French Algeria suggest a similar substantive content in these issues. Support for the free flow of United Nations information (if we may interpret 5002 in this manner); the right of individuals or bodies "to establish and control educational institutions" (3005); and the right of any individual "to benefit from the protection of moral and material interests resulting from any scientific, literary or artistic production of which he is the author" (vote 3007, which has its highest loading on rotated factor 6) can be interpreted as legitimate cultural concerns or ideals of the Western nations.

Politically, the voting on these issues is related to the East–West alignments of unrotated factor 1. (Refer to the loadings of these items on that factor in Table 5.1.) But substantively the Western humanitarianism issue is quite distinguishable from the Korean War or Chinese United Nations membership. Scandinavians that vote with the Russians on Communist Chinese membership will vote with the West on Western humanitarian issues, while American cold war allies in Asia (Japan, Iran, Thailand, Turkey, and to a lesser extent the Philippines) will not.

Finally, both vote 8010 on Syria and vote 8034 on Cyprus, the highest contributors to rotated factor 7, reflect varying support for UN-circumscribed "mediation in the Near East." Russians and Arabs were pleased with the time limit of three days set for King Saud's individual mediation attempts in Syrian–Turkish border tensions and the proviso that British negotiations be undertaken in view of the "right of self-determination" of the people of Cyprus. Interestingly, the two votes represent compromises of Russian and American positions which neither opposed. On both of these votes Asians usually abstained while Latin American and Western European nations were very split, somewhat along North–South lines, anti-colonials favoring both resolutions.

Figure 5.2, the "map" of rotated factor scores on cold war and self-determination issues, suggests that while geopolitical pattern-

Figure 5.2. Rotated Factor Scores on Cold War and
Self-Determination Issues at the 12th General Assembly

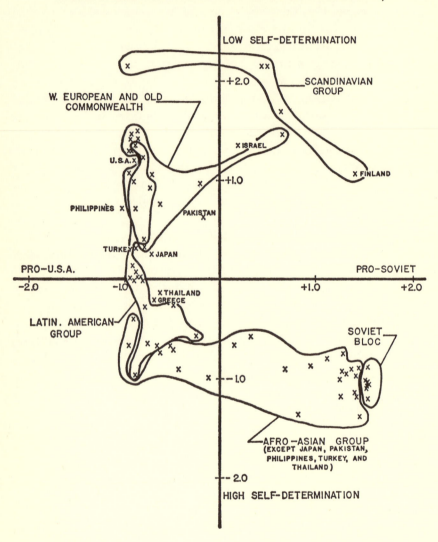

ing of states still held to a certain extent other explanatory factors
were also involved: military alliances with the West badly split the
Afro–Asians, while jealously independent Latin Americans like
Mexico and Argentina were much more anticolonial than
countries like Brazil and Honduras. Substantively, too, rotated self-

determination and cold war factors can easily be distinguished from less homogeneous but more East–West and North–South alignments. Nonetheless, these two unrotated geopolitical alignments underlie or explain about two thirds of the votes at the United Nations, justifying succinct political and behavioral descriptions in such terms.

Comparing roll calls for their general substantive content and for their relationships to geopolitical alignments is a valuable way to assess the interrelationship between cognitive and behavioral analyses of the same phenomenon. By seeing to what extent an issue may behaviorally be described as East–West or North–South or substantively be associated with the cold war or self-determination, we can assess more accurately UN members' perceptions of an issue and the degree of its polarization along such alignments. Furthermore, votes *not* loading heavily on rotated factor 1 or 2 reveal issues and perceptions not to be confused with the cold war or self-determination. For example, the issues of supranationalism (including UNEF) and commitment to UN activities in South Africa produced votes distinct from self-determination or the cold war as usually perceived. Western humanitarianism likewise did not correspond very highly with pro-Western cold war positions.[11]

Because rotated factors can be distinguished from unrotated ones, we would expect cold war votes at the United Nations to evidence important deviations from East vs. West or North vs. South regional groupings. Differences among states *within* these groupings also occur with respect to their commitment to anticolonial policies in the UN and to its mediation efforts. Regarding colonial questions, since 1947 we have seen continual wide differences among Latin American states, especially with regard to issues involving self-determination. The more extreme deviants, and the direction of their departure, may be seen in Figures 5.1 and 5.2. South Africa has repeatedly produced reactions that are not of the typical self-determination sort because Old Europeans have been split over what to do.

11. By definition, factor scores for these rotated factors correlate zero with each other; using *revised* rotated factor scores, self-determination and supranationalism are moderately correlated with cold war factor scores (both r's are in the middle 0.50s). Although both the revised cold war and South African interventionism scores show similar correlations with the North–South alignment, each is also more highly correlated with East–West voting.

Regarding East–West competition, several additional points can be made. First, Soviet victories continued to occur on dimensions along which they were in a majority position even back in 1952. On this and the other issues on which they sided with the majority (e.g. South Africa or Suez), considerable American or liberal Western support was also required. On other major issues, such as the cold war or Western humanitarianism, the Soviets usually were in a minority.

Besides the need to clearly distinguish the different super-issues at the United Nations before judging the extent of or the increase in Soviet power, this review of the issues discussed at the Twelfth Session also suggests a point made earlier about the Seventh General Assembly. It is a majority of underdeveloped countries at the UN, not the Soviet Union, which "wins" on self-determination issues. The Soviets sometimes tag along, pretend they are leading the anti-imperialist camp, or try (along with the extreme colonial powers) to destroy moderate decolonializing achievements. One fairly frequently finds evidence of their duplicity in this regard. Although strongly backing increased Afro–Asian membership on the General Committee the Soviets are rarely willing to commit themselves regarding contributions to UN causes (such as UNEF or the Special Fund) heavily favored by their underdeveloped or Southern allies. As such, UN supranationalism attempts cut across both self-determination and the cold war.

East and West can sometimes, as in the case of Cyprus, be drawn together by the incorporation of each other's symbols—such as self-determination—into a resolution without seriously hampering negotiation. In 1957 the Soviets and the West were both drawn toward the newer countries, and therefore in one sense toward each other, when they agreed to grant the more recent members a greater role in UN affairs. But many of the shared interests of the Old Europeans and Russians are negative ones, including budgetary hesitations and skepticism regarding moderate self-determination resolutions. Certainly many substantive concerns overlap in the United Nations (see Figure 5.2 and Table 5.2); they have since 1947.

Yet to assess the integrative contribution of shared voting victories (or defeats) one has also to assess shared interests, perceptions, loyalties, and intentions—the determinants of voting behavior. Smaller UN members probably did feel increasing respect for the

UN and its Secretary-General as they became more powerful. The Soviets were finding the United Nations more useful, but shared few victories with the West or sympathies with the Secretary-General. The Western states were able to hold their own on cold war questions, perhaps grew in their respect for the Secretary-General, but became increasingly divided about the usefulness of the UN itself for positive action in any substantive area.

# CHAPTER 6

# Issues and Alignments
# at the Sixteenth General Assembly

### IMPLICATIONS OF THE CONGO CRISIS

The Congo crisis is "postcolonial" in many of its international aspects as well as its internal aspect. It illustrates vividly that most of the new states do not measure the issues of international politics with Cold War calipers. The meaningful choices are not between the "free world" and the "communist world," nor between democracy and authoritarianism, nor between the economic systems of the East or West. Insofar as these options are incorporated into issues inviting choice between one or the other of the two opposing blocs, most of the postcolonial states are neutral. And if the Cold War is conceived as the development of spheres of influence by East and West, all new states want to "keep the Cold War out of the Congo." [1]

The exceptional degree of early Russian commitment to a UN military force for the Congo (ONUC) is sometimes overlooked. *"Here was an international armed force precisely of the sort that the U.S.S.R. had heretofore opposed.* The Soviet vote in favor of its establishment was above all an extension of its policy to befriend the African states. . . . It could not very well fail to support this first showdown on colonialism in Black Africa." [2]

As ONUC strengthened its hand in the Congo, the Soviets were faced with a dilemma. They had to choose between giving out-

1. Robert C. Good, "Congo Crisis: The Role of the New States," in Arnold Wolfers, ed., *Neutralism* (mimeo., 1961), p. 2.
2. See Chap. 10, entitled "The Congo: The Last Straw," of Dallin's *The Soviet Union*, p. 141 (our emphasis).

right military support to Lumumba, thus greatly increasing the chances of conflict with the West and more moderate Afro–Asians,[3] or the more inactive and frustrating course of trying to influence events from the outside. Caution and the dictates of political strategy prevailed.

> Even when it attacked the United Nations action, it reluctantly complied with U.N. decisions and refrained from massive uni-lateral support for its friends. It refrained from vetoing several resolutions sponsored by neutralist states it was seeking to be-friend. Yet it was precisely the small and unaligned powers on whose support the Secretary-General hinged *his* policy, and successfully so. Logic would have invited the Soviet Union once again to 'go it alone.' But in the age of "coexistence," Moscow deemed it essential to fight for the sympathy and sup-port of the underdeveloped world.[4]

Russian attacks on Hammarskjold, his death, the election of U Thant, and the successful weathering of the immediate financial crisis followed. With the easing of the Congo conflict, a milestone had been passed. An Afro–Asian Secretary-General, a two-thirds majority in the United Nations for the "developing countries" (without Soviet support), and continued balancing of cold war inter-ests (as in Cuba or the Congo) by a majority of states preoccupied with their own problems of unity, power, and development all characterize the emerging postcolonial period of the United Nations. How much the issues and alignments of earlier years have changed remains to be seen.

### IMPORTANT ISSUES AT THE SIXTEENTH SESSION

Because of the large number of roll calls at the Sixteenth Session, which continued in three parts until June 1962, selecting important roll calls by the same criteria used in earlier chapters would have

---

3. Good, p. 37, neatly summarizes the positions of radical, moderate, and conserva-tive (Brazzaville) Africans regarding the kind of government desired in the Congo and the role the UN ought to play there. None of them wanted Soviet intervention. Although Rajeshwar Dayal of India, the highest UN official in the Congo after Bunche's recall, supported Lumumban legitimacy, he also was against outside inter-vention.

4. Dallin, pp. 145–50.

produced about 80 votes. Factor analyzing a great many more roll calls than the 63 votes chosen for 1952 would make their description and analysis more tedious than necessary for the desired description of major voting components. In order to keep within an upper limit of 70 votes for the analysis, roll-call votes in plenary session were sometimes omitted from the analysis when they produced virtually the same alignments as did other votes on a similar subject. Additionally, committee selections were limited usually to a maximum of one vote per agenda item or conflict situation. As before, committee votes were chosen only when not reflected in plenary voting on the same subject. The seventy votes described below nonetheless capture all important plenary alignments and issues (53 out of a total of 75 plenary roll calls) and the most important, unduplicated committee votes (17 out of a total of 121 committee votes).

## Special Political Questions

Indians and race conflict in South Africa, Palestine, nuclear testing and disarmament, and membership questions before the Sixteenth Assembly were much the same as they had been in 1957. Mauritanian membership and trouble in Oman were the only new issues meriting roll calls that came before the Special Political Committee.[5] With respect to South Africa, however, attention was centered primarily on treatment of the native population, rather than "persons of Indian and Pakistani origin"—the latter were unpopular citizens of many new African states.

During the general debate in the Assembly, Liberia moved that Foreign Minister Louw's speech on conditions in South Africa be stricken from the record, an indication of the intensity of passion that has continued to develop in Assembly discussions of South African conduct. After some maneuvering, "a motion of censure against the government of South Africa, or its delegate" was approved (vote 8004, 67-1-20). Old Europeans either abstained or did not participate (considered also as an abstention). A few Latins and pro-Western Asians also abstained. Later, a key plenary vote on

5. The sources for the following description of resolutions and votes include the *Annexes* and *Official Records of the General Assembly* for the Sixteenth Assembly; "Issues before the Sixteenth General Assembly," *International Conciliation*, No. 534 (September 1961); and "Issues before the Seventeenth General Assembly," *International Conciliation*, No. 539 (September 1962).

paragraphs recommending diplomatic and economic sanctions (8022) failed to get a two-thirds majority (48-31-22) because of general Western opposition and Asian abstention. Nonaligned Asians generally did support a request that the Security Council consider expelling South Africa from the UN (52-30-18, vote 8023); but the same nonaligned Asians again abstained on vote 8024 and vote 8025 asking for an embargo on arms (a Soviet initiative) or one on petroleum (a Pakistani initiative). The final result was the passage of a somewhat more moderate resolution calling on individual states to take actions open to them in conformity with the Charter.

While all other African states had united in condemning South Africa, voting on the withdrawal of foreign troops and self-determination for the British protectorate of Oman did not produce solid African support. Old Europeans generally opposed the final resolution to this effect (8027); Latins abstained; Soviets and Arabs were in favor; pro-Western Asians abstained; Brazzaville and Monrovia countries were divided.[6] The Casablanca powers failed (33-21-29) to obtain a two-thirds majority.

Except for vote 0018 in committee, positions on Palestine refugees corresponded roughly to earlier alignments. Several Old Europeans, several Latins, four Asians, and three Brazzavillians abstained on 0018; except for Israeli opposition, the rest of the UN's members supported in committee an amended American resolution, (1) noting "with deep regret" that repatriation or compensation of refugees had not been effected; (2) noting the precarious financial position of the United Nations Relief and Works Agency for Palestine Refugees

6. This is our first mention of African political groupings at the United Nations. Professor Hovet suggests that African representation "has been divided into at least two major factions, the Casablanca group and the Brazzaville group. In caucusing within the U.N., there is an African caucus of all the members, except, of course, South Africa. At the same time there are caucus meetings held by the Casablanca group and the Brazzaville group. . . . The unity of the Casablanca group resulting from the January 1961 meeting of Ghana, Guinea, Mali, Morocco, United Arab Republic, Libya, Provisional Government of Algeria, and Ceylon (these last two were not African UN members) created a major division of the African states, as most of the rest of the African states attended the conference in Monrovia in May 1961. In many senses the Casablanca group constitutes a more militant African position, and the other factions, such as the Brazzaville (ex-French colonies south of Algeria), represent the more passive position toward Pan-Africanism and other issues." Thomas Hovet, Jr., "African Policies in the United Nations," *American Behavioral Scientist, 5* (1962), 29. For a more detailed analysis of these groupings see also his *Africa in the United Nations.*

in the Near East (UNRWA); and (3) requesting a reconstituted Conciliation Commission to intensify its efforts. Plenary votes on Palestine (8045, 8046, 8047, and 8048) failed to reconstitute the Conciliation Commission and found varying degrees of Western unanimity (Latin Americans still being divided on this issue), the usual Casablanca and Soviet opposition, and some Western support from Asian and Monrovian powers. For some reason (Spanish Sahara?) Spain persistently supported the Arab position.

Finally, membership questions included China (votes 8029, 8030, 8031, 8032) and the admission of Mauritania (vote 8007). Membership for both Outer Mongolia and Mauritania was suggested by the Security Council in October 1961. The Soviet Union abstained on the Mauritania vote; the United States did likewise for Outer Mongolia; China was absent. According to her delegate:

> In the circumstances with which the Security Council was confronted the Chinese delegation reluctantly came to the decision that its opposition to Outer Mongolia's entry should not be made a pretext, however meagre and unjustifiable, for the non-admission of a new State (Mauritania) which my delegation particularly desires to see within the ranks of this Organization.[7]

In other words, a deal: China did not veto Outer Mongolia; Russia did not veto Mauritania, to whose admission most Arab states (especially Morocco, who claimed sovereignty over that area) strenuously objected. The Brazzaville states were generally favorable toward postponing discussions of Chinese representation.

Another major topic of discussion in the Special Political Committee was the report of the United Nations Special Committee on the Effects of Atomic Radiation (UNSCEAR), established in 1955. A joint resolution appreciating the work of UNSCEAR and urging specific organizations to increase their radiation data collection and reporting (similar in alignment to 8037 and therefore not included) passed in committee by a 75-0-17 majority; a weaker but still positive resolution sponsored by Czechoslovakia (votes 0003 and 8006) failed to achieve a two-thirds majority. Pro-Western states usually abstained or voiced objections.

7. Quoted in Department of State Publication 7413, *U. S. Participation in the U. N.: Report by the President to the Congress for the Year 1961* (Washington, U.S. Government Printing Office, 1962), p. 190.

## Political and Security Affairs

Concern with the problem of nuclear testing and disarmament showed itself in several ways at the Sixteenth Session. All but Soviet bloc countries (including Mongolia), Cuba, and Mali joined in an appeal (8008) to the Soviet Union not to detonate a 50-megaton hydrogen weapon. The five great powers were joined only by their closest allies in objecting to a resolution (8009) sponsored by five Arab–Asians and Yugoslavia regretting the resumption of tests and urging that no tests be conducted pending negotiations to prohibit them. (A reference to "general and complete disarmament" was rejected in committee, 36-43-22, when the Brazzaville countries and several Asians joined most of the pro-Western states [vote 1010].) The Soviet bloc and most Casablanca powers were the main objectors to a 71-11-15 endorsement (vote 8010) of the U.S.–U.K. position on the need for controlled inspections. Most Western and Brazzaville states abstained on a 55-0-44 resolution calling for a denuclearized zone in Africa (vote 8012). Pro-Western states (excluding the Brazzaville group) were unable to defeat (55-20-26) a Casablanca powers' initiative (8016) declaring the use of nuclear weapons contrary to the Charter. (As might be suspected, Japan voted with the Afro–Asian majority.) Finally, on the spread of nuclear weapons, more moderate neutrals (e.g. Sweden, Tunisia, and Cambodia) passed a "non-nuclear club" request to prevent further dissemination of nuclear weapons. Westerners and Brazzaville states, except for some Europeans with neutralist tendencies, did not support the resolution (vote 1023), which passed by a comfortable majority.

An invitation to the Peoples' Democratic Republic of Korea to UNCURK discussions if they bound themselves to UN decisions failed (vote 1026, 63-18-19) to get the support of the Soviets and most non-allied, non-Brazzaville Afro–Asians. The final Assembly vote (8054) produced a similar alignment, with greater unity within each of the caucausing groups.

In the last roll call at the first part of the Sixteenth Session, Western and pro-Western Asians succeeded in passing a resolution (vote 8055) deploring Soviet and Hungarian disregard of Assembly resolutions on the situation in Hungary. And at the resumed Sixteenth Session Cuban complaints of American aggression found the same pro-Western states (as well as the Brazzaville group) abstaining on a Charter reaffirmation (vote 8064, 39-0-61). A similar roll call

(8063) was omitted from the analysis. The final (seemingly innocuous) resolution (8065) was defeated, 37-45-18 by pro-Western states. The Brazzaville powers abstained.

A resolution in the First Committee's report on Algeria called for resumed negotiations for an independent, territorially unified Algeria. Some of the Brazzaville states abstained, as did most Latin Americans. Among Old Europeans, Scandinavians, Austria, and Ireland sided with the Afro–Asian majority (vote 8044).

## Economic and Financial Questions

Questions relating to economic development again occupied the Second Committee. Nevertheless, the voting alignments were not always the same. In committee, for instance, Afro–Asian and Soviet states succeeded (45-36-10) against fairly solid Western objections in passing a request that the Secretary-General consult member states on the advisability of holding a conference on trade problems, especially primary commodity markets (vote 2002). After an amendment in plenary session making clear that Secretariat investigations and consultations would not prejudice the issue whether the conference would be held (vote 8038—Afro–Asians vacillated, the Soviets voted against the amendment), the final resolution was passed without a roll call. The richer Old Europeans (again excluding Scandinavia) had abstained on the final committee vote (2005, 81-0-11). Also in the committee, Old Europeans formed virtually the only opposition to ECOSOC consideration of establishing a special agency of industrial development (vote 2010).

The same states were alone in favor of deleting a request for Secretariat action on the possibility of an international conference regarding patents and developing countries (vote 2015). In another interesting economic vote, after much debate, only the communist countries and a few Old Europeans (e.g. Belgium, Portugal, Australia, Austria) opposed the hope that international assistance and capital should equal one per cent of the combined national resources of the economically advanced countries (vote 8039).

The final development topic that appeared in roll-call voting was "population growth and economic development," an issue with religious and moral implications. After several procedural votes, a vote (8041) to refer the matter to the Second Committee at the next session of the Assembly failed (47-25-24) to receive the two-thirds majority required for such a specific allocation of responsibility.

## Social, Humanitarian, and Cultural Questions

Thailand, Malaya, Ireland, and El Salvador succeeded in putting the "Question of Tibet" on the Assembly's agenda (vote 8001) and passing a resolution declaring that Tibetan suppression violated the Universal Declaration of Human Rights, including self-determination (vote 8043). Nonaligned Asian and Casablanca powers generally abstained; pro-Western states (except for France and South Africa, with reservations of their own) supported the resolution; the Soviets, of course, opposed discussion of the issue; while the Monrovia states remained somewhat skeptical.[8]

None of the Third Committee roll-call subjects reached roll-call status in the plenary session. Three of the thirteen committee votes were included in the present analysis. First of all, on vote 3001 the Soviets supported and Arabs protested a provision in a Draft Convention on Consent to Marriage allowing exceptional marriages without the presence of one of the parties involved. Remaining states in all continents seemed divided on the issue. In what the Soviet Union called "a choice between freedom to spread war propaganda and racial hatred or prohibiting it" (vote 3007), most pro-Western states demurred at limiting the freedom of speech, while the Soviets and other Eastern states favored restriction. Another vote on provisions for a draft convention on Freedom of Information (3013) divided Western and Eastern states. English-speaking Westerners, Soviet allies, some Asians, and all Arabs favored making optional specific legal safeguards for the "right of reply."

## Trusteeship and Non-Self-Governing Territories

A major result of deliberations in the Fourth Committee at the Assembly's Fifteenth Session was a "Declaration on the granting of independence to colonial countries and peoples." Originally suggested by the Soviet Union, a draft submitted by 43 Afro–Asian states was finally passed by an 89-0-9 majority. Only Australia,

8. Bailey, *The General Assembly*, Chap. 10, examines the Tibetan issue in great detail.

Belgium, the Dominican Republic, France, Portugal, Spain, South Africa, the United Kingdom, and the United States abstained on a call for "immediate steps" to transfer "all powers to the peoples of [dependent territories], without any conditions or reservations." Early in the Sixteenth Session, the Assembly approved a special Committee of 17 to review the implementation of the Declaration. Heavily weighted toward anticolonial representation (the Committee on Information is half and half), this new committee was widely interpreted as the "overseer of decolonization.

The concerns of the Fourth Committee included Algeria, Western Irian, South Africa, Southern Rhodesia, Angola, and, most lengthily, Ruanda–Urundi. On a resolution so phrased as to recall the Declaration of Independence, a request (8011) to redress "the legitimate grievances of the Algerian prisoners," sponsored by Pakistan, found only Japan, China, and Israel in abstention among Eastern states. A Soviet amendment to the resolution establishing the Committee of 17, proclaiming "1962 the year of elimination of colonialism," produced solid opposition from pro-Western states and, for the most part, Afro–Asian abstentions. The final resolution (virtually unanimous) showed abstentions by France, the United Kingdom, South Africa, and Spain. Portugal did not participate in the voting; the United States voted in favor.

Despite the unanimity in establishing the Committee of 17; the Eastern states were badly split over the next topic. All three roll calls on Western Irian (8019, 8020, and 8021) produced small majorities (less than the required two thirds) for Dutch and Indonesian negotiations based "on the principle of self-determination of peoples in accordance with the Charter of the United Nations." Western and Brazzaville states differed sharply from remaining UN members on the proper interpretation of self-determination regarding Western Irian.

A number of other matters must be mentioned. Portuguese noncompliance with Trusteeship Charter obligations was also discussed. Brazzaville countries and a fair number of Latin Americans did not support Old European efforts to replace "condemns" by "regrets." Despite or because of the instruction to the Committee on Information from Non-Self-Governing Territories to examine political and constitutional information as well as the economic and social information required by the Charter, the Soviet states, France, England, South Africa, and Spain opposed renewing the Committee's mandate

(8037). A moderate resolution by Sweden on South West Africa drew some Arab–Asian abstentions, although it failed to get more than 26 affirmative votes from Western allies (vote 4009). Virtually unanimous votes occured on the final resolutions.

The Assembly decision to request the Committee of 17 to "consider whether the territory of Southern Rhodesia has attained a full measure of self-government" produced extremly bitter protests from the United Kingdom. The plenary vote (8066) found Old Europeans opposed, Latin Americans abstaining, and almost all the remaining UN members in favor. Similar voting alignments (with more disunity among the Latin states) occurred in plenary discussions that "deplored" the denial of equal political rights there (8068, 8073, 8075).

When it was proposed that the subcommittee on Angola report to the Security Council and the General Assembly through the Committee of 17, Western ranks were sufficiently solid and Afro–Asians sufficiently divided for a majority (37-44-20) to vote against the measure (8058). Similarly, a request that the Committee of 17 consider Angolian independence failed to receive a two-thirds majority (8059). A Bulgarian and Polish resolution, condemning the "colonial war pursued by Portugal" and recommending an arms embargo (vote 8056), failed (26-43-32) to receive a simple majority.

When, in October 1961, Belgium asked the Assembly to note that "persons suspected of having committed the crime" of murdering the Prime Minister of Burundi had already been apprehended, only Old Europeans seemed to find this information relevant to a resolution asking the UN Commission for Ruanda–Urundi to investigate the assassination (vote 4001). Despite this inauspicious beginning, the discussion in the Fourth Committee and at plenary sessions about the future of Rwanda and Burundi did achieve a fairly high degree of concurrence. Paul Henri Spaak presented the Belgian point of view. He was successsful in amending an Afro–Asian resolution to state that "after independence Rwanda and Burundi will enjoy sovereign rights" (vote 4021). Though this was seemingly a trivial statement, the Belgian delegation voted for the final resolution, probably because of the success of such modifications.

Fearing unrest in the two new countries after independence, the Belgian government argued that it would be a violation of the new governments' sovereignty to prohibit the possible use of Belgian troops stationed there to maintain public order. Russian attempts (such as 8069) to insist on a "1 July 1962" deadline for troop removal were opposed by pro-Western states and supported only by scattered Afro–Asians. The modified troop withdrawal request (4023) found six procolonial powers and the Soviet bloc in abstention. Seven Old Europeans (including the United States, but not Belgium) abstained on part of the revised withdrawal request (vote 8070), while only the Soviet bloc abstained on the final plenary resolution (excluded here because similar to 8008). On this resolution the Soviets, not the colonial countries, were isolated.

### Administrative and Budgetary Concerns

We have included six administrative and budgetary roll calls in the factor analysis. All but one of the Fifth Committee roll calls were either virtually unanimous or again repeated in plenary session.

A vote authorizing the Acting Secretary-General to commit up to two million dollars for possible "emergency measures" in Rwanda and Burundi was opposed by France and the Soviet bloc. Twelve additional states (mostly Old Europeans or Latin Americans) abstained (vote 8071).

On a resolution (8049) submitting to the International Court of Justice the question whether Congo and UNEF expenses constituted regular "expenses of the Organization," France and Soviet countries objected, while a majority of Afro–Asians abstained. Belgium, France, Madagascar, and the Soviet countries (Cuba abstained) opposed an authorization of up to $120 million for 1962 Congo expenses. A majority of Latin and Afro–Asian states supported the resolution (8051). Soviet countries again objected to UNEF apportionments weighing more heavily on the bigger UN contributors; Casablanca and Monrovia countries either abstained or favored the authorization (vote 8052). A similar alignment (with more Monrovian and less Latin American support) characterized an authorization of $200 million in UN bonds, to be repaid over a period of years out of the regular budget of the United Nations (vote 8053).

### Legal Questions

Perhaps because of the implied recognition of Communist China, all Western and allied states opposed an attempt by Ceylon, Czechoslovakia, Guinea, India, Indonesia, and Poland to stipulate that "all countries" be invited to a conference on consular relations. The amendment to the Report of the International Law Commission lost by a 28-50-15 majority (vote 8033).

## VOTING DIMENSIONS IN 1961

The unrotated factor pattern is presented in Table 6.1; state positions on the first two unrotated factors are summarized in Figure 6.1. Several results are very striking. First, East–West voting dominated the issues before every committee of the United Nations, with the possible exception of budgetary concerns. This one voting alignment accounted for more than half (52.8 per cent) of all the important votes in our analysis. As part of the 83 per cent of all the voting variations that could be explained by nine underlying voting components, nearly two thirds (64 per cent) of the interpretable voting variation consisted of this alignment. As Figure 6.1 makes clear, Latin American states and pro-Western Asians were regularly opposed to Soviet states and to most of the Afro–Asians; the Brazzaville states, and to a lesser extent several additional Asian states were the only powers with voting positions bridging the gulf between East and West.

The second unrotated voting factor was again a North–South super-issue on which Soviet countries and some colonial powers tended to vote the same way regarding arms control, the Committee on Information from Non-Self-Governing Territories, economic aid, Rwanda and Burundi, and budgetary questions. As such North–South voting accounted for only about 13 per cent of the general variation in important votes at the Sixteenth Assembly. Only five votes out of 70 analyzed did not correlate at more than a 0.50 level with either North–South or East–West voting. In fact, not a single important roll call analyzed had a voting communality less than 0.66, suggesting that nine distinct voting components can explain more than two thirds of any important roll call in 1961.

Turning to the rotated factor pattern (Table 6.2), we see that for most votes only four substantive factors provide an adequate interpretation: even after rotation, only four distinct voting components had eigen values greater than 2.5. With a λ of 22.7, the first rotated voting component may again be called self-determination because it consists mostly of votes on South Africa, Angola, Southern Rhodesia, and Ruanda–Urundi (now Rwanda and Burundi). The

# Table 6.1. Dimensions of Voting in 1961: Unrotated Factor Matrix

|  | | | | FACTORS | | | | | |
| ROLL CALLS | 1 | 2 | 3 | 4 | 5 | 6 | 7 | 8 | 9 |
|---|---|---|---|---|---|---|---|---|---|
| 8004. Censure South Africa | .63 | .33 | —.36 | .02 | .09 | —.03 | —.11 | —.11 | —.00 |
| 8022. Sanction South Africa | .84 | .25 | —.28 | —.13 | .01 | —.01 | .05 | .06 | —.03 |
| 8023. Security Council & S. Africa | .88 | .28 | —.22 | —.13 | —.04 | —.03 | .00 | .01 | .07 |
| 8024. No arms to South Africa | .83 | .22 | —.15 | —.21 | —.05 | .04 | .18 | .07 | —.02 |
| 8025. No petroleum to Africa | .85 | .21 | —.20 | —.16 | —.03 | —.00 | .20 | .11 | —.05 |
| 8027. Oman self-determination | .84 | .06 | —.16 | .26 | —.11 | —.05 | —.02 | —.01 | .10 |
| 0018. Reconstitute Pal. Con. Com. | .38 | —.03 | —.00 | .04 | —.11 | —.57 | .32 | .49 | —.14 |
| 8045. Reconstitute Pal. Con. Com. | .72 | —.01 | .01 | .39 | —.07 | —.24 | .01 | .14 | —.20 |
| 8046. Protect Arab refugees | .77 | —.02 | .07 | .38 | —.13 | —.18 | —.00 | .03 | —.17 |
| 8047. U.N.R.W.A. | —.64 | .20 | —.03 | —.32 | .33 | —.22 | .11 | .16 | .17 |
| 8048. U.S. Palestine Resolution | —.70 | .22 | —.02 | —.28 | .26 | —.17 | .11 | .22 | .08 |
| 0003. Czech Res. on UNSCEAR | .81 | —.09 | .01 | —.12 | —.12 | —.02 | —.07 | —.04 | —.06 |
| 8006. Czech Res. important? | —.87 | .05 | .02 | .03 | —.03 | —.02 | .16 | .00 | .00 |
| 8007. Admit Mauritania | —.77 | .17 | —.14 | —.28 | .16 | —.04 | .05 | —.16 | —.00 |
| 8029. China question important? | —.74 | .19 | —.49 | .04 | —.21 | —.10 | .09 | —.16 | .00 |
| 8030. China declaration | .67 | .15 | .54 | —.25 | .05 | .17 | —.17 | .16 | .07 |
| 8031. Seat People's Rep. of China | .63 | .16 | .55 | —.32 | .02 | .11 | —.15 | .14 | —.00 |
| 8032. Representation of China | .74 | —.13 | .45 | —.27 | .15 | .12 | —.12 | .15 | .02 |
| 8008. Stop 50 megaton bomb | —.55 | .64 | .17 | —.03 | —.34 | .04 | —.14 | .09 | —.02 |
| 1010. General & complete disarm. | .88 | .04 | .03 | —.11 | —.08 | .05 | —.03 | —.09 | —.16 |
| 8009. Regrets tests; need treaty | —.01 | .86 | .12 | .15 | .10 | .18 | —.04 | —.06 | .07 |
| 8010. Regrets rejection of US-UK | —.70 | .50 | —.07 | —.04 | —.17 | —.08 | .11 | —.07 | .02 |
| 8012. Denuclearize Africa | .70 | .06 | .43 | .17 | .06 | .10 | .24 | —.14 | .07 |
| 8016. Charter bans nuclear weapons | .87 | .31 | —.11 | —.11 | .04 | .05 | .06 | —.07 | .04 |
| 1023. Form Non-nuclear club | .67 | .10 | .41 | .17 | .19 | .12 | .22 | —.19 | .01 |
| 8044. Question of Algeria | .68 | .16 | .43 | .12 | .14 | .03 | .27 | —.20 | .04 |
| 1026. N. Korea & UNCURK | —.75 | .32 | —.25 | .02 | —.22 | —.05 | .11 | —.11 | .13 |
| 8054. Report of UNCURK | —.88 | .25 | —.18 | —.01 | —.08 | —.00 | .14 | .08 | —.01 |
| 8055. Deplores Hungary on disrespect | —.92 | .07 | .04 | .20 | —.04 | —.04 | .05 | .04 | .05 |
| 8064. Noninterference in Cuba | .86 | —.08 | .23 | .09 | —.01 | —.06 | —.10 | .09 | —.06 |

# Table 6.1. Dimensions of Voting in 1961: Unrotated Factor Matrix

| ROLL CALLS | FACTORS | | | | | | | | |
|---|---|---|---|---|---|---|---|---|---|
| | 1 | 2 | 3 | 4 | 5 | 6 | 7 | 8 | 9 |
| 8065. Friendly relations with Cuba | .92 | .05 | .10 | —.11 | —.00 | —.02 | .00 | .12 | —.09 |
| 2002. Hold trade conference | .88 | .23 | —.06 | —.17 | —.09 | —.03 | .15 | —.06 | —.03 |
| 2005. Help primary producers | .44 | .41 | —.10 | .25 | .41 | .08 | .14 | .16 | .37 |
| 8038. Study trade conference | —.74 | .37 | —.03 | —.17 | —.14 | .00 | .07 | —.06 | .11 |
| 2010. Special int. devel. agency | .57 | .38 | —.42 | .34 | .21 | —.02 | —.12 | .12 | —.04 |
| 2015. Conference on patents | —.58 | —.21 | .36 | —.37 | —.16 | .05 | .28 | .00 | —.21 |
| 8039. Aid with 1% GNP | —.25 | .74 | .09 | .01 | —.14 | —.08 | —.28 | .16 | .05 |
| 8041. Population & econ. devel. | .53 | —.13 | .38 | —.23 | .00 | —.17 | .27 | .04 | .25 |
| 8001. Tibet on agenda | —.83 | .31 | —.03 | .04 | .10 | .02 | .15 | —.04 | —.01 |
| 8043. Resolution on Tibet | —.79 | .44 | —.17 | —.06 | .06 | —.03 | .19 | —.02 | .00 |
| 3001. Absentee marriage legal | —.02 | —.38 | —.33 | —.17 | .50 | —.28 | —.11 | —.16 | —.33 |
| 3007. Disallow "hatred and hostility" | .78 | .17 | —.31 | —.15 | .03 | —.05 | —.16 | .04 | —.02 |
| 3013. Safeguard right of reply | .68 | —.17 | .10 | —.07 | —.29 | —.07 | .17 | —.26 | —.16 |
| 8011. Algerian prisoners | .78 | .30 | .10 | —.15 | .04 | .08 | .34 | —.04 | .06 |
| 8017. 1962 end of colonialism | .91 | —.05 | —.05 | —.19 | .07 | —.01 | .03 | —.01 | —.04 |
| 8019. W. Irian self-determination | —.74 | .11 | —.25 | —.34 | .13 | .17 | —.04 | —.03 | —.08 |
| 8020. Commission on W. Irian | —.78 | .09 | —.26 | —.31 | .09 | .14 | —.10 | .01 | —.07 |
| 8021. Indian res. on W. Irian | .76 | .01 | .24 | .40 | .08 | —.08 | .05 | —.10 | .09 |
| 8035. Regrets Port. non-compliance | —.83 | —.29 | .20 | .09 | .04 | .02 | —.07 | .00 | —.15 |
| 8037. Renew CINSGT | —.26 | .84 | .15 | .08 | —.04 | .14 | —.03 | .07 | —.07 |
| 4009. Swedish res. on South Africa | —.80 | —.12 | .34 | .18 | —.05 | .01 | .17 | .03 | —.07 |
| 8066. Ask SC 17: S. Rhodesia SGT? | .87 | .32 | —.27 | —.05 | —.03 | —.00 | .03 | —.01 | .04 |
| 8068. S. Rhodesia on agenda | .84 | .34 | —.25 | —.04 | —.04 | —.06 | .05 | —.07 | .03 |
| 8073. "1 man 1 vote" S. Rhodesia | .86 | .24 | —.16 | —.14 | —.10 | .02 | .09 | —.07 | —.01 |
| 8075. Regret UK acts on S. Rhodesia | .73 | .40 | —.30 | .10 | .06 | .03 | .04 | —.10 | .02 |
| 8056. Condemn Portugal re Angola | .92 | .04 | —.05 | —.13 | .02 | —.07 | .03 | —.01 | —.07 |
| 8058. Report on Angola | .80 | .03 | —.03 | —.08 | .04 | —.10 | —.07 | —.02 | .11 |
| 8059. Angola & SC 17 | .89 | .16 | —.08 | —.00 | —.00 | —.10 | —.05 | —.06 | .02 |
| 4001. Burundi Prime Minister | —.88 | —.24 | .18 | .01 | .04 | .02 | .06 | .11 | —.05 |
| 4021. Rwanda & Burundi sovereign | —.82 | .01 | —.12 | .09 | —.05 | .11 | .12 | .09 | —.09 |

## Table 6.1. Dimensions of Voting in 1961: Unrotated Factor Matrix

| ROLL CALLS | FACTORS | | | | | | | | |
|---|---|---|---|---|---|---|---|---|---|
| | 1 | 2 | 3 | 4 | 5 | 6 | 7 | 8 | 9 |
| 8069. Evacuate R. & B. by 1 July '62 | .95 | .02 | —.01 | —.11 | .00 | —.10 | .00 | —.04 | —.03 |
| 8070. Rwanda & Burundi evacuation | .30 | .40 | —.05 | .21 | .46 | .29 | .16 | .03 | —.49 |
| 4023. Rwanda & Burundi evacuation | —.30 | .73 | .06 | .20 | .04 | .19 | .01 | .31 | —.18 |
| 8071. $2 million to S.G. for R. & B. | —.24 | .66 | .26 | —.16 | —.22 | —.00 | .03 | —.08 | —.30 |
| 5004. Five Sec. members/ country | .57 | .56 | .07 | —.02 | —.33 | .01 | —.13 | .02 | —.03 |
| 8049. Congo expenses and ICJ. | —.74 | .39 | .20 | .14 | .14 | —.19 | .05 | —.08 | .00 |
| 8051. Congo cost | —.42 | .55 | .43 | .07 | .12 | —.37 | —.22 | —.20 | —.01 |
| 8052. UNEF expenses | —.50 | .45 | .43 | —.02 | .13 | —.33 | —.24 | —.19 | .06 |
| 8053. Budget for year 1962 | —.39 | .60 | .29 | —.21 | .16 | —.28 | —.02 | —.15 | —.14 |
| 8033. "All" attend conference | .91 | —.06 | .06 | —.15 | .01 | —.04 | —.18 | .03 | —.02 |

Roll-call variance accounted
for by factor (eigen values) $\lambda=37.0$ $\lambda=7.8$ $\lambda=4.2$ $\lambda=2.4$ $\lambda=1.8$ $\lambda=1.4$ $\lambda=1.4$ $\lambda=1.1$ $\lambda=1.0$

economic component of Afro–Asian self-determination demands is also clear from the high loadings of votes 2002, 2010, 2015, and 5004 (trade, aid, patent inquiries, and Secretariat posts).

Perhaps because of the threat of newer, more radical African states in great numbers, Latin Americans were much closer to the Old European position on many of these self-determination issues. Thus on vote 8066 (a request that the Committee of 17 study Southern Rhodesia), the Latins abstained from the usual anti-European voting that we have found previously to characterize self-determination issues. Perhaps also because of clearer Soviet initiatives (e.g. vote 8069 on troop evacuations from Rwanda and Burundi), the Latins tended to side with at least the more liberal Old Europeans on many of the issues loading heavily on factor 1.

This tilting of self-determination issues away from an anti-European alignment closer to an East–West alignment also accounts for the frequency of cold war related issues loading heavily on the first rotated factor. Soviet disarmament moves increasingly produced an East–West response (votes 8006, 1010) on the question whether the use of nuclear weapons was a crime against Afro–Asian humanity. Similarly, Eastern countries saw Cuban independence as a self-determination issue in the way that Hungary and Tibet

## Figure 6.1. Unrotated Factor Scores on the East–West and North–South Issues at the 16th General Assembly

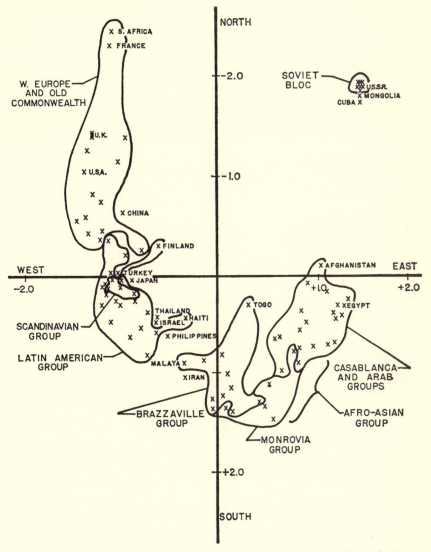

(especially votes 8001 and 8055) were not. Factors 1 and 3 are plotted in Figure 6.2.[9]

9. Revised self-determination and cold war scores correlate 0.80 and 0.85 respectively with unrotated East–West factor scores. Revised cold war and self-determination scores are moderately intercorrelated ($r = 0.41$) suggesting that the two factors have been increasingly interrelated.

# Table 6.2. Dimensions of Voting in 1961: Rotated Factor Matrix

**FACTORS**

| ROLL CALLS | 1 | 2 | 3 | 4 | 5 | 6 | 7 | 8 | 9 |
|---|---|---|---|---|---|---|---|---|---|
| 8004. Censure South Africa | .77 | .02 | .00 | .17 | .16 | .08 | —.11 | .03 | —.09 |
| 8022. Sanction South Africa | .88 | —.10 | .19 | .13 | .05 | —.11 | .03 | —.03 | —.11 |
| 8023. Security Council & S. Africa | .91 | —.06 | .25 | .16 | .06 | —.07 | .06 | —.06 | —.00 |
| 8024. No arms to South Africa | .82 | —.12 | .28 | .08 | —.05 | —.15 | .14 | —.15 | —.11 |
| 8025. No petroleum to S. Africa | .84 | —.14 | .24 | .11 | —.02 | —.20 | .11 | —.13 | —.14 |
| 8027. Oman self-determination | .67 | —.19 | .15 | .51 | .17 | —.06 | .09 | —.07 | .02 |
| 0018. Reconstitute Pal. Con. Com. | .24 | —.08 | .09 | .19 | —.01 | —.85 | —.02 | —.03 | .03 |
| 8045. Reconstitute Pal. Con. Com. | .43 | —.12 | .19 | .65 | .08 | —.33 | —.06 | —.02 | —.13 |
| 8046. Protect Arab refugees | .45 | —.12 | .23 | .71 | .03 | —.22 | —.03 | —.07 | —.08 |
| 8047. U.N.R.W.A. | —.33 | .28 | —.18 | —.67 | .18 | —.18 | —.18 | —.01 | .09 |
| 8048. U.S. Palestine Resolution | —.38 | .32 | —.21 | —.65 | .13 | —.21 | —.10 | .06 | .01 |
| 0003. Czech Res. on UNSCEAR | .60 | —.25 | .40 | .30 | —.14 | —.03 | —.01 | —.04 | .06 |
| 8006. Czech Res. important | —.64 | .25 | —.44 | —.33 | —.05 | —.02 | .05 | —.01 | .00 |
| 8007. Admit Mauritania | —.37 | .28 | —.40 | —.59 | —.08 | .13 | —.18 | .02 | .03 |
| 8029. China question important? | —.22 | .20 | —.83 | —.30 | —.10 | .05 | .01 | .15 | .09 |
| 8030. China declaration | .34 | .13 | .86 | .12 | .00 | .03 | .15 | —.09 | .00 |
| 8031. Seat People's Rep. of China | .33 | .16 | .84 | .08 | —.09 | —.01 | .11 | —.09 | .01 |
| 8032. Representation of China | .33 | —.17 | .87 | .12 | —.01 | —.03 | .01 | —.11 | —.01 |
| 8008. Stop 50 megaton bomb | —.22 | .79 | —.21 | —.16 | —.12 | .04 | .30 | .20 | .06 |
| 1010. General & Complete disarm. | .69 | —.16 | .42 | .33 | —.18 | .01 | —.01 | —.10 | —.08 |
| 8009. Regrets tests; need treaty | .24 | .76 | —.04 | —.02 | .25 | .20 | .17 | —.13 | —.23 |
| 8010. Regrets rejection of US-UK | —.26 | .59 | —.51 | —.32 | —.09 | .00 | .12 | .01 | .05 |
| 8012. Denuclearize Africa | .31 | —.03 | .48 | .42 | .05 | .01 | .11 | —.52 | —.10 |
| 8016. Charter bans nuclear weapons | .85 | —.02 | .29 | .17 | .07 | .01 | .04 | —.19 | —.09 |
| 1023. Form Non-nuclear club | .31 | .00 | .47 | .38 | .09 | .06 | .01 | —.53 | —.19 |
| 8044. Question of Algeria | .35 | .07 | .46 | .36 | .05 | —.00 | .02 | —.58 | —.12 |
| 1026. N. Korea & UNCURK | —.29 | .37 | —.67 | —.32 | —.04 | .07 | .15 | .05 | .14 |
| 8054. Report of UNCURK | —.47 | .35 | —.58 | —.43 | —.03 | —.04 | .11 | .12 | —.05 |
| 8055. Deplores Hungary on disrespect | —.72 | .31 | —.47 | —.22 | .07 | —.00 | .07 | .08 | .03 |

# Table 6.2. Dimensions of Voting in 1961: Rotated Factor Matrix

**FACTORS**

| ROLL CALLS | 1 | 2 | 3 | 4 | 5 | 6 | 7 | 8 | 9 |
|---|---|---|---|---|---|---|---|---|---|
| 8064. Noninterference in Cuba | .48 | —.17 | .57 | .49 | .03 | —.13 | —.01 | —.07 | —.02 |
| 8065. Friendly relations with Cuba | .67 | —.15 | .54 | .29 | —.04 | —.17 | .02 | —.09 | —.08 |
| 2002. Hold trade conference | .83 | —.06 | .31 | .19 | —.11 | —.11 | .07 | —.23 | —.04 |
| 2005. Help primary commodities producers | .44 | .11 | .11 | .03 | .67 | —.04 | .11 | —.25 | —.19 |
| 8038. Study trade conference | —.34 | .48 | —.41 | —.45 | —.09 | .07 | .14 | .03 | .12 |
| 2010. Special int. devel. agency | .67 | .06 | —.09 | .30 | .43 | —.05 | —.08 | .13 | —.29 |
| 2015. Conference on patents | —.60 | .05 | .03 | —.38 | —.51 | —.10 | .09 | —.14 | .01 |
| 8039. Aid with 1% GNP | .06 | .78 | —.07 | —.10 | .12 | .02 | .18 | .26 | .03 |
| 8041. Population & econ. devel. | .23 | —.16 | .51 | .05 | —.02 | —.26 | .07 | —.43 | .25 |
| 8001. Tibet on agenda | —.49 | .43 | —.47 | —.39 | .05 | .05 | .01 | —.04 | —.12 |
| 8043. Resolution on Tibet | —.32 | .48 | —.56 | —.49 | .03 | —.01 | .03 | —.02 | —.10 |
| 3001. Absentee marriage legal | .01 | —.38 | —.08 | —.18 | —.03 | —.03 | —.74 | .12 | —.14 |
| 3007. Disallow "hatred and hostility" | .82 | —.13 | .22 | .13 | .06 | —.03 | —.08 | .13 | —.02 |
| 3013. Safeguard right of reply | .45 | —.26 | .23 | .40 | —.39 | —.05 | .01 | —.27 | .09 |
| 8011. Algerian prisoners | .69 | .01 | .35 | .09 | —.01 | —.11 | .17 | —.44 | —.13 |
| 8017. 1962 end of colonialism | .72 | —.30 | .45 | .19 | —.04 | —.08 | —.07 | —.13 | —.05 |
| 8019. W. Irian self-determination | —.32 | .16 | —.35 | —.65 | —.12 | .20 | —.07 | .22 | —.10 |
| 8020. Commission on W. Irian | —.36 | .16 | —.38 | —.63 | —.10 | .18 | —.06 | .29 | —.06 |
| 8021. Indian res. on W. Irian | .37 | —.09 | .35 | .63 | .23 | —.05 | —.02 | —.33 | —.03 |
| 8035. Regrets Port. non-compliance | —.85 | .05 | —.20 | —.15 | —.12 | .06 | —.11 | .14 | —.02 |
| 8037. Renew CINSGT | .04 | .84 | —.11 | —.11 | .08 | .07 | .23 | .02 | —.24 |
| 4009. Swedish res. on S. Africa | —.84 | .19 | —.21 | —.10 | —.10 | —.05 | .08 | —.09 | —.04 |
| 8066. Ask SC 17: S. Rhodesia SGT? | .91 | —.04 | .16 | .21 | .09 | —.05 | .06 | —.07 | —.06 |
| 8068. S. Rhodesia on agenda | .90 | —.00 | .13 | .22 | .06 | —.06 | .02 | —.12 | —.04 |
| 8073. "1 man 1 vote" S. Rhodesia | .86 | —.07 | .23 | .20 | —.07 | —.04 | .09 | —.15 | —.05 |
| 8075. Regret UK acts on S. Rhodesia | .82 | .05 | .02 | .23 | .18 | .04 | .01 | —.12 | —.16 |
| 8056. Condemn Portugal re Angola | .76 | —.21 | .40 | .25 | —.05 | —.12 | —.07 | —.12 | —.04 |
| 8058. Report on Angola | .65 | —.17 | .37 | .24 | .10 | —.05 | —.07 | —.10 | .10 |
| 8059. Angola & SC 17 | .77 | —.09 | .31 | .34 | .06 | —.05 | —.06 | —.11 | .02 |

## Table 6.2. Dimensions of Voting in 1961: Rotated Factor Matrix

**FACTORS**

| ROLL CALLS | 1 | 2 | 3 | 4 | 5 | 6 | 7 | 8 | 9 |
|---|---|---|---|---|---|---|---|---|---|
| 4001. Burundi Prime Minister | —.85 | .06 | —.22 | —.30 | —.07 | —.04 | .00 | .09 | —.01 |
| 4021. Rwanda & Burundi sovereign | —.58 | .14 | —.49 | —.30 | —.05 | .00 | .11 | .14 | —.14 |
| 8069. Evacuate R. & B. by 1 July '62 | .75 | —.20 | .42 | .31 | —.03 | —.11 | —.08 | —.15 | .02 |
| 8070. Rwanda & Burundi evacuation | .30 | .19 | .09 | .10 | .12 | .04 | —.15 | —.13 | —.81 |
| 4023. Rwanda & Burundi evacuation | —.05 | .70 | —.14 | —.09 | .16 | —.08 | .26 | .15 | —.44 |
| 8071. $2 million to S.G. for R. & B. | .01 | .75 | —.04 | —.11 | —.35 | —.01 | .10 | —.03 | —.14 |
| 5004. Five Sec. members/country | .64 | .41 | .21 | 28 | —.10 | —.02 | .24 | .04 | .03 |
| 8049. Congo expenses and ICJ. | —.51 | .61 | —.32 | —.20 | .11 | —.02 | —.13 | —.10 | —.01 |
| 8051. Congo cost | —.28 | .83 | —.01 | —.00 | .07 | .01 | —.30 | —.08 | .17 |
| 8052. UNEF expenses | —.36 | .76 | .02 | —.11 | .07 | .06 | —.29 | —.06 | .23 |
| 8053. Budget for year 1962 | —.12 | .76 | —.03 | —.29 | —.10 | —.06 | —.27 | —.13 | .01 |
| 8033. "All" attend conference | .65 | —.23 | —.56 | .29 | —.02 | —.04 | —.08 | .01 | .06 |

Roll-call variance accounted for by factor (eigen values) $\lambda=22.7$ $\lambda=8.7$ $\lambda=10.2$ $\lambda=7.6$ $\lambda=1.8$ $\lambda=1.4$ $\lambda=1.6$ $\lambda=2.4$ $\lambda=1.6$

An important reason for identifying the second rotated factor as UN supranationalism comes from the heavy loading of crucial UNEF and Congo budgetary questions on it. The usual anti-Soviet aspect of this enhancement of UN authority again appears in several rebuffs to Soviet policy (votes 8008, 8009, 8010). The Russians also refused to support capital and technical assistance, the renewal of a somewhat moderate Committee on Information from Non-Self-Governing Territories (vote 8037), or constructive and peaceful decisions on the future of Rwanda and Burundi (votes 4023, 8071, and 8072, discussed above).

While Hungary and Cuba increasingly were becoming East–West or self-determination issues (from different points of view), cold war and membership questions again produced a distinctive and frequent voting component. Korea, Cuba, Hungary, Tibet, and a universal invitation to a conference on consular relations were "issues in transition" between distinctive cold war voting in the Assembly and the larger overall East–West division of opinions and policies. All these issues loaded fairly heavily on either or both of the first and third rotated factors. The peculiarity of the less extreme Soviet position on the cold war dimension of Figure 6.2 comes in their abstentions on votes 8031 and 8032 (previously mentioned) because the wording did not exclude the possibility that *both* Nationalist and Communist China be allowed to remain in the General Assembly. The Soviets were "moderates" in the cold war

Figure 6.2. Rotated Factor Scores on Cold War and Self-Determination Issues at the 16th General Assembly

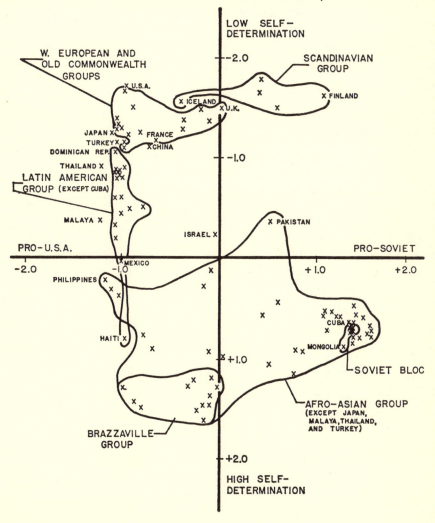

membership issue only in the sense that they were not willing to vote unconditionally for Communist Chinese membership (neither, of course, would Communist China).

With a lambda of 7.6, the fourth rotated factor is clearly composed of Palestinian and Western Irian mediation attempts. Arab–Soviet coalitions continued to operate on these questions; Old European and Latin states were still divided on them, but to a much lesser degree. Looking at the votes again and the relevant factor scores, it is clear that what distinguishes these issues from the general East–West tenor of self-determination issues (note the heavy loadings of all of them on the unrotated first factor) is no longer Western divisions but, instead, the divorce of the Brazzaville countries from their fellow Afro–Asians.[10]

We may describe the remaining five voting components in lesser detail. Factor 6 reflects residual Latin, Benelux, and Scandinavian misgivings about the composition of the Palestinian Conciliation Commission (vote 0018); similarly the ninth rotated factor is essentially limited to colonial doubts about Rwanda and Burundi (vote 8070). About half of the Old European states were isolated in their hesitancy about commodity regulations (vote 2005), perhaps because of the definite anti-Common Market flavor of Second Committee discussions (factor 5). A more peculiar coalition of the Soviet bloc and several Latin Americans appeared in voting on marriage rules in the Third Committee (vote 3001, factor 7). Finally, the coalition of conservative Westerners with conservative Afro–Asians (the Brazzaville group) on votes 8012, 1023, and 8044 is probably due to "French concerns" for nuclear testing and Algerian problems (factor 8).

African and, to a lesser extent, Asian problems certainly dominated Assembly discussions at the Sixteenth Session, as they probably did the year before. By June 1962 only Portuguese colonies, notably Angola, seemed clear examples of enduring foreign-controlled colonialism. African-based white minorities in Southern Rhodesia and South Africa remained major problems before the UN. They represent postcolonial problems of difficult proportions for the West;

10. Revised Palestine scores correlate 0.92 with the East–West alignment. When estimated only from roll calls with moderately high factor loadings (i.e. "revised"), Palestine scores lost a good deal of their distinctiveness: correlations with other revised scores were 0.60 with self-determination, −0.47 with supranationalism, and 0.76 with the cold war.

Africans may tend to see them as examples of neocolonialism, a phobia peculiar to most new countries in varying degrees.[11]

Structurally speaking, smaller groupings such as one on Angola, one on South West Africa, and more prominently, the Special Committee of 17, have proliferated in an attempt to perform the Assembly's tasks. The unwieldy nature of the large Assembly was already a problem when Hammarskjold appointed an Advisory Committee to consult with him during the Suez Crisis. The same procedure was followed in the Congo operation. Similarly, membership subgroupings seemed remarkably solid on most of the issues before the Assembly. For many of the newer nations and some of the older ones (namely Latin Americans) caucusing groups were foci of political action and negotiation.[12]

We have suggested that substantively Afro–Asian postcolonial problems are and will be the highlights of coming General Assemblies. Structurally, investigations and decisions by committees and caucuses appear more prevalent than in the "period of the Secretary-General." As the epitome of this gradual development, the key issue in the debate on the appointment of a new Secretary-General was not so much who he should be, but who his principal *advisers* in

11. Robert Good has presented an excellent summary of the reasons for such continuing interpretations in his "State-Building as a Determinant of Foreign Policy in the New States," in L. W. Martin, ed., *Neutralism and Nonalignment* (New York, Praeger, 1962), pp. 3–11. Seymour M. Lipset, *The First New Nation,* Chap. 2, makes the same point about the early history of the United States: the need of a newly independent country for national identity, neutrality, and autonomy, as reflected in the well-known phrase, "America's advantage from Europe's distress."

12. Thomas Hovet maintains that several of the African groupings in the United Nations decide many of their national foreign policies in their respective caucuses, that only on a few major issues are advance instructions received from home. He reports, for instance, that some African delegates had not even been instructed how to vote on Chinese membership! See his *Africa in the United Nations,* Chap. 7.

Two other examples of caucusing activity will suffice. In conversation, a UN diplomat suggested a major reason for Afro–Asian moderation on the Rwanda–Burundi issue (besides Spaak's moving plea) was U Thant's affirmation before the Afro–Asian caucusing group that the United Nations could not possibly afford in money, material, or personnel another operation of Congo scope in Rwanda–Burundi. A Latin American diplomat stressed that the strategy of his caucus group on the same issue was silently to abstain or oppose, en masse, until the Afro–Asians consulted them on *their* point of view. The point in the text is not that committees and caucuses are new developments in New York (they certainly are not), but that cohesion, intra- or inter-caucusing group negotiations, and the delegation of labor to smaller committees are increasingly required with the growth of the Assembly's membership, its work load, and the burdens of an increasingly politicized Secretariat.

the Secretariat should be! The number of Westerners declined; Afro–Asians increased.

In terms of voting alignments, the remarkable prevalence of East–West voting does suggest that the United Nations is in the midst of a struggle for control of the organization, as Jackson has contended.[13] But the battle is between coalitions we have labeled "East" and "West," not communists and noncommunists. The presence of newer, more radical, more powerful (in voting strength) African groupings has pushed most Latin Americans toward the Old European position which they usually rejected in 1952 and 1957. Only the Brazzaville group, with clear ties to France, bridged the gap between East and West on some issues. North–South voting continued as a secondary theme.

Amazingly enough, the number of frequent and distinct voting dimensions actually decreased from earlier years. In fact only four rotated factors had eigen values greater than 2.5 in an analysis of 70 roll calls. In 1947 the same criterion, when applied to only 48 roll calls, suggested five fairly frequent rotated voting components. In 1952 and 1957, six rotated factors had $\lambda$'s above 2.5, even though the number of important votes analyzed each year was again smaller than in 1961.

The argument is not that differences do not exist in African policies and priorities (the Brazzaville group often differed from their fellow Africans), but that, with different emphases, the main voting dimensions in 1961 could be interpreted in ways similar to previous ones. In this interpretation, *there has not been an evolving complexity and fluidity of important super-issues before the General Assembly*. Continuity and even simplification seem more valid summary emphases.

For instance, self-determination and certain cold war issues were much the same East–West kinds of phenomena that they had been in 1947. A separate factor of cold war membership questions, on which Western countries were still split, also appeared. Asian states had not greatly changed their positions; conservative Africans tended to support the pro-Western Asians; radical Africans followed radical Asian and Arab positions. Palestinian voting, although more solidified, again appeared as distinctive, with West Irian positions

13. See Chap. 2 above.

reflecting similar viewpoints. Brazzaville support for the Western position gave it the small majority that it has usually had. Soviet and Arab protests continued as they have in concert since 1952.

The final frequent voting dimension which we called small power or UN supranationalism also again appeared. The same states tended to object to small power attempts (usually but not always supported by the United States) to increase the authority of the Assembly and of the United Nations. Congo and UNEF budget issues found the same alliances of Soviet countries and the most conservative colonial or neocolonial countries (South Africa). Other examples of Soviet obstructionism or immoderation appeared, with some support from the most radical Afro–Asians, on the renewal of the Committee on Information from Non-Self-Governing Territories, the future of Rwanda and Burundi, and certain economic questions.

In addition, the less frequent factors included some scattered misgivings about the Palestinian Conciliation Commission; similar doubts about Rwanda and Burundi (by some Old Europeans), and commodity regulations (by other Old Europeans); disagreements about marriage rules; and objections to French concerns for nuclear testing and Algerian problems. Most of these factors could be viewed as partial aspects of Western European distrust of some newer Assembly members, or vice versa.

# CHAPTER 7

# The Development of
# United Nations Issues and Alignments

The historical dimension of this study allows one to compare and contrast the issues and alignments of the present period with those of earlier years. On some of these issues national policies have shown considerable change; on most, however, the continuity has been even more remarkable. A review of the main findings of previous chapters will help to clarify and extend their implications.

### THE CONTINUITY OF UN CONCERNS

Voting alignments have never been more varied than they were before and during the years in which Assembly members were first faced with committing themselves to positions on a large number of issues, many of which had not previously occupied their attention. The most arresting and least expected finding of this study is the continuity of the main super-issues revealed in Assembly voting. On comparing the relatively simple factor matrices for the Sixteenth General Assembly with those for earlier sessions, it is *not* true that "the simple formula of East–West confrontation, which was replaced by the East–Neutral–West confrontation, has been superseded by a complex and fluid pattern of international relations." [1]

Although the variety and length of the Assembly's agenda have grown, the same major behavioral voting dimensions have appeared from 1947 through 1961. The East–West and North–South voting dimensions have been clearly identifiable in the unrotated factor matrices and the maps from related factor scores that have been presented for all the years we have studied. During the "honeymoon"

1. For the context of these remarks by U Thant, recall the discussion in Chap. 1, above.

period, then, these alignments and some of their potential consequences could have been perceived, even though generally they
were not.[2] Certainly by 1952 the General Assembly had become,
what it is today,

> a prime political forum for the nations which remain outside
> the East–West camps and pursue their own goals of political
> independence, economic improvement, and racial dignity. In
> this situation what might be called the North–South conflict
> cuts across the East–West issues and makes its own powerful
> demands on American diplomacy, at the same time offering
> frequent opportunities for the Soviets to seize the political
> initiative.[3]

That the East–West and North–South conflicts are clearly perceived by a good many practicing diplomats can be seen from interviewing them or quoting their statements. U Thant's position has
been made remarkably clear in these terms: "I am not neutral in
the fight for the reduction of North–South tensions, which reveal
themselves as more fundamental than the East–West ones, and I
may not be altogether objective when it comes to evaluating the usefulness and importance of the organization which I serve." [4]

The continuity of UN concerns is even more remarkable in terms
of the substantively interpretable rotated factors that have been
identified. For at least three of the four years studied, we have

2. Thomas Hovet, in what may be only a slight understatement, has suggested that
"the only allusion at the San Francisco Conference [in 1945] to the possibility of blocs
and groups or to the implications of 'bloc voting' was . . . when Mr. Molotov . . .
discussed the majority voting procedure of the conference," objecting to the near
majority held by the United States, the Latin Americans, Liberia, and the Philippines
(*Bloc Politics in the United Nations*, pp. 1–4). In *The United Nations as a Political
Institution*, Nicholas suggests that the three main problems discussed at the San
Francisco Conference were regional security organizations, trusteeship questions, and
the veto. In an early East–West controversy, the United States and the Soviet Union
quarreled over who should preside at Conference meetings. The Latin Americans
promoted Argentine membership over East European objections, and they were especially active in preserving the right of collective self-defense for regional (e.g. inter-
American) organizations. On trusteeship and colonial territories the Soviets often
sided with the ex- or anticolonial countries. And finally, almost all the small powers
objected to the veto provisions agreed to at Yalta by the great powers (a North–South
issue we would call small power or UN supranationalism).

3. Bloomfield, *The United Nations and U.S. Foreign Policy*, p. 10.

4. *United Nations Review* (April 1963), p. 12.

reinterpreted East–West and North–South voting and additional unrotated voting dimensions to identify (1) *self-determination* or (2) *cold war* issues (distinct from 1952 onward); (3) frequent attempts by the U.S. and the small powers to increase UN *supranationalism;* and (4) distinctive voting on *Palestine* and similar problems. Votes distinguishing liberal or conservative Western positions on colonial issues, particularly regarding *intervention against South African racial policies,* also regularly appeared. The names that have been suggested for the main voting components at the various Assemblies are presented, along with a brief mention of their specific content, in Table 7.1 below.

Table 7.1. The Continuity of Issues before the General Assembly (select rotated factor names, 1947, 1952, 1957, 1961)

|  | 1947 | 1952 | 1957 | 1961 |
|---|---|---|---|---|
| *Cold war issues* | F1. East vs. West (Cold war and colonial) | F5. Cold war (Korea and membership) | F1. Cold war (Korea, membership, testing) | F3. Cold war (membership) |
| *Self-determination* |  | F1. Self-determination (economic and colonial) | F2. Self-determination (economic and colonial) | F1. Self-determination (South Africa, East vs. West) |
| *Palestine questions* | F4. Palestine partition | F3. Palestine and Tunisia | — | F4. Palestine and West Irian |
| *UN supra-nationalism* | F6. Genocide (supranationalism) | F2. Supranationalism (repatriation, moderation) | F3. Supranationalism (UNEF, testing) | F2. Supranationalism (Rwanda and Burundi, UNEF, Congo) |
| *Anti-intervention* | F5. SW Africa (trusteeship) | F4. Indians and race in South Africa | F4. UN commitment (South Africa) | F9. Evacuate Rwanda and Burundi |

In 1947, the rotated factor pattern still did not distinguish most of the colonial issues from general East–West issues and the cold war. By 1952, however, anti-Old European voting on self-determination issues was quite different from cold war voting positions. In 1957, this trend continued, with Chinese membership questions the main evidence of the cold war struggles in the United Nations. Self-determination alignments continued on many economic and colonial issues. Typically, self-determination questions have produced fairly unified Old European minorities with most Latin American states somewhere between the European and the anticolonial position. Perhaps because of the sudden influx of unaligned African states, Latin American states moved closer to the Western position on East–West issues in 1961. Cold war voting (again mostly on membership questions) was again distinct from the self-determination issues occupying the Assembly.

Fourteen years after Palestine partition Israel's relations with her neighbors were still a principal concern of the General Assembly. Even as recently as 1952 Soviet bloc nations did not always side with the Arab countries on these issues. But as the Soviets began to vote more and more with the Moslem states on Palestine and issues like UN mediation of Tunisian and West Irian independence, the Latin states moved closer to the American position. In 1961 a sharp split between the Brazzaville group and other Africans prevented these issues from appearing solely as self-determination concerns, while heightening their similarity to cold war alignments.

Attempts by the smaller members of the United Nations to impose their will on the larger and wealthier powers, including most of the colonial states as well as the Soviet Union, appeared in all four of the Assembly sessions studied. Although in 1947 a Convention on Genocide produced the sole example of this alignment, since then many of the most significant decisions of the Assembly have had a supranationalism aspect, often linked to a fear of war among the great powers (e.g. regarding genocide and Suez).[5] In 1952 a Korean prisoner repatriation compromise suggested by India loaded heavily on a supranationalism factor, as did several moderate decolonialization measures. In 1957, the appropriations for UNEF also revealed an underlying conflict over a supranational role for the UN. Similarly, at the Sixteenth Session (the fall of 1961 and the spring of 1962), fateful decisions about Rwanda and Burundi,

---

5. American aloofness from the Genocide Convention recommended by the Assembly suggests that the American vote for speeding up its discussion is not good evidence of commitment to small power supranationalism. Inis Claude, *Swords into Plowshares*, p. 399, attributes this reticence to a domestic reluctance to support the development of international standards of economic and social policy. America's continued reluctance to subscribe to the Conventions of the International Labor Organization reinforces this view.

UNEF, and the United Nations Force in the Congo appeared to hinge on supranationalism concerns of the United States and most smaller nations.[6]

Special problems arising from intervention in colonial or ex-colonial African territories have also produced distinctive voting dimensions since the beginning of the United Nations. When liberal humanitarianism, Charter principles, or political pressures have moved Latins, Scandinavians, and the United States away from their usual self-determination alignments toward intervention in South African domestic affairs, the most noninterventionist Latins and Europeans have found themselves in an even smaller minority. In 1947, and also in 1957, some East European states had somewhat similar reservations on these and related issues. Depending on the severity of the situation and the action called for in the resolution, the result has been that racial problems in South Africa and trusteeship status for South West Africa have appeared as either self-determination (East–West) issues or anti-interventionist alignments isolating a few Northern powers and occasional conservative Latin support. Factors for 1947, 1952, and 1957 distinguishing the anti-interventionists are listed in the fifth row of Table 7.1. In 1961, all roll calls on South African policy had either become controversial self-determination issues or were virtually unanimous. Anti-interventionist Europeans were again isolated, however, in their reservations regarding the evacuation of Rwanda and Burundi. Several unimportant committee roll calls on African questions evoked a similar alignment.

Although the conflicts underlying UN voting were not identified as such in the theoretical literature discussed in Chapter 1, it should not be inferred that proof of their existence is solely dependent on the body of statistics presented in this book. One reason for confidence in the overall interpretation of continuing Assembly conflicts is the remarkable stability with which the factors have appeared.

---

6. Although there is a fairly high correlation between supranationalist voting and a country's smallness, the United States is a significant exception. This position is in part due to widespread (but often vague) support for the UN from the American public and its leaders, the preeminence of United States influence, and repeated coincidences of the American national interest and the UN's peacekeeping concerns. Changes in two of these variables—decreasing Congressional support and declining American influence—suggest that American commitment to UN supranationalism is likely to diminish, at least relative to earlier positions.

If the first analysis could be thought of only as a way of generating interpretive hypotheses, certainly the results for the next three analyses must be taken as at least partial confirmation of these interpretations.

Another more important reason for confidence in the findings comes from the ease with which practitioners of the diplomatic art understand such descriptions. In fact, for at least some of them, predictions of voting outcomes must be made in terms of how likely it is that an issue will conform to one of several basic factors or conflicts in Assembly voting. In the words of one experienced diplomat:

> Pakistan . . . as a member of CENTO [likes] to vote with the the West, but is also sensitive to Afro–Asian opinion, particularly sensitive to opinion in Moslem countries and strong on self-determination (Kashmir). A Western canvasser can therefore safely count on Pakistan's vote in a direct East–West controversy (Cuba, Hungary) but must make separate calculations if relevant racial, religious or colonial factors are involved. For example, in a "colonialist" issue where the "Moslem" factor tells on the "colonialist" side (Cyprus), or where the Kashmir issue comes into play (Goa), the West may reasonably expect Pakistan's support. On the other hand, on a straight racial issue (*apartheid*), or an issue where a Western power is, or has been, in conflict with Moslem populations (Suez, Algeria, Tunisia, Israel), Pakistan will be the most anti-colonial Afro–Asian. On such issues where both anti-colonialism and the cold war are involved—for example the Soviet moves on the liquidation of colonialism—accurate prediction of a Pakistan vote becomes impossible.[7]

In this view anticolonialism, the cold war, Moslem questions (like Palestine), and intervention against South Africa on questions of apartheid correspond to factors we have discussed. Only supra-

7. Conor Cruise O'Brien, *To Katanga and Back*, p. 18. In interviews at the United Nations several diplomats concurred with the interpretations offered in this paragraph. One of them even felt the distinctions were obvious ones. If they are, other analysts have certainly had difficulty in agreeing on any particular set of them. Content analysis of Assembly debates and further interviewing of Assembly delegates, together with further roll-call analyses similar to those presented above, should prove useful in ascertaining diplomatic perceptions as well as ways to predict what O'Brien calls the "impossible."

nationalism, perhaps the dominant issue in the Congo crisis, is overlooked.

A final means of validating the continuity of such factors is given in Table 7.2. There, factor scores derived from factor patterns for four different sessions are intercorrelated. For both the first two unrotated factors and the five most frequent rotated ones, continuity from year to year is quite high: only one correlation out of seventeen for proximate years is below 0.50 in magnitude, while only four correlations between adjacent Assemblies are below 0.70. Realizing that at least four years have elapsed between the sessions being studied, remembering that newer Assembly members and newer issues are likely to change voting alignments, and allowing for problems of measurement error, we nonetheless find a general rule. From one Assembly to another, *at least half of the variance in policy positions (factor scores) can be explained by similar voting alignments from a previous period in the history of the United Nations.* For some alignments (e.g. East–West voting on self-determination), predicting three quarters of future roll-call variance does not seem out of the question—if we can be sure which roll calls will load on which factors, and to what extent.

Correlations between the earliest and most recent appearances of an alignment in our data suggest, for the most part, an even higher degree of super-issue continuity. For long-time members of the Assembly, East–West factor scores from the Second Session are almost identical with those from the Sixteenth! The actual correlation is an astonishingly high 0.88. For self-determination alignments, the analogous correlation is almost as high: $r = 0.84$. Cold war and, to a lesser extent, North–South alignments have remained remarkably similar.

Even examining some of the smaller correlations between Assembly sessions gives the impression of recognizable super-issue continuity. Genocide alignments in 1947 correlate moderately with supranationalism scores in 1961 ($r = 0.53$), probably because fewer Old Europeans are willing to go as far in the antisupranational direction on UNEF and ONUC as they did on less significant questions regarding the Genocide Convention. Arab states have also been increasingly skeptical about UN supranationalism. From 1947 to 1952, 1952 to 1957, and 1957 to 1961, however, supranational

# Table 7.2. Correlations between Factor Scores from Different General Assemblies *

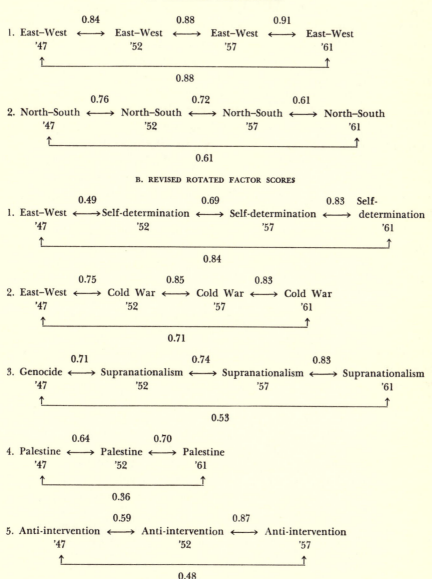

1. East–West '47 ←→ (0.84) East–West '52 ←→ (0.88) East–West '57 ←→ (0.91) East–West '61

0.88

2. North–South '47 ←→ (0.76) North–South '52 ←→ (0.72) North–South '57 ←→ (0.61) North–South '61

0.61

B. REVISED ROTATED FACTOR SCORES

1. East–West '47 ←→ (0.49) Self-determination '52 ←→ (0.69) Self-determination '57 ←→ (0.83) Self-determination '61

0.84

2. East–West '47 ←→ (0.75) Cold War '52 ←→ (0.85) Cold War '57 ←→ (0.83) Cold War '61

0.71

3. Genocide '47 ←→ (0.71) Supranationalism '52 ←→ (0.74) Supranationalism '57 ←→ (0.83) Supranationalism '61

0.53

4. Palestine '47 ←→ (0.64) Palestine '52 ←→ (0.70) Palestine '61

0.36

5. Anti-intervention '47 ←→ (0.59) Anti-intervention '52 ←→ (0.87) Anti-intervention '57

0.48

* Data are taken from Appendix. In each correlation, data are from only those countries present at both sessions.

alignments have undergone relatively slight alterations (the lowest correlation being 0.71).

Most dramatically, the 1952 shift of the Soviet bloc in the Arab direction on Palestine related questions, and, less dramatically, the growing Latin American support for Palestine resolutions, explain the rather marked change in Palestine alignments from 1947 to 1961. Stronger intervening links suggest, however, that the identity of the super-issue was preserved, even if alignments did change. Anti-interventionist alignments, for which reliable factor scores in 1961 are not available, also show considerable continuity.[8]

To recapitulate, these findings suggest that at least five distinct, interpretable, and relatively frequent voting alignments have regularly appeared in Assembly voting: self-determination, the cold war, supranationalism, Palestine problems, and anti-interventionism, particularly regarding South African policies. The cold war and self-determination have partly reflected East–West voting alignments, as have Palestine questions more recently. Supranationalism, and perhaps anti-interventionism, have more nearly resembled North–South voting differences. The fact that the voting alignments on these issues in any particular year are largely uncorrelated among themselves means that knowing an unidentified state has a particular score on any one of these super-issues (say, the cold war) does not help to predict its position on self-determination and supra-nationalism issues. All five super-issues need to be accounted for in any comprehensive analysis of voting conflicts within the United Nations.

### THE CHANGING PROMINENCE OF UN CONCERNS

While the substance (but not the particulars) of UN concerns and related geopolitical voting alignments have reappeared with remarkable continuity in important Assembly roll calls, our second main finding is that East–West voting has increased since the

8. Two other low correlations deserve at least passing notice. The 0.49 association between rotated East–West scores in 1947 and 1952 self-determination scores reflects the composite nature of the 1947 factor (which is also used in the cold war row of Table 7.2) and the exceptional anti-Old European alignment at the Seventh Session. The 0.61 correlation between 1957 and 1961 North–South scores, while moderately high, indicates the somewhat ambiguous nature of this alignment—all four rotated factors had considerably more continuity between the Twelfth and Sixteenth sessions. Anti-interventionist scores for 1947 and 1957 correlate about 0.50.

beginning of the United Nations. Together these conclusions seriously question U Thant's "evolving complexity" interpretation of voting alignments in the General Assembly. The trend toward more East–West voting behavior (in which anticolonial and cold war elements are partly fused) is clear. Figure 7.1 indicates that in 1947 just over 40 per cent of the common variation in important roll-call votes was interpretable in East–West terms. By 1961, after a fairly steady rise, this figure was approaching 70 per cent. If present trends continue, voting according to East–West reflexes will actually reach 70 per cent in the next few years. North–South voting, on the other hand, has steadily decreased from more than 20 per cent of the common voting variance in 1947 to less than 15 per cent in 1961. Together these two behavioral dimensions have accounted for at least 65 per cent of the common voting variance in all four

Figure 7.1. The Prominence of East–West and North–South Components of Important Assembly Votes in 1947, 1952, 1957, 1961 (cumulative per cent of common variance) *

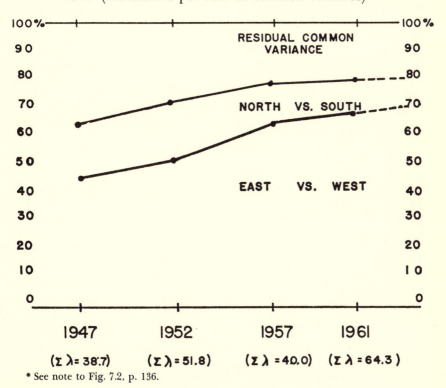

* See note to Fig. 7.2, p. 136.

Figure 7.2. The Relative Prominence of Certain Principal Components of Important Assembly Votes in 1947, 1952, 1957, 1961 (cumulative per cent of common variance, after rotation) *

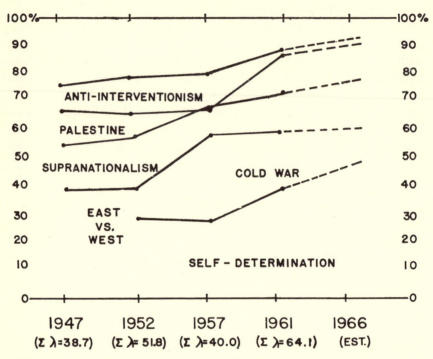

* For 1961, percentages include estimates for 7 important plenary votes not included in the factor analysis (see note 13, Chap. 2). The remaining data may be derived from the unrotated factor patterns presented in Chaps. 3, 4, 5, 6.

of the years we have studied. It seems reasonable to predict that four fifths of all generalizable voting variance will soon be interpretable in these terms.[9]

9. Several cautions are in order in interpreting these results. First of all, until we have examined why nations voted the way they have, we cannot be very sure that present trends will continue. Secondly, data have been analyzed for only four of sixteen Assembly sessions: the lines connecting the data points are plausible ones at best, otherwise gratuitous. Thirdly, the number of votes summarized is rather small; if one strongly East–West vote had been omitted and a highly North–South vote included in its place in our set of important roll calls, the data points for that particular year would have varied about 2%. More omissions would have compounded the error. This problem is more serious regarding the smaller issue category subdivisions presented in Figure 7.2 below. In defense of presenting Figures 7.1 and 7.2, it should be noted that the trends described have been fairly stable ones over

Plotting the relative prominence of our different rotated factors again confirms and amplifies these conclusions. In Figure 7.2 we see that East–West issues (more particularly self-determination and the cold war) have accounted for from below 40 to nearly 60 per cent of interpretable voting variance after rotation. As we can also see, a distinctive cold war factor was more frequent in 1957 than in either 1952 or 1961. Supranationalism alignments have continued to occur on about 15 per cent of important UN votes. What is more striking, however, is the exhaustiveness of the five most recurrent voting alignments that we have singled out for attention. Including more frequent East–West issues, these five voting dimensions have accounted for from 75 to nearly 90 per cent of the common voting variance in the years studied—and the trend is an upward one.

### CHANGES IN PARTICULAR ALIGNMENTS AND ISSUES

Because of the prominence and continuity of East–West and North–South voting in the Assembly, we shall here summarize changes in state voting positions in these terms. In effect we shall be looking for the "deviant cases" in the overall pattern of continuity of East–West and North–South alignments established in Table 7.2. For those wishing to conduct further analyses of this sort, more detailed data on national policy positions within the UN can be found in Appendix 2.

Figure 7.3 presents the movements of selected states on East–West and North–South unrotated voting dimensions for 1947, 1952, 1957, and 1961. A dozen states somewhat typical of their respective groupings have been chosen to illustrate the trends in voting positions presented. They are the five permanent members of the Security Council, and also Argentina and Mexico from Latin America, Sweden from Scandinavia, India, Egypt, and Ethiopia from the Asian, Arab, and African states. For 1961 the voting position of the Republic of the Congo (Brazzaville) has also been plotted.

For each of the years studied, factor scores derived from original standardized ranks have been plotted for these states. It will be

---

the four years studied—each roll call in itself represents the positions of more than 50 states on a particular issue. The larger set of roll calls used in Chap. 9 also leads to a similar interpretation of substantive trends in the concerns of the General Assembly.

# Figure 7.3. Position of Select States on East–West and North–South Voting Dimensions in 1947, 1952, 1957, 1961

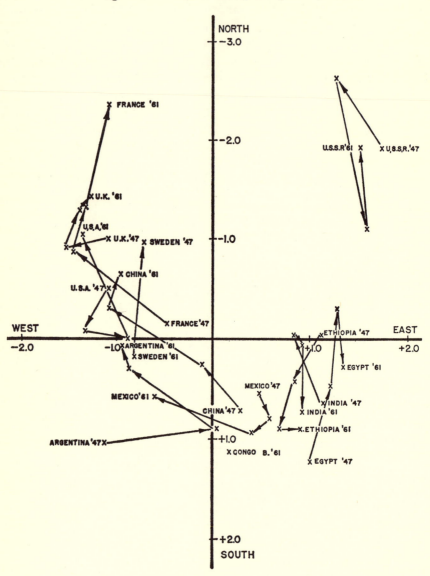

recalled that a factor score of zero indicates the average score on a particular dimension; extreme scores represent greater isolation from the majority position. With these facts in mind, voting trends of the major UN groupings and states may be summarized as follows.

The Soviet states have not moved closer to the majority position on East–West voting; on North–South issues they were extremely isolated during the Korean War, much closer to the majority position in 1957, but not in 1961.

Among Latin states, Mexico (and Haiti) have identified themselves considerably with Afro–Asians on both North–South and, to a lesser extent, East–West issues. Most other Latin states (including Argentina) were also very Eastern in voting on self-determination issues in 1952 (see Figure 4.2 in Chapter 4). The increasing prominence of Afro–Asian states in 1957 seems to have caused the Latin Americans (Argentina in 1957, Mexico by 1961) to move closer to the position of Old Europeans on both East–West and North–South issues. As Figure 6.2 of Chapter 6 also graphically illustrates, the Brazzaville powers have become the new "Latin Americans" of the General Assembly: generally pro-West or neutral on cold war issues, yet strongly anti-European on self-determination concerns.

The Scandinavian states have maintained a fairly consistent pro-colonial stand on self-determination issues in the Assembly, but in 1961 they were more Southern than they had been in any previous year. Although generally pro-West on East–West issues, their position on Chinese membership in 1957 and 1961 (except for Iceland) has been sharply differentiated from that of most other Old Europeans.

Asian states can usually be distinguished as Eastern or Western in their orientations. In 1947, Chinese voting was very similar to India's; by 1957, however, China had moved considerably North–West to become closely identified with the Old European states on *both* North–South and East–West issues. In 1961, similar voting positions were taken by Thailand, Malaya, Japan, and several other pro-Western Asians. The Eastern Asian states have generally remained in the South–Eastern portion of the geopolitical space we have been describing.

Egypt, as a fairly typical Arab state, has been closer to the Northern position on North–South concerns, and generally closer to the

Soviet position on East–West concerns. Her self-determination voting score has not been as high as that for most other African or Arab states because of a tendency (shared with other Casablanca powers, but not Ethiopia since 1947) to vote with the Soviet Union and the more extreme colonial powers against more moderate decolonialization attempts. A similar "turning back" toward the opposition characterized Soviet voting on Chinese representation during the Sixteenth Assembly. The Soviets were not willing to support resolutions which did not make it clear that the Peoples' Republic would actually *replace* the Republic of China in the United Nations (see Figure 6.2, Chapter 6).

Finally, the Western great powers have moved in easily comprehensible paths. Close to the majority position on both East–West and North–South issues in 1947, by 1961 France was, except for South Africa and Portugal, the most isolated Northern power on North–South issues. The United States moved closer to the majority position on North–South issues in 1952 and 1957, returning to a more isloated position in 1961. Relative to the other members of the UN, the United Kingdom's position has been much the same on both North–South and East–West issues for the four years studied.[10]

### STAGES IN UN DEVELOPMENT

Although the most recent years at the United Nations have brought into prominence the caucusing group and committee processes in the Assembly, it has been a "gradual evolution," [11] as was true earlier with respect to the role of the General Assembly

10. In making these and other trend statements in this book, we are assuming factor scores to be cardinal numbers, with a similar zero point and meaningful ratios; otherwise the points for different years could not be plotted together and movements described. Although the United States and the Soviet Union have remained in very similar East–West positions during the years we have studied (thus adding some measure of confidence to our results), one could still argue that the "average" state (with a factor score of zero) has moved East during the last fifteen years, bringing the United States and most other Old European states with it. For example, in 1947 it was difficult for the anticolonial countries to establish a Committee on Information from Non-Self-Governing Territories; by 1961, the Committee was rejected by the more extreme anticolonial states as too conservative in its approach.

11. Thomas Hovet, Jr., "United Nations Diplomacy," *Journal of International Affairs, 17* (1963), 35. The whole issue of this journal was devoted to "Diplomacy in Transition" and discusses the developments mentioned here in much greater detail from an institutional and procedural viewpoint.

and of the Secretary General. The three phases have been high-lighted by such specific events as the Uniting for Peace Resolution, Hammarskjold's role in the Suez crisis, and developments in a post-colonial Congo crisis. Similarly, there has been a remarkable continuity of super-issues and related voting alignments. A preoccupation with the East–West conflict on a regional and perhaps racial basis has increasingly been in evidence. Self-determination issues with their political, economic, and racial components have continued to arise frequently in the postcolonial age. The clash between East and West on these and related matters has apparently become more marked, although significant supranationalist achievements along North–South lines serve to bridge the widening gap between East and West.

The determinants of voting behavior, the resulting distribution of policy positions and power in the Assembly, and related consequences for the political system in the United Nations will now be our principal concerns. This analysis will add other interpretations to the developing issues and alignments that have been uncovered so far.

PART II

The Context of U.N. Politics

# CHAPTER 8

# Party Politics in the General Assembly

## DOMESTIC POLITICS AND INTERNATIONAL POLITICS

A number of attempts have been made in recent years to construct rigorous models of the international system, among the more precise of which are various models of international equilibrium and other examples of systems analysis.[1] Most of those efforts have been directed to the application of models derived from economics or the natural sciences. It may be, however, that we have overlooked a number of possibilities from closely related aspects of political science. For example, there is a substantial body of theory about competitive national political systems which might profitably be applied to international politics.

Our discussion has dwelt at length upon the issues and alignments in the Assembly, in much the same way as studies of national legislative bodies have done.[2] Despite this, the parallel between domestic and international politics may not be fully apparent. National systems are characterized by institutions empowered to make, execute, and interpret decisions binding on their citizens. Though these institutions are not entirely absent from the international system, they are undeniably weak. But in any society cooperative behavior does not depend solely on the actual or potential threat of physical sanctions applied by authority. Nor would such institutions guarantee cooperation. In their comparative study of political integration, Karl W. Deutsch et. al. found the establishment of common governmental institutions and a "monopoly of violence" often more of a hindrance

---

1. See especially George Liska, *International Equilibrium* (Cambridge, Harvard University Press, 1957), and Morton Kaplan, *System and Process in International Politics* (New York, John Wiley, 1957).

2. In particular see Duncan MacRae, Jr., *Dimensions of Congressional Voting* (Berkeley and Los Angeles, University of California Press, 1958).

than a help.[3] Of the wars between 1820 and 1949 involving more than 31,000 casualties, at least half were internal rather than international.[4]

Rules of order are often followed, in both local and international society, because of various kinds of expected gains or losses. A reputation for morality and law-abidingness can be useful, and the contrary reputation damaging. In this respect the United States has an important asset not lightly to be squandered, for to much of its international audience the word of the American government carries a certain presumption of sincerity. Similarly, rules may be followed so that others will also comply on matters of common interest. Despite their hostility, the United States and the Soviet Union regularly avoid certain forms of threatening behavior (sinking "spying" trawlers, "spoofing" each other's radar). On another level, interference with the regular channels of international commerce and postal exchange is generally avoided even though short-term gains might accrue from interference. Retaliatory interference might well produce losses for all parties.

Nor is even the threat of sanctions by other powers all that restrains an actor. Conflict may be mitigated by consensus about proper procedures or by normative considerations. It is sometimes fashionable to allege that law and morality are illusory forces in the world arena, but those who characterize international politics as amoral and lawless sometimes mistake their own *prescription* for true *description*. As in domestic politics, it is highly likely that at least occasionally governmental leaders are influenced by moral considerations.[5] The restraints on biological and chemical warfare form a fine mixture of ethical and strategic considerations.

Furthermore, what Talcott Parsons calls "an underlying structure of cross-cutting solidarities" produces restraint.[6] Even some firmly

3. *Political Community and the North Atlantic Area* (Princeton, Princeton University Press, 1957), p. 105.

4. See Lewis F. Richardson, *Statistics of Deadly Quarrels* (Pittsburgh, Boxwood Press, and Chicago, Quadrangle Books, 1960), pp. 32–50.

5. Allegedly a major factor in the late President Kennedy's decision not to attack Soviet missile bases in Cuba without warning was his conviction that such a course would be morally wrong.

6. "Order and Community in the International Social System," in James N. Rosenau, ed., *International Politics and Foreign Policy* (New York, Free Press, 1961), p. 126. Also see his article "Voting and the Equilibrium of the American Political System," in Eugene Burdick and Arthur J. Brodbeck, eds., *American Voting Behavior,* (Glencoe, Free Press, 1959).

anticommunist governments in Latin America long refused to apply sanctions to Castro—in part because of their established cultural and political ties with Cuba which cut across the communist–noncommunist dimension. We shall discuss these and other sources of restraint in the following pages. It simply is erroneous to think of international politics as anarchic, chaotic, and utterly unlike national politics. We shall examine some of the similarities, as well as some differences, between national competitive systems and the international system.[7]

The world could be thought of as a political system in which the major blocs are analogous to two parties that compete for the favor of the uncommitted voters. (Depending upon their size and cohesion the uncommitted voters might of course be thought of as composing a third party. We will present evidence on this below, especially in Chapter 10, but the presentation immediately following does not depend importantly on any choice between the two- and three-party alternative formulations.) Each "party," including a leader and loyal party members or "partisans," tries to convince "voters" that it is best able to fulfill their needs and respect their normative prescriptions.[8] At this stage of the analysis we shall consider a voter, whether

7. Hans Morgenthau's position that a theory of international politics is but a specific instance of a general theory of politics is well known. For example, see his "The Nature and Limits of a Theory of International Relations," in W. T. R. Fox, ed., *Theoretical Aspects of International Relations* (Notre Dame, University of Notre Dame Press, 1959), p. 15. Several recent pieces have examined the similarities of other political systems to international politics. For comparison with primitive societies and developing nations see Chadwick F. Alger, "Comparison of Intranational and International Politics," *American Political Science Review,* 57 (1963), 406–19; Roger D. Masters, "World Politics as a Primitive Political System," *World Politics,* 16 (1964), 595–620; and Fred Riggs, "International Politics as a Prismatic System," *World Politics,* 14 (1961), 141–81. Perhaps the strongest dissent from this kind of attempt is represented by Stanley Hoffmann in his "International Relations: The Long Road to Theory," *World Politics,* 11 (1958), 346–77. Hoffmann maintains that, unlike national systems, the international system is insufficiently integrated to permit comparison. Though we are well aware that there are major differences, we would maintain that whether they are so great as to destroy the value of comparison is a question to be investigated rather than pronounced upon. Even Hoffman agrees that after much more research comparison could be valuable.

8. Bailey, *The General Assembly,* refers in passing to an "embryonic" party system in the Assembly, but then dismisses the idea on the ground that because voting alignments differ so greatly on different classes of issues one cannot really call it a party system. Perhaps his conclusion results from his greater familiarity with the relatively homogeneous British parties than with heterogeneous American parties where shifting alignments from one issue to the next are commonplace. Peter H. Merkl

neutral or partisan, as equivalent to the government of a particular nation. The United Nations is, obviously, a major arena of competition—it is where the parties do vie for votes, and where the one nation—one vote principle holds. In fact, by providing a forum where the parties must participate in a continuing electoral competition for the allegiance of the neutrals, the United Nations performs a major function in preserving the system's stability. But the United Nations is not the only arena for this kind of competition. By stretching the analogy somewhat we may extend the case to the competition for foreign military bases and allies. Those readers who are disturbed by the one nation—one vote simplification may imagine some kind of "weighted voting" system at work either inside or outside the Assembly.

In applying these ideas to politics in the General Assembly, a deliberative body, we are making our analogy to domestic politics at the level of the national legislature. Thus our voters are equivalent to "elected" representatives who must have a base of power in a local constituency and who ultimately must satisfy (or control) their constituents. But their role as political actors requires them to try to influence other legislators by some combination of bargaining, coercion, and persuasion. Certainly the system is such as to provide some "representatives" with far greater extraparliamentary means of coercing their fellows than is true in national systems. But their ability to achieve their own goals, and to satisfy their constituents, depends heavily on their success in the international "legislative" arena.

Naturally there are differences between national systems and the international model here suggested. There are no periodic elections at which all the legislators must submit themselves for the approval of their constituents, and no regular intervals between the fairly large-scale turnover of representatives. No two of the major democratic countries hold their elections at the same time, and many coun-

("Formation and Cohesion of Supranational Parties in the Consultative Assemblies of the Council of Europe and Western European Union," paper presented to the annual meeting of the American Political Science Association, September 1962) reports that the German delegation is reputed to have the strongest organization of any national delegation to the European bodies, and the Socialists to have the strongest organization of any supranational party. They are, however, the *least cohesive* of their respective groups. Moral: the lack of an obvious party structure does not mean the absence of powerful informal ties.

tries, democratic or totalitarian, are subject to coups which may change the nature of the "representative" at any time. If all representatives were elected simultaneously, the incentives for agreement within the parties might be substantially greater.

As in legislatures, many major votes occur during every session of the Assembly. These skirmishes are quite comparable to votes in a national legislature; no vote results in the kind of complete victory that would eliminate one of the parties from the electoral process. Nor, in the General Assembly, do we often see even such minor victories as could by themselves visibly affect the world distribution of political power. Whatever the reasons such victories may not occur in national legislatures or in the stalemated larger arena of international conflict, the reason they do not occur in the United Nations is that the representatives in that body have carefully avoided giving it the necessary *authority*. This encourages use of the Assembly as a propaganda forum as well as an arena for close political bargaining. Many varied interests are represented, but often there is little incentive to force compromise for the achievement of a common parliamentary program, partly because enforcement of a decision might be virtually impossible.[9]

Seymour Lipset suggests that a major contributor to the emergence of radical politics is the existence of effective channels of communication, informing voters of a potential community of interest and possibilities for joint action.[10] The United Nations, as a forum for promoting debate and the international exchange of ideas, certainly serves as an important means of facilitating communication among the underdeveloped nations. In both the UN and national legislatures the attitudes of individual voters on substantive issues are the subject of public communication in a way that they are not at the individual level in democratic societies—the vote is open, not secret. When the ballot is secret it protects a subordinate from reprisal by his superiors, and it equally protects him from social ostracism by his fellows.[11] A laborer in the "reddest" mining area can vote con-

9. See Arthur N. Holcombe, "The Role of Politics in the Organization of Peace," Commission to Study the Organization of Peace, 11th Annual Report, *Organizing Peace in the Nuclear Age* (New York, Commission to Study the Organization of Peace, 1959), p. 79.

10. *Political Man* (Garden City, Doubleday, 1960), p. 238.

11. See Stein Rokkan, "Mass Suffrage, Secret Voting, and Political Participation," *European Journal of Sociology*, 2 (1961), 132–52.

servative without his choice becoming known to his coworkers unless he wishes to make it known. Party or bloc members in national assemblies or the UN generally have no such protection. Yet even here there are differences between the two on some procedural matters. In the UN, elections of officers—the Secretary-General, the President of the Assembly, committee chairmen—and the filling of vacancies on bodies like the Security Council are always subject to secret ballot.

## LEGITIMACY AND CONSENSUS

In referring to some of the differences between national competitive systems and the international one we have also alluded to some of the similarities. In a more systematic examination of the similarities we shall draw heavily on analyses of the American system, both because it has been intensively studied and because observers agree that it is characterized by much underlying diversity.

In making this comparison we shall be presenting a set of hypotheses about how nations might behave in the United Nations *if* international politics were much like politics within nations. This is in the spirit of "theory as a set of questions," alerting us to variables and relationships we might otherwise overlook. The exercise might usefully be thought of as involving two basic types of questions. The first includes inquiries about the degree to which international politics is like competitive domestic politics, questions which in effect ask whether the similarities are sufficient to make comparison valuable. Though we will have a general answer, not all of the suggested correspondences will be fully established or fully disproven. In particular, it is easier to show structural similarities in two systems than it is to establish the functional similarity of those structures. The second involves questions about the behavior of states and the stability of the international system. Because of intensive research on Britain, the United States, and other countries we know something about the operation and stability conditions of national systems, though we certainly do not know enough. But granted that a useful degree of similarity is suggested by our first set of questions, the subsequent inquiries will, in addition to providing some answers, suggest further research on both kinds of systems.

Most voters, including all the neutrals and even many of the partisans, prefer a world of continuing competition and no final resolution of the East–West division. They probably have preferences as to the party they would wish to see win in a showdown, but it is far better for their self-perceived interests that neither party eliminate the other.[12] This is not merely because of a fear that final victory would be achieved only by the military destruction of at least one antagonist, with the concomitant destruction of many neutrals and partisans. More important, in a competitive world there are many potentialities to be exploited by the voters. Their importance, whether as neutrals or as needed allies, is far greater than their strength would warrant in a world without East–West conflict. Furthermore, they can use their votes on East–West questions to bargain for concessions on other dimensions. Competition between the great powers is likely to produce concessions to the neutrals and the offer of substantial favors in the form of foreign aid, support for anticolonial movements, and help in the achievement of other goals such as security from a local enemy. As we shall see below, conditions of competition may also serve to moderate the ideologies or platforms of the major parties; insofar as the original ideology of neither party appeals to the needs of a neutral, this moderating influence is likely to result in a nearer approximation of his wishes.

Not only does competition provide the neutral with eager suitors for his favor, it furnishes him numerous opportunities to seek actively the fulfillment of his wishes. By the promise of his vote, or the implicit or explicit threat to give it to the other party, he may significantly influence the platform or performance of one or both of the parties in his favor. His influence may be dependent upon his ability to maintain his lobby in some kind of uncommitted position. This is analogous to a major question about interest group politics in national systems—under what conditions will a lobby be more influential as a partisan than with a foot in both camps? The partisan may or may not have substantial control over the politics of his

12. For evidence that this applies to partisans as well as to neutrals see Lloyd Free, *Six Allies and a Neutral* (Glencoe, Free Press, 1959), pp. 33–35. Free cites numerous interviews with members of the Japanese Diet who affirm their attachment to the Western alliance but nevertheless believe that the continuance of East–West competition serves Japanese interests by making the Americans sensitive to Japanese needs. A similar situation surely applies to Poland, where many Polish Communists are well aware that even their limited independence is due to the existence of a rival to the Russians.

leader; the uncommitted may, by playing his hand shrewdly, influence both leaders.

This is not very different from what goes on in democratic national politics, where neither the neutrals nor, in most cases, even the partisans will aid in the elimination of either party. No matter how deeply committed a party is to achieving final victory over its opponents, when it discovers that victory is not a real possibility for the foreseeable future it must become active in a different kind of politics. In Ernst Haas' terms, the result would be "a delicate negotiating process, with the world organization the forum, not of a community conscience or a concert of power, but of counterbalancing forces unwilling to seek a showdown, fearful of alienating friends or neutrals, and therefore willing to make concessions." [13]

Yet the system's stability may be quite fragile. Though neutral voters may much prefer a world where neither party wins final victory, even more vital may be the desperate necessity, in case one side *does* win, of being on the winning side. Thus if either side appeared to be winning one might witness an extremely powerful "bandwagon" effect far in excess of that in stable democracies where no one expects the victors to take drastic reprisals on their former opponents.

In domestic politics, of course, stability is maintained not only by a realization that the long-term interests of most voters depend on the maintenance of an effective opposition, but by a normative element as well. Concepts of legitimacy as well as of interest restrain the partisans. Even Communist parties, in nations where they constitute a major segment of the parliamentary opposition, must at least pay deference to generally accepted norms.

If the idea of competition and competing forces is ever to be legitimatized, it must be through the recognition that all voters share at least some interests in common. A principal mutual interest in the current international arena, though not the only one, is the avoidance of general war. Probably every government can conceive of some conditions to which war is preferable, but also of many other

13. Haas, "Regionalism," p. 240. Cf. also Haas' comment ("Dynamic Environment and Static System," p. 281) : "If the Western political process be conceived, not as dispassionate debate, capped by voting and subject to judicial review, but as the articulate defense of rival group interests in permanent confrontation and subject to cumulative compromises, the UN process is not so very different."

outcomes which are definitely more desirable than war. Unavoidably there is considerable overlap of the views of the two sides, so there are many circumstances both would prefer to general war. The balance of terror, if it remains stable over a long period, may eventually convince each side of its inability to destroy the other at an acceptable cost. From there, and recognizing their mutual interest in avoiding war, each may eventually acknowledge the legitimacy of the opposition and, though not approving of the opposition's policies, may grudgingly admit its right to exist and, within limits, to proselytize. Such a development would be aided by the above mentioned conscious recognition by the neutrals and many of the partisans that their own interests are best served in a system where two or more opposing parties exist. Some such recognition seems to have occurred in the internal politics of England and America.[14] The existence of the United Nations, and the "right" of the other side to take its case to the world body, may eventually contribute to some such development.

Even short-run stability, without the legitimization of the opposition, depends on some degree of consensus on basic values as well as immediate interests. At present there is a *limited* common "frame of reference" between East and West. Without such a consensus, in fact, the idea of competition for the favor of voters would make little sense. As Talcott Parsons has pointed out, both the Communist and Western ideologies place high value on each of the following: economic productivity, political autonomy, and equality.[15] What is more, the elites of the emerging nations, even when they are not confirmed believers in either Marxism or Western liberalism, usually accept these same values. This might not have been the case. Neither productivity nor equality is highly regarded in the traditional cultures of much of Asia and the Middle East, but in most countries

14. Both the Democrats and the Federalists, in the early years of the American republic, regarded themselves as the true interpreters of American doctrine. Only slowly did they become willing to tolerate opposition. Cf. William N. Chambers, *Political Parties in a New Nation: The American Experience, 1776–1809* (New York, Oxford University Press, 1963). The peaceful coexistence controversy within the communist camp does not involve the legitimacy of opposition, but at least turns around the question of whether international politics must be a long-term "system" with "illegitimate" members.

15. "Polarization and the Problem of International Order," in Quincy Wright, William Evan, and Morton Deutsch, eds., *Preventing World War III* (New York, Simon and Schuster, 1962).

the men in power are those at least nominally committed to modernization, not the traditionalists.

Obviously there are sharp limits to this basic consensus. In the world at large conflict arises over two values: socialism vs. free enterprise, and the political freedoms of liberal democracy. Even here, however, the differences can be exaggerated. Western states have, in recent decades, abandoned or restricted free enterprise in many areas of their economies; free enterprise is often valued largely as an instrumental goal, a means of securing political freedom, rather than an aim in itself. Communist societies, on the other hand, give a kind of deference to liberal democracy. However restricted political liberties may be at present, full freedom is promised for the day when the state withers away. Communist leaders are often highly cynical in discussing that day, but the acknowledgement that such a state is desirable does at least show that freedoms are *valued*. Every apparently liberal statement that they make tends, by encouraging popular hopes, to strengthen this very tenuous consensus.

One point should nevertheless be very clear: the existence of a limited value consensus does not preclude, and in fact may produce, the sharpest kind of conflict. Agreement that certain goods are to be valued may only intensify conflict over their distribution. Power over the sharing of *jointly* valued goods is surely a primary goal in current international politics—*who* is to have productivity, political autonomy, or equality? In this sense it will be important to watch the extent to which the underdeveloped states employ the UN as an agency for redistributing wealth. To a substantial degree their efforts have so far been directed more to using the UN as a means of promoting development than to slicing the existing pie differently.[16] Some use of the UN as a redistributive agency could be beneficial on the ground that peaceful change is better than violence. But the continued value of the organization itself may well depend upon

16. One exception is constituted by some modest increases in assessments for technical assistance, voted by the non-European majority. A more serious exception is perhaps the effort to shift the price structure on trade in primary commodities, and another is the attempt to shift most of the expenses for peacekeeping operations onto the great powers. Quite possibly the real reason for the underdeveloped states' restraint on this point is simply the knowledge that they lack the power to enforce redistribution. For a trenchant critique of the idea that consensus on what is to be valued is necessarily conflict-reducing see James Patrick Sewell's "Comment" on Parsons, *Berkeley Journal of Sociology, 6* (1961), 135–46.

keeping the redistribution conflict within "the limits of consensus." [17]

The growth of consensus may depend crucially on a balance of initiatives and rewards. In an overall sense the bases of power may be very unequally distributed, but it is important that the fruits of power, and even power itself, vary among different countries and different policy areas.

> In the course of studying cases of successful amalgamation, we found that it was apparently important for each of the participating territories or populations to gain some valued services or opportunities. It also seemed important that each at least sometimes take the initiative in the process, or initiate some particular phase or contribution; and that some major symbol or representative of each territory or population should be accorded explicit respect by the others.[18]

### ISSUES AND IDEOLOGY

If the parties are to woo voters successfully they must be concerned both with making promises and seeing that their performances, their records, are such that their promises seem plausible. Each party may vary emphasis on the two elements, and each may stress different aspects (the Soviet Union, for instance, was willing to accept a bad blot on its record of international action when it moved against Hungary), but both are nevertheless important. And if a substantial number of voters do not share their ideological goals, the partisans' arguments are likely to turn away from ideological discussion in favor of particular pragmatic platforms and promises. Parties may become increasingly reluctant to commit themselves openly to the goals of a particular set of voters if there is another large set of

17. Inis Claude has suggested that we think of consensus less as positive agreement than as the absence of major disagreement. He talks about "probing the limits of consensus" in cases, such as policy toward South Africa's apartheid regime, where those limits are still not clearly defined. A certain "consensus" exists so long as the Western powers' opposition to near-sanctions is not severe enough for them actually to vote against Afro–Asian resolutions. The Afro–Asians continually try to push those limits back, but they want to avoid outright Western opposition. See his Chap. 1 in John Stoessinger et al., *Financing the United Nations System* (Washington, D.C., The Brookings Institution, 1964).

18. Deutsch et al., p. 55.

voters whose goals are competitive (e.g. American reluctance to make an unequivocal commitment to colonial powers or to anticolonialists).

As ideologies are deemphasized they are likely also to become more ambiguous, giving rise to a split between an esoteric ideology for the inner party members which remains relatively pure and internally consistent and an exoteric, or public, ideology designed to appeal to or at least not to offend a wide variety of sentiments.[19] In recruiting new party members, American Communists, for instance, place little emphasis on the class conflict elements of traditional Marxist thought but rather play to the desires of special groups wanting free speech, civil rights, or the avoidance of "imperialist" war. Yet this difference between the esoteric and exoteric ideologies may cause a nearly intolerable strain producing either a weakening of even the leadership's attachment to the ideology or a situation where it is impossible for the party to hold most of its special interest converts.[20] In the former case conflict between "revisionist" leaders and those who wish to hold fast to the basic ideology is certain.

All these possibilities can be discerned both in the history of the American Communist Party and on the present-day international scene. Of course, in current international politics neither party seems really to anticipate the continued existence of both parties throughout the foreseeable future of the polity. The hope of final, though peaceable, victory, eliminating the need for any subsequent elections, may circumscribe the true, as compared with the apparent, modification of ideology. Once "absolute power" was achieved the forces of ideology would reassert themselves. Yet a contrary hypothesis is also plausible—the real fear of annihilation may induce a party to make its ideology subservient to the pursuit of survival.

The fear of alienating neutral voters may contribute to the formation of party platforms in other ways. In an effort to appeal to competing groups, parties may make quite inconsistent promises, analogous to platforms which call both for more welfare spending

19. Gabriel Almond, *The Appeals of Communism* (Princeton, Princeton University Press, 1954), pp. 68–74, distinguishes between esoteric and exoteric communications.
20. See George Liska, *The New Statecraft* (Chicago, University of Chicago Press, 1961), pp. 48, 206–07.

and for lower taxes. Or a party may select only certain elements of its ideology for campaign emphasis. It is likely to ignore those issues which seem so divisive that almost any position the party might take would alienate more voters than it would attract. The United States government, which stands to antagonize voters whatever its position on colonialism, would surely be not unhappy to see the whole matter dropped. The Soviets, however, who depend upon quite a different set of partisans for their basic support, stand to make a net gain by being anticolonial, so they play up the issue as much as possible.

Unity may be promoted by narrowing the extremes of polarity through crosscutting solidarities. Insofar as voters who adhere to one party belong to or are emotionally attached to organizations including many voters of the other party, they may reduce their demands for fear of losing those with crosscutting solidarities or of causing disbelief in the ranks about the extremists' charges against the other party. There are rather few of these solidarities between the blocs at present; examples are Poland's cultural and emotional predilections for the West and Cuba's political ties to the Soviet bloc while remaining linked by cultural ties with the other Latin American states. Such other nongovernmental bonds as those of the Holy See with Roman Catholics in Eastern Europe also should not be ignored. Many more attachments exist, however, between neutrals and members of the two major blocs. They include formal organizations like the Nordic Council and the British Commonwealth, as well as nongovernmental bonds like Yugoslavia's Communist party ties, and links between neutralist and pro-Western Moslem nations. The role of these crosscutting solidarities may well expand. As discussed in Chapter 1, a kind of developing cooperation and contact across many lines is precisely what adherents to the functionalist school of analysis expect.

Party competition not only may affect the issues chosen for stress and the positions taken, it can give rise to a tendency to avoid the explicit discussion of policy. Attention and effort may be concentrated on the politics of nominating and electing men to office. Heterogeneous groups who could not be brought together on any explicit set of policy statements may nevertheless be able to combine for the purpose of winning elections and distributing offices.

It is of course difficult to draw a sharp distinction between procedural and substantive issues. The meaningful procedural issues are usually important, after all, because how they are resolved will have potentially serious effects on substance. Yet within democratic nations procedural issues arise fairly often on major matters. Discussion of substantive matters under a procedural guise often serves important functions. It can mask the intensity of feeling and the depth of disagreement on substantive matters. It also provides cross-pressured states with an opportunity to avoid committing themselves too publicly. A representative who would not dare to oppose a measure openly may feel he can safely vote to return it to committee for "further study." Presidential nominating conventions in the United States are often hotly contested affairs, yet the delegates must always be acutely aware of the need to maintain party unity agains the external opposition. Many of the key votes at these conventions occur on "procedural" matters, as on which of two competing state delegations to seat.[21] The procedural vote is then often a means of expressing disagreement and reaching decisions without damaging too badly whatever underlying consensus exists.

At least three kinds of procedural issues arise repeatedly in the Assembly: questions of agenda—whether and when to consider an issue; credentials—seating new states or recognizing a new government as entitled to replace the representatives of its predecessor; and "importance"—whether an issue constitutes an "important" matter and therefore requires a two-thirds majority for passage. By these criteria procedural issues have more often been the subject of "important" votes (important here in terms of the criteria for inclusion in the factor analyses) in recent years than previously. The proportion of procedural votes rose from 8½ per cent in 1947 and 6 per cent in 1952 to 18 per cent in 1957 and 14 per cent in 1961.[22] And this was despite the fact that one might have expected procedural votes to be common in the early years as precedents were established for the orderly transaction of parliamentary business. Thus there is evidence that delegations are beginning to adopt

21. Perhaps the most striking recent cases are the Republican national convention of 1952 and that of the Democrats in 1964.

22. In 1947, however, we excluded from the factor analysis ten roll-call votes on the admission of new members, each vote on a different state and with virtually the same alignment. Inclusion of these "spite votes" would reverse the trend. For data on *all* (not just important) roll-call votes, however, Thomas Hovet found no clear trend in the proportion of procedural votes from 1946 to 1958. Cf. *Bloc Politics*, p. 18.

parliamentary methods which seek not to increase dissensus unnecessarily.[23]

We shall refer below to the effect of various distributions of attitudes among the population, but it is important also to recognize the effect of various *intensities* of preference. If those who hold the most extreme attitudes also hold them most intensely, a serious threat to the system's stability exists, especially if the extremists are numerous.[24] The influx of new voters, the emergent nations, into the international arena has meant not only that most voters now prefer a "middle" solution to cold war problems, but that most voters are relatively apathetic in a particular sense. That is, the particular issues presented by the two parties' ideologies really have little appeal to them, so that they would not care greatly which was the victor. Their strong preferences are reserved for what are to them private matters—the independence, unification, and development of their own countries, by whatever methods. They are thus not apathetic toward politics in general, but merely to the issues presented by the parties. As noted above, in their eyes the achievement of their goals may depend upon the absence of a clear-cut victory for either side. This necessity for two-party competition might, in the long run, be turned into a virtue, as the existence of the competitors took on important aspects of legitimacy in the neutrals' eyes.

One is here reminded of the argument by the authors of *Voting* about the role of the "independent" or, more accurately, the apathetic voter.[25] If the majority of voters held strong preferences the system might quickly become unworkable; only so long as most voters are relatively uninvolved in the ideological arguments of the partisans is the peaceful resolution of conflict possible.

### THE ELECTORAL SYSTEM

Institutions also are relevant. It has often been said that single-member constituencies promote the emergence of two parties since

23. Party cohesion in legislative voting is higher on such issues than on more substantive matters. See Julius Turner, *Party and Constituency* (Baltimore, Johns Hopkins University Press, 1951), p. 53.

24. See Dahl, *A Preface to Democratic Theory*, Chap. 4.

25. Bernard Berelson, Paul Lazarsfeld, and William McPhee, *Voting* (Chicago, University of Chicago Press, 1954), pp. 314–15.

small minorities in any district cannot hope, by themselves, to gain power.[26] Do the "single-member districts" of the international system (one country, one government) make a similar contribution?

Federalism, it is sometimes alleged, contributes to the stability of a system threatened by many potential cleavages.[27] Nowhere in the American federal government is there a single locus of power, not even the Presidency, whose commands will receive obedience from officials everywhere. National leaders can control the nomination of local candidates only by enlisting the support of local leaders, and they are often unsuccessful. Federalism, reinforced by the electoral college, forces parties to have a decentralized structure appropriate for campaigning on a state-by-state basis. This encourages them to make contradictory promises, or at least to emphasize different aims in different areas. These factors reinforce the tendency noted above for the parties in a two-party system to concentrate on winning elections rather than on making explicit policy formulations. And the fact that national, state, and local elections are staggered is likely to prevent a party from getting complete control throughout the nation—there is always a new election taking place somewhere. The staggering of Free World elections contributes to a similar decentralization in the international arena.

By forcing partisans to avoid emphasizing issues which might divide the polity these institutional factors can contribute heavily to the long-run stability of the system, even if they sometimes exasperate the partisans. And the federal system, superimposed on a political system characterized by regional cleavages, contributes to the maintenance of long-run competition in another way. Just because there are various state elections as well as national ones, each party can depend on a safe home base from which it can hope to expand. Under competitive conditions the existence of safe regional bases may contribute to the moderation of party policies. Because the leaders know their regional bases are secure they feel free to neglect their home interests in order to woo the uncommitted, and often people in the home area find there is little they can do to remedy the neglect. If regional demands should become too forceful, however,

26. This allegation is also disputed, but for an argument in its favor see Lipset, *The First New Nation*, Chap. 9.

27. Several of the hypotheses in this section are derived from Austin Ranney and Willmoore Kendall, *Democracy and the American Party System* (New York, Harcourt Brace, 1956), pp. 490–99.

or should the leaders of either party despair of attracting the neutrals, these regional home bases could of course become disruptive forces leading to possible "civil" war.

### THE DISTRIBUTION OF PREFERENCES

Whether the two parties will become more or less extreme in their stands is a crucial question. Currently there is some evidence that the international party leaders have moderated their cold war policies, at least those parts which are explicitly stated. Most of this can be seen as an attempt to win the support of neutrals and to hold the less extreme partisans. But whether these developments merely represent temporary tendencies, likely to be reversed in the near future, depends in large part upon the underlying distribution of voters' preferences. This leads to discussion of a variable which could promote system stability, but could also lead to the breakdown of the system and either conflict or the emergence of a polycentric system.

As Anthony Downs has shown, *if* voters favor moderate or middle-of-the-road policies the two parties' policies will converge toward the center.[28] The possible loss of extremists will not deter their movement toward the center and toward each other because there will be so few voters to be lost at the margin compared with the number to be gained in the middle. This situation is illustrated in the following figure. The horizontal axis measures degree of preference for some policy, the extent to which economic control ought to be centralized, for instance, with zero representing no centralization and 100 complete central control; the vertical axis indicates the number of voters preferring any given policy position. If voters' preferences are such that most voters are found at a single mode around 50, then both party 1 and party 2 will tend, over time, to move toward that mode.

28. *An Economic Theory of Democracy* (New York, Harper, 1957), p. 118. We owe to Chap. 8 the method of presentation and many of the insights in the following paragraphs. Donald E. Stokes has made a penetrating criticism of the Downs model ("Spatial Models of Party Competition," *American Political Science Review*, 57 (1963), 368–77). Among his points are: (1) More than one dimension (issue) may be politically relevant, with different preference distributions for each dimension. (2) The salience of various dimensions may change over time. (3) Leaders, partisans, and neutrals all may have different perceptions of salience and preference distributions. We have, however, tried to take these points into account.

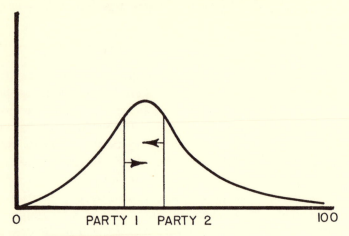

But if preferences are distributed bimodally, as in Figure 8.2, the outcome is likely to be quite different. Attempted shifts to the center may meet with the refusal of extremists to support either party if both become alike, or at least similar. Since the potential loss at the margin to a third party is so great, the parties may retain quite different programs.

Figure 8.2. Two-Party Divergence When Preferences
Are Distributed Bimodally

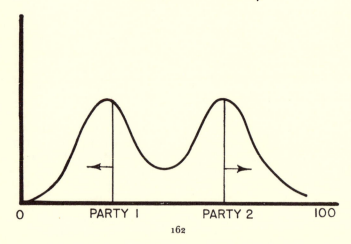

The apparent moderation of some Soviet and American cold war policies might be traced to a world preference pattern like that indicated in Figure 8.1, which the bloc leaders have just now begun to comprehend fully. But if we introduce a dynamic element, the moderation may be traceable to a shift in the world preference pattern caused by the "enfranchisement" of new voters. As the African and Asian countries have achieved independence and admission to the United Nations they have become new voters for whom the parties must compete. Whereas at the end of World War II preferences were distributed bimodally as in Figure 8.2, by the end of the 1950s the addition of new voters to the ranks had created another peak toward the center.

Figure 8.3. Two-Party Convergence with the Creation of a Single Center Mode by the Enfranchisement of New Voters

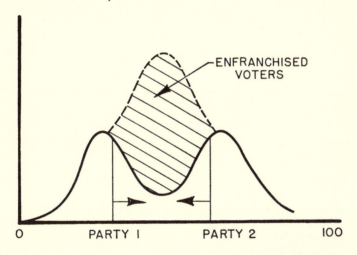

Figure 8.3 illustrates one possible outcome of the enfranchisement of new voters. With the emergence of a new single mode at the center, the parties' policies move toward each other. But the result need not be that above, for the size of the center mode is crucial. If it were much smaller, not significantly higher than the modes at 1 and 2 and separated from each of the original peaks by a valley, the most likely outcome would be not the convergence of 1 and 2 but the creation of a third party, a "neutral bloc."

Any of these outcomes can of course occur only if both parties actually play the parliamentary game; that is, only if both do in fact seek to achieve voting majorities. This need not happen in the international system so long as either side retains some hope of attaining its majority through extraparliamentary methods, as by picking off opposing states one by one through subversion. In the period between 1957 and 1959 Moscow seems actually at times to have regarded the UN as an organization it might eventually come to control. The events of 1959 to 1961, especially the Russians' inability to direct the Congo operation, seem to have burst this bubble. But on several occasions, once its defeat on a particular issue was clear, the Soviet Union refrained from vetoing or opposing a resolution sponsored by the underdeveloped countries. When it could not win on some dimensions it sometimes backed down from positions that might have prejudiced its efforts to win majorities on other issues.[29]

If the Russians were to give up serious attempts to win majorities —and thus lose a major incentive to adopt moderate centristic stances—there would be no reason to look for two-party convergence. One party, such as the West led by the United States, might indeed move toward the middle to pick up votes without encouraging similar behavior by its opponent. In such a case the mean position of the whole Assembly would shift eastward, but the attitude distribution would remain bimodal. Some assessments of the current international situation would argue that this is roughly what has happened, and in the following chapters we shall examine our data with this possibility, as well as more hopeful ones, in mind.

A WORLD OF MANY ISSUES

Finally, it is time to deal more explicitly with a major finding of Part I—the multidimensional voting pattern of the Assembly. In this chapter we have been speaking largely as though there were only one basic alignment. Given the pervasiveness of East–West issues in recent years (nearly 70 per cent of the common variance in 1961) this is not as unrealistic an assumption as it might be. Yet we must bring other issues into the analysis, especially in light of the rather complex configuration that appears on the rotated factor pattern.

Any proliferation in the number of issues brought before the UN

29. An excellent example is the Soviets' reluctance to continue their insistence on a *troika*.

should, in the long run, contribute to stabilizing the system. As long as the United States saw the UN primarily as a forum for promoting Western cold war interests, the independents and neutral-leaning partisans found themselves in a relatively weak bargaining position. But now, with the greater prominence of supranationalism and self-determination issues, many nations have substantial freedom of maneuver.[30] They can bargain and engage in logrolling, exchanging support on security issues for votes against colonialism. As the authors of *The American Voter* declare,

> If an electorate responds to public affairs in terms of one or a few well-defined and stable ideological dimensions on which there is little movement of opinion, political controversy will be relatively tightly bounded and the possibilities of party maneuver . . . relatively circumscribed. But if an electorate responds to public affairs in a less structured fashion, politics will be more fluid, party strategy will include or may consist primarily of exploiting new dimensions of opinion, and the likelihood of party alternation in power will be greater.[31]

To the extent that there are a number of voting dimensions, or super-issues, we must modify the two-party (or three-party) model implicit in the earlier parts of this chapter. If there are two major super-issues or uncorrelated dimensions there are by definition at least four different coalitions, of which two operate on each dimension. Only a multiparty model or, if the groupings were too informal or inflexible to merit the term parties, a multigroup model, would then suffice. In fact the present situation probably falls somewhere between the two-party and the multiparty characterizations. There are a number of dimensions, but (in the unrotated factor analysis) the East–West alignment is much more prominent than the others. We shall return to this point in the following chapters. In any case, U Thant's view, cited Chapter 1, emphasizes the growth of a multidimensional pattern of issues, with a new importance attached to what we have termed the North–South conflict. One implication of this view is that leaders and partisans of both major cold

30. Note that this decline of cold war prominence occurs on the *rotated* factor pattern, and implies additional freedom for the small powers from the great ones. But the increasing pervasiveness of the East–West alignment on the *unrotated* pattern impels a less optimistic assessment. Cf. Chap. 10 below.

31. A. Campbell, P. Converse, W. Miller, and D. Stokes, *The American Voter* (New York, John Wiley, 1960), p. 550.

war blocs may some day decide that they share a common interest in preserving their wealth from confiscation by an aroused underdeveloped bloc.

If the proliferation of issues contributes to stability by making bargaining possible, it may also help in other ways. A cumulative pattern of compromises and concessions can set up expectations of peace, stability, and coexistence which will constrain the leaders. Even if concessions are made purely as temporary expedients and not out of any desire to promote such expectations, they are likely to give rise to hopes that it will be costly to disappoint.[32]

The rise of issues other than the cold war may make it possible for some partisans even of the tightly organized Communist bloc occasionally to deviate from the party norm. One can hardly conceive of the Soviets tolerating deviation on a major cold war threat in the near future, but on other matters a vote against the bloc, or an abstention, might possibly be overlooked. By providing opportunities for deviation on issues that are not central to the Soviet Union's security we may contribute to a wholesome precedent. Once deviation is tolerated at all it may be difficult to stop it short of a certain fluidity even on more vital matters.

The United States could conceivably gain on another way from the proliferation of issues, properly controlled. The West is in many ways conservative, seeking to restrain the pace and scope of economic and social change. Conservative groups traditionally have maintained themselves in part by yielding significantly to the program of their opponents, but also by promoting issues not directly bound up with class or status issues. Essentially conservative parties tend to emphasize "style" issues like efficiency in government or morality, or to stress personality in their campaigns.[33] To protect their own positions and to avoid disruption of the society they must prevent the lines of political division from becoming identical with those of economic cleavage. Both the Republicans and the British Conservatives expect to get about one third of the working class vote; their ability to do so both indicates a significant substantive consensus and helps to maintain their societies' basic procedural consensus.

32. Note, however, that to serve this function the issues must be ones about which there is *disagreement*. Matters about which there is consensus contribute in other ways. See Haas, "Regionalism," p. 250.

33. Lipset, *Political Man*, pp. 281–82.

# CHAPTER 9

# Who Initiates, With What Success?

The models presented in the last chapter suggest why several ideas drawn from the study of domestic political institutions are relevant to the understanding of world politics in the General Assembly. The model's hypotheses about the conditions of consensus and stability will be applied to the main conflicts in the General Assembly in the chapters below. Included in these discussions will be an appraisal of changes in the distribution and intensity of policy positions, changes in the environmental influences on these positions, the distribution of legislative success, and the resulting consequences for the stability of international politics.

Commentators taking a political pluralism approach to international politics will argue that a proliferation of issues in the Assembly, the growth of crosscutting allegiances, and a greater diffusion of power are more likely to produce a cumulative pattern of compromises and concessions among Assembly groups than are the claims and counterclaims of a bipolar world. Since we have already considered trends in the proliferation of Assembly voting dimensions in previous chapters, we shall focus on the pattern of victories, compromises, and defeats that has developed in the General Assembly, substituting the political conflict categories of Part I for less discriminating functionalist distinctions among Assembly issues. We shall ask which groups of nations take which kinds of initiatives, with what degree of success or failure. These findings will help us to assess whether changes in the distribution of legislative influence have contributed to an increasing pattern of responsiveness and compromise within the Assembly.

## MEASURING LEGISLATIVE SUCCESS

A particular advantage of the distinctions made in Part I about the different conflicts pervading the General Assembly is that they allow and even suggest the possibility that the distribution of power and initiative will vary from one issue area to another. Such indeed has been the finding in some recent studies of the distribution of power in certain arenas of domestic American politics. In the present chapter we shall focus on differences in the distribution of legislative success on roll calls dealing with self-determination, the cold war, UN supranationalism, and Palestine questions. In passing, reference will also be made to the kind of successes recorded to date on questions related to intervention in South Africa. Taken together these distinctive conflict dimensions account for approximately 80 per cent of the common variance in Assembly voting; the remaining factors of general interest (see Table 7.1) have not regularly reappeared through time or have not occurred with sufficient frequency for comparative analysis.

The principal items for the analysis of legislative influence in the Assembly will be those important roll calls with their highest loadings on one of the substantive conflicts in the Assembly mentioned above. In order to enlarge the set of votes being analyzed, we have added all other roll calls similar in substance and alignment to the important ones already included.[1]

Results will also be more reliable if roll-call sponsorships and successes are grouped in some meaningful way: the groups to be discussed correspond to or include most of the principal caucusing groups in the Assembly, projected backward in time to the beginning of the General Assembly. In deciding on these groupings, evidence from the factor score maps in Part I and certain other analytical and environmental considerations were taken into account.[2]

Latin American and Arab regional caucusing groups, for example, have attempted to act in concert, at least since the beginning of the United Nations. Their history of cooperation and consultation argues for including both groupings. Starting with only Liberia and Ethiopia in 1945, the African grouping (which for our purposes will exclude the Arab states of North Africa) has more recently grown in

1. In two assignments of the previously omitted roll calls to main issue categories, over 80 per cent of these roll calls were identically classified. Palestine and related questions were the most difficult ones to distinguish.

2. In the maps of Part I, only caucusing groups already in existence were shown. Analytical convenience and the tasks of Part II require the backward projection of such groupings, as well as redefinitions of a nonoverlapping sort.

size, self-consciousness, and formal organization, although some of its leaders have known each other since the League of Nations.[3] In geopolitical terms, African states have almost always been Southern on North–South issues, and they have usually been more East than West. Separating geographically and racially different Asian states from Arabs and Africans also seemed appropriate. (Israel and China were excluded because they are not members of the Afro–Asian caucusing group.) Within this region, however, we would not expect political activity to be as coordinated as among members of the Arab and African caucusing groups. These distinctions will allow an exclusive and exhaustive differentiation among Latin, Arab, African, and Asian roll-call initiatives.

The Soviet caucusing group is of course the most cohesive in the General Assembly. Except for Yugoslavia in 1947, both Finland and Yugoslavia (which are sometimes considered East European states in Assembly practice) have been excluded from this group. On voting maps they are quite distinguishable from the Soviet Union; neither do they caucus regularly with the bloc. At the Sixteenth Session Mongolia, but not Cuba, was considered a member of the Soviet bloc.

All members of the West European, Scandinavian, and Benelux caucusing groups were also identified as Old Europeans, along with the United States and the older members of the British Commonwealth. This follows from the usefulness of such a grouping in describing the factor score clusters mapped in I.[4]

Donald Matthews' "index of legislative effectiveness" suggests one way that legislative power can be measured.[5] The first step in such an approach is to determine for each roll-call loading on a

3. See Kock and Triska, "Asian–African Coalition," for details.

4. Alker's decision to work with an aggregate Old European group is in part supported by Russett's effort to delineate sociocultural regions of the world on a similar inductive basis. He found that a group including Scandinavia, the United States, and the Old Commonwealth showed a very high homogeneity and differentiation from other groups. Turkey's pattern was much more like Asia's than like the Western Europeans', confirming its inclusion in the Asian group. Cf. "Delineating International Regions," in J. David Singer, *Quantitative Research in World Politics: International Yearbook of Political Behavior Research,[6]* (New York, Free Press, 1966).

5. See Donald R. Matthews, *U.S. Senators and Their World* (Chapel Hill, University of North Carolina Press, 1960), pp. 278–79. "Legislative effectiveness" is a "batting average" concept. The graphs displayed in the text below have the advantage of showing both relative and absolute directional power ratings: "batting averages" *and* total number of successful initiatives.

factor, say, supranationalism, the positive or negative direction of the *initiative* along the supranationalism dimension. Both the correct super-issue classification and the direction of the resolution along that issue may be identified by comparing a roll call with sets of votes known to correlate highly with the main issues in the Assembly. Graphically the number of initiatives that a group of states made or shared will be shown as a hollow bar form pointing in either a "positive" or a "negative" direction. Finally the number (or fraction, for jointly sponsored resolutions) of these resolutions that succeed by a simple or, if required, a two-thirds majority will also be plotted on the graph by shading on the same bar form the number of successful initiatives. The *ratio of shaded initiatives to total initiatives* would be what Matthews calls an index of legislative effectiveness.[6] Since more attempts and successes mean longer bar graphs, *absolute values of the number of successful initiatives* will also be apparent.

There are both advantages and disadvantages to the legislative success method of power measurement.

1. As in other roll-call studies, roll calls included in the set to be analyzed are considered equally significant initiatives. Even more arbitrarily, when sponsors are from different regions, equal credit for the initiative is assigned to each region. It seems rather inequitable, for example, to give credit for half of a success on a colonial question to the Old Europeans (e.g. the United States) and the other half to Latin Americans (e.g. El Salvador), when the United States may be assumed to be more than an equal sponsor. Nonetheless, the presence of a Latin cosponsor was considered important enough by the United States to solicit it.

2. A related problem is that resolution sponsors may be, to varying extents, "satellites" of a great power.[7] By grouping states so that a whole region gets legislative credit, our measures do not need to distinguish satellites *within* regions. Regional groups such

6. Like Matthews, we have not usually included amendments (unless the subject of roll calls themselves) in the analysis. Thus when a resolution has been watered down by other states the sponsors will get credit for the legislative success only if they still vote in favor of their original resolution. In the several cases where this has not been the case the amending powers have been credited with the initiative.

7. See Robert Dahl, "The Concept of Power," *Behavioral Science, 2* (1957), 201–15. Dahl also suggests treating states whose positions change with the tide of opinion (chameleons) as powerless (p. 213) even when they vote with the majority. By studying initiatives made considerably before the final vote is taken we are reducing the chances that chameleons will appear as influence wielders.

as Latin Americans, Asians, and Old Europeans that are considerably cross-pressured and divided on certain issues may present initiatives interpreted by the Assembly in either or both directions along an issue continuum. Including the *direction* of the influence attempt allows us to see when groups are considerably divided on a particular issue and which elements (e.g. pro-Western Asians) are more successful in their (usually shared) influence attempts.

3. Some students of roll-call analysis have suggested that states with the more intermediate voting positions along an issue dimension will appear more powerful because they are usually closer to the majority position, not because they have exercised more influence.[8] Yet in our data on some issues (like intervention in South Africa) the more moderate states (Old Europeans and some Asians) were most successful, while on East–West issues the extreme Old Europeans were most frequently successful. Therefore the fact that "scale positions" (factor scores) and legislative influence are sometimes related is, instead of a liability, an important help in distinguishing on what issues moderate or extreme groups usually prevail.[9]

4. A related problem is that legislative influence in a more general sense involves more than just the ability to introduce resolutions that receive the required majorities. Diplomats will argue that both the ability to get states outside one's group to sponsor a resolution and the ability to influence the wording of the resolution *before* it is introduced are often more important. Propaganda purposes might even require that a state get a whopping majority *against*

8. See Duncan MacRae, Jr. and Hugh D. Price, "Scale Positions and 'Power' in the Senate," *Behavioral Science, 4* (1959). As noted earlier, Dahl's notion of majority-inclined "chameleons" implies this result. James March, "Influence Measurement in Experimental and Semi-Experimental Groups," *Sociometry, 19* (1956), 260–71, imaginatively handles "chameleons" in an experimental situation by partial correlational techniques. The closeness of an individual's preference orderings to the final group decision is measured, *controlling* for the original undiscussed distribution of preferences in a group.

9. Within the UN, conflict occurs between moderate and extreme groups in the drafting of resolutions for which a variety of sponsors is desired. Sponsors and co-sponsors from Asian, African, and Latin American states are relatively attractive because they are not completely identified with either extreme on an issue: "In [the influence] game it is important to have 'good sponsorship,' that is to say, sponsorship from as far outside the circle of one's known committed supporters as possible. Thus on a hypothetical Latin question, finding Mexico or Brazil out of reach . . . and if even Peru proved sluggish, the US specialist in hemispheric solidarity . . . would turn with a sigh to El Salvador." Similar remarks might apply to France and the Soviet Union. See Conor Cruise O'Brien's perceptive and polemical chapter, "A Delegate at the General Assembly," *To Katanga and Back,* p. 26.

itself if it wants evidence of the incapabilities of the Assembly and justification for actions outside of the United Nations. And, of course, winning resolutions in the Assembly does not insure that the resolutions will have influence outside the Assembly. Communist Chinese intervention in Tibet, Soviet intervention in Hungary, and South African rejection of Assembly directives come immediately to mind. Even milder resolutions have been obeyed only by states that perceive compliance to be in their national interests. In most cases sanctions for not doing so are relatively weak. Other limits of roll-call methods for measuring success will be discussed below.

5. Finally, the small number of roll calls loading on different factors means that the data objectively summarize only a few relatively important decisions. But since there are often several sponsors of a single resolution, the number of overt acts involved is certainly much larger than merely the number of roll calls loading on a particular factor.

### THE DISTRIBUTION OF LEGISLATIVE SUCCESS

Data on legislative effectiveness on the (rotated) East–West conflict in 1947 and self-determination issues for the Seventh, Twelfth, and Sixteenth General Assemblies are presented in Figure 9.1 (self-determination was in 1947 not a distinct voting factor). There appear to have been remarkable changes in initiative and influence. When we recall that the rotated East–West factor in 1947 contained a good many votes on incipient cold war issues like the Greek border dispute (the main source of Old European successes for the factor), the growth in the total number of anticolonial self-determination initiatives becomes clear. Self-determination was by far the most pervasive super-issue at both the Seventh and the Sixteenth Assemblies. Even during the relatively peaceful Twelfth Assembly self-determination roll calls were more common than any other super-issue.[10]

10. Results about the pervasiveness of different super-issues in Assembly roll calls based on the more comprehensive set of roll calls used for the present analysis are remarkably similar to those portrayed in Figure 7.2. If anything, self-determination appears to be even more common than indicated by the $\lambda$s of Part I. For 1961, using more committee votes means that supranationalism and anti-interventionism (South Africa) were more frequent and Palestine questions less frequent than Figure 7.2 suggests.

There have been significant shifts in the balance of initiatives and successes by the major Assembly groups on self-determination questions. As the data clearly show, the situation has changed from relative Old European dominance on merged cold war and self-determination concerns (in 1947 Old Europeans succeeded in declaring the establishment of a Committee on Information from Non-Self-Governing Territories to be an important question requiring two-thirds majorities) to a situation where the Soviet bloc, Asia, Africa, and the Arab countries share most of the voting victories. From the Second Session (when the most notable Asian victories were committee votes on the treatment of Indians in South Africa) through the blistering anticolonial and anti-Yankee resolutions of the Seventh Assembly to the nearly successful Afro–Asian sanction resolutions against South Africa at the Sixteenth Session, we can see how much greater the influence of the Afro–Asian states has become, more even than mere ratios of effectiveness would suggest. In 1947 the Committee on Information from Non-Self-Governing Territories had not even come into existence; in 1952 Afro–Asians and Latin Americans were not able to insure the continuing existence of the Committee; in 1961 the Soviet bloc and a few Afro–Asians had begun to question the usefulness of the Committee while almost all Old Europeans were voting to retain it! In 1961 the vote was not even along self-determination lines.

Similarly the balance of power on South African questions changed a good deal. Whereas in 1947 India failed to get a two-thirds majority for roundtable discussions of the treatment of Indians in South Africa—an East–West question—by 1957 condemnations of South African failure to respect UN resolutions on the same subject were relatively easy to pass. In 1961 the treatment of Indians in South Africa was not nearly as controversial an issue as apartheid in general and in the Seventeenth Assembly *sanctions* against the South African government's policies were passed.

If issues seem to have gone through phases of development, so also have the initiatives of the various regional groupings. Old Europeans in 1947 were especially interested in East–West questions, many of which had to do with the emerging cold war. At the Seventh Session their activity on self-determination was even more frequent, but almost wholly unsuccessful. By 1957 they seem to have realized their ineffectiveness in this area and confined their initiatives almost entirely to different dimensions. In the Sixteenth Session Cuba,

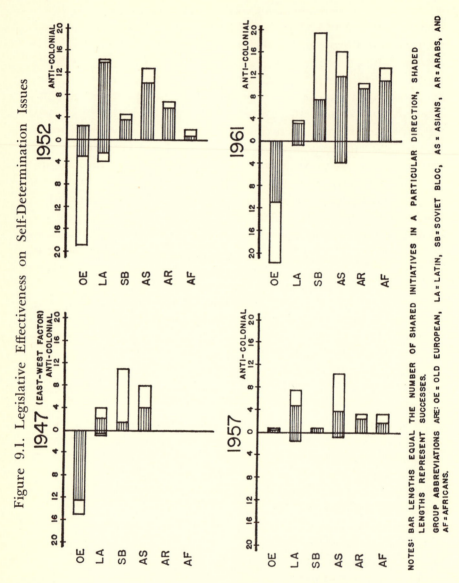

Figure 9.1. Legislative Effectiveness on Self-Determination Issues

NOTES: BAR LENGTHS EQUAL THE NUMBER OF SHARED INITIATIVES IN A PARTICULAR DIRECTION, SHADED LENGTHS REPRESENT SUCCESSES.

GROUP ABBREVIATIONS ARE: OE = OLD EUROPEAN, LA = LATIN, SB = SOVIET BLOC, AS = ASIANS, AR = ARABS, AND AF = AFRICANS.

Hungary, and Tibet began to appear as self-determination alignments even though public opinion within the Old European countries continued to view them as cold war concerns: hence a renewed
set of initiatives. Soviet initiatives on East–West subjects at the

Second Session were largely frustrated; realizing the crippling impact of communist cosponsorship of anticolonial resolutions and the special concern of the underdeveloped world for these questions, the Soviets refrained from initiatives on self-determination issues until the Fourteenth or Fifteenth Session. In 1961 East European countries like Czechoslovakia increasingly and inconspicuously appeared among a large number of cosponsors of anticolonial resolutions. Figure 9.1 also reveals the early and continued prominence of Asian (especially Indian) self-determination initiatives, the increase until 1952 of Latin initiatives and the decrease thereafter, and the development of Arab and later African preoccupation along similar lines.

Clearly Old European states, and to a much lesser extent some of their Latin and Asian allies, have never initiated a major part of the Assembly's resolutions on self-determination questions; on such issues there has developed in the Assembly an overall distribution of power favoring Afro–Asians and, to a lesser extent, their communist allies. As the number of unsuccessful anticolonial initiatives and the occasional successful procolonial initiatives indicate, however, it is more appropriate to describe self-determination as an issue area within the United Nations where Afro–Asians have almost monopolized the initiative, but where they often have had to compromise their proposals or risk the chance of defeat.

In Figure 9.2 we see that until after 1957 Old Europeans and Latin Americans (the West) were generally completely successful in passing their cold war initiatives; the Soviet bloc, with some Indian support on the question of Chinese membership, remained legislatively ineffective. The tendency of the United States and other Old Europeans to share as widely as possible their initiatives on cold war issues is also apparent from the small number of fractional successes for certain (pro-Western) members of the Asian, Arab, and African groups. In 1961 Latin support continued, and Malaya, Thailand, Japan, the Philippines, and Turkey were among those cosponsoring resolutions on Chinese representation, Tibet, and Korea. Unlike previous sessions, however, at the Sixteenth Assembly several Africans and Arabs joined the Soviet Union in passing resolutions declaring the immorality of atomic weapons and the desirability of denuclearizing Africa. Several Mongolian paragraphs (but not the entire resolution) on Cuba also evoked heavy Assembly support.

# Figure 9.2. Legislative Effectiveness on Cold War Issues

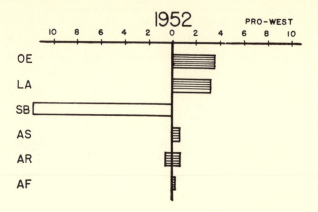

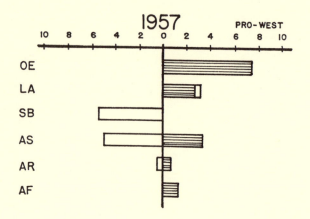

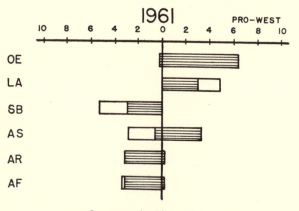

See notes in Figure 9.1

With the United States finding it increasingly difficult to muster support for its position on Chinese representation and with the Soviet Union attempting with some success to turn issues like nuclear testing, Cuba, Tibet, and Hungary into anticolonial resolutions, it is clear that at least after the Sixteenth Session (if not before) American dominance of the Assembly on cold war questions had declined. Resolutions by both East and West had often to be worded in a fashion pleasing to some or all of the Afro-Asian group of states. The side doing so while holding the support of its other allies was increasingly effective.

If the Western states and their allies have been successful on a smaller and smaller number of cold war issues, Afro–Asians and to a lesser extent Latin Americans have more often prevailed over a large set of self-determination roll calls. In neither case, however, is the current situation one of complete domination by the interests of either side. The more extreme resolutions are often defeated or withdrawn before the vote rather than risk defeat. Compromise resolutions taking into account the interests and amendments of several of the main groupings in the Assembly are those most likely to receive two-thirds majorities.

The distribution of legislative initiatives and successes on Palestine and related issues shows that a similar pattern of compromises has developed within the Assembly on a very different set of substantive issues. The long, empty bar of Arab initiatives against the partition of Palestine in 1947 (see Figure 9.3) shows the magnitude of their failure to defeat the combined efforts of Western and Eastern Europeans and most Latin Americans to partition Palestine. By 1952 Asian allies of the Arab states (themselves also representing Moslem populations) were still not able to modify the Palestine situation or to speed up Tunisian independence, but with Soviet help these states did defeat an American resolution commending the work of the Conciliation Commission. Old European and Latin victories were limited to committee roll calls.

The Sixteenth Session saw the reappearance of a factor relatively specific to Moslem concerns. An American resolution on the work of the Conciliation Commission was successfully amended in committee (cold war alignment) by Arabs and Asians to request the President of the General Assembly to reconstitute the Conciliation Commission. This amendment, however, did not receive the neces-

# Figure 9.3. Legislative Effectiveness on Palestine and Related Issues

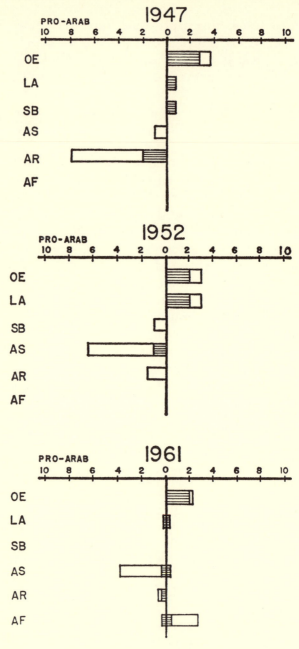

sary two thirds in a plenary roll call. A somewhat emaciated American resolution continuing the Commission finally passed the Assembly without opposition. In a committee vote on another Moslem question Asians, Arabs, and Africans passed a modified resolution on Algerian self-determination. The Casablanca states, however, could not block Mauritania's admission to the United Nations (see Chapter 6).

It will be recalled that West Irian was also a question involving the "self-determination" efforts of Moslem Indonesia. On an issue where alignments were not necessarily fixed by past allegiances, it appears that the result of intensive lobbying was to produce votes not too dissimilar from the Palestine issue. Both a resolution introduced by India on negotiations for independence of the area and one introduced by the Brazzaville powers calling for the self-determination of the Papuan population of West Irian received bare Assembly majorities. Neither side, however, could muster two-thirds support. After such inconclusive results the United States, in the person of Ambassador Ellsworth Bunker, was able to mediate, somewhat as it has tried to do in the Palestine situation.

In attempting to summarize the distribution of successes on Palestine related questions in the Assembly, it is clear that since around 1952 the major change has been in the ability of the Arab states and their allies to prevent some of the UN's activities in the Moslem world from following the course that the United States, and originally the Soviet Union, wanted them to follow. Since partition the Soviet bloc has usually avoided initiatives on Moslem questions and has supported the Arab parties. This Moslem partial veto power, however, has not been effective enough to prevent all Western-backed mediation attempts in the area, like the Palestine Conciliation Commission, nor has it had a negative effect on supranationalist instruments like the United Nations Emergency Force. Arab–Asian initiatives have not been fully successful, but their cooperation with Western or Soviet powers has on occasion enabled them to obtain important concessions regarding Tunisia, Algeria, Palestine, and most recently, West Irian.

Supranationalism issues have increasingly moved to the heart of UN politics. In 1952 the nonaligned members of the United Nations directed their attention toward a Korean settlement, toward greater UN control of decolonialization, and toward the flow of international capital. Many of the roll calls on these subjects reflected cold war and

self-determination perceptions and alignments. But a major ac-
complishment for the Southern powers in the United Nations, along
with some of the smaller Old European states and the United
States, has been the formulation, initiation, and successful negotiation of solutions to economic and political problems—solutions that
received support from UN members which transcended cold war,
Arab–Israeli, and anticolonial alignments. Besides the Korean resolutions in 1952, appropriation votes and related resolutions on
UNEF and ONUC have been the most conspicuous decisions increasing the supranational role of the United Nations in peacekeeping operations. At the Sixteenth Session, widely shared supranationalist initiatives occurred on UNEF, ONUC, the bond issue,
regulating international trade, Rwanda and Burundi, and nuclear
testing. The existence of this alignment has repeatedly been demonstrated on questions involving international economic cooperation,
more moderate resolutions easing with UN assistance the birth pains
of new nations, and attempts of the underdeveloped world to prohibit the use of nuclear weapons.

Three remarkable aspects of these supranational issues are brought
out by Figure 9.4: (1) the uniform success supranational resolutions
have had; (2) the high degree of crossregional sharing of the
initiatives involved; and (3) the virtual absence of antisupranational initiatives. Among the great powers the Soviet Union has
been most consistently opposed to an increase of UN supranationalism; it has neither shared in supranationalist initiatives nor wholly
refrained from opposing them. The only antisupranational initiatives
out of more than 50 relevant resolutions have been Soviet or Soviet-
instigated requests for separate votes on genocide and the UN bond
issue, and two unsuccessful amendments designed to restrict the flow
of information between states and to exonerate the Soviet resumption of nuclear tests. In spite of these actions, however, the limited
extent of active Soviet opposition is worth noting. Even Soviet
objections have been a matter of degree, depending in part on the
unpopularity of their position and the centrality of the issue.

A detailed examination of resolutions loading on the distinct
anti-intervention factor also reveals the existence of a stable two-
thirds majority with positive initiatives shared by Old Europeans
and Afro–Asians. Although often disagreeing, no colonial states have
gone so far as to *propose* anti-intervention resolutions.

Figure 9.4 Legislative Effectiveness on U.N. Supranationalism

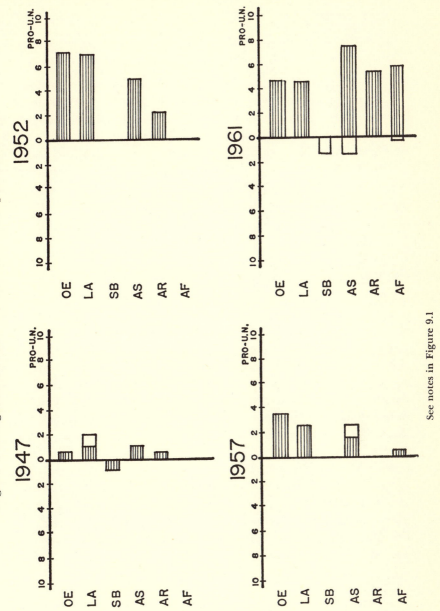

See notes in Figure 9.1

181

THE DECENTRALIZATION OF POWER IN THE GENERAL ASSEMBLY

In *A Preface to Democratic Theory,* Robert Dahl has characterized the American political system in terms of *minorities rule.*

> Elections and political competition do not make for government
> by majorities in any very significant way, but they vastly increase
> the size, number, and variety of minorities whose preferences
> must be taken into account by leaders in making policy choices.
> I am inclined to think that it is in . . . not minority rule but
> minorities rule . . . that we must look for some of the es-
> sential differences between dictatorships and democracies.[11]

As applied to the United Nations, this point of view suggests several
interesting interpretations of the political process in the General
Assembly.

Dahl's model implies that only on those broad basic issues on
which there is considerable consensus among their active members
do majorities "rule." [12] The present study has found two distinct and
important issue dimensions on which a high degree of procedural
(and to a large extent substantive) consensus exists in the United
Nations: UN supranationalism issues and certain colonial intervention questions not involving sanctions. These voting dimensions
are to be distinguished from the cold war, self-determination, and
Palestine related issues into which they sometimes degenerate. The
rather remarkable procedural consensus on these issues is that, within
the Assembly, important resolutions should not be introduced *against*
the majority position. A few nations (the more extreme colonial
powers, the Soviet bloc, and occasionally the United States on disarmament questions, etc.) will disagree with the supranationalist or
interventionist powers, but on almost every resolution along these
dimensions, two-thirds majorities have nonetheless prevailed within
the Assembly. To this extent there has been substantive as well as
procedural consensus.[13]

11. Dahl, *A Preface to Democratic Theory*, p. 132.
12. Ibid., pp. 132–33.
13. This result is not a tautology because supranationalist and South African
questions were first identified from the rotated factor matrices, and *then* initiatives
were counted and assigned a "direction" on the basis of an individual's voting position
and the pattern of Assembly responses to the resolution. Even recent Soviet actions
against the power of the Secretary-General and against UN peacekeeping activities have
stopped short of pressing their initiatives to a vote that would surely fail.

Even outside the Assembly, defeated minorities have occasionally been willing to accept the majority view in their policies, at least to some extent. Russia did eventually support the Korean repatriation compromise suggested by India; and, however reluctantly, the British, the French, and the Israelis have (for other reasons as well) acquiesced to UN demands on the Suez issue, another supranationalist concern. A primary goal for the future is to encourage further concessions from the major Northern states outside the substantive consensus—South Africa and the antisupranationalist Communists and Old Europeans.

Secondly, Dahl suggests that active minorities rule on the specific day-to-day controversies of political life. There are two senses in which it can be said that the winning groups in the Assembly are *initially* minorities. In terms of different regional or functional interests lobbying for their particular causes, this suggestion is not at all radical. Cosponsors of resolutions in the Assembly rarely come from more than two or three regions of the world. If they do, they are usually atypical: either the most pro-Western, pro-Arab, or pro-Communist states in each of the regions. It is also true that on almost any particular controversial issue, those most directly involved and willing to introduce and actively support resolutions are usually only a minority, or at least less than two thirds of the Assembly membership. Ex-colonial countries, for example, do not form an automatic majority in the Assembly; neither do the Arab states, Old Europeans, American allies, Communist countries, nor even, until quite recently, underdeveloped states.[14] We have seen, of course, that ex-colonial states had enthusiastic Latin support in 1952 for self-determination measures, but certainly by 1961 Latin states could not always be counted on to back Afro–Asian initiatives if either a competition for power or Western persuasion suggested that their interests lay elsewhere.

A third major emphasis in Dahl's view is that minorities, not a

14. Hovet, *Bloc Politics in the United Nations*, p. 127, includes only 48 out of 82 UN states in this category (1958). One could argue that Iceland and Japan, among others so classified, cannot be thought of as underdeveloped; in 1961, the influx of African states would give a numerical two-thirds majority to these countries, *if* they had the support of the Soviet bloc and *if* the Brazzaville countries could be counted on to act as though they were not being heavily assisted economically by France. On some issues, of course, it is easier to get a two-thirds majority. Our point, however, is that simply defined economic or regional interests per se do not produce two-thirds majorities; these have to be worked for.

single minority, rule the United States, in a *decentralized political system*.[15] One of the main implications of the voter's paradox, upon which Dahl partly relies in his argument,[16] is that only if all possible policy alternatives can be placed on a single dimensional continuum on which individuals have a favorite policy position at one point (and less and less attractive alternatives farther away from that point), can consistently rational, nondictatorial majority rule prevail. When policy preferences cannot be placed nicely along a single dimension, choice must be considered from a multidimensional framework, and minorities must on occasion prevail in determining collective preferences.

In the General Assembly we have seen the early proliferation and continuous existence of several distinct and contested super-issues within the United Nations on which different initiators sometimes succeed. The spread of voting victories on these dimensions symbolizes the decentralization of effective power in the Assembly. Thus by 1961 every group except the Soviet bloc was making a substantial number of initiatives, with a high frequency of success, on at least two super-issues. For Latins, Asians, Arabs, and Africans these issues were self-determination and supranationalism. Old Europeans as a whole were still fairly successful on supranationalism and the cold war, and retained a strong influence over Moslem questions—although the Arab states have been able to exert considerable influence. Even the Soviet bloc found itself on the winning side for about half of its self-determination and (for a much smaller total number of initiatives) cold war moves. Altogether there has been a gradual decentralization of power and an increase in the need for compromise on a remarkably stable set of basic Assembly conflicts.

The wider sharing of power on cold war, Palestine, and self-determination issues suggests that a larger number of Assembly minorities are willing to compromise their positions or bargain for additional votes in order to achieve quasi-legislative support. Some of the resulting alignments have appeared on supranationalist or colonial intervention dimensions.

Thought of in terms of a multiparty or multifaction model, chances for regional group success seem to have increased, despite

15. Dahl, pp. 132–33, 151.
16. Ibid., pp. 127–30; see also R. D. Luce and H. Raiffa, *Games and Decisions* (New York, Wiley, 1957), Chap. 14 and the references cited there.

the apparent narrowing of the viable number of voting dimensions on which crosscutting allegiances can come into play. A remarkable consequence of this kind of political process is that there are usually more successes than failures on Assembly roll calls (the bar graphs in Figures 9.1 to 9.4 show this to be the case). In a political body where bargaining, compromise, and responsiveness to the primary demands of other parties is repeatedly practiced, the chances for political stability and peaceful change have significantly increased.[17]

### LIMITATIONS OF A CONSENSUS–COMPETITION MODEL OF UN POLITICS

In game theory terms, politics in the UN consists of a set of potentially paramount contests, such as anticolonialism or the cold war, each with different antagonists, different rules and techniques for winning the game, and changing but usually positive goal values to be divided among the players. Several aspects of these contests have already been discussed: the kinds of issues loading on them, states' positions and intensities, and general probabilities of success. In later chapters the effects of domestic and international environments on these positions will also be described.

Prior to and concurrent with any of these particular contests, however, what may be called a "metagame" goes on to determine under what set of rules and perceptions an issue is to be debated, if at all, in the UN context. Within the limits of a national foreign policy, diplomats continually try to define new and old issues in cold war, supranationalist, or self-determination terms in order to enlist the necessary support from the alignment that is then perceived as the most relevant to and/or auspicious for their own particular goals. Conor Cruise O'Brien's caricature of the American view of how to influence Ireland's position typifies this line of thought:

> IRELAND: Refused to join NATO. . . . Is, however, strongly *Roman Catholic* and therefore *anti-Communist*. Political leaders . . . are conscious . . . of ties with . . . Western European countries, but obliged to take into account *anti-British* and *anti-colonial* elements in electorate.

17. Deutsch et al., p. 112, find chances for peaceful cooperation and change increased when leaders succeed in making "compromises which . . . satisfy at least some of the major needs and aspirations of each major group concerned."

CONCLUSIONS: Absolutely safe on East–West issues. *Needs watching on 'colonial' issues* and following tactics are suggested: Emphasize pro-Communist character of relevant "independence movement" (Algeria, Cyprus, etc.); stress absolutely no parallel between historic movement for Irish freedom and Communist-led risings in uncivilized countries; say passage of Afro–Asian (or other undesirable) resolution would damage free world . . . ; produce *sensible, relevant missionary* (Roman Catholic) if available and if vote is of sufficient importance. . . . This delegation is likely to cast some 'anti-colonialist' votes to placate home opinion. In such cases, however, delegation will probably be *helpful on procedural votes,* provided significance of these is not clear to general public.[18]

The existence of a metagame in Assembly politics implies many uncertainties about the findings that have so far been presented. First of all, it should not be assumed that knowledge of the voting dimensions and general probabilities of success on them will enable the observer to *predict* which resolution, with which wording and sponsorship, is most likely to succeed in Assembly politics. If many nations decide to see the financial crisis in cold war rather than supranationalist terms, the consequences will be very different, even if particular cold war voting positions have been favorably modified. Before future consequences and alignments can be predicted, we must know how the metagame will come out, what perceptions of a complex environment will prevail. Clearly the intention so far has not been nearly that ambitious. In an after-the-fact manner, the analysis has attempted to explain positions on a multitude of roll calls in terms of a few basic underlying policy predispositions. Measures of the relevance of particular votes to these basic issues (factor loadings) have been derived, not predicted. These super-issues have in turn been interpreted using the knowledge of the variously worded particular issues and voting positions common to them. Similarly, drawing on the insights of modern students of the domestic power process, we have attempted to interpret trends in successes and failures on these basic issues in terms of the implications for peaceful settlement of outstanding issues resulting from the growing decentralization of power in the Assembly. Such interpretations must necessarily remain tentative, however, until the

18. O'Brien, p. 19 (emphasis in the original).

relationships between Assembly politics and world politics are better understood.

A major additional problem lies in the appropriateness of conclusions about future world instability drawn from Assembly behavior. But uncertainty about such inferences—in brief the problem of the political significance of both conflicts and consensus in the Assembly—need not prevent us from cautionsly comparing Assembly power distributions and their implications with analogies in wider or narrower arenas, as Hoffmann maintains.[19] Actually, many of the problems we have come up against are also present in the study of national political systems, and a comparison of methodologies, provisional findings, and remaining issues should be theoretically worthwhile. One of these problems is the *degree* to which legislative consensus of a procedural or substantive sort must exist before the stability and adaptability of a national or an international system are assured.[20] Whether or not this consensus will frequently be seen in polarized legislative roll calls also remains unclear. Compare, for example, the British and American systems in this regard. In both systems, as in the General Assembly, roll calls are rarely used to express consensus. That the kinds and degree of requisite consensus for international community may not be too different from that required for a primitive or developing society is suggested by the facility with which such models and their implications can be used in the study of international relations.[21]

A related problem has to do with making legitimate worldwide inferences from data on successes and failures in the General Assembly. Voting for merely propaganda reasons is less likely to occur on issues of major importance, where UN action will have detrimental or advantageous consequences. On such issues, e.g. Palestine, UNEF, and ONUC, inferences comparable to those drawn from the study of domestic legislatures are more likely to be valid. On other issues, such as self-determination and nuclear testing, Assembly results to a considerable extent reflect the distribution of *preferences* and *intensities* in world politics more than they do the

19. Stanley Hoffmann, *Contemporary Theories.*

20. Both Dahl in *Who Governs?* and Deutsch et al. in *Political Community in the North Atlantic Area* have begun to address themselves to this question.

21. See Alger, "Comparison of Intranational and International Politics," and K. Deutsch, P. Jacob, H. Teune, J. Toscano, and W. Wheaton, *The Integration of Political Communities* (Philadelphia, Lippincott, 1964) a study of metropolitan, national, and international integration.

actual *power* relations involved. Legislative victories on Hungary and Tibet have not corresponded to the actual course of events there, although to varying extents other cold war and self-determination questions have corresponded to (and even influenced) the actual political processes involved. On the other hand, Assembly policies toward Communist China and sanction resolutions against South African racial policies have not brought about desired changes in either domestic or international conduct. Clearly, comparisons of relative attention, commitment, and compliance behavior toward the national and international levels would be extremely rewarding.[22]

Related to the question of generalizing Assembly power relationships on roll-call votes is the knottier problem of the subjective costs and satisfactions involved. We have argued that the absence of automatic two-thirds majorities (except on early cold war questions) makes bargaining necessary and mutually profitable for the parties involved. Most members win on some of their favored resolutions. But the plain and obvious fact is that on some issues it is patently easier to recruit the required majorities than on others. A careful study of influence relations, in addition to counting the number of successes and failures in a particular area, should also bear in mind the cost of the influence attempt for its originator, as well as the "opportunity costs" foregone by the state yielding to the influence attempt.[23] One gets the impression, for instance, that the United States is working harder and harder for its cold war majorities; on the Chinese membership issue the results seem to have been extremely satisfying, although their effect has been more to deprive the Communists of respectability than of power in international relations.[24] Since 1952 the underdeveloped countries have continued to win

22. A relevant research proposal along these lines is Harold Guetzkow, *Multiple Loyalties* (Princeton, Princeton University Press, 1956).

23. John Harsanyi has presented an extension of Dahl's earlier work on power that takes into account the relative opportunity costs of both participants involved. Clearly, if less of an effort produces more of a policy change, this person's "power," in a schedule sense, is higher than that of the individual who succeeds in achieving the same relatively easy to obtain result at great cost to himself. John Harsanyi, "Measurement of Social Power, Opportunity Costs, and the Theory of Two Person Bargaining Games," *Behavioral Science*, 7 (1962), 67–80.

24. Marshall Singer and Barton Sensenig, "Elections within the United Nations," *International Organization*, 17 (1963), 901–25, have also found a continued but more difficult dominance of the United States on Assembly elections and cold war issues (defined in a way similar to the unrotated East–West factor).

most, but not all, self-determination issues in the Assembly. The trend seems to be toward harsher and more stigmatizing resolutions, with majorities that are easier to obtain. It is clear that Afro–Asian victories have become more damning than the expiration offered by a successful Scandinavian deletion of a phrase or two in the resolution. Paradoxically, it appears likely that Scandinavian mediation attempts, for example, are more likely to change the situation in South Africa than General Assembly sanction resolutions. Until the Security Council can be made to enforce a sanctions resolution or to expel South Africa (which seems to be the African strategy), it is a moot point whether the partial satisfaction of hollow victories in the Assembly assuages the Africans' anger or only intensifies their concern for further action and decreases the chances of peaceful change in the area.

In their article on the "Two Faces of Power" Bachrach and Baratz express the belief that the "dynamics of non-decision-making" are not uncovered by counting successful decisions, even when they are weighed or estimated, as to their importance or significance—as we have tried to do.[25] It is very clear that many policy aims in the Assembly do not reach roll-call votes or, if they do in committee, the sponsor anticipates the Assembly reaction and avoids repetition of an embarrassing failure for his resolution. Withdrawing resolutions that probably will not get a majority is a very common practice, frequently referred to by diplomats, and it explains why there are more successes than failures in Assembly roll-call voting. The implication of the existence of such metagame decisions is that indices of legislative effectiveness do not adequately measure the strength of the veto power of Assembly groups.

Evidence in this chapter on visible power distributions cannot be considered reliably to indicate future or potential power configurations until the dissatisfactions of the colonial powers, the basic frustration of Arab purposes brought about by the creation of Israel in 1947 and 1948, and the disappointments of communist states on cold war and especially supranationalism issues have been more carefully assessed.

25. Peter Bachrach and Morton Baratz, "Two Faces of Power," *American Political Science Review, 56* (1962), 947–52. In his *Preface to Democratic Theory*, (Chicago, University of Chicago Press, 1956), Dahl has talked about a similar problem, the scheduling of alternatives.

Historical analyses can help make some of these metadecisions visible. On self-determination questions, for example, 1952 appears to have been nearly the last year in which the colonial powers attempted to obtain Assembly support for their own policy views. Subsequently, Belgian, British, and French behavior outside the Assembly has indicated a greater dissatisfaction and independent resolve than the lack of Assembly initiatives suggests. Arab resolutions on Palestine itself are also rarer than they were in 1947, although related Moslem concerns frequently reappear in the voting. Except for the Chinese representation question, cold war ambitions and dissatisfactions (e.g. regarding Berlin) have not been especially prominent among recent Assembly voting concerns, although the larger world political context as well as repeated Soviet–United States conflicts along East–West lines indirectly suggest the presence of more fundamental antagonisms. The strength of national resentments on such issues and the extent of unwilling compliance can profitably be subjected to further research.

Despite these reservations, it is worth noting that the preoccupations of the Arab countries with Palestine questions in 1947 and of the Soviets with the East–West conflict in the same year seem to have decreased as they have achieved victories on other issues.[26] Initiatives by Afro–Asians on both supranationalism and self-determination questions have also begun to show a similar differentiation of interests.

In this chapter we have attempted to measure the intensity of policy commitments on major international issues and the decentralization of power within the Assembly by looking at the number of roll-call initiatives and successes on competitive and more nearly consensual issue areas. The next chapter will describe another measure of intensity and an attempt to infer prospects for the stability of the international system from trends in the distribution of these intensities.

26. The "ups and downs" of Soviet attractions to the UN are discussed in Chaps. 5 and 6. The study group of the Egyptian Society of International Law, after describing a phase of "faith, hope and expectation," one of "indifference and resentment," and one of "self-reliance and cooperation," suggested late in 1956 that the UN's handling of the Suez crisis, "is certain . . . to go far toward restoring the confidence of Egypt in the UN as an instrument of peace." See the Carnegie Endowment Series volume, *Egypt and the United Nations* (New York, Manhattan Publishing Co., 1957), p. 67.

# CHAPTER 10

# Intensity and Attitude

## MEASURING INTENSITY

In Chapter 8 we sketched an outline of what one kind of stable international political system might look like, and examined generally the present condition of world, and specifically UN, politics. Let us now examine somewhat more closely the trends in a few of the factors most closely affecting stability—social and political factors, not military–technological influences. In doing so we must address ourselves further to the distribution of intensities as well as to the distribution of preferences. We must know not only what states hold a given attitude, but how strongly they hold it.

Our search for a satisfactory measure of intensity was not easy. One possibly valid means of ascertaining which governments felt most strongly about a given issue would have been simply to ask their delegates. Clearly that solution was out of the question. For events ten or fifteen years past, delegates' familiarity with their governments' policies, and their memories, simply could not be trusted. Even for recent events there must be reservations on this score, for the reliability of such perceptions is often a subject of political controversy.

Another possible solution was to examine the behavior of the delegates as reflected in the official record. In particular, who speaks most often on a given topic? We could count the number of speeches by each national delegation on all the issues which loaded heavily on the major factors as identified in the unrotated and rotated factor patterns. The assumption obviously would be that those who held a position with the greatest intensity would speak most often. There are some flaws in this technique: the major powers, particularly the United States and the Soviet Union, tend to speak frequently on virtually everything. Thus this measure would be likely to find the big powers the most intense on every issue, and this is probably not true in reality. Second, taciturnity and loquaciousness may indicate not intensity of conviction but personality differences. A single cogent, powerful, carefully prepared speech may indicate a far deeper concern than several casually delivered addresses.[1]

One other possibility was to create an index which combined both speechmaking and parliamentary activity. We experimented with the following index, assigned to each delegation with regard to a particular issue as follows:

3. Sponsors resolution, or sponsors amendment, or gives two or more speeches
2. Speaks once
1. Doesn't speak, but at least votes
0. Fails to vote

Despite the attractions of the combined index, we finally decided simply to count speeches. The reasons were these:

1. Counting speeches was a cumulative process, and each speech could be recorded separately and weighted equally. Compiling the index, however, required judgments as to what constituted a particular "issue." One issue might be the subject of much speechmaking and parliamentary maneuvering, another might be dealt with quickly and simply. It would be unfair to count each equally as an issue unit for constructing the index.

2. The index itself seemed artificial and not easy to justify. Why count introducing a resolution as equal to introducing an amendment, or as equal to speaking twice? Or how better justify any other weighting?

3. Counting speeches produced a highly skewed distribution. In 1947, for example, two states delivered 25 or more speeches on North–South issues, 17 additional states spoke ten or more times, and the remaining 38 nations spoke nine times or less. Use of the composite index, however, produced a nearly normal distribution of "intensities": few states consistently failed to vote at all, and just as few took an active part in the debate or parliamentary maneuvers on virtually every subject. While a case might be made for either of these distributions, it seemed to us that the skewed distribution

1. Yet another possibility would have been a content analysis of debates, looking for extreme language.

—a few states very interested, most relatively apathetic—was the more accurate reflection of international reality.[2]

4. Though the shape of the two distributions was different, the two indices—speeches and the composite index—actually produced nearly identical rankings. In a test on North–South issues in 1947, both indices found the same states high and the same states low; the rank order correlation coefficient of the two rankings was a very high .88. Given this similarity in results, the relative ease with which the speech measure could be compiled told heavily in its favor.

We suggested in Chapter 8 that for various reasons the stability of the international system could be increased by the proliferation of issues, by a shift away from preoccupation with the cold war. In terms at least of the super-issues—the factors, those groups of issues which produced distinct voting alignments—this certainly has not happened. The unrotated factor analysis found four super-issues with lambdas greater than 2.5 in both 1947 and 1952, but only three such issues in 1957 and 1961. Similarly, the number of rotated factors with lambdas above 2.5 rose from five in 1947 to six in 1952 and 1957, and then fell to four in 1961.

More striking is the relative increase in the prominence of East–West issues and the decline in North–South. As we saw in Chapter 7, East–West issues accounted for about 45 per cent of the common variance in 1947, 51 per cent in 1952, 64 per cent in 1957, and 68 per cent in 1961. North–South issues always constituted the second most common alignment, but they declined from about 20 per cent in 1947 and 1952 to 15 per cent in 1957 and 13 per cent in 1961. To put it another way, in 1947 East–West alignments were twice as common as North–South alignments; by 1961 they were five times as common. By 1961 the East–West confrontation had come to dominate the Assembly in a way it had not done previously. There is no evidence of an emerging alliance between the West and Communist "haves" against the underdeveloped "have-nots"—in fact, quite the contrary.

Issues which in earlier years had loaded on the North–South

2. Campbell et al., p. 97, found that the distribution of Americans' intensity of partisan preference was highly skewed.

factor turned up on the East–West dimension in 1961. Palestine, a major component of the North–South dimension in 1947, is a striking example. Here most of the change can be traced to the shift of the Soviet Union to a militantly pro-Arab position. Also, in earlier years some of the colonialism issues loaded on the North–South dimension: Nauru Trusteeship in 1947, Morocco and Somaliland in 1952, a few votes on the Cameroons and South Africa in 1957. But of all the colonialism votes in 1961, only two votes on Rwanda–Burundi were characterized by a North–South alignment. In 1961 virtually all of the issues which loaded on either the rotated cold war or self-determination factors were to be found loading fairly heavily on the unrotated East–West factor.

Another way of measuring prominence is to count the frequency of speechmaking on a super-issue. In 1947 and 1952 approximately twice as many speeches were made on East–West as on North–South issues. By 1957 the ratio rose to three to one, and by 1961 five times as many speeches were made on East–West issues as on North–South problems. These data on frequency of speeches almost exactly parallel our data on frequency of votes.[3]

It is difficult to explain these striking findings in light of common assertions that the North–South conflict is a new one, a dimension that has only recently come into prominence. Since these assertions are usually made by Americans, perhaps the viewpoint can be traced to a peculiarly American perspective on world politics; the United States is newly concerned with North–South issues. Figure 10.1 shows the number of speeches made by the average UN member and by the United States, on both East–West and North–South issues.

The United States has always been far more interested in both North–South and East–West issues than the average UN member. In 1947 and in 1961 it made about four times as many speeches as the average member on East–West issues, and about two and one-half times the average in the intervening years. But on North–South issues, until 1961, the U.S. spoke only about twice as often as did the average member. In 1961, however, the level rose to between five and six times the average.

Through 1957 the United States was able to get its way on East–West issues with relative ease, but by 1961 it sometimes had to work

3. These findings are further supported by very similar proportions of initiatives (cf. Chap. 9).

Figure 10.1. Speeches on East–West and North–South Issues

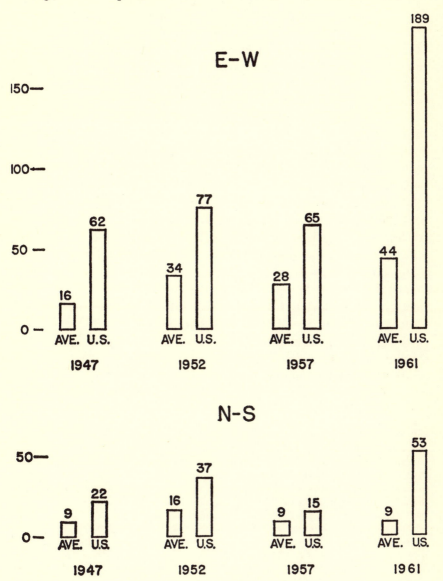

quite hard to achieve its accustomed majority. Paradoxically, the difficulty in rounding up votes on East–West issues may be at the root of the greater interest in North–South problems. To get support on things it thinks important, the United States has had to bargain and has had to show more concern regarding issues important to other states. As the United States delegation began to take a new interest in North–South issues, American analysts began, for the first time, to notice a voting alignment that has in fact existed since the beginning of the organization.[4]

Nevertheless the relative emphasis on North–South issues, both in number of speeches and in number of votes, has declined rather sharply. East–West issues have increased significantly as have supranationalism issues on the rotated factor pattern (up from about 16 per cent of the common variance in 1947 to about 27 per cent in 1961). While the United States continues to hold a prosupranationalism position (perhaps only so long as it expects to be able to use the resulting new powers against the Communist bloc) there will be a rise in the attention given to issues on which the United States and the Soviet Union conflict. Although many Europeans desert the United States on supranationalist issues—this plus the division of the Soviets from the Afro–Asians is essentially why the voting alignment is distinct—the two major bloc leaders more than ever find themselves opposed. This is true even when 1961 is compared to 1952, at the height of the Korean War. The polarization of attitudes in the General Assembly is on the upswing, not on the decline.[5]

---

4. Cf. Chap. 7.

5. One significant qualification to this conclusion stems from our use of speeches and roll-call votes. On a few highly divisive issues there is evidence that both sides endeavor to prevent the topic from reaching a formal vote. The neutrals now try very hard to exclude strictly cold war issues from Assembly consideration, and particularly to avoid cold war divisions where the United States and the Soviets vote on opposite sides. On subjects like nuclear testing their aim is to produce resolutions on which both great powers will vote in favor or abstain. Thus the cold war dimension was relatively infrequently represented in our analysis of the Sixteenth Session, partly because of the neutrals' efforts not to have it discussed. Similarly, Hadwen and Kaufman, p. 95, report that the underdeveloped countries, in their advocacy of a Special United Nations Fund for Economic Development (SUNFED), worked ardently to avoid a roll-call vote all during the years when it was under discussion. They knew they could win a vote, but could not implement it against the will of the major contributors. This phenomenon probably does not occur often, but to the extent it does our sample of roll calls, and thus of speeches, does not adequately reflect the concerns of the Assembly.

But to modify this gloomy conclusion there remain other trends in the *rotated* issues and alignments which appear more compatible with a stable system. Almost as striking as the rise of East–West conflict is the drop in the pervasiveness of the rotated cold war alignment. To some degree this shows up in the amount of variance accounted for by the cold war factor. Cold war and self-determination were indistinguishable in 1947. In 1952 the cold war issue accounted for 11 per cent of common variance; in 1957 it rose to 29 per cent and in 1961 fell again to 19 per cent. And unlike earlier years, the votes which in 1961 loaded most heavily on the cold war factor were on the procedural issue of seating Communist China, rather than on more straightforward substantive matters.

A far clearer indication of this trend, however, is the relative decline in speechmaking on the cold war. Figure 10.2 shows speeches by the United States, the Soviet Union, and the Assembly average for the three years in which cold war and self-determination have been distinct. The increasing disinterest of the Assembly in cold war issues stands out. The Americans and the Soviets delivered more than twice as many speeches on cold war issues in 1961 as in 1952; after a brief rise in 1957 the average General Assembly member actually gave fewer cold war speeches in 1961 than in 1952. The ratio of the Soviet–American score to the mean score rose from about three to one in 1952 to eight to one in 1961.

Further support for this argument comes from relating the number of speeches on any super-issue to the percentage of common variance in the voting accounted for by that issue dimension. The result is a kind of overall intensity score for the entire membership, with speechmaking weighted by each issue's pervasiveness in Assembly voting. We find that between 1952 and 1961 this "intensity score" rose by about 50 per cent or more for most of the major unrotated and rotated dimensions (from 40 to 65 for East–West, 48 to 70 for North–South, and 48 to 83 for self-determination). The trend has been toward more speeches per issue—a consequence, perhaps, of the enlarged membership of the Assembly. But for cold war issues the trend in "intensity scores" has been downward; the index has declined from 33 to 27. Not only have the underdeveloped states been very successful in preventing cold war issues from coming to a vote in the UN, they have to a large degree discouraged even the *discussion* of such matters in the international forum.

As implied by the overall intensity scores, a different trend is

Figure 10.2. Speeches on Cold War and Self-Determination Issues

## SELF-DETERMINATION

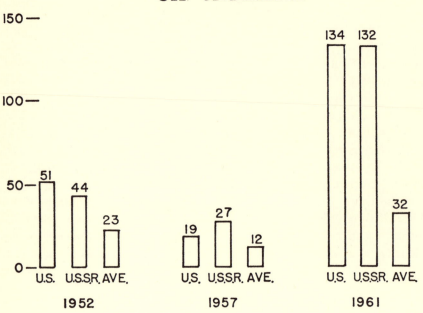

## COLD WAR

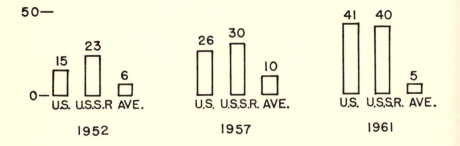

discernible on self-determination issues. Instead of declining, the mean number of speeches has risen by nearly 50 per cent since 1952. In 1961 the average Assembly delegation talked six and one-half times as much about self-determination problems as about cold war issues. Although they delivered eight times as many speeches as the average member on cold war issues, the Russian and American speech totals were only four times greater than average on self-determination. But even this marks a substantial increase, as the major powers themselves were forced, in order to hold the attention of other states, to devote much more of their attention to the Assembly's preoccupation with self-determination and the end of colonialism.

Interviews with diplomats from the nonaligned states indicate that the avoidance of cold war issues stems from a combination of boredom with the subject and irritation. They see Soviet, and especially American, emphasis on the cold war as preventing the nonaligned countries from obtaining the prominence they desire for their own concerns, especially their efforts (on issues that often load on the supranationalism dimension) to *limit* the cold war in areas where they are frightened by its implications—nuclear testing and the

## Table 10.1. Speeches per Issue

|  | 1952 | | 1957 | | 1961 | |
|---|---|---|---|---|---|---|
|  | CW | S-D | CW | S-D | CW | S-D |
| U.S. | 15 | 51 | 26 | 19 | 41 | 134 |
| U.S.S.R. | 23 | 44 | 30 | 27 | 40 | 132 |
| Yugoslavia | 16 | 42 | 18 | 19 | 6 | 70 |
| China | 6 | 21 | 13 | 14 | 5 | 17 |
| Israel | 2 | 34 | 6 | 14 | 3 | 22 |
| Old Europeans | 5 | 26 | 9 | 11 | 4 | 37 |
| Latin Americans | 4 | 16 | 6 | 12 | 3 | 20 |
| Soviet bloc | 11 | 18 | 11 | 10 | 8 | 26 |
| Asians | 5 | 23 | 14 | 13 | 8 | 37 |
| Arabs | 4 | 27 | 7 | 9 | 3 | 37 |
| Africans | 2 | 26 | 11 | 11 | 2 | 33 |

Congo, for example. The avoidance of cold war issues is not due primarily to the admission of new African states, except as they provide a potential nonaligned majority. It is true that in 1961 there were far more African states than previously, and that collectively they showed the same low level of interest in the cold war as Ethiopia and Liberia had nine years previously. But as Table 10.1 shows, with the exception of the two super-powers, *every* group evidenced a lower level of interest in the cold war in 1961 than in 1957, and in most cases lower than in 1952. This is true not only of the neutrals but of the Old Europeans and the satellite states of the Soviet bloc.

We hypothesized in Chapter 8 that bloc leaders would increasingly be forced to turn away from cold war issues if they were to retain their influence among the mass of "voters." That development has not yet occurred, but the forces which would produce it are plainly evident. It seems plausible to expect that in time the bloc leaders will, like their followers, shift their public emphasis from cold war issues to the kind of problem on which they are likely to strike a more sympathetic chord in the Assembly.

### THE ROLE OF THE MIDDLEMAN

Earlier we hypothesized that if those who hold the most extreme attitudes also hold them most intensely, a serious threat to the system's stability exists, especially if the extremists are numerous. The converse might read: For the system to be stable there should be a body of neutrals who are relatively intense about their neutralism; that is, who maintain a middle position and who do so with some degree of involvement, with an active effort to uncover ground of agreement between the extremes and to produce solutions. And the smaller the body of such neutrals is, the more intense must be their commitment to a middle ground if they are to exert a significant stabilizing effect.

First, let us examine the distribution of attitudes along the East–West and North–South dimensions. The following graphs resemble the curves presented in Chapter 8. Across the horizontal axis appear the factor scores, or positions of various countries on East–West or North–South questions. Along the left vertical axis is *number of countries;* on the right vertical axis is the average *intensity* of attitude, the mean number of speeches on topics loading heavily [6] on the given super-issue. The jagged *solid* line represents the distribution of attitudes, the number of states within each range of factor

6. Correlation between the individual vote and the super-issue of .50 or greater.

Figure 10.3. Distribution of East–West Attitudes

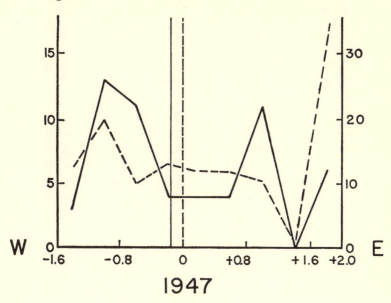

1947

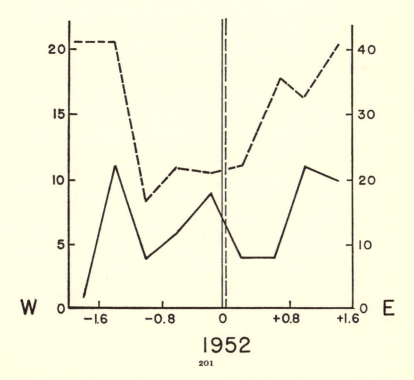

1952

scores. The jagged *dashed* line shows the average intensity for states within that range.

Two other lines have been added. In both figures the *dashed* line rising vertically from zero marks the *mean* or *average factor score*. The *solid* vertical line, on the other hand, represents the *median;* that is, the state which finds itself with exactly half the Assembly on either side. The direction and distance from the mean to the median can be interpreted as one indicator of the strength of the majority. It shows how far from a middle position (the mean factor score) the more powerful side may depart and still retain 50 per cent of the vote.[7] Figure 10.3 gives the data for East–West factor scores, and Figure 10.4 the data on North–South positions. We shall look first at the *solid* jagged lines for the distribution of factor scores.

### Figure 10.3. Distribution of East–West Attitudes

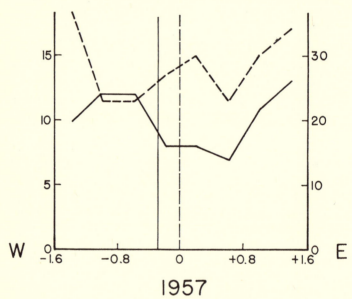

1957

7. If the two sides were equal the mean and the median of the distribution would be identical. By one definition a distribution is unequal or *skewed* to the degree that the mean and the median differ.

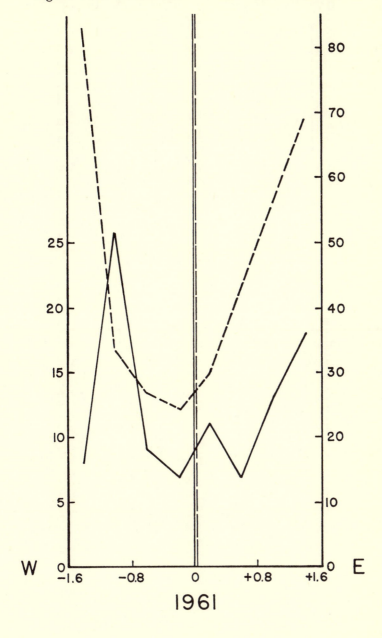

Figure 10.3. Distribution of East–West Attitudes

1961

Figure 10.4. Distribution of North–South Attitudes

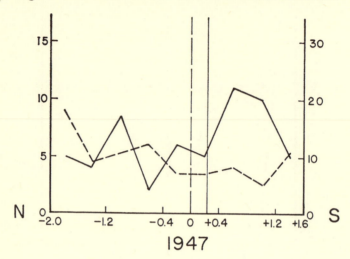

1947

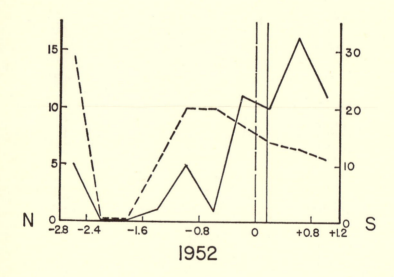

1952

Figure 10.4. Distribution of North–South Attitudes

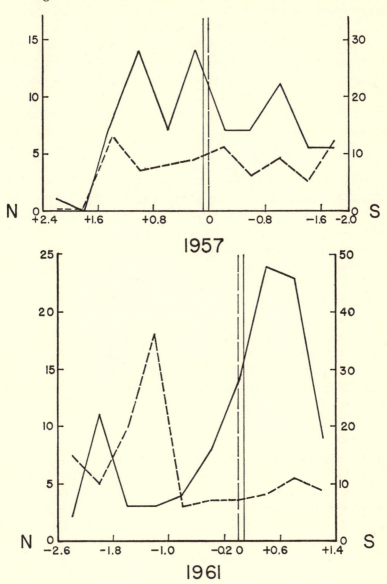

Figure 10.3 illustrates a clear case of a "three party" system. Throughout the period since 1947 there has been a substantial middle group on East–West issues, usually located somewhat to the east of center. But the relative size of this center group has been declining quite steadily—particularly as the East's voting strength has grown. Furthermore, the composition of the center party has been far from constant. In 1947 the "central" peak (actually well to the East of center) represents the position of India, most Arabs, and some other Afro–Asians. By 1952 these same Afro–Asians are to be found in a position nearly as far East as the Soviet bloc, and they stay substantially there from then on. Their place as a "center" group is taken mostly by Latin Americans in 1952 (West of center this time), by a mixed group of Latins, Asians, and some Arabs in 1957, and substantially by the newly admitted Brazzaville Africans in 1961.[8] For purposes of UN voting, at least, the group of Afro–Asians typified by Egypt, India, and Indonesia is not a moderating center group on most East–West issues. Rather it makes up, with the Soviet bloc, the Eastern party. The central, balancing group is to be found elsewhere—and it is diminishing in size.

The development of North–South voting has been more complex. In 1947 there is some evidence for the existence of a third party, composed of some Latins and Western Europeans. During the 1952 session the South seems largely to have controlled the Assembly, though a substantial collection of Europeans and (this time) Asians is still to be found near the center. And in 1957 this same group, augmented by most Arabs, is as large as the "revived" Northern group. But by 1961 the moderate group seems to have evaporated. Few states were prepared, at least on the issues which arose in the General Assembly, to go on record as being very North or even as belonging to any very clearly defined moderate group. To be sure some Europeans group near the middle, but numerically they are swamped by the South.

It might perhaps be argued that the absence of a middle group on North–South issues is partly compensated for by the near consensus at the South end of the axis. Over two thirds of the membership show scores between —.2 and +1.4. A fairly small minority could perhaps be overridden without disastrous conse-

8. For the precise composition of these and other positions on the East–West spectrum see the appropriate maps in Chaps. 3–6, and the factor scores listed in the Appendix.

quences. Such a hopeful evaluation is of course belied by the composition of the "small minority": among others, France, the United Kingdom, the United States, and the Soviet bloc, all with scores greater than −1.0.

Thus on the two principal dimensions of UN voting, East–West and North–South, the evidence points to increasing bipolarity, not to the rise of a third party. On East–West issues the self-styled Afro–Asian "neutrals" in fact generally are to be found with the Soviet bloc. (This is not to imply that Afro–Asians are simply following the Soviet lead; on many issues it is substantially a case of the Soviets taking up causes already dear to Afro–Asian hearts.) On those issues where the North–South alignment prevails the Afro–Asians depart very sharply from the Soviet (and European) position, and take the great majority of UN members with them.

Though these features present a rather dim prospect from the vantage of our particular theoretical tower, a certain brightness would be restored if we found that even though the true neutrals were few in number, they felt rather intense about maintaining their middle position; that is, if they were active in a balancing, compromising, and mediating role. For this we must turn again to our intensity data, combined with the information on direction of attitudes (factor scores). Let us now look at the dashed jagged line in Figures 10.3 and 10.4.

In Figure 10.3 for the East–West dimension, consistently it is the extremists who turn up with the highest intensity scores, the most startling case occurring in 1961. Now to some extent the states at the extreme Western end of the spectrum are few; one would therefore not be surprised by their apparent intensity.[9] But this only partly ex-

---

9. It might be hypothesized that our measure of intensity, number of speeches, tends to be an artifact of the number of states holding a given policy position. Thus if there are many states substantially in agreement on a matter, they can divide up speaking assignments among themselves, with no single state making a great number. But if they constitute a small minority each will have to make many speeches if the group is to hold up its end of the debate. Something of this sort often happens in parliamentary systems. In Britain, for instance, a Liberal Party M.P. can almost always get the eye of the speaker and be recognized, for it is considered that he represents a distinctive point of view which should be heard. Analysis of the debates might find that our liberal M.P. spoke often and therefore seemed quite intense about his convictions. But that might or might not be the case; the alleged "intensity score" could have been largely a product of his uniqueness, not his intensity. In our data, however, this tendency does not apply with any regularity. The average correlation between intensity and number of states is actually slightly positive (.18) over the four dimensions and four years.

plains the high intensity scores even of Western states. It does not in any sense explain the high scores of the Easternmost states who, even though fairly numerous, are always among the most frequent speech-makers in the Assembly. Nor does it explain the reticence of the middle powers who, though perhaps seen, tend seldom to be heard. The principal exception to this pattern occurs in 1957, when the centrists indeed have quite high intensity scores—but they are not too numerous in 1957, so one would expect them to speak often. And it most emphatically does not apply to 1961, when the third party was numerically at its nadir. Though hardly numerous, nations near the middle of the East–West scale on the whole spoke on far fewer occasions than did those at either end.

In terms of our theory of a stable competitive system it is not necessarily a serious loss simply that the neutrals are not *intense*. We referred, after all, to findings and hypotheses about democratic politics which suggested that a large body of apathetic neutrals helped support the system. By their own lack of interest they dampened the intensity of the extremists, and helped prevent the lines of clevage from becoming too clearly demarcated. But the key is in the requirement of a sufficiently *large* body of apathetic neutrals that both sides will modify their stances in order to court it. A small group of intense, mediating neutrals may fulfill one important condition for stability. A large group of apathetic neutrals contributes in quite another but still significant way. It is when the neutrals are both few *and* apathetic that the greatest threats to stability exist. And this was precisely the situation in 1961, on a voting alignment which accounted for 64 per cent of the interpretable variance in Assembly voting. Note that this discussion applies not simply to issues important in the cold war, where there is perhaps a significant body of neutrals, but to the whole complex of issues, including both cold war and self-determination problems, which make up the unrotated East–West factor.

Prospect and retrospect on the pattern of North–South relations are slightly less grim. As a look at the graphs will show, in at least the first three of the four years a more or less well-defined center group is discernible with an intensity level not seriously lower than that of the extremes. Nor is this, especially in 1957, a function of the number of states to be found in the center factor score ranges. In 1957 the center group is more intense than one would expect merely from its size, and the extremists, particularly at the South end, are less so. (This is not true for those at the very end of the South axis, but is decidedly so for the aggregate in the next-to-most-extreme position.) By 1961, however, this pattern too has shifted toward more bipolarity and the extremists at either end show up as the most intense. (That this does not apply to the very Northern end is simply because South Africa refused to participate in many of the discussions.) There is little indication of many center states making a serious effort as intermediaries. A very high peak of intensity does occur well to the North of center, and represents to a large degree the debating activities of the United States. Obviously American UN delegates were trying to play the role of honest brokers. Yet their voting record still is very different from that of the majority of the Assembly on North–South issues, which makes one doubt whether the Americans are near enough to the middle to perform a mediating role effectively.[10]

These comments have been directed to the unrotated factor pattern, which in some ways is the most significant, since with the East–West dimension it gives the basic voting alignment that is by far the most common in the Assembly. It is not unreasonable to demand that mediating and compromising forces show up on this common alignment if they are to be effective. Nevertheless, as virtually every observer knows, states' positions on particular issues within the basic East–West dimension are determined by many different influences. Certainly the Afro–Asians are the most involved on self-determination questions, and the Soviets go along and try to lead a movement useful for damaging the West. And on the cold war it is clearly the Soviet Union which, on the Eastern side, is the most involved. While Communist and Afro–Asian views usually meet sufficiently to permit a coalition on East–West issues as broadly defined, two separate and not necessarily parallel issue conflicts nevertheless underlie it. The rotated factor pattern allows us to distinguish these two conflicts, and the next group of graphs presents an analysis of attitude distribution and intensity on the cold war and self-determination rotated dimensions. We present first the patterns of distribution and intensity on the cold war, and then a

10. Of course, were the United States actually to shift its very great weight (as measured by influence over other delegations) very much farther South the isolation of the Northerners would be extreme.

Figure 10.5. Distribution of Cold War Attitudes

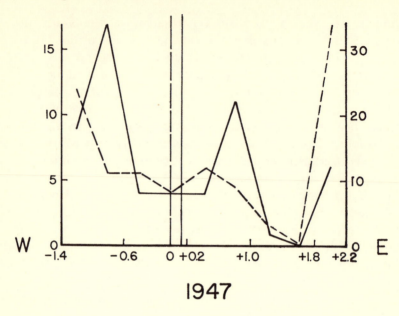

1947

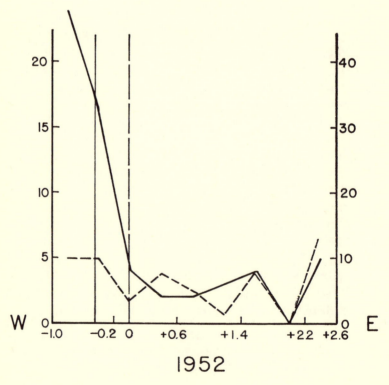

1952

Figure 10.5. Distribution of Cold War Attitudes

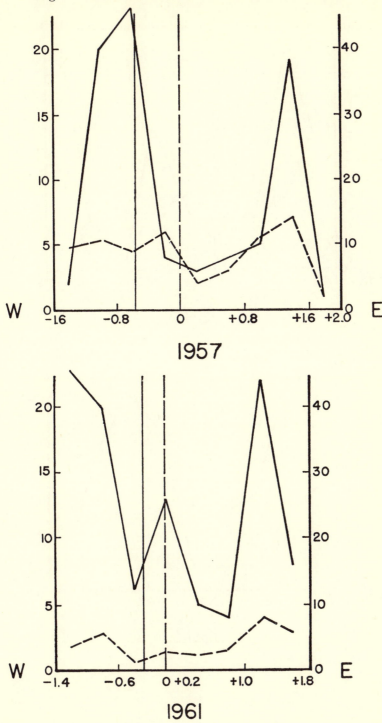

1957

1961

Figure 10.6. Distribution of Self-Determination Attitudes

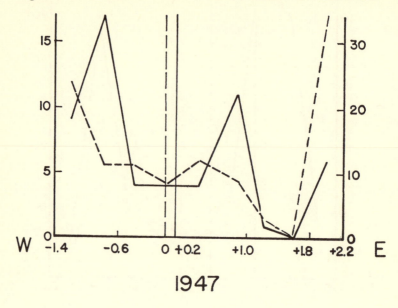

1947

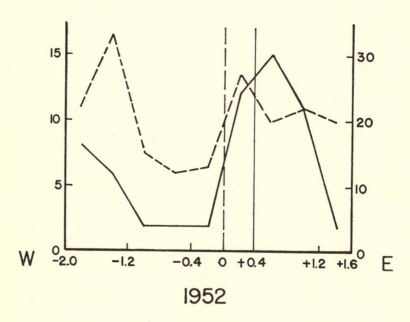

1952

Figure 10.6. Distribution of Self-Determination Attitudes

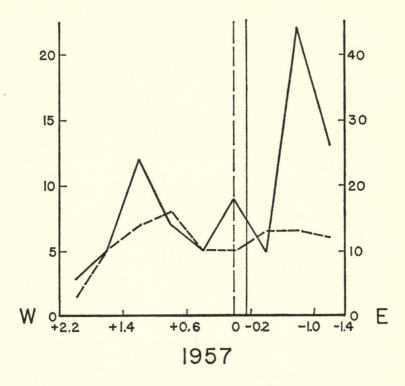

1957

similar pair of figures for self-determination. The 1947 graph in the first figure is repeated in the second, since cold war and self-determination issues were not distinguishable in the Second Session.

The cold war patterns closely resemble those we found for East–West, except that since purely cold war issues were not much discussed in the Sixteenth Session all intensity scores are low. In 1947 there was a distinct center group of Arab and Asian states; in later years this center group all but disappears as the Asians and Arabs generally show up farther to the East. Bipolarity is especially striking in 1957, in the aftermath of Suez and Hungary. It appears muted by a quite small center group in 1961, but this is partly deceptive. Although this group is composed mostly of Africans who can be considered truly center, it also includes the United Kingdom: the British, despite an otherwise regularly Western voting pattern, favored admission of Communist China. To consider them "center" on other cold war issues would be quite misleading. The implication that the most extreme Easterners are less numerous than those in a

Figure 10.6. Distribution of Self-Determination Attitudes

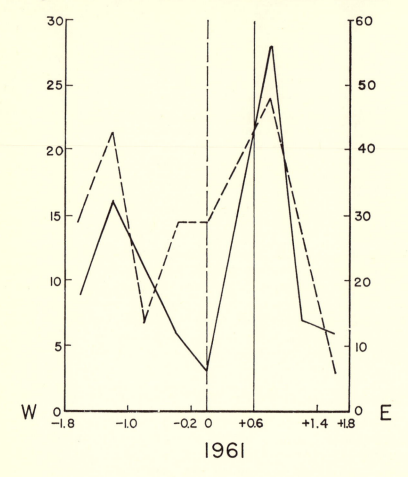

1961

position slightly nearer the middle is also misleading. The Soviet bloc abstained on the resolution favoring Chinese admission because it did not specify the expulsion of Taiwan. Since the proposal simply was not extreme enough for them, it is obvious that the Communist states should properly be considered at the Easternmost pole. The intensity scale gives some impression of bipolarity in 1961, and the infrequency with which cold war issues were discussed makes it impossible to draw any firm conclusions from the graph.

There is reason to feel that the division of the Assembly is not quite so severe on self-determination problems although, as was true on the unrotated East–West dimension, bipolarity exists and without doubt is growing. In 1957 there was a significant middle group of some intensity. By 1961 the middle group had disappeared, leaving only two major peaks, but most states on the Eastern side were not at the farthest extreme. The largest group of states, as well as the most intense, is to be found well in from the right. Even so, we have earlier mentioned evidence that, despite the relative stability of the factor score *distributions,* most or all of the Assembly has shifted to a more anticolonial position. Measures which seemed too radical for the majority in 1947 are now seen as too reactionary. Furthermore, the composition of the very Eastern group is changing. Until 1961 the states which were most demanding about self-determination were those of the Soviet bloc. Since the Russians really were exploiting the interest of the Afro–Asians on this issue, one could take some comfort in the fact that those most immediately involved on the Eastern side, the Afro–Asians, were not as far out. But by the Sixteenth Session quite a number of Africans, concerned about South Africa and the Portuguese territories, overtook and passed the Soviets in their demands. A small group composed of Israel, some Latins, and a few pro-Western Asians (Malaya, Cyprus, and Pakistan) is trying to maintain a mediating position (factor scores between −0.6 and +0.2), and they speak fairly often in such a role.

## TRENDS

Let us sum up some of our findings to this point about where the international political system, as reflected in the Assembly, has been and where it may be going. The most disquieting finding is perhaps the prominence of the East–West conflict, which now accounts for well over half of the roll-call voting and related speech-making.

It is disquieting in view of another finding, not fully recognized in previous analyses, that there are a significant number of uncorrelated dimensions which characterize UN voting. Knowing a state's allies on one dimension does not help in predicting with whom it will ally on another. Each delegation or caucusing group must maintain certain cooperative contracts with every other delegation or group, since it may expect to vote with them on at least one controversial issue or set of issues. This whole pattern of shifting vote alignments can contribute a fluidity and flexibility to the system. Bargaining—the exchange of support on one issue for backing on another—is facilitated.[11] But the more overriding East–West issues become, the more flexibility is lost. Cooperative contracts with states opposed to one on East–West questions may weaken because they are used less often. As the East–West alignment becomes more frequent relative to other dimensions, bargaining becomes more difficult.

Furthermore, we found a clear and growing bipolarity on East–West and North–South issues. Bipolarity accurately characterizes both the distribution of attitudes alone, and the distribution of intense attitudes. From the evidence, true neutrals or middlemen are neither very numerous nor very intense.

Some more hopeful signs arose when we looked at the rotated factor pattern. There remain a number of distinct dimensions, distinct enough to permit and even encourage bargaining. Supranationalism is an increasingly important dimension. Perhaps most encouraging was the decline, at least within the Assembly, of the cold war. To say that strictly cold war divisions are far less common in the UN does not necessarily indicate that they are so in the world at large. The particular exigencies of UN politics undoubtedy discourage, to a growing degree, discussion of cold war matters in the Assembly. Certainly the nonaligned states are trying to keep the cold war out of the Assembly. This is reflected in the increased prominence of supranationalist issues, which are often attempts to limit the cold war in certain areas of special interest to the neutrals. But because these efforts are opposed by one or both of the major powers (by definition when the votes show up on the supranationalism dimension) they are more nearly attempts to *suppress* than to *mediate* the cold war. Maybe depriving the great powers of a propaganda forum on this subject will help reduce overall international tensions, but in a way it could actually make the settlement of cold war disputes more difficult. The UN was, after all, designed as an arena for discussing the major issues dividing nations.

The cold war political pattern nevertheless remains essentially

---

11. Flexibility is of course lost if bargaining ceases. It is conceivable that a state, frustrated by its inability to gain support from a bloc on an issue of particular importance to it, might retaliate by always voting against the recalcitrant bloc. Such behavior, if it became widespread, would be reflected in the collapsing of several dimensions into a single one.

bipolar, possibly of the "loose bipolar" sort. This is not quite so true of the self-determination division, though even there bipolarity is present and probably increasing. The factor score distributions do not provide much evidence that the major bloc leaders, especially the Soviets, are allowing themselves to be pulled very near the middle to pick up votes. Perhaps because the UN has so little power to enforce its decisions, the pressure on the great powers to play the parliamentary game is meeting with only limited success. But still there is a mediating group, rather intense if not numerous, which attempts to mitigate the conflict. And only recently have some of the most extreme Eastern states been the ones most directly involved —the Afro–Asians rather than the Soviet bloc. The future will depend in part upon the continuing strength of various ties which still bridge the gap between the colonial and ex-colonial worlds.

# CHAPTER 11

# World Politics in Assembly Policies

Quincy Wright has noted that international politics can be treated "as a deterministic system, permitting prediction, or as a voluntaristic system permitting choice and control."[1] Our analysis has combined a voluntaristic study of the influence of the main groups or parties in the General Assembly with a more deterministic view of the pressures resulting from the distribution of general policy preferences of nations and their populations. Diplomatic activity has been voluntaristically interpreted as the attempt to reinforce or change policy positions by rewording resolutions and reshaping perceptions of world events in terms of issues on which policy predispositions are favorable to the party concerned. In the preceding chapter we analyzed some of the destabilizing consequences that might be predicted from trends in the distribution of these predispositions and the intensities with which they are held by Assembly members. Again we have not determined why these policy preferences and intensities are as they are, but have assumed them as previously determined by some other process related to the political world in which the Assembly operates.

Whether we employ a two-party or a multiparty model of Assembly politics, it is clear that policies taken there to a large extent reflect broader national foreign policies. The usual mechanism for translating these policies into resolutions, speeches, and votes in the Assembly is the diplomatic communication from the national foreign offices. When a delegate is not specifically advised in this manner, he relies on more general instructions, his own personal initiatives and obligations, and a number of national, regional, and caucusing group loyalties and attitudes. Some idea of the degree of personal freedom exercised by the diplomats themselves can be obtained on an impressionistic basis by interviewing them. On issues

1. Quincy Wright, *The Study of International Relations* (New York, Appleton-Century-Crofts, 1955), p. 495.

that are not of material significance, for instance, many of the smaller or newer states receive very few instructions. The specific influence of personal interpretations and national instructions on each of the issues in the Assembly is, however, as difficult to uncover systematically as is the content of each diplomat's official correspondence. Many of the important conversations and documents are lost or never officially recorded.

To explain UN voting positions one is thus forced deeper in the "funnel of causality," [2] back from the voting act to those regional, social, economic, and political forces affecting national foreign policies. As reviewed in Chapter 1, a number of environmental variables have been suggested as relevant to Assembly voting. The most suggestive list used in studies of voting behavior in international organizations appears in a paper by Ernst Haas on the International Labor Organization.[3] Haas' environmental variables included geographic location, economic development, political system, and alignments in the cold war. As measures of geographic location, we shall use the regional variables defined in Chapter 9; except for the Asian grouping, their similarity to caucusing group identifications also will help us to see how strongly such loyalties or their more distant geographic counterparts affect Assembly voting. Rather than Haas' four-fold classification of the stages of economic development, we have chosen a single index of average income in a society, per capita Gross National Product for the year 1955 measured in United States dollars.[4]

United Nations members were further classified as to the degree of competitivenesss of their respective political systems.[5] "Competi-

2. The notion of a "funnel of causality" whose principal axis is a time dimension toward the center of which at any time period are those causal events that are theoretically relevant, personally conscious, and perceived as increasingly political is presented in Campbell et al., *The American Voter*, Chap. 1.

3. "System and Process in the I.L.O."

4. The paucity of available and comparable data required that data on this and the racial composition variable introduced below be for only one year somewhere near the middle of the period we are studying. These variables occasionally include estimates when accurate figures are not available. Data and sources may be obtained from the Yale Political Data Program.

5. Partly because Haas' data were unavailable, we have modified the classifications given by Gabriel A. Almond and James S. Coleman, eds., *The Politics of the Developing Areas* (Princeton, N. J., Princeton University Press, 1960), pp. 532 ff. on the basis of consultations with area specialists and by using R. H. Fitzgibbon and Kenneth F. Johnson, "Measurement of Latin American Political Change," *American Political Science Review*, 55 (1961), 515–26. These classifications correlate about 0.90 with an earlier set of categories suggested by Alker in "Dimensions of Voting."

tive" systems are those in which two or more parties compete without government interference. "Authoritarian" regimes are those where competitive party politics are either nonexistent or rigidly controlled by the government. States satisfying neither of these conditions are grouped in a residual category. Among such "semicompetitive" states we would include Mexico, and, until recently, Pakistan and Indonesia, where a good deal of competition existed within a single party or nonelective parliament. Military alliances with the United States or with the Soviet bloc were used as measures of cold war political alignments. Bilateral or multilateral defense treaties, such as the United States has with Japan, Nationalist China, SEATO, NATO, and the OAS, were taken as evidence of this kind of Western allegiance. Soviet military allegiance was restricted to members of the Warsaw Pact and, in 1961, Mongolia. In 1961 neither Cuba nor Spain was considered to be a formal military ally of a cold war antagonist.

Several other variables suggested by the literature on international organization and relations were included in the analysis: colonial status, cumulated post-World War II foreign aid from the United States and from the Soviet bloc, the percentage of a nation's total foreign trade with the Western Big Three or with the Soviet bloc, and the racial composition of UN member states.[6] In defining colonial status an attempt was made to include among the colonial and ex-colonial states only those with comparatively recent and relevant experience. Since within the Assembly the Soviet Union is not generally considered a colonial power, colonial powers were defined as those states having extra-European colonies at some time since 1918; ex-colonial states were likewise those states that had been

6. Hans Morgenthau, *Politics among Nations* (2d rev. ed. New York, Knopf, 1956), for example, discusses similar variables under such opposite headings as military, economic, and cultural imperialism, or cultural and functional approaches to world community, pp. 54–59 and 486–502. See also K. W. Deutsch, "Toward an Inventory of Basic Trends and Patterns in Comparative and International Politics," *American Political Science Review, 54* (1960), 34–57, and B. M. Russett, "The Calculus of Deterrence," *Journal of Conflict Resolution, 7* (1963), 97–109. Other possible environmental variables could be derived from a comprehensive analysis of the major value allocation practices of international society. Harold Lasswell, for example, has suggested a number of value categories that should be relevant to international politics: wealth, power, respect, skill, physical well-being, moral rectitude, affection, and intellectual enlightenment. For examples of how these variables can be operationalized see his *The Future of Political Science* (New York, Atherton Press, 1963).

extra-European colonies for any period since 1918, just before the end of World War I and the birth of the League of Nations. The two racial variables used were percentage Negro population and percentage population of European descent.

Moslem population as a percentage of the total population was also included. Such a variable is more useful as an indicator of cultural patterns than as a measure of religiosity per se. As suggested by O'Brien, Moslem identity was expected to correlate with voting on Palestine and related issues.[7]

### THE EFFECTS OF WORLD CLEAVAGES ON ASSEMBLY POLITICS

Although causally rather distant from roll-call votes, variables like per capita G.N.P., colonial past, military alliances, and racial composition should be highly correlated with Assembly voting alignments. First, it is clear that among as well as within nations characteristics like wealth, color, the impact of a colonial past, and economic ties with the great powers are very unequally distributed. Such cleavages correspond to what sociologists call the stratifications of a society. Second, data on patterns of initiation, discussion, and voting in the General Assembly also reveal a good many cleavages which may correspond to these stratifications. Third, on issues like self-determination or the cold war we know that different strata or their "party representatives" in the Assembly feel a sense of identification and shared interests as a result of such common ties and background. In sociological theory such a sense of identity is characteristic of social classes; it typically finds political expression.

---

7. Several other environmental determinants of voting positions were tested but because of low correlations they will usually be omitted in the discussion below. Air distance to the United States turns out to be a poor indicator of Western ties—aid and trade are much superior. Per capita G.N.P. generally exceeded total G.N.P. in its correlations with East–West, North–South, self-determination, or supranationalism alignments. Perhaps logarithms of G.N.P. would have given a better measure of overall national power potentials than unlogged G.N.P.'s. Total foreign aid from the U.S. since World War II was found to be more closely correlated with pro-American voting positions than aid since the previous UN session analyzed. Perhaps *changes* in voting positions are more closely related to short-term aid commitments. Regionally, recent aid figures also do not reflect massive Marshall Plan assistance to Western Europe. Finally, percentage Christian population was found to be a poorer indicator of European culture (in the UN context) than the Old European group variable. Its superiority to European racial percentages as an interval scale measure of European culture, especially in Latin America, should not be overlooked.

The authors of *The American Voter* have defined the condition of active and conscious discord between social strata as "status polarization." Measuring status polarization with a correlation coefficient of the relationship between political preferences and sociological cleavages, they suggest that "variation in the status polarization of a society reflects variation in the intensity and extent of class identifications among its members." [8] They mention several factors contributing to high polarization which are present to a remarkable but varying extent in the General Assembly: (1) *Class awareness and identification.* Regional, alliance, and economic ties are very frequently mentioned in the course of Assembly debates. (2) *A high level of conceptualization.* Well-rationalized thought processes are the trademark of a good diplomat. (3) *High political involvement.*[9] This is obviously true to varying degrees of all but the purely ceremonial members of certain delegations.

Because of the variety of causes of international conflicts it seems quite reasonable to generalize the status polarization concept to other cleavages in international society that are of potential political relevance. Economic, ideological, social, or military polarizations of Assembly voting are worthy of our concern.

The multiplicity of possible environmental polarizers suggests another way of relating cross-pressures to the likelihood of serious international conflict. The potentially damaging effects of high income polarization, for example, may be offset by additional polarizers with opposite effects. States with different per capita incomes, but shared ethnic or cultural allegiances, are likely to become less hostile toward each other (exhibiting what sociologists call a "withdrawal effect" or psychologists label the "reduction of cognitive dissonance"). Two

8. Pp. 338 ff. Chap. 12 of *The American Voter* on "Membership in Social Groupings" and Chap. 13 on "The Role of Social Class" are highly germane to the present discussion. A very similar approach is Johann Galtung's application of James Coleman's work on community polarization (*Community Conflict*, Glencoe, Free Press, 1957) to international summitry: "Summit Meetings and International Relations," *Journal of Peace Research*, 1 (1964), 36–54.

9. Sidney Verba, "Assumptions of Rationality and Non-Rationality in Models of the International System," *World Politics*, 14 (October 1961), 93–117, has suggested the somewhat related hypothesis that high involvement will increase the number of predispositional or nonlogical (personality oriented) effects on decision-making. If these personality traits are national characteristics, then his point of view converges with the one being suggested above. Verba also suggests that personality will become less important as the actors' information, skills, and sense of influence and of responsibility increase.

polarizers, like income and race, may both correlate quite highly with the same alignment without correlating appreciably with each other. The political consequences of social, economic, and psychological cleavages that are perceived to reinforce each other are much more serious. Racial, economic, and alliance variables all reinforcing the same cleavage would be a greater cause for alarm. Perhaps, for example, broader East–West cleavages reflect just such a trend.

Environmental variables may be highly correlated with particular voting dimensions in a way that appears to limit opportunities for political maneuver; they may also influence trends in the bipolarization of Assembly voting positions and intensities and the prominence of Assembly concerns. Even when correlations between per capita G.N.P. and self-determination voting are constant, it is possible for both the distribution of national incomes and national self-determination voting positions to become more or less bipolar. Thus the bipolarization of the national characteristics of Assembly members may explain why policy positions are similarly bipolarized and why certain issues have become more prominent or less prominent in Assembly politics. It may be necessary to explore such explanations for Assembly trends if correlational evidence does not prove sufficiently adequate.

Changing environmental polarizations might also affect the *number* of distinct super-issues appearing in the Assembly, a fundamental characteristic of the Assembly's political system and of the metagame being played to change the issues and stakes of Assembly politics. The collapse of several voting dimensions into a single overriding conflict also suggests destabilizing consequences. In 1956, for example, the Suez crisis nearly brought Arab–Israel differences, anticolonialism, and the cold war together. Several other dimensional trends of this sort deserve our particular attention—the increasing pervasiveness of East–West and self-determination voting, and the decreasing frequency of North–South and cold war alignments. The accentuated bipolarization of positions on the alignments and stronger intensities of feeling about them can also be put into a worldwide, environmental perspective. Where differences are great, are keenly felt, and where other policies and policy determinants reinforce these cleavages, "total politics" threatens the basic consensus of a pluralistic political system.[10]

10. Berelson et al., *Voting*, p. 319.

Elaborating on this view, several questions need to be answered regarding environmental influences on stable and changing distributions of policy attitudes in the General Assembly:

1. To what extent are voting alignments environmentally polarized?

2. Do the polarizing variables reinforce or tend to cancel out each other's effects?

3. Can related trends in the bipolarization of voting positions and intensities [11] be explained by environmental bipolarizations? If so, which variables—regional, economic, social, or political—seem to have brought them about?

4. Can changing polarizations be used to account for changes in the prominence of certain dimensions—tendencies for some to disappear and for others to merge?

5. Depending on the extent to which Assembly arguments serve to build up or let off steam, which voting polarizations are most likely to erupt into violent conflict outside of the Assembly? Given the large amount of literature by social scientists on the United Nations, the lack of systematic studies of the environmental determinants of voting in the General Assembly and of their consequences for the limitations and opportunities of UN conflict resolution procedures is surprising.

### THE POLARIZATION OF EAST–WEST VOTING

Figures 11.1 and 11.2 show the degree to which the environmental variables polarized East–West and North–South alignments from 1947 to 1961. If we bear in mind the importance of diplomatic and personal intervening variables, we may consider these environmental polarizers as multiple determinants of voting positions.[12] Product-

11. See Louis Guttman, "The Principal Components of Scaleable Attitudes," in Paul Lazarsfeld, ed., *Mathematical Thinking in the Social Sciences* (Glencoe, Free Press, 1955), pp. 216–57. He suggests that the intensity component is logically derivable from attitudinal positions. Thus correlations with attitudes might be expected to recur in some form when intensities are considered.

12. It should be clear that considering environmental variables as "determinants" of voting positions is a (useful) analytic distinction. Until systematic attempts have been made to test for the relative importance of each of these variables and to control for the effects of the intervening variables, *causal* inferences can not be assured. See Alker, "Dimensions of Voting," Chaps. 8–11, for the beginnings of causal analysis using multiple regression techniques. Looking at unpredicted residuals from such an analysis is a valuable way of improving one's explanations and taking into account the impact of intervening variables. Nonadditivity and the ordering of variables along the funnel of

moment coefficients of correlations (r's) between a wide range of theoretically relevant environmental variables and East–West and North–South voting positions were calculated for each of the four years studied.[13] In Figure 11.1 correlations with Western voting appear above the zero line and those with Eastern positions apear below it.

Regional variables in most cases correspond to caucusing group identifications. On the basis of the maps in Part I and the interpretation of the East–West conflict offered there, we would expect the Soviet bloc and the Arab states to be most Eastern in their voting. Old Europeans and Latin Americans should be farthest West. These expectations are borne out, with remarkable regularity, for each year in the analysis. The Soviet bloc and Old Europeans (a much larger group) were the highest polarizers (r's were around .50 and .60 respectively) of East–West voting.

Among regional groups Latin American states fluctuated considerably in their East–West positions: in 1952 many more Latin states took Eastern positions than usual. The small number of African states before 1961 and the Western allegiance of the Brazzaville states have together prevented Africa per se from becoming a polarizing force in the East–West conflict. Nonetheless, in 1961 the African states were voting considerably East of all Latin Americans and Old Europeans. Asian location has also not correlated highly with voting on this dimension. The *within-group* polarization of Asian states, due in large part to the military alliances with the West, prevents such an outcome.[14] As Figure 11.1 shows, Latin Americans in the early years of the UN, and Afro–Asians in more recent years, have

---

causality have also to be taken into account. See Alker, "The Long Road to Mathematical Theories of International Politics: Problems of Statistical Nonadditivity" (paper delivered at the Annual Meeting of the American Political Science Association, Chicago, September 1964).

13. Although other measures of association could have been used to gauge polarizing effects, the present choice, which measures the degree of linear relationship between two variables, has the advantage of being interpretable, when squared, as the percentage of voting variance explained by the environmental variable. For variables with skewed frequency distributions, nonlinear relationships sometimes have higher explanatory power; in the present context, however, only linear polarizing effects will be studied.

14. For a discussion of the various possible combinations of within-group and between-group (ecological) correlations that go into worldwide correlations such as those presented in Figures 11.1 and 11.2 see Alker, "Regionalism versus Universalism in Comparing Nations," in B. Russett, H. Alker, K. Deutsch, and H. Lasswell, *World Handbook of Political and Social Indicators* (New Haven, Yale University Press, 1964).

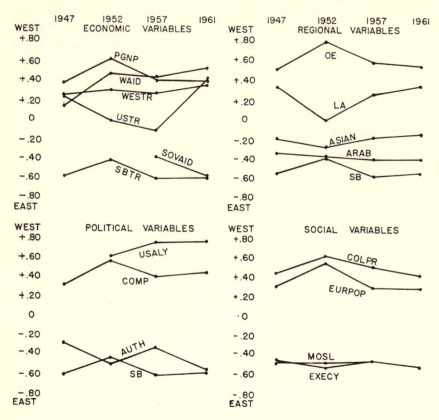

Figure 11.1. Environmental Polarizations of East–West Conflict

been the groups most subject to East–West cross-pressures in an otherwise regionally polarized General Assembly.[15]

We would expect economic variables like U.S. trade and the Western Big Three trade (USTR and WESTR in the figures), Soviet bloc trade (SOVTR), and cumulated per capita American, Western, and

15. If we allow for the split of Africans into Casablanca and Brazzaville groups and allow one degree of freedom to estimate the location of each of eight regional or caucusing groups, voting positions on the predominant East–West conflict in the Assembly can be interpreted by a linear multiple regression equation with a multiple correlation coefficient of .88. Squaring this number means that 78 per cent of East–West voting positions can be "predicted" by knowing a state's group memberships and an overall measure of each group's East–West position. This and other multiple correlations given below are presented in Alker, "Dimensions of Conflict in the General Assembly," pp. 655–56.

Soviet aid (USAD, WESAD, and SOVAD respectively) economically to polarize the East–West conflict. In Figure 11.1 we find considerable polarization—not quite so high on the Western side as with the regional variables—and a polarization that has remained remarkably stable through time. Of these six indicators only American trade has fluctuated significantly with respect to East–West alignments, probably because of the sharp Western swing among America's closest trading partners, the Latin Americans.[16]

A final economic determinant of the East–West controversy whose strong correlation with Western voting positions was not entirely expected is per capita G.N.P. (PGNP). On reflection the association is obvious: Soviet bloc per capita incomes are considerably lower than those of most Old European states, and Western Latin Americans are, on the average, wealthier than Eastern Afro–Asians. Nevertheless, intense Latin anti-Western voting on the question of economic self-determination at the end of the Korean War helps explain the 1952 peak in this and other polarizations (see Chapter 4). Whether Latin or Old European actions were to blame is a different question.

According to diplomatic and scholarly opinions on world politics, all the social and political variables included in the present analysis (race, colonial status, political system, and military alliances) should polarize East–West voting in the UN. Among the social variables, it turns out that colonial powers (COLPR) and ex-European colonies (EXECY) have been moderately and rather continuously polarized against each other. These colonial status polarizations are about 0.50 in magnitude for each of the four sessions, explaining about one

16. Our evidence is insufficient to determine the extent to which votes in the Assembly are "bought" with aid and trade, but in general we do find higher trade and aid polarizations with Soviet economic links than with Western ones. The 1957 dip in Soviet aid polarization does not imply a decreased polarization at the individual national level. Soviet aid was so narrowly directed that the "Eastern" countries receiving it, such as Syria, India, and Egypt, were not numerous enough to increase the overall East–West polarization. Reciprocal influence relationship in these cases might best be called economic or political "interdependence."

Of the polarizing variables we have mentioned, surely trade and aid can be manipulated far more easily than regional identity, level of economic development, racial composition, and the political competitiveness of a foreign state. Changing a state's policy predispositions in this way would not necessarily alter the pervasiveness of Assembly voting along the East–West dimension, as would changing the perceived relevance of these predispositions.

quarter, or together at most half, of the East–West conflict. Before 1957 the European racial composition of states (EURPOP) seems to have induced Western voting to about the same extent as did former colonial status. In the Twelfth Session, and thereafter, Old European group membership or former colonial status appeared to be more highly correlated with Western voting.[17] The presence of more "Eastern" Europeans and more "Western" non-Europeans in the Assembly accounts for the racial depolarization. Until 1961 there were too few Negro states (NEGPOP) in the Assembly to produce linear correlations with any voting dimensions. In that year the Brazzaville states often voted with the West, thus continuing the Negro racial depolarization of East–West voting.

A common claim is that the East–West conflict is one of democracy (COMPET) versus authoritarianism (AUTHOR). But actually the correlations are only moderately high; military alliances with the United States (USALY) and in the Soviet bloc are strongly correlated with voting positions in this conflict. Between 1947 and 1952 there does seem to have been a slight increase in democratic and authoritarian polarization of the East–West conflict, but the finding of overall continuity in this regard is again impressive. As the number of states with which the United States is militarily allied has increased, however, the alliance polarization coefficient of Assembly politics has risen to 0.78, indicating that in 1961 around 60 per cent of Assembly East–West voting positions could be predicted just from knowing these alliance relationships. Communist alliances are of course smaller in number, and by themselves have not polarized Assembly voting to quite the extent that Western ones have (unless, of course, one considers them to have caused the Western alliances in the first place).[18]

17. For most Assembly sessions the regional Old European variable is correlated around 0.60 both with being a colonial power and with percentage of population of European descent. Although together these variables might statistically describe more than half of East–West voting, they seem only moderately to reinforce each other. Only about eight Assembly members have populations of European descent, *and* are Old European states, *and* have been colonial powers—and therefore are not likely to be cross-pressured on self-determination issues. In fact, these same states are those which usually will not vote for the anti-apartheid resolutions characteristic of the "anti-interventionism" factor in Assembly voting described in Part I.

18. The reader may consider the regional variable *SB* to indicate Soviet military alliances. (Adding Yugoslavia and/or Communist Cuba to *SB* because of military interdependence would increase East–West polarizations.)

### THE POLARIZATION OF NORTH–SOUTH VOTING

Although by definition East–West and North–South voting dimensions are completely uncorrelated with each other, we may expect that several environmental variables which correlate with one are likely to correlate with the other. A correlation of 0.70 with one axis means, however, that not more than half of the variability in an explanatory variable will be related to any other independent axis. With such a proviso we may expect that geographical distinctions which highly polarized the East–West geopolitical conflict will also correlate with North–South voting in the General Assembly.

Specifically, recall that the wealthier and more powerful Western and Eastern states, the Old Europeans and the Soviet bloc, were identified in Part I as Northern powers. On the basis of the maps in Part I we would expect Asians, Arabs, and especially Latin Americans before 1961 to polarize North–South voting in a Southern direction. Looking at Figure 11.2, we find that these regional polarizations have occurred, with considerable regularity.

Two interesting trends are brought out by the data. First, the extreme Northern isolation of the Soviet bloc on some Korean War issues (the anti-Soviet polarization of North–South voting in 1952 is 0.80) is seen from Figure 11.2 to have been the high point of its isolation on this dimension. In 1957 new Soviet policies and greater Arab support made for much less anti-Soviet polarization on North–South issues, but subsequent frustrations, ending with ONUC (see

---

A look at some of the intercorrelations among the East–West related economic–political–environmental variables suggests a reinforcing effect on Eastern leanings and a cross-pressuring effect on Western identifications. After estimating internal bloc trade, trade with the Soviet bloc correlates above 0.90 with bloc membership. As dichotomous (0 or 1) variables, Old European and Latin American group memberships correlate 0.33 and 0.54 respectively with the pattern of American military alliances in 1961. Outside their respective camps, Soviet trade shows a higher East–West correlation than does Big Three trade, although neither relationship is strong.

Taken together in a linear fashion, six aid, trade, and alliance variables explain just as much East–West voting (78 per cent) as the eight regional variables referred to in note 15 above. Although pro-Soviet variables are more highly intercorrelated with each other than pro-Western ones, on a worldwide scale the pro-Soviet variables are not merely the opposites of pro-Western ones. In fact, postwar U.S. aid and U.S. alliances, postwar Soviet aid, trade, and alliances all make "significant" contributions toward explaining East–West voting. *Between* East and West there are some cross-pressures at work.

Chapter 6) heightened the anti-Soviet North–South division of the Sixteenth Assembly. We have already noticed how Latin Americans "deserted" the West in 1952; looking at the North–South conflict we see a rather strong (about 0.60) pro-Southern Latin American polarization in 1952 and 1957. With the arrival in quantity of African Assembly members, the Latin Americans shifted West and North and now no longer lead the Southern camp.

Currently then, on North–South issues, it appears that Latins, Asians, and Arabs least polarize the Assembly and are more susceptible to cross-pressures. Arabs, for instance, have sometimes voted with the Soviet Union on North–South issues in return for support on Palestine questions. Asian allies of the United States have increasingly taken Northern as well as Western positions (viz. Nationalist China); Latin Americans, in differentiating their point of view from that of the newer African states, have also been under alliance pressures to move to the West and the North.

Regarding the high anti-Soviet polarizations of Assembly North–South voting, differences between Russia and Communist China, which our voting analysis does not reveal, might influence both these states to try to gain Southern support by balancing maneuvers. But other than occasional Soviet Northern abstentions (as on Palestine questions in 1952) the Russians' strategy does not seem to have been to minimize North–South differences. Rather, they have tried to persuade Afro–Asians and even Latin Americans that anti-Old European self-determination questions are really involved in a particular situation and thus to turn attention away from North–South issues.

Old Europeans, on the other hand, have not always been very united in their attitudes on North–South issues, although all of them have taken more or less Northerly positions. On development, decolonialization, and disarmament issues they have frequently been unable to agree with Southern positions. Their strategy appears to have been to increase the number of anti-Soviet votes on cold war related questions or moderate decolonialization resolutions.

Both the Soviet bloc and Old Europeans were less subjected to depolarizing cross-pressures on these issues than Arab–Asians and, more recently, Latin Americans. The degree to which pressures *within* these groupings correspond to the overall North–South conflict will be discussed in the following chapter.

## Figure 11.2. Environmental Polarizations of North-South Conflict

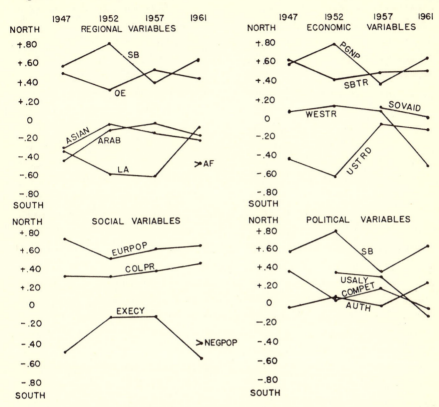

The content of the economic issues loading on the North–South conflict suggests that this conflict rests in part on a cleavage between rich nations and poor ones. From the new interest in this aspect of the North–South conflict, one could expect an increasing polarization of North–South voting along economic lines. The data in Figure 11.2, however, show that wealth has always polarized North–South voting to a moderate degree, with approximately the same magnitude since 1947. Just as the North–South dimension of Assembly politics has existed ever since the founding of the United Nations, now we see that this dimension, like the East–West conflict, has regularly taken on rich-versus-poor connotations.

It is not completely clear what North–South polarizations we might expect from the trade and aid variables, except that pro-Soviet or anti-Soviet economic ties should be especially relevant when the Soviet bloc itself (as in 1952 and 1961) is bearing the major brunt of anti-Northern policies. Such an effect appears on top of a steady Northern bias in Soviet trade. Soviet aid figures, which omit transactions within the Soviet bloc, reveal no North–South polarization in the rest of the world. Comparing Figures 11.1 and 11.2 it also turns out that trade with (and within) the Soviet bloc has had the same fluctuations in North–South polarization as the closely related Soviet bloc regional and caucusing group variable.

U.S. trade in 1952 and Western Big Three aid and trade have peak polarizations corresponding to the anti-Soviet regional polarizations of 1952 and 1961. Another more moderate trend in trade effects is probably attributable to the 1957 entrance into the General Assembly of more Afro–Asians trading with France and England. Before then Latin American contacts were sufficient to give American trade a Southern hue; by 1961 trade with the Western Big Three continued to be more Southern than Northern, although American trade per se had lost its polarizing effect. Over time there has been a slight decline in U.S. aid as a Northern force. The Marshall Plan and early NATO assistance have been augmented by Southern aid. But neither Soviet bloc nor Western aid seems clearly to distinguish Northerners from Southerners; we find that *trade, not aid,* better explains economic influences on the North–South conflict.[19]

Racial variables and colonial status correlate quite strongly with the North–South conflict. From Figure 11.2 we see that anti-

19. Weak Soviet and American North–South aid correlations suggest that aid has not been or could not very well be coercively manipulated to change short-run North–South alignments. A more basic convergence of political interests occurred in the Korean and Congo situations. One might argue however that the higher polarization and peculiar distribution of *trading* relationships suggest that both the within-group economic interdependence of the Soviet bloc and between-group Western trading relationships in primary products with newer UN members may perpetuate the North–South division. Issues of economic self-determination and primary commodities trade were specific components of North–South voting in 1952 and 1961 respectively.

Regional variables account for 78 per cent of North–South voting. Seventy per cent of North–South voting can also be "explained" by a six-variable regression equation involving trading relationships, per capita G.N.P., Communist politics, ex-colonial status, and European racial ties. Only Soviet trade with their allies and Western trade with their ex-colonies seem to have sizable but opposite effects on North–South voting; compared with East–West alignments fewer cross-pressures appear to be drawing North and South together. The same overall conclusion also emerges in the following chapter.

European voting on the North–South dimension has been quite continuous and, to our surprise, a more potent polarizer of Assembly votes than the more obvious variables derived from a nation's colonial past. A pro-Negro Southern polarization also becomes visible in 1961, but it would be difficult to say whether the leaders of Negro nations have become more or less politically conscious. Either the *larger number* of new Africans in the Assembly in 1961 or the *intensification* of racial identities would explain the results. We shall return to the effect of changes in the Assembly's membership later in this chapter.

Probably because of the increasing supranationalist, anti-Soviet flavor of North–South voting in 1961, we see a divergence in the way Communist and American military alliances affect the North–South voting dimension. The United States became pro-supranationalist and took some of its allies along; the Communists have always been opposed. Another interesting political finding is the lack of North–South polarizations on the basis of differences in political systems. Democracy and authoritarianism per se do not discriminate North–South voting position. Communist alliances (sb), however, give the same kind of reinforcing Northern polarization effects as Soviet bloc trade.

### ENVIRONMENTAL POLARIZATIONS OF SUBSTANTIVE ISSUES

The rotated factor patterns of Part I were presented in order to clarify both the component issues of the East–West and North–South conflicts and to explain some of the remaining voting variances left unexplained by the first two unrotated dimensions. Granting that the rotated factors can be interpreted more succinctly in terms of the specific issues loading on them, it would also be methodologically and substantively encouraging if the rotated factor scores showed clearer polarizations regarding some of the important stratifications in world politics. Because they are sometimes intercorrelated the revised rotated factor scores are also likely to reflect real world differences more accurately. Very high polarizations along racial, regional, economic, or ideological lines suggest, however, that cleavages in the Assembly coincide with a greater chance of violent conflict along these lines.

## Figure 11.3. Select Environmental Polarizations of Self-Determination Alignments

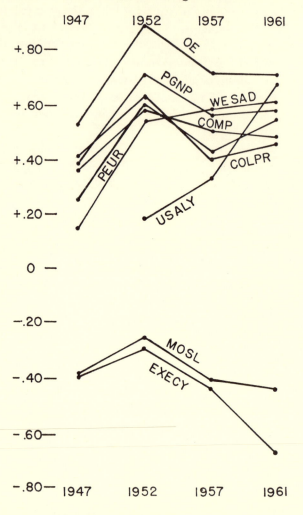

The cold war and self-determination issues both have important East–West components. Nonetheless we would expect trade, aid, and alliances to be the main cold war polarizers, while anti-European, anti-rich, and anticolonial polarizations of the self-determination conflict would seem more likely. On the basis of existing theory, however, it is hard to predict which stratifications among the plausible ones will be strongest, and what trends have occurred

## Figure 11.4. Select Environmental Polarizations of Cold War Alignments

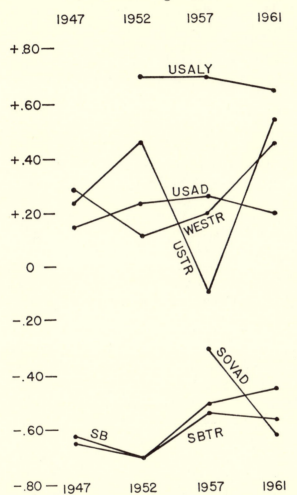

in these relationships. For these purposes a look at the cold war and self-determination correlations is appropriate. The highlights of the following discussion are illustrated in Figures 11.3 and 11.4.

### Cold War Polarizations

For the cold war, let us compare Soviet and Western aid, trade, and alliance polarizations. Since 1952, U.S. military alliances have consistently polarized cold war alignments at about the 0.70 level.

As the Chinese representation issue has increasingly become the basis of UN cold war alignments, since 1952 the anti-Soviet bloc polarization has decreased from 0.70 to a moderate 0.45 in 1961. More noncommunist states, especially newer Assembly members, have supported membership for Communist China. While the anti-Soviet bloc polarization of cold war alignments has decreased, polarizing effects of Soviet aid and trade have increased. Unless forced to do so, few states have been willing to enter into Soviet military alliances, with their accompanying loss of freedom; trading relationships have provided a more satisfactory and more reciprocal form of interdependence than aid or alliances. Between 1957 and 1961 Soviet aid has become more highly correlated with cold war alignments, while the Soviet trade cold war polarization declined to the middle 0.50s.[20]

Throughout the 1950s American and Western trade and aid patterns showed smaller polarizations with cold war alignments than either Soviet aid and trade or cold war military alliances. In 1961, however, the cold war relevance of Western trade ties increased to something like the Soviet level. Western aid failed to correlate highly with cold war alignments ($r = 0.36$), suggesting that Western or American aid has not been a particularly effective cold war polarizer. In effect both Afro–Asian and European splits over the representation of China have helped continue the depolarization of America's cold war aid in the United Nations. The Alliance for Progress and the continued aid of Western military allies in Asia may reverse this trend as more pro-Western states begin to receive economic "rewards." A rising aid polarization of cold war voting may in part be due to increasing Congressional criticisms of U.S. foreign aid programs.

It is clear that a good many more cross-pressures exist on Western than on Soviet states on cold war membership issues. Western-leaning states can take their choice of aid, trade, or alliances (which are only moderately intercorrelated variables) and maintain a fair amount of cold war flexibility; even Old Europeans and NATO are divided

20. Of the six cases between 1952 and 1958 when a country's foreign policy underwent a marked procommunist shift, five were preceded by a sharp increase in trade with the Soviet bloc. Cf. B. M. Russett, "Cause, Surprise, and No Escape," *Journal of Politics, 24* (1962), 14.

on Chinese representation.[21] We must expect that the more consistent pressures of Soviet aid, trade, and alliances leave less room
for discretion on cold war issues. Differences within the Soviet bloc
involving Communist China do not appear in Assembly voting
behavior; nonetheless, they do add some degree of choice on cold war
issues for communist and noncommunist states outside the Assembly.

### Self-Determination Polarizations

We know that colonial status, per capita G.N.P., and Old European identification correlated moderately with the East–West conflict; further analysis shows, however, that the polarizing effect of
these variables has been on self-determination issues rather than cold
war issues. All three variables since 1957 have had correlations with
cold war alignments around or below 0.30. Old European group membership had a phenomenal polarizing effect on self-determination
issues (with a correlation of 0.90) in 1952; since then the correlations
have been in the 0.70s. With self-determination scores, percentage
European population has correlated, on the average, around 0.50;
cold war alignments, however are completely unrelated to European
racial composition (the r's average about 0.05). Colonial or ex-
colonial status has also contributed to self-determination polarizations, with average coefficients in the 0.50s; since 1952 their average
cold war polarizations have been around 0.30. Since 1952 wealth
differences have correlated in the 0.60s with self-determination alignments, certainly higher than their relationship to cold war positions.

An interesting polarization differential also occurs regarding political democracy: political competitiveness polarizes self-determination
alignments (r's average about 0.50) more than it does the cold war
(r's average about 0.30). Paradoxically, the higher relationship is a
negative one: being democratic correlates with taking *anti*colonial
positions, at least in the UN context. Apparently, democracies are
more likely to be colonial powers and to be *anti*-self-determination
than Woodrow Wilson's moving pleas for democratic self-determination would have us believe.

The analysis of the preceding paragraph confirms our expecta-

---

21. Cross-pressures on cold war membership issues are also suggested by the
inaccuracy of multiple regression analyses of this dimension. Group variables together
account for only 30 per cent of unrevised cold war voting alignments in 1961.

tion that the two main components of East–West voting—self-determination issues and the cold war—are distinguishable in their environmental polarizers as well as in their characteristic substantive content. Colonial status, per capita G.N.P., European influence, and political democracy all polarize self-determination alignments to a greater extent than the cold war.

We should inquire, however, whether the aid, trade, and alliance polarizers of the East–West conflict and of the cold war also affect self-determination alignments. In general, these polarizers are not specific to the cold war but, as we would expect, they have usually correlated with self-determination alignments to a lesser extent. The difference is clearest for Soviet bloc aid, trade, and alliance relationships; these countries do not have a history of ties with the Latin and Afro–Asian worlds. In 1947 cold war and self-determination issues were merged in a single alignment. From 1952 to 1961, Soviet trade, aid, and bloc membership had low polarizing effects on self-determination alignments: in 1961, for example, the relevant coefficients were all below 0.30 in magnitude. During the same period corresponding cold war polarizations were around 0.50 or higher.

Western aid, trade, and alliance variables show surprising and more complicated differentiations between cold war and self-determination alignments. Whereas U.S. and Western aid have not polarized cold war alignments on a worldwide basis, as some would expect, cumulative postwar American and Western aid does show a significant anti-self-determination effect (apparently procolonial or less anticolonial friends are successfully either bought or rewarded).

Western aid polarizations do not correspond to trade or alliance effects on self-determination alignments. Unlike the Soviet bloc, the United States and the Western Big Three trade with both anti-colonial and procolonial states. As more ostensibly cold war issues have been perceived by Assembly majorities along self-determination, anti-Western lines, however, American alliances have increasingly polarized self-determination voting. Before 1961 the alliances polarized cold war alignments more than self-determination ones; at the Sixteenth Session self-determination alignments were as highly polarized ($r = 0.72$) by American alliances as cold war votes ($r = 0.66$).

## Palestine Polarizations

Select environmental polarizations of Palestine related issues are presented in Figure 11.5. Despite reservations about the distinctiveness of Palestine related questions in 1961 (the same interrelationships with self-determination existed in 1952, but to a lesser extent) we see several continuous Palestine polarizations in Figure 11.5. The

Figure 11.5. Select Environmental Polarizations of
Palestine Alignments

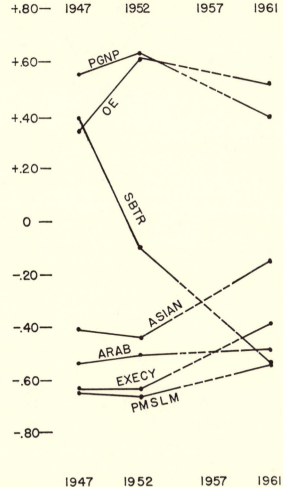

## Figure 11.6. Select Environmental Polarizations of U.N.
## Supranationalism Alignments

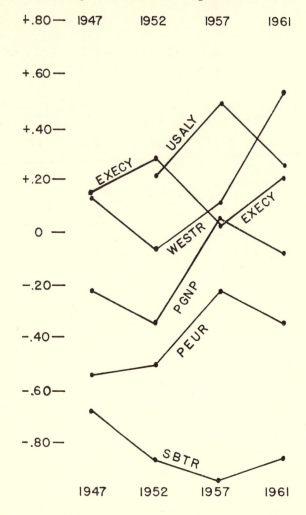

Arab group has regularly polarized these questions at about the 0.50 level. (An Arab and nonaligned Asian grouping would have produced a higher correlation because these groups have usually voted together on Palestine related issues.) It also appears that U.S. alliances and Soviet trade are moderately correlated with positions on Palestine questions, but not so highly as with the cold war. Anti-European and anti-wealth polarizations are fairly strong on these questions, but not to the same degree as on self-determination issues.

A noticeable correlation between "anti-Arab" voting and political democracy suggests another relationship distinguishing Palestine questions from the cold war. Democracies in the UN have been especially sympathetic to anti-Moslem interests in Western New Guinea. The similar high correlation between democracy and a procolonial position on self-determination questions suggests, however, some justification for the Arab protests against the procolonial views of Old Europeans on Moslem questions.

The variety of cross-pressures in both the "pro-Arab" and "anti-Arab" directions on these issues clearly corroborates what we have already found—the considerable room for bargaining and compromise these issues contain. In 1961, for example, democracy, American alliances, Moslem populations, and Soviet trade all correlate with each other around or below 0.30 in magnitude. Added together, variables can help explain a good deal of Palestine voting; but such polarizers do not seem to reinforce each other in the world arena.

## Supranationalism Polarizations

Supranational issues have been North–South issues to a considerable extent. We should therefore expect some but not all North–South variables to account for supranationalism positions, with better discrimination. More strongly than was the case on all North–South issues taken together, in Figure 11.6 we see a growing anti-Soviet polarization on supranationalist issues since 1947, with correlation coefficients in the upper 0.80s. U.S. aid and alliances have not greatly polarized supranationalist voting except in 1957 when cold war aspects of this controversy increased aid and alliance supranationalist polarizations to 0.26 and 0.51 respectively. For 1947, 1952, and 1961 Western trade, rather than aid and alliances, had a considered pro-supranational correlation (0.55 in 1961), somewhat stronger than the North–South polarization due to Western trade (0.43 in 1961). These findings suggest that both communist recalcitrance and economic interdependence with the West help explain supranationalist tendencies in most national foreign policies.

The small *pro*-supranationalist correlation of an ex-colonial past is in strong contrast to the Soviet *anti*-supranational polarization. This finding strengthens our earlier interpretation of a split between ex-colonial countries and the Soviet bloc on supranational issues, which the Soviet Union has seriously misjudged. Even more clearly than was the case with North–South voting, the extreme anti-Soviet polarization of voting on supranationalism suggests that few cross-pressures have pulled the bloc toward the majority. Among the pro-supranationalism majority, a variety of conflicting pressures does not insure strong continued support for supranationalist programs. Low national income, for example, correlates much more highly with Southern and self-determination voting than with supranationalist positions. Not all ex-colonial states are strong supranationalists either: Arab ex-colonial states since 1947 have been skeptical of UN peacekeeping operations.

### Changes in the Distinctiveness of Assembly Issues

The high polarizing effect of a Western alliance on both cold war and self-determination issues requires further comment about the distinctiveness of these two issues. Chapters 6 and 9 noted a tendency for the Soviet bloc and its allies to frequently succeed in making issues like Hungary, Cuba, and Tibet—which to the West are of pure cold war vintage—appear as anti-Western or anticolonial questions. Although the rotated *factors* presented in Chapter 6 were themselves uncorrelated, a merging of the cold war and self-determination issues on other than Chinese membership questions was suggested. This occurred when issues with low loadings (usually under 0.25) were excluded from the calculation of *factor scores*. By correlating the revised rotated factor scores presented in the Appendix we can see a rising trend. In 1952 the correlation was only 0.29; by 1957 it was 0.43. In 1961 the revised cold war and self-determination factor scores were correlated even more highly with each other ($r = 0.48$). This same trend reflects the rapidly growing Western alliance polarization of self-determination questions in the General Assembly. The rising military polarization of self-determination alignments and the accelerated merging of self-determination and cold war issues suggest increased expectations of violence in postcolonial world politics.

Turning from the trend toward the merger of these two voting dimensions, are there similar developments regarding supranationalism and Palestine conflicts? In 1947 both Palestine and supranationalism were closely related to the North–South conflict in the Assembly. Since then Palestine issues have increasingly evoked East–West alignments, as Russia has supported Arab demands on Moslem questions. In 1961 Brazzaville states usually voted with the United States and France both on cold war membership questions and on West Irian. Thus the distinction between Palestine questions, and East–West ones has become quite blurred. Just cutting those roll calls loading below 0.25 from the calculation of Palestine factor scores produced a correlation of 0.76 between the revised Palestine scores and the revised cold war scores. The similarity of cold war and self-determination environmental polarizers to those polarizing Palestine voting would lead us to expect this result. The particular concerns of Arab and Moslem states on these questions, however, partially explain the differentiation of Palestine related polarizations from those more directly influencing either cold war or self-determination positions.

Supranationalism, on the other hand, has continued as an anti-Northern and particularly anti-Soviet concern. Only in 1957, when the Soviets supported the Arab states in their refusal to pay for UNEF and received some Arab support on disarmament proposals, did supranational issues look very much like East–West conflicts. With the isolation in 1961 of both the Soviet Union and several colonial powers on ONUC and UNEF, supranational votes were again anti-Northern alignments. Supranationalism has thus increased its distinctness as a North–South issue in the Assembly. A clearer substantive identity has also emerged. In 1957, revised supranationalism scores were correlated 0.52 with cold war scores and 0.48 with self-determination scores; by 1961 these correlations had dropped to only 0.16 and 0.22 respectively. Thus, supranationalism is more likely than the Palestine dimension to remain as a distinct alternative to anticolonial and cold war alignments in Assembly politics.

### POLARIZATIONS IN THE ENVIRONMENT OF THE ASSEMBLY

Remembering the bifurcation of the rotated East–West factor of 1947 into self-determination and cold war alignments before 1952, an overriding impression from Figures 11.1–11.6 is the continuity of environmental influences on Assembly voting. In almost every figure, the high polarizers have continued to polarize voting alignments.

On East–West and North–South dimensions, only a few variables showed changes in their polarizing effects, often with similar cleavages coming to take their place. From a closer analysis of rotated voting components, explanations such as the Russian shift on Palestine issues and the cold war aspects of 1961 self-determination issues were found even for those changes.

If, on the whole, changes in environmental polarizations do not seem sufficient to account for the growing bipolarity of East–West voting positions and speeches, as well as the increase in self-determination roll calls and initiatives in the Assembly, what does? In the growth of parliamentary parties, added voting cohesion and polarization can often be accounted for by the growing effectiveness of party organizations, which may or may not be associated with destabilizing political consequences. As quasi-parties in the Assembly, East and West have developed into more clearly defined groups. But again we may ask, why have these sides appeared to coalesce?

A simple answer is perhaps the most disarming one. If voting positions have been similarly related to their environment through time, *changes in the distributions* of the positions must result from *changes in the environment* affecting these positions.[22] The most dramatic change in post-World War II politics has obviously been the independence of something like fifty new nations. Membership in the United Nations has been a much sought-after symbol of this independence. From 1947 until 1961 the General Assembly approximately doubled its size from 56 to 104 members.

In effect, this growth in the Assembly's membership has increased some groups' representation more than others. From the groups we introduced in Chapter 9 trends in proportionate membership are shown in Figure 11.7. Among Western powers Latin American states have most clearly declined in relative strength. In 1947 they constituted by far the largest regional group in the Assembly— together with either those farther to the East or the West their 35 per cent of the membership could virtually command a two-thirds

22. This point of view is suggested by Haas, "Revolutionary Nations in the UN: Dynamic Environment and Static Systems." In terms of the enfranchisement of new voters analogy suggested in Chap. 8, the implication of the present analysis is that *environmental* polarizations, not *policy* polarizations, are more determinative of international instability.

Figure 11.7. Trends in the Regional Composition of the
General Assembly 1947–1961

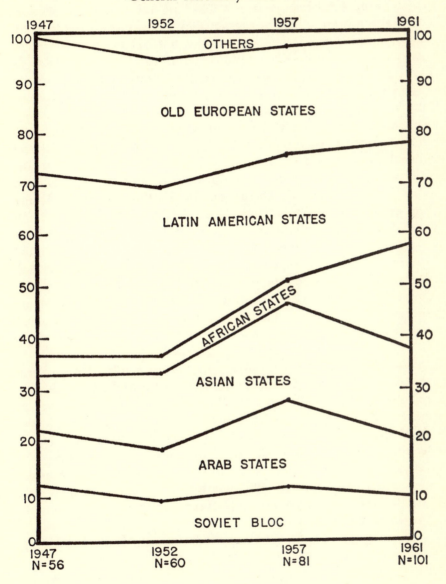

majority. By 1961, however, there were as many Old Europeans and a constantly rising number of Africans. Old Europeans needed most Latin American votes as a blocking third in the Assembly; Afro–Asians were able to pass resolutions in committee without Latin support if the Soviet bloc agreed and not too many pro-Western Afro–Asians deserted their regional positions. As we have seen, in 1961 Latins frequently voted with the Old Europeans against Afro–Asian and Soviet initiatives; these states plus Western allies formed the Western party in the Assembly.

Among Eastern states, Asian and African nations have increased their shares of Assembly membership; Arab states and the Soviet bloc have maintained their existing representation. In 1961 the sharp rise in African membership corresponded to more marked anti-Western voting on African questions. With the Soviet Union supporting the anti-imperialist cause, the Assembly dealt at length with South Africa, Southern Rhodesia, and Portuguese colonialism.

In 1947 the Soviet bloc sometimes failed to support anticolonial causes, and was able to get only neutralist abstentions on cold war issues. By 1961 its pole of the East–West conflict was greatly augmented by the Arab and African Casablanca powers and by many of the nonaligned Asian states. Taken together, the states consistently voting against the West on these issues may be considered the Eastern party in the General Assembly.

When states at the poles of the East–West conflict have agreed, or when from both sides they have been forced to disagree with the policies of the middle powers, North–South alignments have occurred. Typically the Soviet Union has been isolated on North–South questions; but with considerable regularity it has been joined by the most anti-interventionist of the Old European states. The Congo and Rwanda and Burundi were important African issues evoking this alignment in 1961. Figure 11.7 also suggests how they and the Soviet bloc have since 1947 been potentially subject to anti-Northern Assembly majorities.

Some of the specific environmental changes resulting from the enlarged membership of the Assembly are depicted in Figure 11.8. Although many other variables have similar distributions, only high polarizers have been chosen for explicit analysis: national per capita wealth, colonial status, racial composition, and cold war alliances.

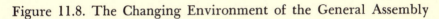

Figure 11.8. The Changing Environment of the General Assembly

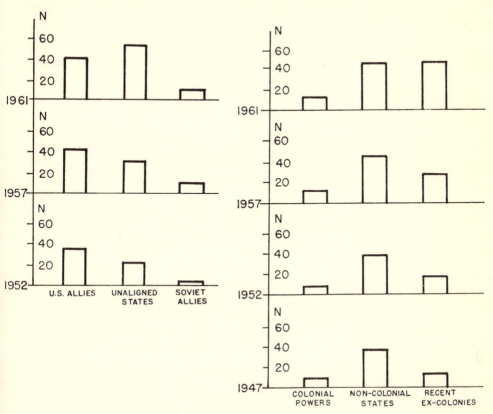

A. THE DISTRIBUTION OF MILITARY ALLIANCES.

B. THE DISTRIBUTION OF COLONIAL STATUS.

Figure 11.8A shows trends in the distribution of military alliances in the Assembly. The striking change has been neither the increase in American alliances nor in Soviet bloc representation; rather more significant is the gradual change from a skewed pro-Western distribution in 1947 to a unimodal shape in 1961 centered on the nonaligned states. This shift helps substantially in explaining the decline in American dominance of the Assembly on cold war issues; it also suggests one reason that cold war issues have recently concerned the Assembly less.

Figure 11.8B, on the other hand, indicates why East–West issues, in particular the special and potentially violent postcolonial self-determination issues, have increasingly preoccupied the Assembly. In the first three years of our study, states that were neither ex-colonies nor colonial powers were the modal group in the Assembly. In this period the relatively few Arab and Asian ex-colonial states had to rely in particular on Latin American willingness to vote against Old European states on economic and trusteeship self-determination issues in order to get significant voting support other than from the Soviet Union. In 1961, however (and even more so since then), the number of ex-colonial states surpassed those with no

Figure 11.8. The Changing Environment of the General Assembly

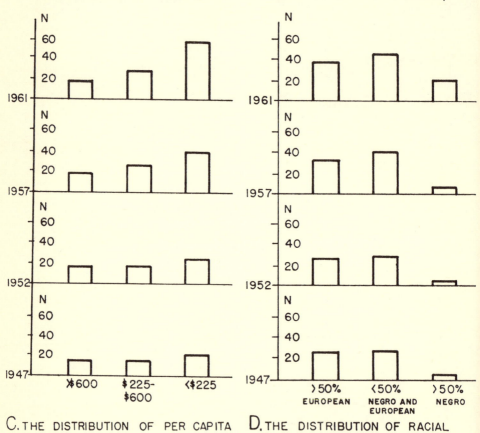

C. THE DISTRIBUTION OF PER CAPITA INCOME.

D. THE DISTRIBUTION OF RACIAL CHARACTERISTICS.

such recent or direct experience. With the noncolonial Soviet bloc joining the ex-colonial states on many self-determination issues, it is not surprising that the remaining noncolonial states (in particular Latin Americans and some of the pro-Western Asians) increased their cooperation with the colonial power minority.

With the ex-colonial rather than noncolonial states carrying the flag of self-determination it is not surprising that East–West speeches, resolutions, and roll calls related to self-determination increased in the Assembly in the same way that cold war related attentions have diminished. With similar and reinforcing effects from wealth and racial divisions (Figures 11.8C and 11.8D above), it also becomes clear why the overall number of self-determination East–West issues has increased to a marked extent, even more than cold war votes have decreased.

Before turning to the figures, however, it is necessary to discuss why, in spite of the anticolonial environment influencing East–West voting, there has been a rise in the correlation of U.S. military alliances with pro-Western voting on East–West issues and a corresponding fall relative to North–South voting. This was the most marked East–West polarization change in Figures 11.1 and 11.2. In addition to the cold war aspects and potentially violent character of many of the anticolonial resolutions, two factors seem important. First, the Soviet bloc has vocally championed the anti-imperialist cause and blamed situations in Angola and South Africa on the NATO powers. Ties between colonial powers and anticommunist allies have thereby been reinforced even when a cold war situation has not been clearly involved. Secondly, as previously suggested, Latin American states, as U.S. allies in OAS, have continued to be pro-West on cold war related issues, but they have *moved* West on self-determination questions, in part because of their loss of power and prominence to the newer African states and in part because of the severity of recent postcolonial self-determination resolutions. A result of this movement has been to bring U.S. alliances and Western voting positions into closer agreement.

As for trends in the distribution of wealth among Assembly members (Figure 11.8C), we see a similar change from the fairly equally distributed set of income levels of 1947 (with the Latin Americans mostly in the lower two levels) to an extremely skewed domination of the Assembly by Eastern and Southern states with per capita GNPs under $225.[23] An economic component of East–West and North–South demands can be expected to increase in the future.

In the 1950s there were very few states in the Assembly with a proportion of Negro population higher than 50 per cent. The dramatic increase in 1961 explains the racial North–South polarization along these lines. The continued representation of non-European and non-Negro populations corresponds to the regularity of anti-European alignments in the Assembly. Continued antagonisms separate both Africans south of the Sahara from Latin Americans and black Africans from the Arab and Asian world. The possibility of a racial triangulation of views may yet confound both colonial European preoccupations with Negro minorities and Communist Chinese attempts to forge an anti-white majority.

### THE VARIETY OF POLARIZATION EFFECTS

An overview of this chapter cannot match the detailed analyses already presented, but it may serve to integrate a variety of findings and methodologies. These methodologies have included discussions of simple and multiple environmental correlations with policy positions, presentations of correlations among policy dimensions, and distributional displays of national characteristics represented in the General Assembly. The principal findings have concerned determinants of voting behavior, their reinforcing and cross-pressuring effects—including trends toward the collapse of certain distinctive issue dimensions—and similarities between distributions of national characteristics and frequency distributions of speeches and related voting positions.

Several general findings emerged. First of all, most *factor scores* can be rather accurately predicted after the fact—using one or a combination of regional and environmental variables far removed in the "funnel of causality" from the last minute instructions and conversations of harried diplomats. Specifically, more than half the

---

23. These results depend to some extent, of course, on the wealth levels used in trichotomizing the data. Trends using the same trichotomous cutting points, however, are less subject to this criticism. As natural cutting points for trichotomizing per capita income, $225 and $600 were first suggested in K. W. Deutsch, C. I. Bliss, and A. Eckstein, "Population, Sovereignty, and the Share of Foreign Trade," *Economic Development and Cultural Change, 10* (1962), 353–66.

variation of national positions on East–West and North–South alignments can be explained by multiple regression equations in which
Western alliances and Soviet bloc membership play the principal role.
The problem of analyzing actual *votes,* however, is considerably
more complicated by the freedom of choice involved in determining
which factor predispositions are going to be evoked by a particular
roll call.

Another finding was the surprising degree to which substantively
interpreted voting components, i.e. revised rotated voting dimensions, were more highly and more specifically correlated with
particular environmental variables than was usually the case concerning unrotated East–West and North–South dimensions. Non-
European states with low levels of economic development and the
experience of colonial rule, for example, appear to have been particularly influential regarding self-determination positions, while aid,
trade, and alliances have been more consistently related to the cold
war dimensions. The ex-colonial and politically democratic states
have tended to agree on supranationalism issues, whereas their
splitting on self-determination questions has been especially marked.

Both multiple and simple environmental correlations have suggested that national positions on several issue dimensions are particularly cross-pressured. Cold war and Palestine alignments are not
as highly polarized as other voting dimensions, nor are they as free
from cross-pressuring influences. Both dimensions have evidenced
decreasing prominence in Assembly politics; part of this trend can
be explained by a withdrawal effect, resulting from competing and
contradictory influences on most national positions. These cross-
pressuring effects, however, seem to have had more impact on noncommunist states than on communist ones. Partly because of this
differential effect, North–South alignments appear to have fewer
bridging variables than the pulls and pushes shaping East–West
positions. U Thant's view of the seriousness of the North–South
conflict in this sense appears justified.

Perhaps in response to a growing prevalence of polarizations influenced by alliance relationships, an increasing correlation between
self-determination and cold war alignments was discovered. Palestine
and cold war issues, on the other hand, grew closer together because
of a dramatic change in Soviet–Arab relationships. Both these trends
probably represent destabilizing changes in the number and fre-

quency of distinctive issues faced by the Assembly. A destabilizing interpretation, however, requires better knowledge of the levels of issue polarization effects that are likely to be seriously harmful.

Except for these merger tendencies, the continuity of environmental polarizers of Assembly positions in the 1952–62 period was especially marked. It was in fact the continuity of these coefficients that led to the study of frequency distributions of national characteristics. Rapidly changing distributions of economically poor nations, ex-colonial states, and politically neutral nations all help explain tendencies for some issues to disappear and for others—like East–West or, more particularly, self-determination questions—to increase in prominence.

By way of conclusion, it should also be recalled that the deterministic language of this chapter is at best provisional; the development of testing procedures for causal relationships is only in its infancy.[24] Voluntaristic diplomatic interpretations and manipulations of Assembly perceptions and predispositions are preached and practiced against a background of changing and stable environmental influences, each of which is in part subject to national controls.

24. The most readable exposition yet to appear of a modest but useful approach to causal inferences in correlational analyses of social science data is H. M. Blalock, Jr., *Causal Inference in Nonexperimental Research* (Chapel Hill, University of North Carolina Press, 1964).

# CHAPTER 12

# Crosscutting Solidarities:
# In Search of the Uncommitted

### GROUP COHESION

To this point in Part Two we have largely been concerned either with propositions about the international system as a whole or with broad trends in the behavior of groups of states. Yet assessment and prognosis—for the system or for groupings—require hypotheses about the behavior of particular states, or "voters." One aspect of this problem is the relation between a single government's constituency and the policies it pursues in the international system. In trying to affect the behavior of another state one government may appeal either directly to the other government or to the constituency beneath it. Thus the American government occasionally, on major issues, negotiates directly with other capitals, usually bargains with other delegations to the United Nations, and also often uses the General Assembly as a propaganda forum to influence world opinion. To examine these problems we may draw upon some of the hypotheses advanced by students both of the behavior of individual voters in national systems and of the behavior of legislators.

According to research on American voting behavior, the individual who is not fully committed to either party is likely to be the individual who is cross-pressured. Now cross-pressuring can occur in a number of ways. As originally derived, the description applied chiefly to sociological cross-pressures. That is, if blue-collar workers tend to vote Democratic and Protestants tend to vote Republican, then the Protestant blue-collar worker may find himself cross-pressured. Protestants will be more likely than other blue-collar workers to vote Republican and, conversely, blue-collar workers will be more likely than other Protestants to vote Democratic. Not satisfied with this level of explanation, later writers applied the cross-pressure hypothesis more explicitly to attitude cross-pressures. Thus an individual may prefer the Democratic party but dislike President Johnson. Or he may like a candidate's stand on civil rights but disapprove of his position on foreign policy questions. Again, he will be more likely to vote against a particular candidate than will someone whose attitudes are almost entirely favorable. Furthermore, the cross-pressured voter is more likely to make up his mind late, to shift allegiances, or even not to vote at all. He is one of the floating voters, those who, by their relative independence, make party competition for their favor meaningful.[1]

To inquire about the importance of cross-pressures in the international arena we need first to look more closely at the voting behavior of particular states. We shall ask which states deviate most strikingly from the voting patterns of their own regional groups. Which Latin Americans vote more East, or West, or North, or South than is the norm for the group as a whole? It seems desirable to examine group deviants because, despite differences, members of various regional groups do tend to share a substantial number of socioeconomic characteristics. Also, in earlier chapters we found a very high degree of unity within most of the caucusing groups (nearly but not quite identical with regional groups) and other writers have emphasized the bargaining and negotiation that precede intragroup agreement.[2] Though few Latins, for example, are as East as most Asians, it becomes essential to know which Latins are relatively East for their group. In this chapter we shall discuss primarily the *unrotated* factor patterns for the sessions we have studied, and principally their East–West and North–South dimensions. By so doing we shall be covering most roll-call votes. In the East–West unrotated factor we have the conflict which is paramount and accounts for more of the voting than any other rotated or unrotated factor; by adding North–South we account for more than would any other two factors. Though the reasons behind voting on

1. The voting studies have elaborated and refined these points. Cf. Paul Lazarsfeld, Bernard Berelson, and Hazel Gaudet, *The People's Choice* (New York, Duell, Sloan and Pearce, 1944) for the origin of the concept as applied basically to sociological pressure, and Campbell et al., pp. 80–88, for a recent careful distinction between the effects of sociological and psychological cross-pressures.

2. Cf. Thomas Hovet, Jr., "United Nations Diplomacy," p. 38.

diverse components of the East–West factor may vary, the voting alignments have not differed too greatly from year to year.

We constructed an "index of divergence" for each group on the East–West and North–South issues in each year. The index is simply the mean deviation from the group average factor score. A highly cohesive group will have a very low mean deviation; a disparate group, a high one. We may then, to find the mavericks in each group, simply identify those states whose factor scores differ from the group average by more than the mean deviation.[3]

### Table 12.1. Group Indices of Divergence*

| GROUP | 1947 | 1952 | 1957 | 1961 |
|---|---|---|---|---|
| *East–West* | | | | |
| Old Europeans | .29 | .17 | .35 | .17 |
| Soviet bloc | .03 | .002 | .02 | .01 |
| Asians | .53 | .52 | .60 | .67 |
| Arabs | .02 | .16 | .29 | .22 |
| Africans | | | .33 | .33 |
| Latin Americans | .51 | .40 | .37 | .33 |
| Average | .28 | .25 | .33 | .29 |
| *North–South* | | | | |
| Old Europeans | .29 | .46 | .54 | .62 |
| Soviet bloc | .16 | .02 | .03 | .03 |
| Asians | .32 | .20 | .47 | .28 |
| Arabs | .13 | .21 | .54 | .24 |
| Africans | | | .39 | .25 |
| Latin Americans | .41 | .16 | .51 | .33 |
| Average | .26 | .21 | .41 | .29 |

* Groups correspond to those in Chapter 9.

3. Arend Lijphart, "The Analysis of Bloc Voting in the General Assembly," *American Political Science Review*, 57 (1963), 902–17, criticizes some previous studies for relying on an index of group cohesion which is not comparable for groups of different size. Both his solution and ours—the mean deviation from the mean—avoid this difficulty.

Virtually all previous analyses (Lijphart's included) either deal with a preselected set of votes which are alleged to consider the same basic issue, or lump all issues together. The findings, especially those of the latter approach, have shown low cohesion for all groups other than the Soviet bloc. Our approach, which considers sets of votes previously identified by the factor analysis as belonging to the same dimension, provides a more discriminating basis for comparing differences in group cohesion *by issue*.

Before turning to the study of individual deviants let us look at the divergence indices themselves. Not surprisingly the Soviet bloc turns out to be the most unified. Except for a few North–South votes in 1947, before the bloc was fully consolidated, the slight deviations can probably be accounted for by mere misunderstanding of the official position. It is notable, however, that deviation is consistently more common on North–South than on East–West issues. On several occasions when the Soviet Union made a quick tactical decision to abstain on a particular economic or colonial issue, producing something like a North–South alignment, bloc communication probably broke down.

Of the others, the Arabs are almost always among the most cohesive. Their unity has disintegrated somewhat since 1947 (when Palestine was so important), but it partly returned in 1961. Quite unlike the Asians, Africans, and Latin Americans, they are more unified on East–West issues than on North–South ones. The Africans, numerous enough to be considered a group only since 1957, are perhaps surprisingly united considering their division in 1961 into two caucusing subgroups (Brazzaville and Casablanca). The Asians, always sharply split on East–West issues, have become more so. Their unity on North–South issues is significantly greater but has fluctuated rather sharply. Latin America too has been rather sharply divided, but has consistently become more unified over the years, especially on East–West colonial attitudes. If one were to delete Cuba from the Latin American group in 1961 the increased cohesion would be even greater. Finally, the Old Europeans, despite the inclusion in this category of Austria, Ireland, and the Scandinavian neutrals, have always been rather highly unified on East–West issues, though their unity on North–South matters is rapidly disappearing.

One feature of these patterns is the tendency for a group to be more unified the nearer it is to an extreme. A look at the maps of unrotated factor scores in Chapters 3 through 6 will show that the Latins have, as a group, been moving West since 1952. Similarly the Old Europeans have shifted slightly West and become more unified. A majority of the Asians has increasingly parted company with the Western oriented states of Turkey, Japan, the Philippines, Thailand, and Iran. These five states together have become more unified as they moved West, and the remaining Asians increasingly united without them (though the average factor score for the non-Western Asians has not changed significantly). On the North–South dimension the Latins were more unified in 1952, when they were farthest south. The Arabs were as a group farthest South in 1947 and in close agreement; in 1957 when the group average was almost precisely in the middle of the North–South axis, Arab voting unity reached its nadir. To some extent extremeness (and unity) are associated with the importance of an issue to a group. Palestine was a key North–South issue in 1947, but was relatively unimportant a decade later.

There are, of course, exceptions. The Arabs have, as a group, shifted slightly to the East and have lost unity. Asian states are basically Southern; no consistent relation between unity and group position on the North–South dimension emerges. The Old Europeans have become more deeply divided on North–South issues as the group average becomes more North; even here, however, a substantial part of the apparent Northern shift is due not to movement of the group as a whole, but to the increasing isolation of France, South Africa, and Portugal.

Thus, with exceptions, there seems to be a general tendency for group cohesion to be associated with extremeness. Given the growing polarization of the Assembly discussed in Chapter 10 this would suggest that the power of cross-pressures to mitigate conflict *between* regional groups may have declined. This conclusion is supported by the lower average divergence index in 1961 than in 1957. Still, that index remained slightly higher in 1961 than in 1947 or 1952.

EXPLAINING DEVIANTS

To gain a proper understanding of the role of cross-pressures, however, we must look in detail at deviant states and try to discover what influences are associated with departure from the group norm. In a sense one is faced with a plethora of explanatory variables. Many influences operate, each of which explains some but hardly all of the voting patterns.

For example, one may try to explain deviation in terms of trade and aid. We earlier found a very high correlation between these economic variables and East–West voting. Within some groups trade and aid work very well as explanations. The three African states farthest West in 1961 were Cameroun, Dahomey, and the Malagasy Republic; they ranked fifth, second, and fourth, respectively, in per capita economic aid received from France. Among Arabs, Jordan, Lebanon, and Tunisia were second, third, and fourth (behind Libya) in per capita aid from the Western Big Three; they were the three most pro-Western states in voting. Turkey, Japan, Thailand, and the Philippines were West of the Asian group by more than a mean deviation. Respectively they ranked second, sixth, seventh, and third as aid recipients among the sixteen Asian UN members.[4]

These pro-Western states received aid exclusively, or virtually so, from the West. The most Eastern states in each of these groups always received aid from both sides. The five Asians who were East of the group average by more than a mean deviation—Indonesia, Afghanistan, Nepal, India, and Cambodia—all were among the top six Sino–Soviet aid recipients in Asia. Iraq and Egypt led the Arabs in Eastern voting and trailed only Syria on aid. Guinea, Ghana, Mali, Somalia, and Ethiopia led the Africans in both departments. Total Sino–Soviet bloc aid to these twelve countries was about $25 per capita at the time the Sixteenth General Assembly met. Every one of these states also received aid from the Western Big Three, though it averaged only about half that from Communist countries.

As we cautioned earlier, it is not easy to say who is controlling whom in this kind of relationship. We cannot say whether one major bloc principally aids proven friends, or whether it to some degree actually buys votes. One would normally expect some combination of the two to operate with different force in each case. Probably it is really a mutually reinforcing process.

But however powerful economic bonds may be as explanations of voting behavior they leave much unaccounted for. The prime example is Latin America. Every Latin state has received aid from the United States—less aid than has been sent to Europe, but more on a per capita basis than has gone to most Afro–Asians. Correspondingly the Latins have been, as a group, more Eastern than Europe but more Western than Afro–Asia. But neither trade with the United States nor economic aid is at all correlated with deviations *within* the Latin American group. Those whose economies are

4. Always excluding Taiwan, which ranked higher both in Westernness and in aid than any member of the Asian group.

most closely bound to the United States are *not* its closest allies in the Assembly.

As we have tried to explain earlier, trade is more than an economic relationship. It tends quite strongly to mirror political and social community. In the modern world there are many possible suppliers for most goods. But few markets are closely analogous to the model of perfect competition, as the products of two sellers are seldom identical, at least in the mind of the buyer. Customs, habits, traditions, and "myths" about the goods or the seller differentiate two seemingly identical products. A seller who speaks the language and understands the mores of his customers has a great advantage over one who does not. Past habits can affect current prices through credit terms. Goods coming across a previously established trade route can be shipped more cheaply than those using a route which has not yet developed much traffic. Thus trade is one, by no means perfect, indicator of political and cultural integration.[5]

Though trade with the United States does not help to explain Latin American voting, trade within the regional group does. We have worked with a crude but simple and objective measure of economic interdependence. In 1954 all countries of the world exported a total of $77 billion worth of goods, of which about 12 per cent went to Latin America. Paraguay, however, sent a third of its total exports to Latin American states, a figure well above the world average. Similarly the Latin American group took .3 per cent of its imports from Paraguay, when the world average was .04 per cent. This difference between actual and world average was, in essence, our measure.[6] One may then construct a simple table with cells

5. The theoretical and empirical literature on this point is voluminous. For a general theoretical examination of these problems and their application to Anglo–American relations see Bruce M. Russett, *Community and Contention: Britain and America in the Twentieth Century* (Cambridge, Mass., M.I.T. Press, 1963), Chaps. 2 and 3.

6. Actually the mathematics of properly computing the trade indices are quite complex, though this is essentially what is done. See I. R. Savage and K. W. Deutsch, "A Statistical Model of the Gross Analysis of Transaction Flows," *Econometrica, 28* (1960), 551–72; and Hayward R. Alker, Jr., "An IBM Program for the Gross Analysis of Transaction Flows," *Behavioral Science, 7* (1962), 498–99. Data computed by Savage and Deutsch for 1954 (the middle year between 1947 and 1961) were used; an examination of data for other years indicated the patterns would not be markedly different.

for countries that export below the world average to their own
regional groups and those whose exports are equal to or above the
world average. In addition one can separate those countries whose
factor scores are equal to or less than one mean deviation from the
group average score, and those whose factor scores are farther away,
either negatively or positively, than one mean deviation. Two such
tables, one for East–West and one for North–South, follow. The
data are for all four years; thus a country which has been in the
UN since 1947 was counted four times, whereas the newest members
were counted only in 1961.

### Table 12.2. Voting Cohesion and Economic Integration with the Group

EAST–WEST FACTOR SCORES

| Exports to group | ≤ 1 Mean deviation from group average | > 1 Mean deviation from group average | Total |
|---|---|---|---|
| ≥ World average | 92 | 55 | 147 |
| < World average | 33 | 35 | 68 |
| Total | 125 | 90 | 215 |

NORTH–SOUTH FACTOR SCORES

| Exports to group | ≤ 1 Mean deviation from group average | > 1 Mean deviation from group average | Total |
|---|---|---|---|
| ≥ World average | 87 | 60 | 147 |
| < World average | 37 | 31 | 68 |
| Total | 124 | 91 | 215 |

For the East–West dimension, then, there is a clear association
between economic integration and voting cohesion. Countries which
trade heavily with their regional groups are more likely to vote with
the group.[7] Trade integration is a particularly good predictor of
Latin American voting on East–West issues. Eleven Latin states sent
a smaller proportion of their exports to other Latins than did the

7. Using Tschuprow's $T$ as a measure of strength of relationship, the association
between trade and voting with the group on North–South issues is much weaker (.05)
than on East–West issues (.14). The former are surely not as important to most
states as are the major cold war and colonialism issues which make up the East–West
dimension; thus there may be much less pressure to maintain group unity. Also, the
North–South dimension is composed of substantively quite diverse issues, and changes
rather significantly in content from year to year. Such diversity would again increase
the likelihood that occasionally certain states would find their interests and perceptions to be different from those of their regional group.

world as a whole. Over the four years analyzed 30 states (counting most twice or more) had factor scores which differed from the group average by more than a mean deviation. In 22 of these 30 instances the divergent state was not closely integrated with the group. Since economic integration usually indicates a certain degree of political community this association may not be surprising, yet it might, on the other hand, have been overwhelmed by great power pressures or a hundred other influences.

Even so, trade hardly explains everything. It does not account for many voting deviations in the preceding tables. A particularly striking exception is Lebanon. Thanks largely to its geographic position and entrepôt trade Lebanon is more closely integrated economically with her regional group than is any other state with its group. Yet in voting Lebanon is consistently one of the most Western, and one of the most Southern, of the Arab nations.

Clearly we must bring in other cultural, political, and economic variables as explanations. Close examination of the deviants suggests numerous complementary hypotheses. Approximately half of Lebanon's population is Christian, a Western characteristic. Excepting only Israel and the oil sheikdoms, Lebanon's per capita income is the highest in the Middle East. It has a free enterprise economy and its political system is by far the most democratic of any Arab country. Lebanon is thus heavily pulled toward the West by a number of crosscutting solidarities. Perhaps its Western voting, despite its commercial relations with other Arabs, can be traced not to any one of these influences but to their unique combination.

In 1961 the four most Western Asians were, in order, Turkey, Japan, the Philippines, and Thailand. All are military allies of the United States. All have free-enterprise economies. The first three are democracies. Turkey has always been a European power as well as an Asian one; part of Turkey is in Europe; the Turkish state is a member of NATO. Japan has been more deeply affected by Western industrial culture than perhaps any other Asian state. The Philippines are predominantly Christian, with English the major language. Turkey, the Philippines, and especially Japan are, by Asian standards, economically well off.

Again it is difficult to single out any particular influence. Alliance may be a major one, but Iran and Pakistan, two other Western allies, are only slightly to the West of the Asian center. A few other

Asian states are as rich as at least Turkey and the Philippines. It would appear that the combination of Western influences, rather than any single one, is largely responsible. The same kind of explanation would apply to Turkey and Japan who, with Afghanistan (whose voting closely parallels the Sóviet Union's), were the most Northern Asians.

Similarly one can explain deviations in negative terms; i.e. the absence of economic and social characteristics which are common to other members of the regional group. Haiti is, in almost every respect, the least Western of the Latin American states. Its per capita income is as low as any in the hemisphere. Its population is black, it does not share the Iberian culture of the rest of the region, and its cultural ties with France are at best tenuous. Four fifths of the population speaks a Creole patois unintelligible to a Frenchman. Even nominally its Christian population is proportionately the smallest of the Latin states (70 per cent) and the Christianity of many is heavily spiked with Voodoo. Commentators have called it just another underdeveloped African country. Thus it is no surprise to find Haiti consistently at the Easternmost edge of the Latin American voting group. Among Old Europeans the Easternmost states are usually either poor (Greece, Portugal in 1961) or those who, as neutrals, are not tied in with Western security arrangements.

### THE REPRESENTATIVE AND HIS CONSTITUENTS

A number of studies of voting in the United States Congress and in state legislatures have found that representatives from districts which are socioeconomically most typical of their parties tend to show the highest degree of party loyalty, and those who come from districts atypical of their parties tend to cross party lines often.[8] To a very substantial degree the same findings have applied in the United Nations, if we consider the national government the representative and its people the constituents. We are nevertheless required to explain a significant number of exceptions. One intriguing possibility is suggested by Duncan MacRae's finding that members of the Massachusetts state legislature whose previous election margins were close tended to reflect constituency socioeconomic characteristics in their votes more closely than did those with wider margins.

8. Cf. Turner, *Party and Constituency,* p. 53.

He indicates that this may be due either to a heightened sensitivity to constituents' wishes resulting from anxiety about reelection or from a general rise in the level of interest in constituencies where there is a continuing political contest.[9]

Quite the opposite conclusion is suggested by Leon Epstein's examination of the characteristics of British M.P.s who defied their parties' stand on the Suez issue.[10] He found that constituency parties in safe districts were much more likely to retaliate against M.P.s who defied the party Whips than were the constituency organizations in marginal districts. It is generally felt in British politics that no candidate can add by his personal characteristics more than 500 votes to what any other candidates from the same party could poll. Thus the party organization in a safe constituency can win with any other candidate—its M.P. needs it more than it needs him. On the other hand, the constituency party of a marginal district may be loath to purge an M.P. and provoke an intraparty battle.

Part of the difference between the findings of MacRae on American politics and Epstein on British politics is surely explicable in terms of differences between the national systems. Local party organizations are usually far more autonomous in the United States than in Britain; a representative is better able to build up a local machine specifically for *his* support. The local party is more closely controlled by the central party organization, and thus more likely to reflect its views, in Britain than in the United States. Because he is more closely tied to the national party, a representative in the British system would be less likely to reflect the socioeconomic characteristics of an atypical constituency than of a typical constituency, regardless of the closeness of his election.

A similar hypothesis stems from David Truman's finding that Democratic Congressmen who come from close districts and have low seniority almost always agree with the Democratic majority leaders.[11] That is, Congressmen who lack power bases of their own follow the party leadership. The converse is shown by the fact that Republican Congressmen who were first elected in a presidential year between

9. Duncan R. MacRae, "The Relation Between Roll Call Votes and Constituencies in the Massachusetts House of Representatives," *American Political Science Review, 46* (1952), 1046–55. Cf. also MacRae, *Dimensions of Congressional Voting*, p. 286.

10. "British M. P.s and Their Local Parties: The Suez Cases," *American Political Science Review, 54* (1960), 374–90.

11. Truman, *The Congressional Party*, pp. 214–24.

1932 and 1948 (i.e. against a strong Democratic national trend) were less likely to agree with the Republican House Leader than were Congressmen first elected in nonpresidential years. Those with independent power bases tended to be either noticeably more conservative or significantly more liberal than G.O.P. Leader Joseph Martin.

On the international scene, according to this line of reasoning, governments most directly faced with a foreign-sponsored alternative to their rule—such as the divided states of China, Germany, Korea, and Vietnam—might be most dependent upon their alliances for support and therefore most extreme in the advocacy of their parties' policies. This does not mean that there would necessarily be great harmony between leader and partisan—both Chinas exemplify just the opposite—but that the dependence of the partisan on the strength of his party for protection would tend to make him at least as doctrinaire, and possibly more so, than his leader.

Clearly these hypotheses imply two alternative strategies for any government, especially to the degree it is uncertain of its ability to remain in power. It may, particularly in a democratic system, decide to build its strength on a policy of full responsiveness to the socioeconomic characteristics of its constituency. Thus a poor, imperfectly Westernized Latin American nation (Bolivia) may vote less with the West than an advanced and thoroughly Europeanized Latin state (Uruguay). Or a country like Taiwan may solidify its position not by mirroring the characteristics of its constituency but by drawing on the strength of one of the major parties. The government of China was, in 1947 voting, quite East and South, as one might expect a poor Asian state to be. But in later years, when the government of Taiwan had become so thoroughly dependent upon American support, it shifted well into the Northwest voting quadrant.

Any government must in some degree respond to the desires of its populace. Yet some do so more than others; some are far more effective in molding and controlling their publics. Our hypothesis about international behavior reads as follows: the more democratic the politics of a nation are, the more closely the government's international behavior will reflect the socioeconomic characteristics of the nation.

Latin America provides an excellent opportunity to test the hypothesis. Most countries there are poorer than virtually all the

European states, though some are richer than most Asians. The ruling elites are often white, but except in Argentina, Uruguay, and perhaps Chile and Costa Rica the Indian and/or Negro population is large and often a majority. In such states as Bolivia and Paraguay Indian languages are spoken by most of the people. Though the cities may be Western in culture, the rural areas frequently are not. The Latins clearly are not Eastern in culture; except possibly for poverty there is little that they share with Asia or Africa. But they are not fully Western either. On the basis of their socioeconomic characteristics one might expect them to vote a little West of center. According to our hypothesis, then, this is where the most democratic, domestically responsive governments should be. Nondemocratic regimes might also be found here, but they might equally incline toward either the Western or the Eastern extreme.

As an indication of the political nature of the regime we shall use the "competitive," "semicompetitive," and "authoritarian" classification introduced in Chapter 11. The following table indicates the degree to which each type of Latin American regime did or did not vary, by more than a mean deviation, from the Latin average on East–West and North–South issues. Each state is counted four times (once in each session) with the exception of Honduras, which was excluded from the 1961 analysis because of high absenteeism.

Table 12.3. Political Systems and UN Voting Behavior:
Latin America

EAST–WEST

| Regime | West | Center | East | Total |
|---|---|---|---|---|
| Competitive | 0 | 17 | 0 | 17 |
| Semicompetitive | 3 | 17 | 5 | 25 |
| Authoritarian | 16 | 13 | 8 | 37 |
| Total | 19 | 47 | 13 | 79 |

NORTH–SOUTH

| | North | Center | South | Total |
|---|---|---|---|---|
| Competitive | 2 | 7 | 8 | 17 |
| Semicompetitive | 3 | 17 | 5 | 25 |
| Authoritarian | 10 | 21 | 6 | 37 |
| Total | 15 | 45 | 19 | 79 |

For East–West voting, at least, the hypothesis is strikingly confirmed. The competitive regimes (Brazil, Chile, Uruguay, Costa Rica after 1947, Argentina and Venezuela in 1961) are *always* near the middle of the Latin group. Though this is not true for North–South voting, it is obvious from the maps in Part I that Latin America is much more clearly Southern than it is Eastern. Thus it is not surprising to find many competitive regimes voting South.[12]

What perhaps is surprising is the degree to which authoritarian regimes are likely to deviate from the norm, and especially in both the Northern and Western directions. As stated earlier, this is not because these countries are more heavily dependent on the goodwill of the American government—there is no correlation, within the Latin American group, of aid or trade with the United States and Western or Northern voting. It may more likely be due to the nature of the support which the authoritarian regime has built for itself. An authoritarian government without a solid mass base is likely to depend on the endorsement of commercial interests, both foreign and domestic, who would not look kindly on too Southern or Eastern a foreign policy.

Asians, Arabs, and Africans are, with the Soviet bloc, normally the Eastern states. According to our theory one would seemingly expect democratic, or competitive, regimes there also to vote near the norm for the group. Such expectations are not quite borne out when we look at a similar table for these nations during the four sessions analyzed.

Table 12.4. Political Systems and UN Voting Behavior: Asians, Arabs, and Africans

EAST–WEST

| Regime | West | Center | East | Total |
|---|---|---|---|---|
| Competitive | 12 | 18 | 4 | 34 |
| Semicompetitive | 5 | 14 | 8 | 27 |
| Authoritarian | 9 | 21 | 15 | 45 |
| Total | 26 | 53 | 27 | 106 |

| | North | Center | South | Total |
|---|---|---|---|---|

NORTH–SOUTH

| Regime | North | Center | South | Total |
|---|---|---|---|---|
| Competitive | 5 | 21 | 8 | 34 |
| Semicompetitive | 6 | 17 | 4 | 27 |
| Authoritarian | 7 | 24 | 14 | 45 |
| Total | 18 | 62 | 26 | 106 |

12. Again using $T$ as the measure, the strength of relationship in the East–West half of the table is .38; in the North–South half it is .23.

The competitive regimes are by far the most likely to deviate from the group norm to vote with the West. This would seem to contradict the findings on Latin America, but only until we examine the deviant cases more closely. Except for two African states in 1961, the competitive states voting West are solely those four we earlier identified as being particularly heavily influenced by Western culture—Lebanon, Turkey, the Philippines, and Japan. In voting with the West, then, their governments probably are in fact being particularly responsive to the socioeconomic characteristics of their constituents. To adopt a center or Eastern position would be to distort the wishes of whatever segment of their populace has articulated foreign policy preferences and to ignore basic ties of economics and culture with the West. This seems especially plausible since in voting West these states are not voting as far West as the Old Europeans, but only West of most other Asians and Arabs.

On the North–South dimension no clear-cut pattern emerges; the variations among different kinds of regimes are not substantial.[13] In a way this corresponds with earlier tables where the variations, in terms of our predicted patterns, were much less striking on North–South than on East–West votes. It may well be that individual governments are subject to lighter pressure on North–South issues. Such issues were, after all, not as prominent in the Assembly, accounting for, at most, only half as many votes and speeches as did East–West issues. Given the lesser salience of such issues both to other governments and probably to the people of the nations themselves, the usual pressures are much weakened and a government is more able to maneuver, to vary its position, to bargain, and to vote in response to interests quite different from those which have the most force on East–West alignments.

One of the most striking features of the North–South pattern is the difficulty encountered in explaining within-group variations. The variables just used successfully as partial explanations of East–West voting—intragroup trade, domestic political system—were not much help on the North–South dimension. Neither do most of the variables which in Chapter 11 were so powerful in identifying North–South characteristics *in the Assembly as a whole* help much. European race, economic development, alliance, Christian religion, trade and aid from the West; all are only very slightly correlated

13. $T$ is equal to .12, as compared with .17 in the East–West portion of the table.

with North voting, and sometimes even negatively within the Latin, or Asian, or Arab, or African caucusing groups.[14]

Only two variables work at all well. One is colonial status, which discriminates powerfully within the Old European and Asian groups. All nine of the Old European states North of the group average in 1961 were colonial powers; only two colonial nations—Italy and the Netherlands—were to be found South of the group average. Among the Asians, four of the five states which had never been colonies—Japan, Nepal, Thailand, and Turkey—were North of their group, and two, Japan and Turkey, were themselves former colonial powers. Of the noncolonies, only Iran was more Southern than the group average. The other variable that discriminates well is aid from the Soviet bloc, which is almost as good a predictor of Northern voting as it is for Eastern alignment. In the Arab group the three highest per capita aid recipients—Syria, Egypt, and Iraq—were in 1961 the fifth, fourth, and second most Northern states. Similarly, Afghanistan was most Northern, Cambodia was fifth, and Indonesia was fourth in Asia.[15] And in Africa the four chief recipients of Soviet aid all ranked in the top six of Northern-voting states.

We may now draw these findings together to form a clearer picture of certain forces operating in the international system. On East–West and, to a lesser extent, North–South voting, governments do indeed tend to reflect certain unmistakable socioeconomic characteristics of their people. Asians, for instance, even if they have substantial sympathies with the West, seldom vote with the West as regularly as do virtually all Old Europeans. But some governments are more likely than others to reflect these characteristics. Regimes faced with strong internal opposition, particularly if this opposition is free to express itself, to mobilize a mass base, and to challenge the government periodically at elections, are much more likely than "representatives" from noncompetitive states to be sensitive to socioeconomic influences. Just what position authoritarian regimes will take is difficult to predict on the basis of the categorizations available.

14. For a discussion of the theoretical implications of analyzing differences within and between units sharing certain characteristics see Hayward R. Alker, Jr., "Regionalism versus Universalism in Comparing Nations," in Russett et al., *World Handbook of Political and Social Indicators.*

15. This is the only instance where Western aid helps to identify Northern voters. Turkey and Japan, second and sixth among Asian recipients of American aid, were the second and third most Northern Asian states in 1961.

Most often they lean in the same direction as the whole regional group, only more so. Thus Latins tend to vote with the West; the authoritarian Latin governments are more likely than others to deviate from the group position, and twice as likely to lean West as East. They usually choose to build their support on interest groups, foreign and domestic, which align them with the Western bloc. Though they may not receive more American aid than other Latin governments, or trade more with the United States, they may nevertheless be more heavily dependent upon these ties than are their fellow South and Central Americans. A few, of which Cuba is the most notable example, build their position at least partly on support not from the pole nearest them, but from the more distant Eastern pole. In either case these are representatives who are more than normally dependent on the support of an external party, as contrasted with broad support from within their own constituencies.

This is equally true when one looks at the Asians, Arabs, and Africans. In about nine tenths of all cases the competitive systems vote either near the center of their groups or toward the West. A state following the latter course is almost always socially, economically, and culturally more akin to the West than are most other nations outside of Europe and the Western Hemisphere. Some authoritarian regimes—chiefly Thailand, Jordan, Iraq until after the 1958 revolution, Dahomey and Ivory Coast among the new Africans— are built upon the support of the more distant Western party. Taiwan, whose voting is so very "un-Asian," is an especially striking case. Most, such as Egypt, Syria, Afghanistan, Ghana, Guinea, Mali, and Iraq in 1961, maintain themselves with substantial assistance from the Eastern party, almost always at least partially in the form of direct economic aid. All these states, because of the nature of their power bases, can better ignore the wishes of some of their own people than of the external allies on whom they to a greater or lesser extent depend.

We find, then, a curious combination of elements from both the British and American political models. If we think in terms of two parties, one Eastern and one Western, most representatives vote as one would expect from certain fairly clearly defined socioeconomic characteristics of their constituents. There are two exceptions. One is where the socioeconomic characteristics are mixed or ambiguous, as in the Philippines. Then a representative, especially if from a constituency where he faces substantial competition, will reflect the nature of his constituents by voting more East than the Westerners and more West than the Easterners. This is essentially the American model (which is not always borne out empirically). The other exception is the representative who does not reflect the characteristics of his constituents. Though from a clearly Eastern district, for instance, he often votes with the West (Thailand). In virtually every case these representatives are not from highly competitive districts—competitive at least in the sense of meaningful mass participation, though there may be some competition at the pinnacle. Such representatives are really dependent, for reelection, on the support of the international party. This situation, with a strong centralized external party to which the representative is attached is (without the antidemocratic implications of our example) more nearly akin to the British model. The international party system is at present sufficiently fluid to include both types.[16]

### SEEKING A BUFFER

We began this chapter, and in fact Part Two, with the hypothesis that if long-term rivalry between East and West was indeed in prospect, the stability of the system would depend upon the existence of a group or groups not fully aligned with either side. The group or groups might take the form of an active, intense, and cohesive neutral body, or might simply include a large number of states which, though neither very cohesive nor very intense about their neutrality, were numerous enough and flexible enough always to constitute a body of floating voters—not very involved in the central East–West controversies, chiefly interested in more parochial concerns, and ready to bargain with both East and West to further their own ends.

In general the search was discouraging, for there was little sign of a middle group growing either in number or intensity. A hope that cross-pressures within a regional or caucusing group might force it to a middle position was, with the significant exception of Africa,

16. The emphasis of this chapter has been that the consequences of similar economic, social, or political conditions may be different in different contexts, and the quest for universal relationships may be disappointing or misleading. In mathematical terms, the relations among the variables are nonadditive; in an explanatory equation the coefficient attached to a particular variable may vary widely, or even change signs, in different contexts. See Alker, "The Long Road to Mathematical Theories of International Politics: Problems of Statistical Nonadditivity."

not borne out. The Scandinavians, in their voting at least, were never appreciably nearer the center than other Old Europeans; they are less so now. The Latins have tended to become more cohesive as they have moved nearer the extremes. The Arabs are quite East and quite unified.

The Asians are far from cohesive and are, on the average, not too near the Eastern pole. This is true because of the severe cross-pressures to which a number of pro-Western Asian nations are subject. The effect of these cross-pressures, however, has not been to modify the positions of Asians as a whole. On the contrary it has been to create an ever widening gulf between the quite Eastern majority and a Western leaning minority. Instead of bringing all Asians toward a less extreme position, the effect of the Western ties of some (and conversely, the ties of others with the Soviets) has been to diminish the compromising and mediating effects of their common Asian bonds.

Possibly the chief hope of a nonpolarized Assembly lies with its largest but weakest grouping: the non-Arab Africans. The African group was reasonably cohesive in 1961. Its divergence index was .33, far better than the Asians (.67) and not worse than the newly coalescing Latins (.33). It is particularly striking to find such high agreement among states in the center. Most sub-Saharan states were able, within limits, to concur on a middle-of-the-road policy on East–West questions. The Latins, by contrast, achieved relative consensus only when a number of former "centrists" shifted West to join the main body of the group. And finally, African agreement is impressive when one remembers that most members of the African group also belonged to a separate caucusing subgroup—Brazzaville or Casablanca.[17] Even these subgroups apparently did not divide African loyalties too seriously. Too much cohesion, of course, could be as dangerous to the system as too little. The virtue of a group of "balancers" is that they form a floating vote, aligning now with one side, then with another, and often being sufficiently uncohesive that some members of the group can be picked off by either side. A too uniform cohesion and rigid noncommitment to either side would deprive the group of its stabilizing value. It must, after all, be able to hold out the prospect of availability to those who seek its support.

Africa provides a perfect example of what it means to be cross-pressured, yet at the same time somewhat remote from the great

17. These subgroups have since been disbanded.

struggle. Economically the states south of the Sahara are almost uniquely vulnerable. Most of them remain in the franc or sterling monetary zones, and are closely bound to their former metropolitan territories. It is not unusual for an African state to carry on two-thirds or more of its trade with the United States–Britain–France; half did so in 1960 or 1961. Such firm ties of current trade mean that virtually all of their capital equipment was made by one of these three great Western industrial powers; thus replacement parts must come from the West. At the same time a number are trying, with some success, to establish aid and trade relations with the communist countries. By mid-1962 Guinea, Ghana, Somalia, Mali, Ethiopia, and Senegal all had received Sino–Soviet bloc aid. And in one crucial economic variable—per capita income—they are very non-Western.

Culturally too, they are cross-pressured. Thanks to the success of Western missionaries in formerly pagan lands, Christians are fairly numerous throughout Africa and actually make up a majority of the population in quite a few states. In Asia, only in the Philippines has Christianity had such a Westernizing impact at least in numerical terms. But at the same time a major Eastern religion, Islam, is strong in Africa, and is the majority religion in several states. Finally, many areas of Africa have resisted acculturation under either of these influences. And of course in color they are non-Western without necessarily feeling more than a negative sort of bond with Asians.

Nor are most of the new African elites irrevocably bound to the political systems of either camp. Most were trained in Western or Western-run schools—unlike Asia, Africa had scant indigenous resources for education. Yet few members of these elites are deeply committed to democracy as it is understood in Europe or the Commonwealth. Few too, despite strong Marxist influences, are orthodox Communists. They may mouth ideologies either of state ownership or of private enterprise, but in many cases this ideology represents less a basic emotional or intellectual commitment than a response to foreign or domestic pressures.[18] The Liberian government, with its dependence on Firestone Rubber, talks about free enterprise; the Guineans, less rich in foreign investments, do not.

18. In 1954 Robert A. Scalapino described neutralism as a curious mixture of ambivalence, distrust, and disinterested tolerance for the competing Western doctrines of Marxism and liberal democracy. "Neutralism in Asia," *American Political Science Review*, 48 (1954), 49–63.

In competing for the allegiance of African voters, then, the West has some important strengths: religion, the Western training of most elites, the cultural residue of colonialism, and current economic ties of trade and aid. The East too has its influences: Islam, some economic ties, and color. But neither West nor East has made a deep impression on Africa. Perhaps most influential in the end will be the uniquely African characteristics referred to by Africans themselves as "negritude." Already there are indications, such as the disbanding of the separate Monrovia, Casablanca, and Brazzaville groups, that African common interests may count for more in the international arena than the interests that divide the continent. This is *not* to imply that African political unity, in the sense of a common government, is around the corner. Such a prognosis would require a totally different study. It does imply that in the international arena a sort of African parochialism may tend to keep the states relatively cohesive as a voting bloc.[19]

Thus prospects may be for an Africa that is apathetic toward many aspects of world conflict and is able to maintain a middle and fairly unified position between the two camps. Africa is not a power in the larger world of international politics; it is still too weak. But in the peculiarly distorted yet intrinsically important arena of the UN it may yet be a moderating force. This cannot happen until "African self-determination" problems—Angola, South Africa, Rhodesia—leave the center stage. While colonialism remains in its most obvious political form, Africans will have extreme opinions, keenly felt. And the elimination of colonialism, when it comes, may occur with such racial violence as to deepen yet further the East–West gulf and throw the Africans irrevocably away from the middle.

If this outcome can be avoided, the Africans may become that group of apathetics, wooed but never won, which can mitigate conflict and provide the basis for a stable order. Essentially, the question is what will be the most prominent dimension of future UN sessions. If it should be the cold war, Africa would seem uniquely suited to play the center position. But over most of the life of the UN the

19. Hovet (*Africa in the United Nations*) also found most African states occupying a middle position on many East–West controversies, especially cold war ones, and he presents convincing evidence that this is indeed due to parochialism and indifference. Most striking is his report (p. 219) that a delegate of one of the older African states, an important official in his own government and an experienced representative on the Main Committee concerned with Korea, did not know that the Korean peninsula is divided into two states, North and South.

trend has been toward a decline in the prominence of cold war issues and an increase of self-determination questions. Some observers believe that colonialism too is a dying issue in the world organization, as the last territories achieve independence.[20] Yet announcement of the birth of the "postcolonial world" may be premature. Still another candidate for prominence in the coming years may be the set of issues involving rich–poor relations. The alignment might not differ greatly from the one which now characterizes supranationalism issues (a dimension which has indeed been growing in prominence) except that the United States is likely to be farther North. If either self-determination or rich–poor questions predominate, the Africans almost certainly will be far from the middle and the role of a neutral balancer will fall to countries alsewhere in the non-European world. Asians, and perhaps especially Latin Americans, may yet find themselves holding the key to peace.

20. Cf. Haas, "Dynamic Environment."

# CHAPTER 13

# Continuity and Change
# in the General Assembly

Among the tasks of historical sociology are the descriptions of different historical international systems, comparisons among international systems, and, finally, comparisons between domestic political systems and international ones.[1] The main conclusions of this study are intended as a contribution to these goals. We have been concerned, for instance, with a particular international system: world politics in the United Nations since the end of World War II. But rather than compare different historical systems in international relations we have focused on similarities and differences between a variety of domestic political systems and a single international system.

This emphasis on one era, which has been called the "international system of the postwar generation," [2] does not imply that within the system significant changes have not occurred. Stressing both continuities and changes should help put the characteristic elements of the era in clearer perspective, while at the same time indicating the likely direction of future international politics as revealed in the United Nations context. Large changes transmitted from one international system to another must result from a series of smaller changes within or at the boundaries of a particular system.[3]

1. Stanley Hoffmann, *Contemporary Theory in International Relations*, pp. 174–75.
2. Richard N. Rosecrance, *Action and Reaction in World Politics* (Boston, Little, Brown, 1963), pp. 261–67.
3. In the jargon of the political science profession, this distinction between "equilibrium analysis and developmental analysis" is a venerable one. See, for example, Harold D. Lasswell, *World Politics and Personal Insecurity*, reprinted in Lasswell, Merriam and Smith, *A Study of Power* (Glencoe, Free Press, 1951). Both Rosecrance and Kaplan have been criticized, somewhat unfairly, for ignoring "transformation rules" or "the mechanism of transition from one system to another," See Hoffman, *Con-*

It is to the analysis of one such system of international relations that we now turn. Our conclusions will be summarized in as general a manner as possible to facilitate comparisons with other political systems, both domestic and international.

### CONTINUITIES IN THE GENERAL ASSEMBLY

Quincy Wright has described international relations as a field in which individuals, groups, nations, and international organizations compete, fight, and cooperate. Preferring this framework to a model drawn from the study of integrated communities, Hoffmann has defined international systems in a way remarkably similar to the approach of the present study:

> An international system is a pattern of relations between the basic units of world politics, which is characterized by the scope of the objectives pursued by these units and of the tasks performed among them, as well as by the means used in order to achieve those goals and perform these tasks. The pattern is largely determined by the structure of the world, the nature of the forces which operate across or within the major units, national capabilities, and patterns of power.[4]

### Issues and Alignments

During the postwar period alliance configurations and national objectives within the Assembly were remarkably continuous. The most obvious continuity has been the existence of East–West and North–South behavioral voting dimensions. On the average, the East–West dimension has accounted for over 55 per cent of the

---

*temporary Theory*, pp. 40–50; George Liska, "Continuity and Change in International Systems" *World Politics, 16* (October 1963), 110–36; Kaplan, *System and Process*, pp. 9–10; and Rosecrance, *Action and Reaction*, pp. 270–73.

4. Stanley Hoffmann, "International Systems and International Law," *World Politics, 14* (October 1961), 207. Footnoted on the same page is the comment "Such a definition corresponds to accepted definitions of domestic political systems, which are characterized also both by the scope of the ends of politics (the United States vs. the totalitarian state, the welfare state vs. the free enterprise state) and by the methods of organizing power (constitutional relations between the branches of government, types of party system) ." The objection to community, equilibrium, or organizational models is spelled out, along with a similar and lengthier definition of the international system, in *Contemporary Theory*, pp. 1–12 and 179–84.

explainable variation in positions taken on important votes, and North–South alignments have underlain about 15 per cent of these votes. Correlational analyses have confirmed the continuity of these same two voting dimensions since the beginning of the United Nations, before the distinction was made either by diplomats or by scholars.

East–West positions in 1947 correlated 0.88 with those in 1961; across the same 14-year period, North–South scores were also quite similar ($r = 0.61$). Looking back at Figure 7.3 (p. 138), Mexico (from East to West in 1961), Argentina (from West to just barely East and back, 1952 and 1957), and China (East to West in 1952) are the only countries that moved across the East–West dividing line. Of the countries not shown in that graph there are relatively few major shifts, and those that have occurred have usually been associated with changes in major environmental variables polarizing East–West positions, such as trade and aid. Cuba is a good example. North–South fluctuations, on the other hand, were mainly Chinese movement to the North and West, Scandinavian leanings to the South and, except for Cuba, disillusioned flirtations of several developing countries with the Soviet bloc.

What objectives have been sought by the different contestants on these alignments? The content of the East–West and North–South conflicts has been suggested by roll calls loading heavily on these factors, by the geopolitical configuration of states' voting positions, and by environmental correlations. High East–West correlations with military alliances, aid, Soviet trade, and colonial status confirmed an interpretation of the merged cold war and anticolonial nature of this conflict. High North–South polarizations by noncommunist, ex-colonial, racially non-European, and underdeveloped states suggested the poor versus rich, anti-European, and anticommunist meaning of Southern voting positions. The correlation between national per capita wealth and Western voting positions suggests that Eastern states are more revolutionary, while Western states, with higher levels of income and industrialization, are more interested in preserving the status quo. We may interpret the North–South conflict and the other less frequent behavioral voting dimensions as attempts by the less powerful allied and nonaligned states in the Assembly to move away from the influence of East–West ties and to achieve some of their own primary anticolonial and developmental goals.[5]

The particular positions of different kinds of states on these two alignments suggest patterns of policy that may recur in other domestic or international contexts. We found, for instance, that the Western superpower, the United States, was less isolated on North–South questions than its European allies and the Soviet Union. This Southern tendency of the United States might well be explained by its relative strength in the General Assembly, which has encouraged it to support many of the *peacekeeping* (but not *developmental*) supranationalist resolutions in the Assembly, resolutions to which some of its allies have not been able to agree. America's commitment to using the United Nations has also been stronger than the Soviet Union's because of its paramount role in establishing the organization and writing the Charter in terms of Western ideals.

Although the West began the postwar period with clear economic and military advantages, the decline of its control over colonial territories in Africa and Asia has allowed states with an anti-great power (Southern) orientation to enter into world politics. Only some of them, those needing external political support or not recently subject to the colonial experience, have remained pro-West on colonial and cold war issues. As the more revolutionary great power, the Soviet Union has found it considerably easier to support and exploit anticolonial feelings for its own purposes; hence the virtual nonexistence of a middle group on East–West issues in the General Assembly.

A further implication of the unrotated factor analysis was that explanations of UN politics in terms of these two geopolitical alignments would necessarily be inadequate. Cold war enthusiasts often see the East–West conflict as the paramount conflict in the United

5. Efforts of small states to increase their power through interstate legislative machinery occurred in both the Hague Conferences and in the battles over the Council's authority in the League and the United Nations. In the convention to write the U.S. Constitution the small states were hesitant to join a powerful union potentially dominated by the bigger states. But after the Connecticut Compromise, assuring the small states of equal representation in the Senate, they tended to ratify the Constitution more quickly than the big states. In supranational terms, these examples suggest that small powers will not always be in the forefront of efforts to strengthen the central authority when their involvement may bring about a loss in power. The one state–one vote principle in all these cases has definitely encouraged small power supranationalism.

Nations; representatives of anticolonial and nonaligned states some-times seem to ignore cold war uses of their policies. Similarly, North–South votes can be further analyzed into supranational or Palestine type issues. Since East–West and North–South factors represent the two most compact and parsimonious ways of sum-marizing Assembly voting behavior, the alternatives were either to add several more unrotated factors to the analysis or to rotate the factor pattern to a simply structured one involving several more factors. In the rotated matrix the first factor was not always the single most frequent voting component but both it and several of the other rotated factors were more likely to have a clearer cognitive significance. Taken together, three or four unrotated factors or four or five rotated factors explain more votes than East–West and North–South voting alone.

The principal *substantive* issues in Assembly voting that emerged from the rotated factor matrix were remarkably clear in content. Whereas some rotated factors seem to have been only momentary conflicts over national and group objectives (such as relations with Spain after World War II, four or five substantive conflicts, with similar voting alignments and content, were found to have permeated Assembly debates during the entire postwar period. Together they have accounted on the average for about 75 per cent of interpretable Assembly voting, a 5 to 10 per cent improvement on an unrotated two-factor interpretation. We have labeled these super-issues self-determination, the cold war, Palestine-related questions, UN supra-nationalism, and anti-interventionism regarding South African racial policies.

Our analyses of trends in speeches, resolutions, and voting posi-tions have depended on the continuity of substantive content and national positions on these super-issues. Fortunately, factor scores from one session of the Assembly to another some years afterward have usually been correlated with each other at the 0.70 level or above. The validity of these distinctions, based as they are largely on roll-call analysis, has also received important corroboration from published scholarly studies and unpublished comments by several UN diplomats before and after the analyses were completed.

Voting alignments on these conflicts have been highly correlated with many of the relevant external variables previously mentioned in theoretical writings about international politics. In fact, it was possible to distinguish among rotated factors on the basis of their distinctive environmental polarizations. Trade, aid, and alliances polarized cold war alignments more than they did self-determination voting. Self-determination polarizers like colonial status, per capita G.N.P., and Old European identity did not appreciably correlate with cold war alignments. On supranational issues the isolation of communist states was made very clear, as were the aspirations of Arab states and democracies on Palestine related issues. Such distinctive polarizations strengthen our prior interpretations of the principal substantive conflicts accounting for national policies in the General Assembly.[6]

If such alignments are determined to a considerable extent by forces outside the Assembly, we would expect issues analogous to these conflicts to have appeared in other contexts. Cold war membership questions, with their potential effect on the distribution of power, and self-determination alignments, for instance, have occurred in the International Atomic Energy Association.[7] Supranationalist issues have continually arisen in bodies like the International Labor Organization and the League of Nations: great powers have generally tried to protect their rights and privileges against the demands of smaller powers for equal stature.

Working primarily with materials about the I.L.O., Ernst Haas concludes his recent, monumental study, *Beyond The Nation-State*, with a similar discussion of supranationalism issues. He emphasizes the economic components of the supranationalism issue as more important than the peacekeeping ones:

> *There will be a continued drift toward supranationality,* though no federal millennium is in the offing. Economic planning,

6. The continuity of these conflicts allows us to hazard certain guesses about the future, e.g. concerning possible positions taken by Communist China if it were to become a member of the United Nations. We may consider France a disgruntled and aspiring second-rank Western power; Communist China has the same standing in the Eastern camp. As mavericks in either camp these two countries have taken similar stands in opposition to the test ban treaty. France's recognition of China and her overtures for cooperation in Southeast Asia also indicate commonly perceived roles in international politics. On noneconomic UN supranational questions, we would expect that Communist China in the UN would behave like France: a Northern antisupranational state.

7. See John Stoessinger's perceptive "Atoms for Peace: The International Atomic Energy Agency," in Commission to Study the Organization of Peace, *Organizing Peace in the Nuclear Age* (New York, Commission to Study the Organization of Peace, 1962), pp. 117–233.

local military operations, and ad hoc disarmament will provide the function. Economic planning is obviously the chief candidate for integrative functions in the future system . . . [but] enthusiasm for this function should not be allowed to be wholly infectious.[8]

Haas sees a gradual evolution toward international community coming about through an unbalanced and partly unplanned pluralistic interregional political process.

The importance of economic supranational issues is also stressed in a recent analysis of stable Western democracies. Once government is reasonably centralized in its judicial, financial, and military functions, "politics are no longer a struggle over the distribution of the national sovereignty; instead they have tended to become a struggle over the distribution of the national product and hence over the policies guiding the administration of centralized government functions." [9]

## Mechanisms of Representation

Representational styles within the different regional groupings along East–West and North–South lines showed noticeable differences. Among Latin American countries, competitive states mirrored most accurately their regional constituency characteristics; national representatives from noncompetitive ("safe") districts tended to be nonrepresentative and to rely on outside support (the United States) to preserve their domestic political position.

Among Africans and Asians, a nearly opposite model of representation on East–West issues seemed at first to apply. Most of these states took the Eastern position that their regional characteristics would lead us to expect. In the manner of those deviant British M.P.s who successfully survived reprisals from their marginally Conservative constituencies for their stand on the Suez issue, representatives of competitive and relatively stable societies—Lebanon, Turkey, Japan, and the Philippines—voted considerably West of their regional averages. In terms of their religious, cultural, and

8. Ernst Haas, *Beyond the Nation-State: Functionalism and International Organization* (Stanford, Stanford University Press, 1964), p. 492.

9. Reinhard Bendix, "Social Stratification and the Political Community," *European Journal of Sociology, 1* (1960), 181–213. Quoted in Robert Alford, *Party and Society* (Chicago, Rand McNally, 1963), p. 338.

economic ties, however, it was suggested that ambiguous constituency characteristics did to some extent explain the Westward leanings of these states.

A companion analysis was performed on North–South alignments. The cohesive force of within-group trading links that bound these regions together in East–West issues revealed no within-region cohesive ties on North–South issues. Their political competitiveness was also not related to how far North or South different states deviated from their regional tendencies. On both North–South and East–West issues, regional groups taking more extreme positions were found to be more united.

### Environmental Influences

Trade and political systems variables were found in Chapter 11 to be moderate polarizers of East–West and North–South alignments. The fact that similar variables polarize voting positions *within* Latin and Afro–Asian regions on East–West issues, but not North–South ones, helps to clarify two steps by which partial international integration may be achieved. One of the essentials, if a balancing group is to mitigate conflict, is that within the two poles there be *differences* which tempt competitors within either polar group to incorporate the middle group's positions as a way of increasing their domestic success.[10] Such balancing possibilities have occurred on East–West issues in the Assembly. The different kinds of representational style among Latin Americans and Afro–Asians have had the impact of bringing non-European competitive political systems closer together on the East–West conflict. Competitive Latin Americans have been *East* of their authoritarian neighbors; competitive Afro–Asians have moved *West* as compared with other members of their caucusing groups.

When such integrative solutions have occurred—and the economic decolonialization and peacekeeping components of the North–South and supranationalism conflict are a few examples—East–West alignments have no longer appeared. North–South related supranationalism issues have given rise to situations where the Southern states have tried to extract Northern concessions by a form of per-

10. See the discussion of Haas, "Regionalism," in Chapter 1 and Alker, "Regionalism versus Universalism," for a description of the possible kinds of within-region and between-region correlations that can account for various worldwide relationships.

missive enforcement, over the objections of a few great powers, on measures where theirs was a nearly certain two-thirds majority. Except for Old European states, on this kind of alignment relevant divisions have been between groups rather than within them.

Colonial status and Soviet aid seem to be the highest within-group discriminators that also polarize the North–South division. The former variable is probably more closely linked to anti-interventionist alignments, the latter to supranationalism issues. The scarcity of relevant within-group North–South polarizers (economic development does not work) offers a reason for U Thant's view of the potentially more serious nature of the North–South conflict.

An important finding about current East–West foreign policies in the Assembly, despite different representational styles, is the similar way in which they can be explained. Either in terms of regional identities or in terms of aid, trade, and alliances, East–West voting at the Sixteenth Session was accurately estimated. (In most cases, the squared multiple correlation coefficients were 0.78.) Even though alliances have changed and Western aid patterns have shifted away from postwar Europe, one or several such vote polarizers have helped maintain remarkably constant national policies in the East–West conflict.

### CHANGES IN THE GENERAL ASSEMBLY

In searching for potential sources of change in the current international system it may be more profitable to concentrate on changes in perceptions of new issues, changes in the distribution of environmental influences on states, and changes in the distribution of power. Without revolutionary wars, national, social, political, and economic characteristics change much more slowly.

### Changing Issues and Alignments

The most striking overall change since the Assembly's inception has been the increase in the pervasiveness of East–West politics. At the Second Session, this alignment accounted for something over 40 per cent of recurring Assembly voting alignment: by the Sixteenth Session, it accounted for two-thirds of interpretable voting patterns. North–South alignments have decreased from 20 to 13 per cent of explainable voting variance. These trends have been accompanied by similar concentrations of speaking efforts. In the first two years covered approximately twice as many speeches were made on East–West as on North–South issues. Even in a rather quiet Twelfth Session, this ratio rose to three to one. By 1961 there were five times as many East–West as North–South related speeches.

Two substantive issues in the Assembly have also increased in prominence: self-determination and UN supranationalism. Cold war, anti-intervention, and Palestine related issues have continued to appear, but less frequently. Changes in the substantive content of these issues can be associated with higher East–West or North–South components, with changing environmental polarizations, or with the changing membership of the United Nations.

Substantively, explicit cold war issues in the Assembly have taken on the nature of debates about the recognition or seating of new members, especially Communist China.[11] Self-determination questions, on the other hand, have changed from early efforts by the ex-colonial countries to build UN machinery for speeding the work of the trusteeship system to concerted legal and extralegal attempts to free Portuguese colonies, and the use or threat of UN sanctions against self-governing or nominally self-governing states in southern Africa.[12]

With the great influx of new small and ex-colonial states and a growing great power interest in the gray areas of the cold war, supranational concerns for drafting universalistic legislation have increasingly become peacekeeping and capital development issues. Substantively, interventionist issues have gradually developed from attempts to assert the legal obligation of South Africa to place South West Africa under the trusteeship system (a battle which has been carried into the World Court) to resolutions condemning South African racial policies in Charter terms. Though the United States is the less revolutionary of the superpowers, it has been acutely aware of the moral pressure exerted by newer members in terms of a Charter the United States was instrumental in drafting, and has been forced to support or to abstain on many such resolutions

11. Before the American Civil War, the United States Senate was preoccupied with analogous membership problems related to the Missouri Compromise, the Kansas–Nebraska Act, and California's potential Civil War position.

12. Haas, "Dynamic Environment and Static System," pp. 307 ff., describes what is probably the same trend as the "elimination" of colonial issues in the Assembly and the increased appearance of Afro–Asian collective security demands.

against a Western nation. Because both the Soviet Union and the United States have tried to gain the favor of the African states on these issues, interventionism has increasingly lost its legalistic flavor.[13]

Figure 13.1 illustrates some of these changes in prominence and substance. It helps to explain how supranationalism alignments have increased and cold war roll calls have decreased, while at the same time East–West rather than North–South voting alignments have come to pervade the Assembly. Although it is not possible to capture completely four distinct dimensions in a two-dimensional picture, Figure 13.1 represents a *projection* into an East–West and North–South plane of the five main substantive issues (and their character-istic attitudes) revealed from the rotated factor analyses. The projection data are in fact correlations between unrotated and revised rotated factor scores. Trends in these correlations are plotted for each of the sessions for which sufficient data were available.[14] Rotated East–West scores in 1947 were used to indicate both anti-colonial and anticommunist positions. From Figure 13.1, it is clear that any attitude can be reflected to the diagonally opposite geo-political quadrant if the "anti" label is changed to a "pro" designation.

Since the Second Assembly antisupranationalism has tended to be a Northern and an Eastern view. At the Sixteenth Session, however, as shown in Chapter 11, its tendency to be identified with colonial attitudes markedly decreased. This trend was also associated with a return to a more nearly neutral position on the East–West dimen-sion.

Other formerly North–South related issues, however, have become increasingly East–West oriented. This trend by and large accounts

13. Voting on a revised version of Khrushchev's original suggestion of a Declaration on the Granting of Independence to Colonial Countries and Peoples (Resolution 1514, of Session XV) also evoked a harsher "interventionist" alignment on which the United States joined a small nucleus of colonial powers.

14. The amount of variance in one of these substantive issues that cannot be explained in East–West and North–South terms can be measured by subtracting the squared East–West and North–South projections from 1.00. One of the main effects of revising the original rotated factor scores was to increase correlations between sub-stantive and geopolitical alignments. The figure corresponding to projections from the unrevised rotated factor scores is similar in its main respects to Figure 13.1, but its "projection" coefficients are not so high. Since the revised rotated scores are inter-correlated with each other, Figure 13.1 also suggests tendencies of substantively distinct issues in the Assembly to collapse into each other and into the East–West conflict.

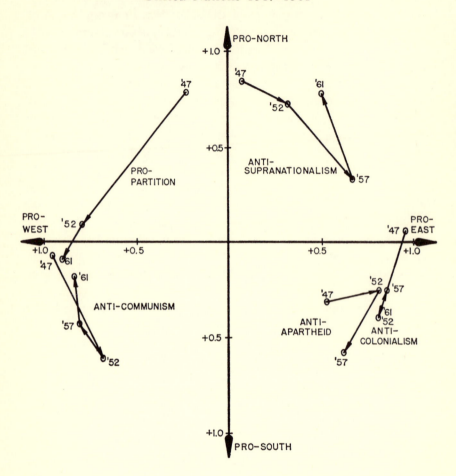

Figure 13.1. Correlations between Various Substantive Attitudes and the East–West and North–South Conflicts in the United Nations 1947–1961

for the overall drop in North–South voting and the rise in East–West alignments in the Assembly. As we noted earlier, Palestine has become more an East–West conflict, as the Russians have refused to side with other Northern powers. This departure from the North–South axis and the approach toward cold war positions is very clear from the "Southwesterly" movement of the pro-partition attitude on Palestine related questions. Cold war attitudes reached the height of their anti-Northern character in 1952 during the Korean War;

they too have since declined in North–South content and moved closer to an East–West alignment.

Self-determination attitudes (anticolonialism and related demands) have continued to be closely related to the East–West conflict; anti-European and anti-rich polarizations on these issues were also higher in 1952. Ex-colonial status has more recently become an especially high polarizer of these alignments, as have Western military alliances. A moderate Southern movement of self-determination positions reflects the anti-Northern "collective security" concerns of revolutionary Eastern states.

Anti-intervention resolutions in 1947 sometimes found the Soviets and the extreme colonial powers voting together against a Southern majority; although this issue has continued to be a mixture of East–West and North–South components (and others as well), its initial disappearance from important roll-call votes in the Sixteenth Assembly also implies a decrease in the pervasiveness of North–South alignments there. A substantively more accurate way of interpreting the rise of the East–West conflict is to say (1) that UN supranationalism has become the only significant North–South issue; (2) that cold war and Palestine related attitudes and alignments increasingly look like East–West alignments and like each other; (3) that anticolonial issues (or more recent similar postcolonial divisions) have continued as East–West issues and increased in frequency.

### Changes in the Distributions of Positions and Intensities

The model in Chapter 8 implied the importance of a symmetrical unimodal distribution of voters' preferences for moderating influences on Assembly conflicts; for a political leadership not committed to changing these preferences, the rational strategy for gaining a majority vote was to move toward the modal policy position. Bimodal distributions, on the other hand, would serve to polarize national representatives in two-party competition, for lack of a middle base of support and for fear of the appearance of a more extreme party which might capture one's original supporters. It was suggested that the enfranchisement of new voters might transform a previously bimodal East–West distribution of voter preferences.

When we differentiated East–West voting into its cold war and self-determination components, however, the relevant environmental distributions of new voters produced *opposite* effects. The number

of states not militarily aligned in the cold war, and therefore pre-
sumably in the middle on cold war issues, has increased to the
extent that they form the modal alliance category. From a modal
*non*colonial group in the Assembly, the distribution of colonial
experiences has become skewed so that now the *ex*-colonial states
are the largest colonial status group in the Assembly. A similar
skewing effect of racial and wealth variables (related also to North–
South alignments) has occurred. When we specify the "evolutionary
potential" of the Assembly in terms of these environmental changes,
it seems clear that cold war votes and speeches (except perhaps by
the protagonists) will occur less often in non-crisis years, just as they
already have done. Postcolonial self-determination issues, on the
other hand, are likely to remain frequent and intense concerns of the
Assembly.[15] Thus in Chapter 11 we saw that *distributional* bipolarizations of national characteristics, more than *environmental* polarizations (as measured by correlation coefficients), explain trends in
issue content, national policies, and Assembly preoccupations.

## Changes in Patterns of Roll-call Successes

A final changing aspect of the political process in the Assembly
has been the greater diffusion of power and the greater opportunties
for most groups to achieve some roll-call victories on issues of special
concern to them. As detailed in Chapter 9, Old Europeans continue
to be successful on a (smaller) range of cold war issues in the Assembly; Afro-Asians have increased the number of their anticolonial
successes; the Soviet bloc has begun to score some anti-imperialist victories in the Assembly and has achieved some success on cold war
related disarmament issues; Latin American prominence on self-

15. In 1961 Palestine related questions were also closely associated with the East–
West alignment, as we have just seen. The effect of new nations on the most relevant
polarizers of those questions is not so clear as with the two East–West components
discussed above. The fraction of Old Europeans in the Assembly has been decreasing,
but the percentage of Arab states has itself not recently increased. The proportion of
democracies in the Assembly may have shrunk slightly since 1952, but the number of
authoritarian or communist states likely to support Arab positions has not rapidly
expanded. Perhaps because of the colonial–ex-colonial polarization of Palestine issues
and the much larger number of ex-colonial states in the Assembly, the Arab states
have recently tried hard to present questions like Oman and Palestine as anticolonial
questions. At the Eighteenth Assembly Arab states succeeded in bringing the Oman
situation to the Fourth Committee, but failed through lack of African and Latin
American support (again like the 1961 alignments) to have Oman labeled as colonial
territory under resolution 1514 (XV).

determination questions has declined, but the region retains the role of a veto group on such issues and has shared in several supra-nationalist decisions; Arab states have even begun to gain some satisfaction on Palestine issues. In a period when East–West align-ments have been increasingly prevalent, partial victories for various sides have resulted from the ability to gain the support of some of those states normally in opposition. Various substantive issues have sometimes been of just this sort—despite East–West voting drawing about equal and opposite responses from East and West, newer con-stellations of allies have helped determine the voting outcome. The decentralization of power in the Assembly, along with greater un-certainty as to which kinds of resolutions will win or be supported on Palestine, self-determination, cold war, and even supranational-ism issues, produces the main pattern of evolving complexity in the General Assembly.

### THE FUTURE OF UN POLITICS: STABILITY OR INSTABILITY

We are now in a position to assess trends toward stability or instability in world politics as seen in the General Assembly from the vantage points suggested by the questions in Chapters 1 and 8. In making this assessment it will be convenient to use two distinc-tions introduced previously—a cognitive–behavioral distinction between rotated and unrotated factor patterns, and a voluntaristic–deterministic distinction in interpreting and explaining positions on these conflicts. Deterministic and distributional considerations, com-bined with an emphasis on behavioral geopolitical alignments, create a set of pessimistic interpretations.

### Pessimistic Considerations

A pessimist would focus on the trends in pervasiveness and on the distribution of positions and intensities of commitment on the unrotated conflicts. The East–West split is increasingly pervasive, increasingly bimodal, and increasingly intense, even in terms of speeches per roll-call vote. The number of states standing between the protagonists in this conflict is dwindling and, as measured by their speechmaking, there are not many intense members of an uncom-mitted East–West "fire brigade." Africa is currently the largest source of middle states, but the intensity of Brazzaville activity to bridge the East–West gap has not been high. At the Sixteenth Session bridging groups between North and South were even rarer, although Scandinavian states were active on some of these issues.

It is possible that a bimodal distribution of intensity and attitude is not so rare in parliamentary bodies as we have assumed. From the voting studies we would expect that bimodality of opinions is less typical of the *electorate* than of the *legislatures* in stable democracies. Little work has been done on environmental distributions or attitudinal polarizations in the electorate, which may pressure voters to more extreme or more moderate behavior. Certainly the tight party discipline of the British Parliament, for example, creates at least the appearance of bimodality—perfect discipline in a two party system would show up as perfect bimodality on roll-call votes. Within a domestic political system tight party discipline presupposes some basic congruence of interests within each of the parties, or the discipline would not be accepted. That discipline is likely to reflect, on the whole, the position of those in the middle of each party, and thus the voting will look bimodal. Whether the underlying distribution of attitudes within the British Parliament is really bimodal is not so certain. May there not really be more M.P.s in the middle, Laborites and Tories together, than at any point on either side? Roll-call votes can give us a misleading impression.

The problem of party discipline on roll-call votes makes it difficult to know whether the apparent bimodality, even the trend to greater bimodality on East–West issues, is sufficient to constitute a real threat to the system's stability.[16] Even though trade, aid, and alliances explain most voting positions after they have happened,

16. The problem of how much polarization is too much, i.e. is likely to be associated with outbreaks of violence, demands further analysis. Whether we look at the kinds of new members in the UN, the environmental polarizations they have changed, the distribution of their votes, or the intensity of their speeches, the point is the same. In remarks that may apply more to the cold war than to self-determination or supra-nationalism cleavages, Alford, p. 339, concludes that "The evidence that the political parties [in stable Western democracies] may come to be more clearly based upon class cleavages is not prima facie evidence of imminent danger to the existing political institutions. *Under conditions of highly developed industrialism*, class cleavages may actually be the cleavages which are most easily compromised. . . . *Regional and religious* loyalties are not easily compromised because they rest on differences of 'values,' not 'interests.' Such cleavages may be inherently more divisive and less flexible than class [or economic] ones" (our emphases).

the extent that votes are influenced by the threat of punishment is not clear. Within the Soviet bloc party discipline involves certain sanctions, to be sure, but the number of votes switched by the threat of curtailment of Soviet aid, trade, or alliances is extremely hard to estimate.

Outside of the bloc, the Soviet Union has found it increasingly expedient to support African self-determination claims, but it does not appear that either Russia or the great bulk of Afro–Asian states has developed a sense of loyalty or obligation to the other. Among Western allies voting positions reflect a greater number of converging interests, but even then trade and aid sometimes represent influence *attempts,* not *rewards* or *sanctions* for previous behavior.

Even if we were to concede that bimodality is to some degree to be expected, the pessimist could still point to the increasing pervasiveness of the East–West conflict. All interests hardly coincide on all such issues; nevertheless the alignments are similar and, to an ever greater extent, have come to dominate the Assembly. North–South questions, defined by a separate and distinct voting alignment, are becoming rarer, as are other unrotated alignments. And the increased East–West component of voting positions on major issues —cold war, self-determination, and Palestine—may by repetition of voting alignments reinforce countries' images of who are their friends and who their opponents. Fewer distinct "parties" on different ends of these alignments have preserved the cohesion and visibility of others.

In our discussion of "party politics" we have sometimes spoken largely in terms of two-party competition, and at other times of a multiparty system. Two-party competition is possible, of course, only in a world where most conflicts form on a single dimension. But whether a two-party system will in fact emerge depends heavily on the distribution of preferences. Two parties may converge toward similar positions, or a third may arise in the center.[17]

A pessimist would also emphasize that the considerable con-

17. Many political scientists have long contended that an electoral system of single-member districts with plurality voting (i.e. no runoffs) tends strongly to produce two-party politics. This is the world "electoral" system at the moment. It is agreed, however, that the tendency to two-partyism is stronger where there is a powerful independently chosen executive, a condition that certainly does not apply in current world politics.

tinuity in environmental polarizations of East–West and North–South issues may perpetuate dangerous East–West or other tensions. He might argue, with some justification, that environmental polarizations have been continually so high that intensities of feeling have run even higher.[18] The enfranchisement of recently independent and bitterly anticolonial states has also heightened these tensions. The East–West division appears bound to increase in intensity, threatening to degenerate into an even more tension-filled and potentially violent conflict. In this kind of situation cross-pressures may no longer compromise positions, divert attentions, or dilute passions:

> The two-party system works best where it is based on an elaborate, cross-cutting solidarity structure, in which men and groups are pulled in different directions only by their diverse roles and interests. Wherever the solidarity structure is polarized by class, race, or religion, and the political lines follow those of social cleavage, a two-party system may intensify internal conflict rather than help to integrate the society. . . .
>
> In general, where the class struggle is superimposed upon a conflict between religion and irreligion, or between different ethnic groups—wherever opposing groups see elections as a fight between good and evil, so that conversion from one political faith to another is almost impossible—a two-party system is more destructive of political stability than is one which center parties can mediate between extreme opponents.[19]

For states potentially near the middle of the East–West continuum, the English type of representative model (primary allegiance to an

---

18. Again we have the problem of how much polarization is too much, and how the UN compares with national legislatures in stable democracies. Hardly any evidence exists, though Leroy N. Rieselbach's study *The Roots of Isolation* (Indianapolis, Bobbs-Merrill, 1965), and a letter from the author show that constituency characteristics (ruralism, ethnic composition, and socioeconomic status) almost never correlated as high as .50 with Congressional voting on a variety of domestic and foreign policy questions over four different sessions. The only constituency attribute which correlated consistently above .40 with any voting dimension was ruralism with a civil rights scale. Regional variables and party alliances were not included in the analysis, but the impression remains that in the General Assembly polarizations are more extreme.

19. Lipset, *The First New Nation*, pp. 308–09.

outside source of support) appears more common than the American model of constituency based representation. Rather than seek victory by moving closer to the uncommitted voter and a slender majority, both East and West have tried, through the admission or non-admission of new members, to increase the number of states committed to their own—essentially unchanged—views.

Such an interpretation denies that world politics has evolved toward greater complexity, fixes on a protracted bipolar conflict between East and West, and, as a result of an intensified bipolarization, questions the possibility of peaceful settlement of East–West differences. In this view the concomitant decrease in North–South alignments reflects a growing crisis of confidence in the UN's peace-keeping and developmental capabilities.

### More Optimistic Views

It is also possible to argue that the bipolarization of East–West politics contributes to international stability. Because other alignments of interest exist even though they are not as frequently expressed, East–West positions must aggregate them, modify them, and somehow integrate them into positions either acceptable or tolerable for "party" members. Some scholars, such as Talcott Parsons and Kenneth Waltz, have argued for the stability of a two-party, bipolar world, even when perceived largely in cold war terms. Rather optimistically, the argument goes that bipolarity and other evidence indicate the beginnings of a viable two-party system, in which each side acts under heavy constraints.

Waltz for example, argues that Gross National Products of the two superpowers will continue to exceed those of other states for several decades, even taking into account differing rates of economic growth. Effective nuclear forces will continue to reflect such economic capabilities. Inherently, then, the world is bipolar, and the variety of recurring crises need not cause panic:

> Intensity and breadth of competition and recurrence of crises in a picture of constant conflict verging on violence. At the same time, the relative simplicity of relations within a bipolar world, the great pressures that are generated, and the constant possibility of catastrophe produce a conservatism on the part

of the two greatest powers. The threat of massive nuclear retalia-
tion greatly reduces the chances of major international conflict.[20]

From a cognitive and voluntaristic view, a more uncertain, more
multidimensional, more pluralistic, and perhaps more realistic
interpretation of UN developments emerges. The cognitive perspective insists that specific substantive and situational issues, not
compact summary voting dimensions, be discussed as the source of
possible violent conflict in the future of world politics. When we
distinguish between the cold war, self-determination, and Palestine
related questions (all of which now contribute heavily to the East–
West voting alignment), an assessment has to be made in specific
terms of: (1) the likelihood of violence on the perimeters of the
Soviet Union, or of Communist China (whose polices and intensities
we have not studied); (2) the likelihood of postcolonial racial
conflict in southern Africa; and (3) the likelihood of conflict on
Moslem questions between Arabs and Israel or between Moslems and
Hindus over Kashmir. On North–South issues, significant possible
future conflict may stem from (1) the likelihood of the violent isolation of all but a few of the Old Europeans on an African intervention
question, and (2) the more divisive possibility of anti-Northern
expropriations in supranational "collective security" or "self-
determination" terms.

Admittedly such a long list does not inspire euphoria, but it does
suggest that the outcomes of these conflicts are in part manageable,
and not predetermined. Each of these possible sources of conflict has
received considerable diplomatic attention. None of them need in-
exorably expand into worldwide conflagrations.

The pluralistic optimist might consider that trends in the pervasiveness, bipolarization, and intensity of the various rotated factors
suggest that not cold war, but more tractable self-determination
issues are most likely to erupt into violent controversy. The cold
war within the UN remains a dangerous preoccupation of its protagonists, but not of most other UN members, and data for 1961

20. Kenneth N. Waltz, "The Stability of a Bipolar World," *Daedalus, 93* (1964),
903–04. Comments in the same volume by Roger Fisher and William Griffith criticize
both the bipolarity assumption and the related feeling of nostalgia. Waltz himself is
aware of problems relating to the spread of nuclear weapons and the related diffusion of military power.

show Palestine related issues not to have pervaded the UN. On all these issues, the effect of supranationalist successes in the Assembly is to provide a stronger set of resources for coping with conflicts that might break out in cold war, self-determination, African intervention, or Palestine related controversies. The significance of such agreements and achievements is not adequately conveyed by a small number of North–South roll calls.

From a cognitive and voluntaristic perspective, changes in the attitudes of various members toward the legitimacy and authority of the UN need to be studied as does the inclusive or exclusive consciousness of ideological, racial, and economic identities. Comparisons of our findings with those from other international or national bodies and historical periods would be important to establish thresholds of imminent danger.

The appearance of an increasing East–West trend may also be a result of our choice of years for analysis. It might be appropriate to study years from the UN's history like 1948, 1950, 1956, and 1960 to see what voting polarizations looked like during the Israeli–Arab War in Palestine, at the beginning of the Korean War, and during the Suez and early Congo crises. It may be, for instance, that 1947 and 1957, like 1963, were quiet years in the Assembly. Anti-Americanism in 1952 at the end of a long and inconclusive war made the Seventh a long remembered Assembly session. The massive influx of African states, the Belgrade Conference, the building of the Berlin Wall, and the resumption of nuclear testing were all recent events at the Sixteenth Assembly Session. Each of these two years is close to a time of bitter Soviet attacks on the Secretary-General. But as Hammarskjold successfully replaced Lie, so it may be hoped that Thant will weather the "crisis in confidence" in the UN associated with his first years in office and the subsequent financial crisis at the Nineteenth General Assembly.

The data we have studied have of course been more appropriate for the study of dissensus than consensus, in that unanimous resolutions or outcomes which did not include formal resolutions have been only inferentially suggested. Furthermore, our method of ranking state's positions has sometimes equated a possibly intense minority "no" with an unhappy but passive "abstain" on some other roll call. Nonetheless, the rotated factors suggested issues on which a kind of near consensus had developed in the Assembly; these were not highlighted by the unrotated analyses, partly because of the substantive variety of North–South alignments.

The more than three quarters of the Assembly's membership that supported principled UN intervention into colonial or apartheid problems may continue to find ways of modifying self-determination resolutions until they are tolerable for most Old Europeans. Similarly, on UN supranationalism issues it is fortunate that the new states in the Assembly have granted greater authority to the UN to intervene in their affairs than have some of the older West and East European powers.[21] Such an interpretation does suggest that, depending on the choices of the actors involved, new self-determination crises may not plunge Africa into a bloody war.

From a voluntaristic point of view, our single most dramatic finding of an "evolving complexity" in General Assembly politics has not been in the increase of the number of different voting issues there, but in the diffusion of voting successes on these dimensions to a variety of groups involved. This diffusion in terms of legislative *success* or effective *power*, not in terms of alignments or speeches, has also been associated with an increase in the number of legislative successes of the Arab, African, and Soviet groups in the Assembly on some issues of special concern to them. Rather than a tightening bipolar struggle between an Eastern and a Western party, however, such findings suggest that the decline of Western power in the Assembly has been associated with the beginnings of a multipolar UN confrontation, in which each of the poles is especially interested in and somewhat influential on particular substantive issues before the Assembly. With this perspective in mind, multiplying East–West alignments and intensities can be explained in terms of a Soviet shift to support the Arab and Casablanca states, the growing unrest of ex-colonial states in the Assembly, and Latin Westward movements away from the African position. Positive support of great power cold war positions by Latins, Arabs, and Asians, however, has not been increasing.

Communist China's admission to the UN and a deeper split between France and the United States could also continue a decentralization of power in the Assembly which may or may not have destabilizing effects. In terms of our findings it would add another

21. On this point see Ernst Haas, "Dynamic Environment and Static System."

voice like that of the Soviet Union to African self-determination demands, it would intensify the discussion of cold war issues with which other states in the Assembly do not want to be preoccupied, and it would pose more problems and opportunities for the Assembly's supranational majority on development, peacekeeping, and disarmament issues. Sino-Soviet differences might also be magnified in their attempts to gain support from both radical and moderate Afro-Asians.

We cannot fully assess the increment in bargaining and peaceful compromises resulting from the diffusion of power in the Assembly, and the greater likelihood that some old issue will be perceived in new ways, without having a better idea of each member's balance between subjective satisfactions and dissatisfactions in the Assembly and its likelihood of resorting to policies of violence outside the UN. A formal success in the Assembly may be only a frustrating experience if the decision is not at least partially respected. The future of Assembly politics is in the perspectives with which its members view conflict situations, in the polarizations they choose to perpetuate, and in the honorable and peaceful compromises they are willing to work for and to accept.

# APPENDIX

# Factor Scores for All General Assembly Members on All Super-Issues

## UNROTATED FACTOR SCORES [a]

| Country | EAST–WEST | | | | NORTH–SOUTH | | | |
|---|---|---|---|---|---|---|---|---|
| | 1947 | 1952 | 1957 | 1961 | 1947 | 1952 | 1957 | 1961 |
| Finland | | | —0.49 | —0.57 | | | 2.29 | —0.33 |
| Sweden | —0.49 | —1.24 | —0.72 | —0.83 | —0.82 | —0.30 | 0.97 | 0.17 |
| Denmark | —0.67 | —1.28 | —0.93 | —1.08 | —1.32 | —0.18 | 1.01 | 0.02 |
| Iceland | —0.65 | —1.18 | —1.09 | —1.12 | —0.75 | —0.05 | 0.32 | 0.15 |
| Norway | —0.22 | —1.16 | —0.84 | —0.97 | —0.81 | —0.07 | 0.94 | 0.10 |
| Belgium | —1.06 | —1.48 | —1.41 | —1.32 | —1.03 | —1.16 | 1.50 | —1.29 |
| Netherlands | —0.96 | —1.53 | —1.48 | —1.30 | —1.23 | —0.35 | 1.28 | —0.45 |
| Luxembourg | —0.88 | —1.60 | —1.48 | —1.44 | —0.97 | —1.12 | 1.36 | —0.58 |
| France | —0.48 | —1.45 | —1.34 | —1.10 | —0.17 | —0.90 | 1.33 | —2.39 |
| Italy | | | —1.50 | —1.34 | | | 1.03 | —0.62 |
| Greece | —1.15 | —0.84 | 0.14 | —1.18 | 0.13 | 0.05 | —1.36 | —0.76 |
| Portugal | | | —1.23 | —0.92 | | | 1.58 | —1.93 |
| United States | —1.07 | —1.32 | —0.91 | —1.36 | —0.52 | —0.08 | 0.00 | —1.06 |
| Canada | —1.45 | —1.42 | —1.20 | —1.19 | —0.90 | —0.03 | 1.16 | —0.38 |
| United Kingdom | —1.10 | —1.54 | —1.40 | —1.26 | —1.02 | —0.93 | 1.31 | —1.44 |
| Australia | —1.28 | —1.63 | —1.40 | —1.28 | —1.17 | —1.10 | 1.31 | —1.43 |
| New Zealand | —1.14 | —1.51 | —1.40 | —1.28 | —1.26 | —0.71 | 1.29 | —0.84 |
| South Africa | —1.32 | —1.53 | | —1.06 | —0.82 | —1.46 | | —2.50 |
| Austria | | | —0.75 | —0.76 | | | 0.17 | —0.28 |
| Ireland | | | —0.20 | —1.17 | | | 0.48 | —0.48 |
| Israel | | —0.40 | —0.53 | —0.61 | | 0.41 | 0.54 | 0.47 |
| Spain | | | —1.21 | —1.07 | | | 0.60 | —1.16 |
| China | 0.28 | —0.13 | —1.08 | —0.96 | 0.73 | 0.25 | 0.32 | —0.66 |
| Argentina | —1.14 | 0.04 | —0.87 | —0.95 | 1.03 | 0.89 | —0.30 | 0.07 |

## UNROTATED FACTOR SCORES [a]

| Country | EAST–WEST | | | | NORTH–SOUTH | | | |
|---|---|---|---|---|---|---|---|---|
| | 1947 | 1952 | 1957 | 1961 | 1947 | 1952 | 1957 | 1961 |
| Bolivia | −0.64 | 0.84 | 0.04 | −0.78 | −0.28 | 0.99 | −1.52 | 0.52 |
| Brazil | −0.65 | −0.06 | −0.72 | −0.81 | 0.46 | 1.20 | −1.19 | 0.21 |
| Chile | −0.46 | 0.25 | −0.73 | −1.02 | 0.01 | 1.05 | −0.99 | 0.24 |
| Colombia | 0.19 | −0.66 | −0.94 | −1.13 | 1.27 | 0.91 | −0.59 | 0.11 |
| Costa Rica | −1.05 | −0.05 | −0.31 | −0.96 | 0.83 | 1.03 | −1.78 | 0.29 |
| Cuba | −0.14 | −0.28 | −0.79 | 1.51 | 0.80 | 0.86 | −0.82 | −1.80 |
| Dominican Republic | −1.12 | −0.59 | −1.15 | −1.12 | 0.90 | 0.73 | 0.09 | −0.40 |
| Ecuador | −0.47 | −0.17 | −0.46 | −0.70 | 0.66 | 0.69 | −1.72 | 0.37 |
| El Salvador | −0.89 | 0.57 | −0.35 | −1.07 | 0.96 | 1.04 | −1.88 | −0.02 |
| Guatemala | 0.83 | 0.97 | 0.34 | −0.92 | −0.29 | 0.42 | −1.62 | −0.23 |
| Haiti | 0.65 | 0.34 | 0.10 | −0.30 | 0.79 | 0.95 | −1.40 | 0.44 |
| Honduras | −0.04 | 0.36 | −0.96 | | 0.71 | 0.97 | −0.41 | |
| Mexico | 0.47 | 0.59 | 0.41 | −0.63 | 0.53 | 0.80 | −0.94 | 0.57 |
| Nicaragua | −1.27 | −0.51 | −1.16 | −1.14 | 0.14 | 0.60 | 0.27 | 0.09 |
| Panama | 0.09 | −0.20 | −0.28 | −1.07 | 0.11 | 0.80 | −1.76 | 0.45 |
| Paraguay | −1.05 | −0.62 | −0.69 | −1.16 | 0.78 | 0.67 | −1.24 | 0.28 |
| Peru | −0.67 | −0.66 | −0.66 | −1.12 | 0.68 | 0.63 | −0.92 | 0.15 |
| Uruguay | −0.74 | −0.17 | −0.38 | −0.90 | −0.36 | 0.80 | −1.62 | 0.60 |
| Venezuela | 0.09 | −0.29 | −0.67 | −0.72 | −0.03 | 0.48 | −1.23 | 0.80 |
| Albania | | | 1.54 | 1.52 | | | 1.12 | −1.94 |
| Bulgaria | | | 1.54 | 1.52 | | | 1.12 | −1.94 |
| Byelorussia | 1.71 | 1.27 | 1.58 | 1.52 | −1.91 | −2.65 | 1.07 | −1.94 |
| Czechoslovakia | 1.73 | 1.28 | 1.58 | 1.52 | −1.70 | −2.60 | 1.10 | −1.94 |
| Hungary | | | 1.58 | 1.49 | | | 1.07 | −1.88 |
| Poland | 1.71 | 1.27 | 1.60 | 1.52 | −1.67 | −2.65 | 0.96 | −1.94 |
| Romania | | | 1.58 | 1.52 | | | 1.07 | −1.94 |
| U.S.S.R. | 1.73 | 1.27 | 1.60 | 1.52 | −1.94 | −2.65 | 1.12 | −1.94 |
| Ukraine | 1.73 | 1.27 | 1.58 | 1.52 | −1.94 | −2.65 | 1.07 | −1.94 |
| Yugoslavia | 1.84 | 0.97 | 1.21 | 1.26 | −1.45 | 0.29 | 0.09 | 0.44 |
| Mongolia | | | | 1.49 | | | | −1.81 |
| Afghanistan | 1.13 | 1.22 | 1.02 | 1.11 | 0.66 | 0.05 | 0.45 | −0.12 |
| Burma | | 0.91 | 1.11 | 0.89 | | 0.01 | 0.11 | 0.56 |
| Cambodia | | | 0.73 | 0.91 | | | −0.03 | 0.36 |
| Ceylon | | | 0.91 | 0.89 | | | −0.11 | 0.72 |
| Cyprus | | | | 0.19 | | | | 0.94 |
| India | 1.12 | 0.83 | 0.92 | 0.92 | 0.65 | −0.05 | −0.06 | 0.71 |
| Indonesia | | 1.21 | 1.14 | 1.30 | | 0.08 | 0.25 | 0.30 |
| Iran | 0.81 | 1.17 | 0.28 | −0.30 | 1.07 | 0.55 | −0.99 | 1.01 |
| Laos | | | 0.12 | −0.13 | | | −0.37 | 0.84 |
| Malaya | | | 0.03 | −0.34 | | | −0.72 | 0.87 |
| Nepal | | | 0.93 | 0.96 | | | −0.03 | 0.46 |
| Japan | | | −0.24 | −0.88 | | | −1.09 | 0.03 |
| Pakistan | 0.79 | 0.92 | −0.35 | 0.21 | 1.50 | −0.06 | −0.40 | 0.77 |
| Philippines | 0.26 | 0.67 | −0.48 | −0.50 | 0.66 | 0.37 | −1.02 | 0.60 |
| Thailand | | −0.14 | −0.29 | −0.62 | | 0.44 | −1.28 | 0.42 |

## UNROTATED FACTOR SCORES [a]

| Country | EAST–WEST | | | | NORTH–SOUTH | | | |
|---|---|---|---|---|---|---|---|---|
| | 1947 | 1952 | 1957 | 1961 | 1947 | 1952 | 1957 | 1961 |
| Turkey | −0.73 | −0.83 | −0.91 | −1.01 | 0.29 | −0.18 | 0.49 | −0.04 |
| Iraq | 1.01 | 0.96 | 0.66 | 1.37 | 1.38 | 0.44 | −0.86 | 0.23 |
| Jordan | | | 0.66 | 0.69 | | | −0.66 | 0.64 |
| Lebanon | 0.97 | 0.82 | 0.42 | 0.62 | 1.40 | 0.75 | −0.91 | 0.64 |
| Saudi Arabia | 1.02 | 1.34 | 1.19 | 0.99 | 1.12 | −0.01 | 0.13 | 0.08 |
| Yemen | 0.97 | 1.29 | 1.21 | 1.18 | 1.11 | 0.20 | 0.38 | 0.14 |
| Sudan | | | 1.19 | 1.03 | | | 0.46 | 0.48 |
| Tunisia | | | 0.71 | 0.72 | | | −0.57 | 0.95 |
| Egypt | 1.00 | 1.20 | 1.29 | 1.33 | 1.22 | 0.47 | 0.31 | 0.27 |
| Libya | | | 0.80 | 0.90 | | | −0.55 | 0.85 |
| Morocco | | | 1.20 | 1.18 | | | 0.28 | 0.66 |
| Syria | 1.06 | 1.11 | 1.37 | 1.23 | 0.99 | 0.21 | 0.68 | 0.38 |
| Ghana | | 0.94 | 1.03 | | | 0.07 | 0.72 | |
| Guinea | | | | 1.26 | | | | 0.66 |
| Mali | | | | 1.33 | | | | 0.40 |
| Cameroun | | | | −0.14 | | | | 0.92 |
| Central African Rep. | | | | 0.10 | | | | 0.78 |
| Chad | | | | 0.23 | | | | 0.95 |
| Congo (Brazzaville) | | | | 0.17 | | | | 1.12 |
| Dahomey | | | | −0.03 | | | | 1.25 |
| Ivory Coast | | | | 0.07 | | | | 1.21 |
| Malagasy Republic | | | | −0.03 | | | | 0.83 |
| Mauritania | | | | 0.28 | | | | 0.88 |
| Niger | | | | 0.14 | | | | 0.97 |
| Senegal | | | | 0.46 | | | | 1.27 |
| Togo | | | | 0.35 | | | | 0.31 |
| Upper Volta | | | | 0.18 | | | | 1.36 |
| Congo (Leopoldville) | | | | 0.62 | | | | 0.95 |
| Ethiopia | 1.12 | 0.85 | 0.67 | 0.90 | −0.05 | 0.40 | −0.89 | 0.90 |
| Liberia | 0.64 | 0.66 | 0.06 | 0.12 | 0.85 | 0.39 | −0.73 | 1.34 |
| Nigeria | | | | 0.57 | | | | 1.10 |
| Sierra Leone | | | | 0.52 | | | | 1.32 |
| Somalia | | | | 0.83 | | | | 0.76 |

a. In most cases blanks indicate nonmembership in the United Nations for the year indicated. Several countries have also been omitted from the factor analysis in the various years because of high absenteeism (see Chaps. 2–6).

## REVISED ROTATED FACTOR SCORES [b]

| Country | COLD WAR 1947c | 1952 | 1957 | 1961 | SELF-DETERMINATION 1952 | 1957 | 1961 |
|---|---|---|---|---|---|---|---|
| Finland | | | 1.40 | 1.09 | | 1.06 | —1.64 |
| Sweden | —0.60 | —0.20 | 0.64 | 0.60 | —1.84 | 1.68 | —1.52 |
| Denmark | —0.75 | —0.63 | 0.50 | 0.44 | —1.80 | 2.13 | —1.81 |
| Iceland | —0.84 | —0.63 | —0.99 | —0.39 | —1.89 | 2.15 | —1.58 |
| Norway | —0.26 | —0.63 | 0.44 | 0.42 | —1.79 | 2.16 | —1.66 |
| Belgium | —1.11 | —0.48 | —0.95 | —0.99 | —1.28 | 1.28 | —1.31 |
| Netherlands | —1.21 | —0.54 | —0.89 | —0.37 | —1.87 | 1.39 | —1.29 |
| Luxembourg | —1.32 | —0.53 | —0.94 | —1.03 | —1.43 | 1.42 | —1.38 |
| France | —0.78 | —0.68 | —0.95 | —0.65 | —1.25 | 1.45 | —1.13 |
| Italy | | | —0.89 | —1.03 | | 1.49 | —1.33 |
| Greece | —0.87 | —0.41 | —0.67 | —0.98 | —1.11 | —0.20 | —1.17 |
| Portugal | | | —0.21 | —0.10 | | 0.97 | —1.38 |
| United States | —1.18 | —0.68 | —0.86 | —0.95 | —1.81 | 1.21 | —1.22 |
| Canada | —1.05 | —0.62 | —0.74 | —1.05 | —1.15 | 1.05 | —1.41 |
| United Kingdom | —1.07 | —0.75 | —0.95 | 0.03 | —1.38 | 1.07 | —1.52 |
| Australia | —0.84 | —0.51 | —0.95 | —0.95 | —1.37 | 1.07 | —1.25 |
| New Zealand | —0.89 | —0.63 | —0.95 | —0.96 | —1.82 | 1.04 | —1.22 |
| South Africa | —1.01 | —0.36 | | —0.81 | —1.70 | | —1.28 |
| Austria | | | —0.62 | —0.18 | | 0.76 | —1.50 |
| Ireland | | | 0.65 | —1.04 | | 1.47 | —1.33 |
| Israel | | —0.25 | 0.18 | —0.02 | 0.04 | 1.36 | —0.26 |
| Spain | | | —0.80 | —0.88 | | 0.32 | —1.53 |
| China | 0.28 | —0.88 | —0.95 | —0.72 | —0.68 | 1.28 | —1.12 |
| Argentina | —0.98 | —0.40 | —0.89 | —1.03 | 1.02 | —0.99 | —0.88 |
| Bolivia | —0.78 | —0.04 | —0.49 | —0.92 | 0.95 | —0.26 | —0.50 |
| Brazil | —0.89 | —0.72 | —0.89 | —1.03 | 1.24 | 0.71 | 0.85 |
| Chile | —0.88 | —0.45 | —0.89 | —1.01 | 0.66 | 0.08 | —0.45 |
| Colombia | —0.21 | —0.56 | —0.93 | —1.05 | 0.87 | 0.98 | —0.86 |
| Costa Rica | —0.82 | —0.42 | —0.95 | —1.01 | 0.76 | 0.03 | —0.61 |
| Cuba | —0.09 | —0.87 | —0.73 | 1.36 | 0.58 | 0.93 | 0.68 |
| Dominican Republic | —0.79 | —0.90 | —0.80 | —1.07 | 0.56 | 0.41 | —1.08 |
| Ecuador | —0.69 | —0.19 | —0.83 | —0.79 | 0.53 | —0.01 | —0.51 |
| El Salvador | —0.51 | —0.60 | —0.91 | —1.07 | 1.04 | —0.01 | —0.88 |
| Guatemala | 0.98 | —0.27 | —0.66 | —0.99 | 0.99 | —0.67 | —0.83 |
| Haiti | 0.70 | —0.96 | —0.88 | —0.99 | 0.90 | 0.01 | 0.79 |
| Honduras | —0.10 | —0.66 | —0.90 | | 1.39 | 1.37 | |
| Mexico | 0.41 | —0.33 | —0.24 | —1.02 | 0.75 | —0.60 | 0.01 |
| Nicaragua | —0.93 | —0.77 | —0.80 | —0.97 | 0.67 | 1.23 | —0.91 |
| Panama | —0.11 | —0.72 | —0.97 | —1.07 | 0.63 | —0.35 | —0.63 |
| Paraguay | —0.72 | —0.64 | —0.93 | —1.05 | —0.27 | 0.14 | —0.82 |
| Peru | —0.72 | —0.83 | —0.83 | —1.05 | 0.17 | —0.00 | —0.85 |
| Uruguay | —1.08 | —0.37 | —0.76 | —1.08 | 0.56 | —0.65 | —0.34 |
| Venezuela | —0.07 | —0.90 | —0.80 | —1.07 | 0.64 | —0.29 | —0.21 |
| Albania | | | 1.55 | 1.37 | | —0.87 | 0.74 |
| Bulgaria | | | 1.55 | 1.37 | | —0.87 | 0.74 |

| UN SUPRANATIONALISM | | | | PALESTINE-RELATED QUESTIONS | | | ANTI-INTERVENTIONISM (AFRICA) | | |
|---|---|---|---|---|---|---|---|---|---|
| 1947d | 1952 | 1957 | 1961 | 1947 | 1952 | 1961 | 1947 | 1952 | 1957 |
|  |  | 0.06 | 0.49 |  |  | −0.98 |  |  | 1.48 |
| −0.25 | −0.37 | 0.94 | 0.72 | −0.85 | −1.30 | −1.26 | 0.86 | 0.07 | −0.49 |
| 0.80 | −0.20 | 0.67 | 0.74 | −1.07 | −1.18 | −1.25 | 0.70 | −0.07 | −0.41 |
| −0.10 | 0.19 | 0.67 | 0.74 | −0.88 | −1.19 | −1.20 | 0.63 | 0.29 | −0.56 |
| −0.25 | −0.20 | 0.67 | 0.75 | −0.96 | −1.18 | −1.23 | 0.86 | 0.21 | −0.50 |
| 1.26 | −1.04 | 0.75 | −0.85 | −0.17 | −0.14 | −1.30 | −1.79 | −2.13 | 2.45 |
| 1.13 | 0.14 | 0.75 | 0.57 | −0.73 | −1.37 | −1.31 | 0.56 | −1.42 | 2.22 |
| 1.24 | −0.90 | 0.33 | 0.54 | −0.00 | −0.97 | −1.31 | −0.19 | −2.11 | 2.03 |
| −0.85 | −0.42 | 0.75 | −1.55 | 0.31 | −1.09 | −1.15 | 0.26 | −1.90 | 2.47 |
|  |  | 0.60 | 0.52 |  |  | −1.06 |  |  | 2.07 |
| 0.49 | 0.12 | 0.00 | 0.10 | 0.76 | −0.15 | −0.78 | −1.64 | −0.75 | −0.68 |
|  |  | 0.40 | −0.99 |  |  | −0.56 |  |  | 1.93 |
| −0.83 | −0.01 | 0.16 | 0.42 | −1.06 | −1.27 | −1.20 | 0.68 | 0.17 | −0.18 |
| −0.07 | 0.44 | 0.29 | 0.44 | −1.06 | −1.09 | −0.94 | −1.26 | −1.49 | 1.77 |
| 1.15 | −0.42 | 0.75 | 0.15 | −0.06 | −1.30 | −1.20 | −1.54 | −2.09 | 2.45 |
| 0.42 | −0.76 | 0.75 | −0.16 | −1.07 | −1.28 | −1.27 | −1.96 | −2.22 | 2.45 |
| 0.07 | −0.17 | 0.75 | 0.43 | −1.26 | −1.30 | −1.19 | −0.98 | −1.49 | 2.22 |
| 0.94 | −0.64 |  | −1.38 | −0.66 | −1.33 | −0.63 | −1.46 | −2.32 |  |
|  |  | 0.60 | 0.37 |  |  | −0.69 |  |  | 0.18 |
|  |  | 0.34 | 0.42 |  |  | −1.02 |  |  | −0.66 |
|  | 0.07 | 0.00 | 0.68 |  | −1.35 | −0.79 |  | 0.35 | −0.35 |
|  |  | 0.33 | 0.03 |  |  | 0.04 |  |  | 1.84 |
| −0.82 | −0.69 | 0.04 | −0.44 | 0.71 | 0.95 | −0.72 | 1.19 | 0.19 | 0.53 |
| 0.28 | 0.61 | 0.75 | 0.48 | 0.96 | 0.47 | −0.39 | −1.44 | −0.96 | 2.08 |
| −0.16 | 0.80 | 0.75 | 0.50 | −0.17 | 0.96 | −0.71 | −0.30 | 0.82 | −0.82 |
| −0.10 | 0.52 | 0.60 | 0.43 | 0.28 | −0.28 | −0.37 | 1.09 | 0.51 | −0.28 |
| −0.07 | 0.63 | 0.25 | 0.50 | −0.57 | −0.16 | −1.26 | 0.58 | 0.66 | −0.49 |
| −0.76 | 0.71 | 0.06 | 0.50 | 1.53 | −0.13 | −1.02 | 0.68 | −1.26 | −0.59 |
| −1.00 | 0.71 | 0.63 | 0.51 | −0.40 | −0.45 | −0.78 | −1.27 | 0.44 | −0.70 |
| −0.94 | 0.25 | 0.01 | −2.34 | 0.71 | −0.59 | 1.44 | −0.61 | 0.19 | −0.67 |
| −0.97 | 0.84 | 0.83 | −0.31 | −0.62 | −0.27 | −0.96 | −1.24 | −1.55 | 1.59 |
| −0.54 | 0.74 | 0.52 | 0.51 | 0.25 | −1.27 | −0.06 | 0.72 | 0.17 | −0.77 |
| −0.98 | 0.40 | 0.64 | 0.27 | 0.22 | 0.80 | −0.82 | −1.56 | 0.69 | −0.78 |
| −0.80 | 0.04 | 0.26 | 0.44 | −1.14 | 0.42 | −0.49 | 0.40 | 0.87 | −0.43 |
| −1.01 | 0.43 | 0.89 | −0.25 | 0.68 | −0.10 | −0.64 | 0.38 | 0.63 | −0.47 |
| −0.83 | 0.51 | 0.31 |  | 0.25 | −0.61 |  | 0.23 | 0.49 | −0.22 |
| −0.94 | 0.69 | 0.51 | 0.48 | 0.24 | 0.02 | −0.47 | 0.22 | 0.74 | −0.40 |
| −0.98 | 0.58 | 0.33 | 0.67 | −0.44 | −0.92 | −1.03 | −1.77 | −0.40 | 0.37 |
| −0.98 | 0.74 | 0.11 | 0.73 | −1.08 | −1.23 | −0.95 | 0.22 | 0.37 | −0.67 |
| −0.91 | 0.49 | 0.40 | 0.73 | −0.58 | −0.66 | −1.05 | −1.11 | 0.15 | −0.61 |
| −0.43 | −0.12 | 0.33 | 0.46 | −0.55 | 0.12 | −1.04 | 0.59 | −0.81 | 0.07 |
| −0.63 | 0.47 | 0,56 | 0.73 | −0.98 | −1.10 | −0.82 | 0.26 | 0.46 | −0.58 |
| −0.96 | 0.36 | 0.33 | 0.93 | −1.06 | −0.24 | −0.43 | 0.22 | −0.91 | −0.35 |
|  |  | −2.72 | −2.56 |  |  | 1.39 |  |  | −0.64 |
|  |  | −2.72 | −2.56 |  |  | 1.39 |  |  | −0.64 |

# REVISED ROTATED FACTOR SCORES [b]

| Country | COLD WAR | | | | SELF-DETERMINATION | | |
|---|---|---|---|---|---|---|---|
| | 1947c | 1952 | 1957 | 1961 | 1952 | 1957 | 1961 |
| Byelorussia | 1.98 | 2.33 | 1.55 | 1.37 | 0.37 | —1.06 | 0.74 |
| Czechoslovakia | 2.01 | 2.33 | 1.57 | 1.37 | 0.34 | —1.08 | 0.74 |
| Hungary | | | 1.55 | 1.36 | | —1.06 | 0.70 |
| Poland | 2.02 | 2.33 | 1.55 | 1.37 | 0.37 | —1.20 | 0.74 |
| Romania | | | 1.55 | 1.37 | | —1.06 | 0.74 |
| U.S.S.R. | 1.95 | 2.33 | 1.55 | 1.37 | 0.37 | —1.06 | 0.74 |
| Ukraine | 1.95 | 2.33 | 1.55 | 1.37 | 0.37 | —1.06 | 0.74 |
| Yugoslavia | 1.96 | —0.27 | 1.38 | 1.39 | 0.86 | —1.10 | 0.76 |
| Mongolia | | | | 1.41 | | | 0.89 |
| Afghanistan | 1.03 | 1.67 | 1.26 | 1.49 | 0.61 | —1.17 | 0.59 |
| Burma | | 1.28 | 1.41 | 1.12 | 0.75 | —1.15 | 0.73 |
| Cambodia | | | 0.81 | 1.10 | | —1.35 | 0.53 |
| Ceylon | | | 1.39 | 1.25 | | —0.91 | 0.57 |
| Cyprus | | | | —0.08 | | | 0.13 |
| India | 0.80 | 1.60 | 1.48 | 1.17 | 0.38 | —0.89 | 0.54 |
| Indonesia | | 1.60 | 1.42 | 1.54 | 0.81 | —0.97 | 0.74 |
| Iran | 0.76 | 0.56 | —0.54 | —1.19 | 0.96 | —0.69 | 0.22 |
| Laos | | | 0.31 | —1.04 | | —0.58 | 0.35 |
| Malaya | | | —0.37 | —1.23 | | —0.64 | —0.39 |
| Nepal | | | 1.47 | 1.39 | | —1.38 | 0.46 |
| Japan | | | —0.72 | —1.10 | | 0.25 | —1.26 |
| Pakistan | 0.51 | 1.36 | —0.17 | 0.51 | —0.10 | 0.62 | —0.39 |
| Philippines | 0.41 | —0.67 | —1.03 | —1.11 | 0.48 | 0.72 | 0.33 |
| Thailand | | —0.87 | —0.64 | —1.23 | —0.49 | —0.15 | —0.93 |
| Turkey | —0.38 | —0.61 | —0.88 | —0.98 | —0.95 | 0.32 | —1.17 |
| Iraq | 0.83 | 0.25 | —0.95 | 1.54 | 0.38 | —0.68 | 0.77 |
| Jordan | | | —0.51 | —0.80 | | —0.71 | 0.76 |
| Lebanon | 0.95 | —0.74 | —0.91 | —0.17 | 0.66 | —0.43 | 0.27 |
| Saudi Arabia | 0.87 | 1.52 | 0.68 | 0.44 | 0.73 | —0.90 | 0.57 |
| Yemen | 0.79 | 1.25 | 1.30 | 1.22 | 0.86 | —0.94 | 0.59 |
| Sudan | | | 1.28 | 1.08 | | —0.74 | 0.56 |
| Tunisia | | | 0.15 | 0.60 | | —0.67 | 0.45 |
| Egypt | 0.74 | 0.64 | 1.31 | 1.44 | 1.01 | —0.94 | 0.77 |
| Libya | | | —0.44 | —0.11 | | —0.91 | 0.92 |
| Morocco | | | 1.11 | 1.34 | | —0.79 | 0.64 |
| Syria | 0.90 | 0.88 | 1.26 | 1.41 | 0.33 | —1.00 | 0.56 |
| Ghana | | | 1.45 | 1.37 | | —0.86 | 0.66 |
| Guinea | | | | 1.57 | | | 0.73 |
| Mali | | | | 1.57 | | | 0.78 |
| Cameroun | | | | —1.00 | | | 1.30 |
| Central African Rep. | | | | —0.18 | | | 1.47 |
| Chad | | | | —0.12 | | | 1.47 |
| Congo (Brazzaville) | | | | —0.17 | | | 1.64 |
| Dahomey | | | | —0.33 | | | 1.27 |
| Ivory Coast | | | | —0.20 | | | 1.20 |

| UN SUPRANATIONALISM | | | | PALESTINE-RELATED QUESTIONS | | | ANTI-INTERVENTIONISM (AFRICA) | | |
|---|---|---|---|---|---|---|---|---|---|
| 1947[d] | 1952 | 1957 | 1961 | 1947 | 1952 | 1961 | 1947 | 1952 | 1957 |
| 2.15 | −2.86 | −2.72 | −2.56 | −1.39 | 0.32 | 1.39 | −0.57 | 0.45 | −0.64 |
| 2.15 | −2.81 | −2.34 | −2.56 | −0.83 | 0.36 | 1.39 | −0.57 | 0.45 | −0.38 |
|  |  | −2.72 | −2.55 |  |  | 1.37 |  |  | −0.64 |
| 2.13 | −2.86 | −2.37 | −2.56 | −0.93 | 0.32 | 1.39 | −0.82 | 0.45 | −0.33 |
|  |  | −2.72 | −2.56 |  |  | 1.39 |  |  | −0.64 |
| 2.10 | −2.86 | −2.46 | −2.56 | −1.58 | 0.32 | 1.39 | 0.01 | 0.45 | −0.38 |
| 2.10 | −2.86 | −2.72 | −2.56 | −1.58 | 0.32 | 1.39 | 0.01 | 0.45 | −0.64 |
| 2.14 | −0.37 | 0.35 | 0.39 | −0.55 | 0.30 | 1.29 | 0.01 | 0.92 | −0.51 |
|  |  |  | −2.44 |  |  | 1.26 |  |  |  |
| 1.08 | 0.92 | −0.12 | −0.69 | 1.30 | 1.42 | 0.87 | 0.46 | 0.97 | −0.39 |
|  | 1.02 | 0.46 | 0.53 |  | 0.08 | 0.88 |  | 0.76 | −0.27 |
|  |  | −0.77 | −0.09 |  |  | 0.96 |  |  | −0.59 |
|  |  | 0.93 | 0.62 |  |  | 0.62 |  |  | −0.27 |
|  |  |  | 0.83 |  |  | 0.19 |  |  |  |
| 0.92 | 0.82 | 0.52 | 0.47 | 1.76 | 1.23 | 0.75 | 1.12 | 0.70 | −0.19 |
|  | 0.76 | 0.78 | 0.31 |  | 1.48 | 1.38 |  | 0.79 | −0.40 |
| −0.41 | 0.85 | 0.72 | 0.75 | 1.62 | 1.46 | −0.14 | 1.28 | 0.88 | −0.67 |
|  |  | 0.94 | 0.68 |  |  | −0.19 |  |  | −0.43 |
|  |  | −0.02 | 0.94 |  |  | 0.22 |  |  | −0.19 |
|  |  | −0.20 | 0.48 |  |  | 1.00 |  |  | −0.62 |
|  |  | 0.71 | 0.72 |  |  | −0.40 |  |  | −0.76 |
| −0.84 | 0.45 | 0.35 | 0.63 | 1.62 | 1.58 | 0.46 | 1.26 | 0.93 | −0.74 |
| −1.04 | −1.00 | 0.40 | 0.05 | 0.01 | 1.11 | −0.45 | 0.19 | 0.87 | −0.78 |
|  |  | 0.37 | 0.42 | 0.73 | 1.16 | 0.23 |  | 0.69 | −0.68 |
| 0.74 | 0.30 | 0.12 | 0.59 | 0.80 | −0.19 | −0.85 | −1.91 | −1.09 | 1.04 |
| −0.70 | 0.38 | −0.47 | −0.35 | 1.55 | 1.49 | 1.52 | 1.08 | 0.80 | −0.74 |
|  |  | 0.15 | −0.14 |  |  | 1.46 |  |  | −0.25 |
| −0.72 | 0.38 | −0.43 | 0.37 | 1.58 | 1.49 | 1.50 | 1.09 | 0.80 | −0.77 |
| −0.14 | 0.81 | −0.13 | −0.61 | 1.58 | 1.49 | 1.52 | 1.08 | 0.99 | −0.40 |
| −0.57 | 0.84 | −0.08 | −0.51 | 1.57 | 1.56 | 1.54 | 1.08 | 0.99 | −0.32 |
|  |  | −0.11 | −0.13 |  |  | 1.43 |  |  | −0.40 |
|  |  | 0.26 | 0.85 |  |  | 1.23 |  |  | −0.28 |
| −0.62 | 0.79 | −0.29 | −0.32 | 1.62 | 1.50 | 1.52 | 1.20 | 0.92 | −0.55 |
|  |  | 0.02 | 0.33 |  |  | 1.51 |  |  | −0.32 |
|  |  | −0.20 | 0.49 |  |  | 1.50 |  |  | −0.40 |
| −0.13 | 0.77 | −0.96 | 0.01 | 1.27 | 1.50 | 1.53 | 1.09 | 0.97 | −0.32 |
|  |  | 0.56 | 0.45 |  |  | 0.64 |  |  | −0.51 |
|  |  |  | 0.45 |  |  | 1.10 |  |  |  |
|  |  |  | 0.16 |  |  | 1.20 |  |  |  |
|  |  |  | 0.08 |  |  | −0.86 |  |  |  |
|  |  |  | −0.16 |  |  | −0.91 |  |  |  |
|  |  |  | 0.26 |  |  | −0.49 |  |  |  |
|  |  |  | 0.43 |  |  | −0.83 |  |  |  |
|  |  |  | 0.80 |  |  | −0.65 |  |  |  |
|  |  |  | 0.79 |  |  | −0.60 |  |  |  |

## REVISED ROTATED FACTOR SCORES [b]

| Country | COLD WAR | | | | SELF-DETERMINATION | | |
|---|---|---|---|---|---|---|---|
| | 1947[c] | 1952 | 1957 | 1961 | 1952 | 1957 | 1961 |
| Malagasy Republic | | | | —0.83 | | | 1.51 |
| Mauritania | | | | —0.87 | | | 1.44 |
| Niger | | | | —0.24 | | | 1.52 |
| Senegal | | | | —0.07 | | | 1.28 |
| Togo | | | | 0.02 | | | 0.97 |
| Upper Volta | | | | —0.13 | | | 1.37 |
| Congo (Leopoldville) | | | | —0.27 | | | 1.23 |
| Ethiopia | 1.14 | —0.11 | —0.12 | 1.15 | 0.51 | —0.98 | 0.76 |
| Liberia | 0.62 | 0.01 | —0.64 | —0.69 | 0.36 | —0.73 | 0.90 |
| Nigeria | | | | 0.78 | | | 0.92 |
| Sierra Leone | | | | 0.51 | | | 1.05 |
| Somalia | | | | 0.86 | | | 0.94 |

| | UN SUPRANATIONALISM | | | | PALESTINE-RELATED QUESTIONS | | | ANTI-INTERVENTIONISM (AFRICA) | | |
|---|---|---|---|---|---|---|---|---|---|---|
| 1947[d] | 1952 | 1957 | 1961 | | 1947 | 1952 | 1961 | 1947 | 1952 | 1957 |
| | | | −0.05 | | | | −0.87 | | | |
| | | | 0.07 | | | | 0.37 | | | |
| | | | 0.06 | | | | −0.83 | | | |
| | | | 0.77 | | | | 0.06 | | | |
| | | | 0.23 | | | | 0.23 | | | |
| | | | 0.81 | | | | −0.71 | | | |
| | | | 0.40 | | | | 0.11 | | | |
| −0.54 | 0.08 | −0.21 | 0.42 | | 0.08 | 1.31 | 0.58 | 1.14 | 0.62 | −0.28 |
| −0.39 | 0.55 | 0.09 | 0.70 | | 1.02 | 0.14 | −0.20 | 0.53 | 0.66 | −0.57 |
| | | | 0.81 | | | | −0.02 | | | |
| | | | 0.86 | | | | −0.06 | | | |
| | | | 0.51 | | | | 0.77 | | | |

b. Revised rotated factor scores were in all but one case calculated from "factors on roll calls" regressions derived according to the equation in Chap. 2, note 20. Coefficients in this equation representing roll calls with loadings less than 0.25 were set to zero and the new factor scores were restandardized to have means to zero and standard deviations of unity. Cold war factor scores for 1957 were recalculated only from roll calls with loadings above 0.35. This exceptional procedure ordered national voting positions considerably more like those of the highest loading cold war alignments.

c. 1947 cold war is actually the rotated East–West factor which contains self-determination questions as well as cold war ones.

d. 1947 supranationalism was labeled a Genocide factor in Chap. 3.

In this index several conventions have been adopted regarding the mention of specific nations, issues, and institutional components of the UN system. Individual countries have been indexed only when they represent specific issues before the General Assembly, or are great powers. Specific information about their voting behavior may be found by referring to pages given for particular issues, classes of issues, or general voting components involved, or to the Appendix. Tables and figures have not been indexed, but can be located from text references.

Specific issues have been indexed only when of major importance; when not indexed they may be found by referring to the appropriate issue classes (e.g. economic) or super-issues involved (e.g. cold war). The same principle applies to voting determinants (e.g. military alliances).

Only the major components of the UN system have been specifically indexed. Information on other international organizations and on General Assembly committees and subcommittees can be found by referring to the issue classes or super-issues involved.